233237

PORTRAIT OF A
PROGRESSIVE

Viscount Addison while Leader of the Lords
(in the possession of the Dowager Lady Addison)

PORTRAIT OF A PROGRESSIVE

The Political Career of
Christopher, Viscount Addison

KENNETH and JANE MORGAN

CLARENDON PRESS · OXFORD
1980

Oxford University Press, Walton Street, Oxford OX2 6DP
OXFORD LONDON GLASGOW
NEW YORK TORONTO MELBOURNE WELLINGTON
KUALA LUMPUR SINGAPORE JAKARTA HONG KONG TOKYO
DELHI BOMBAY CALCUTTA MADRAS KARACHI
NAIROBI DAR ES SALAAM CAPE TOWN

Published in the United States by
Oxford University Press, New York

© Kenneth and Jane Morgan 1980

All rights reserved. No part of this publication may be reproduced, stored in a retrieval system, or transmitted, in any form or by any means, electronic, mechanical, photocopying, recording, or otherwise, without the prior permission of Oxford University Press

British Library Cataloguing in Publication Data

Morgan, Kenneth Owen
   Portrait of a progressive.
   1. Addison, Christopher, *Viscount Addison*
   2. Statesman – Great Britain – Biography
   I. Title   II. Morgan, Jane
   941.083'092'4   DA566.9.A/   79-41131

ISBN 0-19-822494-X

Printed in Great Britain by
Lowe & Brydone Printers Limited, Thetford, Norfolk

To Our Mothers

Preface

The career of Dr Christopher Addison, Viscount Addison of Stallingborough, was one of unusual length and importance. After a distinguished career as a doctor he entered politics in his early middle age in 1910 and served in Liberal, Coalition, and Labour governments from that of Asquith to that of Attlee. Alone of British politicians he was directly involved in post-war reconstruction, first after 1918, then after 1945. He died in 1951 at the age of eighty-two still very much in harness. As Minister of Munitions, then of Reconstruction, and, most important, as the first Minister of Health under Lloyd George, he initiated programmes of major long-term importance. After joining the Labour party in the early twenties he was to prove an influential Minister of Agriculture under MacDonald. Finally he was Leader of the Lords and a senior Cabinet figure for six years under Attlee. Twice during his career—in 1921, when he resigned from the Lloyd George Coalition over housing policy, again in 1931 when he opposed the National Government and lost his seat in the landslide election of that year—Addison's political career seemed to be over. Each time he came bounding back to complete forty years of active politics in peace and in war of an interest and variety almost equalling that of Lloyd George himself.

Yet Addison's career has, hitherto, received no worthwhile study. The late R. J. Minney's biography, *Viscount Addison, Leader of the Lords* (1958), was very unsatisfactory, particularly for Addison's career up to 1939. It was based on only a small sample of his papers. Nor has Addison's work as a departmental minister received due recognition. Studies of British social policy during and after the first world war have frequently treated Addison, most unfairly, as a scapegoat, especially over housing. The role of the treasury in frustrating Addison's creative and innovative policies, has not been properly discussed. As for Addison's important achievements as a Labour Cabinet minister in 1930–1 and 1945–51, these have scarcely been seriously treated by historians at all.

Now, however, it is possible to take a fresh look at his career. His papers have been available in the Bodleian Library for some years, while those of Lloyd George, MacDonald, and other contemporaries are also easily accessible. In addition, the opening up of the public records now enables us to examine Addison's long career as a Cabinet minister in depth down to the end of 1948. Our main concern has been to discuss his record as a politician and a policy-maker. His highly distinguished earlier achievements as a medical doctor are only summarized briefly as we are not qualified to discuss them in detail. The essential purpose of this book is to portray Addison as a major figure in the British progressive tradition, in the evolution of the British left from the radicalism of the years before 1914 to the democratic socialism of the later twentieth century. It tries to do belated justice to a creative and important political figure whose achievements have hitherto been grossly neglected or misrepresented. We hope that Christopher Addison will no longer be one of the forgotten men of modern British history.

We are particularly indebted to the Dowager Lady Addison for all her encouragement, for valuable information about her late husband, and for the unrestricted use of his papers. We are also very grateful for assistance from the third Viscount Addison and Mrs Isobel Cheshire, Addison's surviving son and daughter. We also received much kindness from Mrs Biddy Joel of High Wycombe. We have greatly benefited from the personal recollections of Addison that were provided by Sir Harold Wilson and Lord Wakefield of Kendal. Those who very kindly offered advice on sources included Dr R. A. C. Parker, Mr Andy Cooper, Professor John Stubbs, Dr Ross McKibbin, and Mr David Marquand. Dr Emanuel Lee generously allowed us to draw on his medical expertise. Jane Morgan is personally much indebted to Mr Rupert Evans of the University of Leicester who supervised her researches, and Kenneth Morgan to The Queen's College, Oxford, for sabbatical leave. Pat Lloyd provided her usual impeccable typing, while the staff of the manuscript department of the Bodleian Library were most helpful in making Addison's papers so fully available. Our final thanks must be personal—to Sara Ruane whose devoted and ever cheerful baby-minding made much of the research in libraries possible; to David and Katherine Morgan for their forbearance while the book was being written; and, finally to our mothers, to whom this book is dedicated and who, we hope, will accept it as a small token of gratitude in return for so much.

Preface ix

K.O.M. and J.M.

Long Hanborough, Oxfordshire,
February 1979

Contents

		Page
	List of Illustrations	xiii
1	The Making of a Politician	1
2	The Making of a Prime Minister	33
3	Munitions and Reconstruction	59
4	The Heyday of the Coalition	90
5	The Break with Lloyd George	120
6	From Liberalism to Labour	149
7	The Second Labour Government	176
8	From Slump to Victory	208
9	Labour's Elder Statesman	238
	Conclusion	276
	Notes	283
	Bibliography	306
	Index	319

List of Illustrations

Frontispiece: Viscount Addison while Leader of the Lords
(in the possession of the Dowager Lady Addison)

Plate 1: Dr Christopher Addison in 1901
(in the possession of the Dowager Lady Addison)

Plate 2: The Overloaded Omnibus: the Ministry of Health Bill, 1919
(in the possession of the Dowager Lady Addison)

The Sacrifice: Addison's resignation, July 1921
(in the possession of the Dowager Lady Addison)

Plate 3: Lord Addison and Mackenzie King, Ottawa, September 1946
(in the possession of the Dowager Lady Addison)

Plate 4: The Commonwealth Prime Ministers' Conference, 1946
(in the possession of the Dowager Lady Addison)

Plates fall between pages 162–163

1

The Making of a Politician

Medical men and women have very seldom reached the heights in British politics. Dr David Owen, who became Foreign Secretary in February 1977, was one of only a small handful of doctors turned politician to make a decisive mark on British political life during the present century. Only one doctor to date has enjoyed a career in politics of prolonged and successful achievement, and that after attaining considerable eminence in the medical profession. He was Christopher Addison who first entered politics as Liberal member of parliament for the Hoxton division of Shoreditch in the general election of January 1910. This marked the launching of a career in public life which was to span the years from the government of Asquith to that of Attlee and to last until Addison's death in December 1951 in his eighty-third year.

Yet Addison was already turned forty when he embarked upon a political career. He was born on a farm at Hogsthorpe, in the marshlands of Lindsey in east Lincolnshire, on 19 June 1869, the son of a tenant farmer. In addition to a smallholding of a few acres, Addison's father also rented a further 200 acres, which were used for grazing cattle. Later, this land was handed on to the elder Addison son, Robert, while the father moved to the north of the county to a much larger farm of 600 acres by the sea at Stallingborough, near Grimsby. Christopher Addison himself was later to manage the farm at Hogsthorpe which he bought in 1919. He had, therefore, a country upbringing, and he retained the outlook and style of a countryman all his life. He was always most at home amongst corn, cattle, and pigs, and the placid, unhurried life of the rural community. In some respects, his later period as Minister of Agriculture was to prove the most satisfying of his career. He always strongly identified with the isolated, bleak farmland of his native county. Years later, in 1916, he noted how repelled he was by the urban, patrician style of Margot

Asquith. 'Perhaps it is an upbringing in the flat Lincolnshire marshes of tenant farmer blood that makes me unresponsive to certain types of conversation.' Margot, he felt, 'must have put me down as a very dull fellow'.[1] Addison, like his later associate, David Lloyd George, was instinctively a populist, an agrarian radical, as rooted in Lincolnshire and the peasantry of the Danelaw as Lloyd George was in Gwynedd. There was, however, an important difference between them. Addison's father was an orthodox rural Conservative as his farming forebears had been in Lincolnshire over many generations. He was deeply alarmed when the young Christopher began to declaim radical sentiments in the family home, for instance about the lot of the farm labourer. Addison's radicalism arose not from his background or inherited tradition but from experience and intellectual conviction.

Addison's parents gave their son an extended education.[2] After attending a local school at Wainfleet, the young Christopher went to Trinity College, Harrogate, at the age of thirteen and stayed there for three years. Much later, in a debate in the House of Lords, Addison severely criticized this school—'a school which ought never to have been allowed to exist'[3]—but this appears unduly harsh. Trinity College, Harrogate, seems to have given him the basis of a broad education in the humanities, in mathematics, and in the sciences, and to have made entry into a profession possible for him. From an early stage, he was fascinated by the medical life. At the age of eighteen, he went to medical school at Sheffield, and then on to St. Bartholomew's Hospital in London. This entailed some financial struggle. The young student tried to live on £1 a week, lunching on a bun and a glass of milk. Characteristically, Addison insisted on paying his father the whole of the £676 that his years of further education cost the family—with 5 per cent interest tacked on.[4] The final repayments were concluded just before his father died. At St. Bartholomew's Hospital, Addison rapidly proved himself a most gifted student, as one of his fellow students, Lord Horder, was later to recall. In the field of human anatomy in particular, he showed himself to be a young man of unusual ability. After a brief period as a doctor at Banstead Asylum in Surrey, a post obtained out of simple financial necessity, Addison made a professional breakthrough in 1893 when he was appointed Demonstrator in Anatomy in the Sheffield Medical School. In November 1895 he was appointed full lecturer; two years later, when the University of Sheffield came into being in 1897, he was appointed

The Making of a Politician 3

the first holder of the Arthur Jackson Chair of Anatomy.[5] This extraordinarily rapid promotion, which saw him elevated to a professorship at the age of only twenty-eight, continued to gain momentum as his national reputation as an anatomist brought growing recognition. He delivered an important paper to the Royal Society in 1898 and gave the immensely prestigious Hunterian lectures to the Royal College of Surgeons in 1901. That year he moved to London to take up a post as special lecturer in anatomy at Charing Cross Hospital, where he later became Dean. In 1906 he moved back to his *alma mater*, St. Bartholomew's, where he received a similar appointment.

Throughout these years, Addison's career as an anatomist was one of consistent and impressive achievement. He became a member of the Royal College of Surgeons, and a Licentiate of the Royal College of Physicians in 1891; two years later he gained a doctor's degree from the University of London. At Sheffield, he was exceptionally active as an administrator, course organizer, and editor of the college journal; in embryo, the flair of the future Minister of Munitions and of Housing was being revealed. At Charing Cross and later at St. Bartholomew's, he established a reputation as a powerful teacher. B. C. Roy, later Gandhi's personal physician, was but one of his notable postgraduate students. Addison was certainly amongst those who launched the systematic teaching of advanced courses in anatomy and physiology in British universities and hospitals.

But it was as a distinguished researcher that he most securely made his name as an anatomist. His main research concerned the abdominal viscera in man. In particular, he worked on locating the position of the abdominal organs and carefully mapping their relation to well-defined lines drawn on the skin surface of the abdomen. He also ascertained the way in which the intra-abdominal organs altered their position or were displaced when they themselves, or neighbouring organs, were enlarged or diminished in size, or subjected to pressure. His surface maps became for generations afterwards the clinician's guide to the position of the underlying abdominal organs and were used throughout the medical world. He published some highly important papers on these themes, especially two in the *Journal of Anatomy and Physiology* in 1899 and 1900.[6] His Hunterian lectures were also a major addition to understanding of the abdominal organs. The most notable of all his publications, 'The Shape and Position of the Pancreas and Adjoining Viscera', described his method of drawing a line, horizontal or transverse, to indicate the average level of the trans-pyloric plane. He thus gave his name to a well-known feature of the human anatomy, 'Addison's Plane'.[7] In the nineteen-forties, doctors were astonished to learn that this owed its name, not to some distant seventeenth-century scientific pioneer, but to a living member of the British Labour government. In these and other respects, then, Addison had established himself securely by his later thirties, as one of the most eminent anatomists in Britain, and a nationally known figure in the profession. In 1904–6 he served as secretary of the Anatomical Society of Great Britain. For the rest of his career, his background as an anatomist enabled him to view social and medical phenomena not only with compassion but also literally with clinical detachment. When a parliamentary deputation surveyed the Nazi concentration camp at Buchenwald in 1945, just before the end of the war, only two of its members were able to withstand the human horrors unveiled there without breaking down completely—Tom Driberg the journalist, and Christopher Addison the anatomist.[8] Addison remained justly proud of his early career as a doctor. In October 1937, when speaking at the annual dinner of the Charing Cross Medical School, he recalled his 'cherished recollections' of his time as an anatomist there and at St. Bartholomew's. He expressed pride that the first two medical men to enter the British Cabinet (himself and Auckland Geddes) had been anatomists. 'He knew of no training which if used properly could be of greater use than medical training.' He instanced his own period at the departments of Education and of Health to illustrate its value to the political life.[9]

Until his mid-thirties, there seemed little likelihood of Addison's moving beyond the secure, placid career of the medical world where he had established such a notable reputation. Yet his thoughts had long moved beyond the narrowly medical sphere. Even as a young boy, he had a close interest in political matters; his reading of John Stuart Mill testified to an early sympathy for Liberalism, while his experiences in the local Methodist Sunday School may have fortified a sturdy, anti-landlord style of rural radicalism. As he worked in the hospitals of London after the turn of the century, Addison became deeply and passionately aware of the poverty and disease so prevalent in the poorer sections of the city, notably in the East End of London. He rapidly concluded that ill health and social and environmental deprivation were intimately connected. His lifelong concern with

The Making of a Politician 5

medical research, with housing reform, and environmental planning began at this time. His closest friend then, and until he died in 1948, was Dr Alexander Macphail, another medical professor, another chess enthusiast, and a devout Christian with a powerful commitment to the social gospel.

Addison's political and social concern was also reinforced by his marriage in 1902 to Isobel Mackinnon Gray. She was the daughter of a wealthy shipping man who had amassed money through trade in India, but unlike her father, a vehement social radical and a convert to High Anglicanism from Presbyterianism with a powerful commitment to Christian Socialism of the Gore/Scott Holland school. There is not much to be said, then or later, about Addison's domestic life. His first marriage, like his second (Isobel was to die in 1934 and he remarried in 1937), was exceptionally happy. They had a house, 'Pretty Corner', built in 1905 at Northwood near Watford in Hertfordshire, where they were to live until after the end of the first world war. It was an attractive, modern, six-bedroomed villa, set in substantial, rather wild grounds, including a tennis lawn and a kitchen garden. When auctioned in June 1920, it realized £6,500. The Addisons had five children, two daughters, Kate and then Isobel, and three sons, Paul (who died at the age of three), Christopher, later the second Viscount, and Michael, later the third. Addison was a loyal husband, a devoted father, socially something of a recluse with a countryman's reserve of manner. His major recreations were chess and bridge (the former of these gave him later an entrée to Bonar Law), and always long country walks at week-ends where the sounds, sights, and smells of the countryside could be enjoyed at leisure. Otherwise, Addison had no hobbies, seldom listened to music or visited the theatre, and devoted his off-duty moments to his professional activities, first as a doctor, then as a politician. It is truer of Addison than of most men that it is in the public man that the real personality is to be found. The private man is, frankly, not of much historical interest.

His first wife admirably blended in with his outlook. She, too, was a country person, most at home in rural Buckinghamshire, never at ease in London, though a loyal supporter of her husband's political career at Westminster. Apart from looking after the household, with the manifold domestic crises that small children bring with them, Isobel Addison supplied a tough core of nonconformist-style radicalism and a basic egalitarianism, that notably strengthened her doctor husband's growing commitment to politics.[10] She had a powerful social conscience, and was generally thought to be closer to the Labour party than to the Liberals, long before her husband moved towards Labour himself. With her husband, Mrs Addison was active in charitable activities in the East End at an early stage, much on the lines of those inspired by Toynbee Hall or by Hull House in Chicago. She took part in Care Committees and Play Garden Committees in poor areas of East London; the plight of children, many of them ill-clad, destitute, and undernourished, was an especial priority both for her and for her husband. A compassionate and self-effacing woman, Isobel Addison was an essential part of her husband's decision to seek fulfilment in the political life.

During the Edwardian years, the content and approach of Liberalism as a philosophy were being dramatically transformed. These were the years of the new collectivist ideas of writers such as J. A. Hobson and L. T. Hobhouse and the group of radicals who formed the Rainbow Circle and brought out the *Progressive Review* in 1896. Through their influence, through social critics like Chiozza Money and C. F. G. Masterman, through the 'social Christianity' associated with the 'forward movement' in the churches and with radical pastors like R. J. Campbell, the traditional commitment of late Victorian Liberalism to individualism and to *laissez-faire* was severely modified. The concept of systematic state action on behalf of social and economic reform, a view often based on an organic rather than on an atomistic view of society, became an increasingly acceptable part of the Liberal creed and programme. This 'new Liberalism' was an important undercurrent in the revival of the Liberal party in the years up to 1905. The electoral landslide of January 1906 seemed to confirm the compatibility of the older Gladstonian Liberalism with the new Liberalism of social reform, despite the known caution of the new Prime Minister, Sir Henry Campbell-Bannerman, on social questions.

The appeal of the new Liberalism to a man of Addison's outlook and profession is self-evident. Public health had been a vital theme in the articulation of the New Liberalism. For example, the poor physique of working-class recruits during the South African War had highlighted the defects of the public health services. An important section of Chiozza Money's *Riches and Poverty* was devoted to ill

The Making of a Politician

health and undernourishment among children, and to the appalling facts of infant mortality. Addison, as an active, socially-concerned doctor, naturally responded to this public debate, fortified by the conviction that he had the skill and knowledge to turn this anxiety about the nation's health to practical effect. Throughout his career, he was always to emphasize that it was concern for health, and especially the plight of the undernourished children of the poor and unemployed, that impelled him into politics. So he sought a parliamentary seat, preferably in London near to his medical work.

In May 1907 he was adopted as Liberal candidate for the Hoxton division of Shoreditch in the East End.[11] Like some other East London constituencies, it had something of a Tory tradition and had been in Unionist hands since 1900. The sitting member in 1907, who had managed rather surprisingly to hang on to his constituency even in the 1906 landslide, was the Hon. Claude Hay, a younger son of the Earl of Kinnoul. From the time of his adoption, Addison began energetically to cultivate the constituency. He represented himself as an 'advanced radical', a champion of social and educational reform and the taxation of the rich, a strong supporter of the 'Progressive' politics of the London County Council with their tinge of municipal socialism, as carried out from 1889 to 1907. Everything that happened between 1907 and the next general election fortified Addison's radicalism. There was the growing commitment of the government to New Liberal social policies, such as Old Age Pensions. There was the advent of Winston Churchill as an advocate of Bismarckian-style social reform. Churchill, indeed, was to write an endorsement of Addison as candidate for Hoxton.[12] There was the new social strategy outlined by Churchill and Lloyd George in 1908–9 including national insurance, labour exchanges, and assaults on poverty and unemployment. Above all, there was Lloyd George's 'People's Budget' of 1909, rejected by the House of Lords, a bold measure directed against the 'old Liberal' foes of the landlord and the brewer, but designed to promote a long-term social programme to which middle- and working-class Liberals could all subscribe. All the developments of these exciting years seemed to emphasize the differences between a reforming government and its die-hard opponents.

The general election came in January 1910, following the Lords' rejection of Lloyd George's 'People's Budget'. For Addison more than most Liberals, this was a crucial challenge for the New Liberalism. He denounced the action of the Lords in rejecting the Budget and forcing the government to dissolve parliament as a constitutional outrage. There was the prospect of a Liberal government being permanently hamstrung by a reactionary second chamber, and of tariff reform being introduced in the wake of this. For Addison, the contrast between 'the peers' and 'the people' was transparently clear. Inevitably, too, his speeches had a powerful social content. The Lords had rejected the Budget primarily because of its proposals for the valuation of land and for the taxation of the unearned increment in land values.[13] This was a theme to which Addison, with his rural background, readily warmed. On the other hand, there were the government's long-term proposals for health and unemployment insurance, for the relief of unemployment and distress and malnutrition. Addison's vigorous oratory, together with the respect he inspired as a distinguished member of the medical profession, went down well in the rough-and-tumble of a working-class East End constituency like Hoxton. 'He says things which are not flamboyant, but which a working-class audience loves to hear .... He has the human touch,' commented one contemporary journal.[14] Claude Hay tried to exploit Addison's work as an anatomist. 'Dr. Addison cuts up bodies. Don't let him cut up the Empire' read one Unionist poster.[15] But this was more than countered by the enthusiastic canvassing work by several of Addison's own medical students in the constituency. The campaign was in many respects a colourful one. The constituency contained 'the Mile', a picaresque no-go area along Essex Street, the haunt of pickpockets and prostitutes. Addison encountered the former at least when his own watch was stolen and later returned by an elderly pickpocket. In the aftermath of his victory, the same pickpocket presented him with Claude Hay's watch (later returned to its owner) as a symbol of triumph. Addison was never a commanding or effective stump orator; he had too much of the pedantic, pedagogic style of the university professor. But he was an immensely energetic and forceful campaigner, who took to politics with great zest. His election agent was an able young law student, Arthur Comyns Carr, himself destined for a distinguished career in law and politics. The outcome was that, in an election which saw the Liberals lose their huge over-all majority of 1906 and become dependent on the support of Labour and the Irish Nationalists, Addison captured Hoxton by 338 votes over Hay. It has been noted that he was the one English

The Making of a Politician 9

Presbyterian returned in January 1910,[16] although in fact Addison, a kind of 'broad Church' deist, attended a wide variety of Protestant churches without commitment and later often accompanied his wife to High Anglican services. However, a nonconformist basis to his radicalism is clear enough.

A second general election soon was now inevitable, since the government, having obtained a mandate for the 1909 budget, was thought to require another to endorse their Parliament Bill designed to curb the veto powers of the House of Lords. Addison was well aware of this as soon as he became a member of parliament. His maiden speech on 24 February 1910 made a good impression. Inevitably, it concentrated on social questions. He strongly endorsed the majority recommendations of the recent Royal Commission on the Poor Law, which would provide for far greater security for working people than would the Tory panacea of tariff reform.[17] Subsequently in this session of Parliament, charged with high political passions, he was active in speaking on behalf of the budget, in denouncing protectionism, and in condemning the pretensions of the House of Lords. He was also energetic in pressing constituency matters relating to the people in his constituency. For example, he acted as spokesman for the grievances of the costermongers and other street traders in Hoxton with regard to their liberty to trade. This was politically shrewd as costermongers were a powerful influence in Hoxton politics, and had tended to vote Unionist in the past. Addison managed to secure promises from Churchill, the Home Secretary, that at least six hundred traders would be saved from eviction from the streets of Hoxton. He was deeply impressed by the sympathetic understanding that Churchill showed a large contingent of hawkers when they met him at the Home Office. 'Whatever happens, I shall always have a warm corner in my heart for Winston.'[18] When in April 1910 a Unionist leaflet was circulated in Hoxton, stating that the new MP had voted for sweated wages, Addison managed to obtain a letter from Ramsay MacDonald, the Labour member for Leicester, stating that he had voted with the Labour member on this issue.[19] This episode, relatively unimportant in itself, shows the range of contacts with leading figures on the left that Addison was building up. Another friend from this period, a lifelong one, was Wedgwood Benn, another Liberal member for an East London seat, who had represented Tower Hamlets since 1906.

This record of the vigorous endorsement of wider radical principles and of careful attention to the needs of his own constituency stood Addison in good stead in the new general election of December 1910. The Union of City Hawkers, for example, now endorsed him even though they had previously supported Hay and had resented the restrictions imposed by the Progressive majority on the LCC on their trading privileges. So, too, did the Postal Porters, and many leading trade unionists in Hoxton.[20] Addison's election platform was that common to most Liberals at the time—the curbing of the Lords' veto through the Parliament Bill, social reform, and the iniquity of tariffs. Although the Hoxton Tories fought hard, and put up a new candidate, F. Francis, Addison held the seat with an increased majority of 694. This victory confirmed a notable swing to the Liberals in London East End constituencies at this election, contrary to the gloomy interpretation of London Liberalism offered by Dr Paul Thompson. Lloyd George wrote to his wife at this time, 'London has once more amazed everybody; the East End actually increased the Liberal majority.' Addison's victory was no doubt what he partly had in mind.[21]

In May 1911 Addison's career was totally transformed. He emerged from the shadowy ranks of the back-benchers to become a key policy-maker. This followed from the National Insurance Bill introduced by Lloyd George on 4 May. Here emerged the theme with which Addison was chiefly to involve himself over the next three years, and to make a new impact upon the politicians and the public at large. In addition, it proved Addison to be a notably effective parliamentarian and lobbyist. Most important of all, it began his long and momentous association with David Lloyd George.

The National Health Insurance scheme, introduced as Part I of the National Insurance Act of 1911, marked the culmination of the social welfare programme of the Asquith government.[22] It was, without doubt, the most far-reaching, expensive, and controversial of all the social policies of the pre-war years. The bill provided the familiar friendly society benefits of medical treatment paid for on an insurance basis jointly by the state, employers, and employees. The first two would pay fivepence a week between them, and the employee fourpence ('ninepence for fourpence' in Lloyd George's graphic phrase). The sickness benefit would be ten shillings a week for men over a period of thirteen weeks, and five shillings a week for the next thirteen

The Making of a Politician 11

weeks, beginning on the fourth day of illness. There would also be a five shillings disability benefit, a thirty shillings maternity benefit, and the right to treatment in a sanatorium. At the end of each quarter, a worker would carry his card filled with stamps to the approved society of his choice (in many cases, his trade union). The government's contribution of two-ninths of the cost of benefit was paid directly to the society on the basis of the number of cards they held and the benefits they gave. The scheme was remarkably comprehensive. All workmen over sixteen years who earned less than £160 per year, the income tax limit, would be compulsorily insured, and all manual workers insured whatever their income. However, anyone of any income could insure voluntarily. The main organs of the scheme were the approved societies, mainly insurance companies and trade unions, who were required to provide personal contact with the insured and who employed the doctors whose services provided the medical benefit.

The National Insurance Bill also created a massive, nation-wide machinery to administer the new legislation. Local health committees were to be appointed to administer the sanatoria, to provide for the representation of Post Office contributors, and to investigate local health conditions. There were also to be National Health Insurance Commissions for England, Wales, and Scotland, responsible to a Board of Commissioners appointed by the Treasury—a measure of administrative devolution which brought protests from civil servants concerned with drafting the bill. A vast new bureaucratic machine of Bismarckian proportions for administering social welfare had thus been created. Through it, men like Arthur Salter, Thomas Jones, Claude Schuster, and Percy Watkins were to establish their careers as public servants. There was to be a major link between the bureaucratic revolution of 1911–12 and the 'palace revolution' of 1916 which brought Lloyd George to the premiership.

The political strategy underlying the passage of this measure to implement national health insurance was highly complex. It entailed playing off the industrial assurance companies against the friendly societies, and both of them against the British Medical Association. It involved trying to detach some of the doctors' rank and file from their own leaders, the executive council of the BMA. It also concerned the world of industrial relations since both private employers and trade union leaders had to be placated. In terms of party manœuvring it meant an arrangement between the Liberal chief, the Master of Elibank, and the Labour party. As a result of this, the latter generally supported Lloyd George's bill (with the exception of some dissentients such as Keir Hardie, Philip Snowden, and George Lansbury), in return for the passage of the payment of members of parliament. The entire strategy of handling the politics of national insurance required a high degree of sophistication and flair. It has been stated that 'only Lloyd George could have got it through'.[23] But, as will be seen, he did so with the vital and decisive help of his essential link between Westminster and the medical profession, Dr Christopher Addison.

At first, the bill was received well both by press and politicians. Mr Punch depicted Lloyd George as 'bringing down the house'. He is shown as observing, while the applause and bouquets rained down, 'Pit and gallery I'm used to, but now the stalls and dress-circle have broken out.'[24] This seeming unanimity did not last long. There were two powerful groups of well-organized, heavily financed adversaries. There were the industrial assurance companies; their counsel was Kingsley Wood, solicitor for the Liverpool Victoria and Royal London Mutual, and later to serve under Addison at the Ministry of Health in 1919–21. These powerful companies were gradually conciliated as control of the new insurance scheme was wrested from the friendly societies. More dangerous for the government, there was the British Medical Association, a vocal representative of wealthier doctors, with as its secretary Smith Whitaker, a man of considerable political guile. During the recess in the summer of 1911, immense opposition built up from the doctors' organization; it was fortified by massive propaganda campaigns in the Unionist press against 'licking stamps for Lloyd George'. To the BMA, the Insurance scheme entailed a massive control of their own professional activities as general practitioners, and a threat to private practice. It was here that Addison, a member of the BMA, and the one distinguished medical man in the Commons, emerged as a significant political figure. With his unique blend of medical expertise and political flair, he emerged as a powerful influence upon the government's Insurance Bill.

He was selected as a member of the BMA's Advisory Committee which began its deliberations at the end of May 1911. His attention was concentrated on two main areas of the Bill, those relating to the

The Making of a Politician 13

operations of the friendly societies and to the medical profession. In general, Addison warmly supported the new measure, as might have been expected. It would advance public health and would also encourage thrift as it would offer inducements for people to join friendly societies. It would provide great security for the receipt of benefits, and additional benefits of which those insured could avail themselves. But the position of the medical profession was crucial. The National Insurance Bill affected the daily work and remuneration of the doctors, whereas almost everyone else involved in the Bill were more or less beneficiaries of it. Addison felt that the medical profession could be persuaded to co-operate with the Bill, but that an agreement would have to be reached between the doctors and the friendly societies whereby the interests of doctors would be protected. As it stood, the Bill, in Addison's view, failed to provide doctors with adequate security and he put down some major amendments to improve it.[25]

His criticisms of the Bill soon reached the ear of Lloyd George. Through the mediation of C. F. G. Masterman, Addison was called in by Lloyd George early on to give his reasons why he thought the Bill to be inadequate. In his memoirs, Addison left a vivid record of this first meeting with the Chancellor of the Exchequer. Lloyd George met him with a smile in a room behind the Speaker's chair in the Commons. 'Masterman has told me a horrible tale of what you say about the Insurance Bill. Let me hear it again.' Addison replied at length, and with much force, that under the existing provisions of the Bill, the medical attendance of eight to ten million people would be worked merely as an extension of the existing club system. 'It simply stank in the nostrils of the whole medical profession and if he tried to impose it on them he would find them solid to a man against it. I should do everything I could to back them up, for we would never get a proper health system established in the country on these lines.' Addison had meanwhile canvassed nearly every member of the House of Commons against the proposals.[26]

From this time on, his contact with Lloyd George became ever closer and more frequent. He introduced a deputation of BMA members to Lloyd George on 18 May to discuss medical objections to the Bill. He was also in close touch with Smith Whitaker, the BMA secretary, in obtaining an accurate reflection of the views of the medical profession. Lloyd George had paid scant heed before this to the views of the BMA. He felt they were not representative of the average GP, especially of doctors in working-class districts. 'A deputation of doctors is always a deputation of swell doctors.'[27] Addison was foremost amongst those who succeeded in convincing him that the feeling against the Bill within the medical profession was not unreasonable and needed to be taken into account in remodelling the Bill. Gradually a process took place by which the opposition of the doctors to the Bill was transformed into opposition to the friendly societies, who were hostile to proposals to transfer the administration of medical benefit from them to local health committees. Addison felt that the composition and role of these health committees were vital to the whole scheme. If local committees were to manage the treatment of the sick, then poor law infirmaries would come under the Bill, and the whole of sickness benefit come under the administration of health committees. Addison also suggested that doctors should be enrolled on district panels from which patients should be able to select their own medical attendants.

His arguments had sufficient impact on Lloyd George to persuade him to leave the entire question of local health committees to a free vote in the House. On 1 August, in the committee stage, Addison argued vigorously on behalf of his amendment to Clause Thirteen.[28] As the Bill stood, medical benefit in relation to Post Office contributors, was to be administered by local health committees; but it was likely that the administration of insured persons would be undertaken by the friendly societies. Thus there might be a welter of seven or eight, or more, different societies, in addition to the local health committees, in any district, all administering medical benefit, which would be totally chaotic. It would be in the interests of the medical profession and also of insured persons generally if the entire medical administration of the system were placed in the hands of the health committees. Addison's speech was reported as having a marked effect upon opinion in the House. Lloyd George at once accepted the amendment and urged the friendly societies to agree to the provision of doctors by local health committees alone. On the division, Addison's amendment was carried by 387 to 15, and it was associated with his name ever after.

The next day, 2 August, Addison moved his so-called 'local option' amendment.[29] This gave discretion to local health committees with regard to the limit of income for the doctors' contract system. At the

The Making of a Politician 15

same time, it provided that persons whose income exceeded the limit of £160 per year would be required, and others would be allowed, to make their own arrangements for medical attendance at their own expense. In the course of his speech he predicted that in two or three years an equitable contract system would be evolved throughout the country. His amendment was carried by 289 votes to 41. It lightened considerably the force of the blow of the income limit of £160 per year for the medical profession. Again, it narrowed the gulf between the doctors and the Liberal government.

Addison's arguments also helped to defeat other amendments to the Insurance Bill. For example, on 1 August the effect of the Bill on voluntary hospitals was discussed. Several amendments were raised to Clause Twelve dealing with insured persons admitted to these hospitals. The opposition spokesman, Austen Chamberlain, claimed that in the case of forty-four Midlands hospitals it was estimated that 60 to 80 per cent of their whole income would be adversely affected by the Bill. Lloyd George tried to allay these fears: he claimed that the Bill would relieve the hospitals of the care of many people too poor to contribute. Addison, however, boldly challenged Lloyd George's view from the ministerial side. Although the number of outdoor patients might be reduced by the elimination of persons able to pay for treatment, the indoor work would be increased by earlier diagnosis and the ascertained necessity for hospital treatment. Lloyd George was more convincing when arguing that, by an amendment to be moved by the government, the sick payment of persons without dependants could be given in the hospital in which they were treated. He retained an open mind as to whether persons with dependants should also pay part of their sick pay to the hospital in which they received treatment. Addison provided some effective opposition to this latter suggestion. He admitted that the scheme would involve the immediate reconsideration of the financial position of the hospitals and a new campaign for their support. But, from whatever source the money came, it should not be drawn from the insurance fund, which was designed to keep the household together during the incapacity of the bread-winner. The force of this objection evidently convinced Lloyd George as the government now withdrew its own amendment.[30]

Meanwhile the Addison amendment, so-called, to Clause Thirteen on the creation of local health committees signalled the first victory of the doctors and the insurance companies over the friendly societies. As Addison recorded,

> The change was received with immense relief by the medical profession and provided me with the first experience of the ups and downs of public life. At first congratulations came in by the multitude but as the agitation against the Act grew in power the tone began to change and a generous measure of vituperation was afterwards dealt out to me for supporting the Act even as amended.[31]

Addison gradually became a popular whipping-boy for the British Medical Association, and remained one, to some degree, for the rest of his career, for all his distinguished services to public health. The *Medical Press* condemned him for putting loyalty to his party ahead of his profession. The Association's journal, the *British Medical Journal*, took the opportunity to criticize his volumes of memoirs, *Four and a Half Years*, in 1934 on such trivial grounds as the quality of the typography and the value of the illustrative plates.[32] Addison himself would not have complained since his volumes included a lengthy and contemptuous criticism of the BMA—'the most hopeless crowd I ever came across'.[33] Beyond these personal aspects, the background to the consideration of the National Insurance Bill in the summer of 1911 was one of mounting bitterness. The Parliament Bill held the centre of the stage at Westminster until it became law on 11 August after a tense confrontation between the Lords and the Commons (reluctantly assisted by King George V). Unionists passionately resented the threatened use of royal creation of peers to force the Parliament Bill through, and the abolition of a permanent veto by the Lords which at last made Irish home rule and other terrors practical possibilities. The Unionist rank-and-file now vented their anger on the previously relatively uncontroversial National Insurance Bill. The original cordiality of the Opposition turned to irresponsible obstruction. More than five hundred amendments were put down in an endeavour to emasculate Lloyd George's bill and deny the government another triumph.

The friendly societies were especially displeased with the Addison amendment as it removed the power to administer medical benefit from their control. They now gained Unionist support in attacking the Insurance Bill. Meanwhile, although individual doctors throughout the country congratulated Addison on his amendment, the British Medical Association officially opposed it. In October 1911 a major

The Making of a Politician 17

victory was won by the government over the friendly societies when they were forced to surrender to the insurance companies after a series of complicated manœuvres. But the official opposition of the medical profession to the terms of service offered by the Bill remained to be dealt with. It has been rightly claimed by Professor Gilbert that the 'suppression of this revolt was the work of David Lloyd George'. But it was also due in no small measure to the strenuous efforts of Dr Addison, whose role Gilbert under-estimates, and who acted for the most part as a go-between for Lloyd George and the representatives of the British Medical Association.[34]

The special meeting of the BMA on 31 May–1 June 1911, which Lloyd George himself had addressed, had unanimously passed the 'Six Cardinal Points' which were to be the minimum conditions under which the profession would accept service under the National Health Insurance Act. They included an income limit of £2 per week for the insured; the free choice of doctor by the patient; the administration of medical and maternity benefits by local health committees; and 'adequate' payment for doctors, later defined as a capitation fee of 8s. 6d. per head per year, excluding the cost of medicine. During his speech and in subsequent discussion, Lloyd George had referred to these points, and had readily agreed to all of them, save for the income limit and for the remuneration of 8s. 6d., the fee which the BMA considered to be adequate payment for each doctor. Free choice of doctor and the administration by health committees of the medical benefit had been guaranteed by Addison's amendment on 1 August. Nevertheless, the secretary of the BMA, Smith Whitaker, was busy for the rest of the year mobilizing professional opinion against the health insurance scheme. This involved obtaining signatures to a declaration stipulating that the signatories agreed that 'in the event of the National Health Insurance Bill becoming law, I will not enter into any agreement for giving medical treatment under the Bill, excepting such as shall be satisfactory to the medical profession, and in accordance with the declared policy of the B.M.A.' By the end of the year, the Association claimed that it had collected over 27,000 signatures.[35]

In August 1911, in accordance with a decision reached at the representative meeting of the BMA, twenty-seven members of the National Advisory Committee on the Insurance Bill resigned. This left only fourteen representatives of the medical profession to advise the government on the administration of the Act. Addison acted forcefully in this crisis. He wrote to the Association setting out his reasons why the Insurance Commission should not be boycotted, and explaining why he and others had not resigned from the Advisory Committee. The proceedings of the BMA stood in danger of bringing the profession into public contempt.[36]

The opposition of the doctors continued throughout that autumn, even though by the end of November nearly all the 'Six Cardinal Points' had either been met or at least acknowledged. The one important exception was the 8*s*. 6*d*. capitation fee. The doctors clearly disliked the Act; but until November there was no suggestion that they would resist its operation. Addison himself wrote a forceful article in the *Daily News* in December which set out reasons why doctors should work under the scheme of the Act. Meanwhile the new Joint Insurance Committee and the English Insurance Commission were now in being. But the opposition of the BMA remained unrelenting. Addison recorded in *Politics from Within*, 'The introduction of the Insurance Act was a prodigious task.... It had to be done in the face of a campaign of opposition that was growing in intensity. For my part, after having carried the original amendment and pledged myself to do what I could to make the Act workable, I was gradually brought into counsel more and more....' He worked ever more closely now with the civil servants who formed the administrative core of the new system—John Bradbury, John Anderson, Claude Schuster, Arthur Salter, an outstanding group with, at their head, that 'magnificent hustler', Sir Robert Morant.[37] During the first six months of 1912, there was virtually no contact between the Joint Insurance Commission and the medical profession, certainly nothing that could be recognized as negotiation. The doctors, in Bentley Gilbert's words, 'assumed they could win their battle by waiting'.[38]

During this period of deadlock, Addison was instrumental in drawing up the plan for the launching of the Insurance Act. In April 1912, he was asked to serve on both the National Health Insurance Commission and the Joint Committee. He wrote a powerful memorandum for Lloyd George in May on the date and method of inaugurating the Act, and consulted Morant, 'captain of the working crew', on technical aspects of the Insurance Commission. Addison urged that benefits must begin no later than January 1913. He set out a scheme under which provisional insurance committees should be organized and officers appointed under the Insurance Commission in each area. He

The Making of a Politician 19

also recommended that tuberculosis dispensaries, with their attending officers, be set up in various localities. This was an aspect of medicine much in the public eye at that time, notably in Wales where David Davies had just launched the 'Welsh National Memorial Association' to fight lung disease: here again was a public body where Addison was a key adviser. One suggestion of Addison's, however, did not find favour with Lloyd George. This was a proposal that the operation of the Act be postponed until October 1913 in view of the problems encountered; Lloyd George was firm that this at least ought to be resisted. Addison's reply to the Chancellor mentioned that he had now decided to resign all professional medical appointments at the end of the session in July so as to devote all his time to social and political work.[39]

A crisis had now been reached. If the medical profession could now hold together and refuse service, the outcries from the insured might force the government to concede the doctors' demands *in toto*, since contributions under the health insurance scheme were due to begin in mid-July 1912. However, four out of six 'Cardinal Points' had now been met, while the income limit for the insured was fixed by statute and unlikely to be changed. A report by the distinguished chartered accountant, Sir William Plender, on the remuneration of doctors, issued on 11 July 1912, showed that the approximately 6*s*. per contribution that Lloyd George proposed to allot to the insurance committees as medical remuneration represented a considerable increase, not only over what doctors usually received from the friendly societies, but also over what they usually earned from the public at large.[40] On this, the Harley Street leadership of the BMA was simply out of touch with its own membership. Even so, the BMA still insisted on its demands for an income limit and a basic 8*s*. 6*d*. capitation fee. At a representative meeting of the Association on 19 July 1912, all negotiations between the government and the doctors were broken off, and a resolution was passed requesting the resignation of all doctors serving on public or governmental administrative boards. Addison deplored this move. In a letter to the secretary of the BMA, published in *The Times* on 17 August, he gave reasons again for not resigning from the Advisory Committee. He had refused to allow the medical benefit of millions of people to be administered by a range of different societies because it would endanger public health. He believed that many medical practitioners were willing to work under the Act if they could satisfy themselves that they would do so under conditions honourable to themselves and the profession, and receive proper remuneration. The quasi-syndicalist proposals put forward by the BMA, claiming to speak for the medical profession, did not represent either the interests or the wishes of the great majority of medical men in the country.[41]

A sum of 6s. remuneration per insured person was perhaps insufficient, but it did provide a basis for further negotiation. The Cabinet's eventual decision in October 1912 was to settle the remuneration issue by providing 9s. (including drugs and appliances) per head per patient. Addison thought this to be a fair offer. In 1946, during the debate in the Lords on the National Health Service Bill, he described himself as one of the main authors of the capitation fee system, though he had since come to recognize its inadequacy and the superiority of a system of state salaries for doctors. He noted in his memoirs, 'This decision to provide extra remuneration marked the first occasion on which I entered the Cabinet Room at No. 10 Downing Street.' He was asked whether, if this money were provided, a sufficient medical service would be obtained the following January when the Act came into operation. Addison said that he was doubtful, 'but I thought that on the whole it would, if the whole power of the government were put into it.'[42]

An entirely new situation was created after 23 October and the government's offer of a second set of terms. The BMA executive and its members were themselves divided, as an official memorandum in the Addison Papers shows. Addison now campaigned around the country, addressing audiences of doctors and appealing to them to join local panels. He strongly endorsed the inaugural meeting of the National Insurance Practitioners held in December for the promotion of the interests of those medical practitioners who were prepared to serve under the Act. In an interview in the *Westminster Gazette*, he declared his faith that the Act would be in full operation on 15 January 1913, as planned. Efforts to wreck it would fail, medical panels would be set up throughout the country on the day appointed for the start of medical benefit, and large numbers of doctors would join. He further claimed to believe that the BMA would eventually participate and regain the confidence of the medical profession as a whole.[43]

A meeting at Birmingham on 9 December saw the first substantial break in the ranks of the opposition to the Act, when a resolution in favour of it was carried. Addison and his friends lost no time in giving the maximum of publicity to an important decision by a large body of medical men in a major city. Even so, a representative meeting of the BMA on 21–3 December again rejected Lloyd George's proposals by a four-to-one majority.[44] Addison condemned the Association as 'men who did not understand how to use their power with moderation and in a responsible manner'. As Professor Gilbert justly records, 'this was more than an act of unwisdom, it was an act of folly'. After all, many doctors had already joined local panels. Contact between the BMA and the Joint Insurance Committee was broken off a second time. But by 10 January, nearly 15,000 doctors had signed contracts with insurance committees. By 15 January, the appointed day, so many panels were complete that it was necessary to institute monopolies in only five areas. In 1913, as later in 1947, the BMA stood on the verge of a historic defeat.

Addison's role as a leading supporter of the Insurance Act did not end with its coming into operation. He and Masterman now worked together in trying to extend insurance coverage to include hospital and specialist services for contributors. He also worked to promote the Act with the doctors. He lectured frequently on its working, and wrote in the *Medical World* on 'The Future of the Panel Practitioner, his aims and ideals'.[46] He resisted attempts to undermine the panel system of doctors set up under the Act and to allow a completely free choice of doctors; he was convinced that this was but a wrecking manœuvre. Complaints had been made that the Act was slow in its operation. Addison replied that this was because of the campaign of obstruction and misrepresentation which it had experienced.

On 31 July 1913 a bill to amend the Insurance Act came before the House of Commons, and Addison was placed on the Standing Committee. Some debate took place on his new clause, tabled to the effect that in any area where, within three months, no local medical committee had been set up, a committee appointed by the panel doctors should be formed for consultation with the local insurance committee. Addison had received many letters from panel doctors supporting this change, and it was accepted. He was also in touch with Alfred Cox, the new medical secretary of the BMA. Cox admitted that, although the ranks of the BMA were still divided, 'there is a growing disposition to face the facts of the case'.[47]

The leading part played by Addison throughout the complex passage of the Insurance Act was recognized when a complimentary dinner was given in his honour on 6 February 1914, with Lloyd George himself in the chair. It was seen by some members of the press as an ostentatious way of exulting over the vanquished doctors. But it was in no sense a party political gathering; it was attended by men from all parties with whom Addison had had contact, including Unionists such as Waldorf Astor. In Lloyd George's speech, he emphasized the important part played by Addison in acting as go-between when he and the doctors were in conflict. Lloyd George declared:

During the few years Dr. Addison has been in the House of Commons, I have depended upon him as much as any man ... and he has never let me down. During the Insurance Act ... I found his advice invaluable.... He was loyal to the Government and to the medical profession at the same time. He is a first-rate fighter. He is a man to go hunting tigers with. I have been hunting tigers with him and we both got out of the jungle.[48]

Addison's own forceful reply at this dinner was later printed under the title *The Health of the People and how it may be Improved*.

The Insurance Act provided Addison with the decisive stepping-stone upon which his lengthy career in politics began. It made him for the first time a significant and influential parliamentarian. It also built up a close and almost lifelong relationship with Lloyd George. Its intimacy at this period was shown in a deeply sympathetic letter that Lloyd George wrote to Addison on the death of his son Paul in 1912; Lloyd George compared it with the tragic death of his own daughter, Mair, five years earlier.[49] For the next decade, Addison's career and that of Lloyd George were inseparably intertwined, in peace and in war. In some ways it may seem a surprising relationship. The unassuming, almost colourless, Addison seems very different from those more glamorous figures from the world of politics, the press, and business, that raffish *demi-monde* with which Lloyd George was so frequently associated. Addison, however, fulfilled another, perhaps more pressing, need for his radical chief. Lloyd George admired his practicality, his persistence and pugnacity, his energy, his unsentimental directness in getting things done, always allied to a real social conscience. In his frequent breakfast meetings with Lloyd George in 1912–14, Addison's role was to supply factual memoranda upon which the Welshman's fertile mind and imagination could play. He also strove to keep their conversations relevant to the theme on hand,

The Making of a Politician 23

amidst the 'score of subjects, domestic, general, personal' that Lloyd George gaily flung forth each morning. As Addison noted in his diary, 'We encourage each other to dream dreams but to base them on existing realities.'[50] Both men combined social radicalism with an artistry in the uses of power less commonly found in politicians of the left. Lloyd George came to depend heavily on Addison's clarity of mind and plain countryman's common sense: he was a political version of those business-orientated 'men of push and go' favoured by Lloyd George at the Ministry of Munitions in 1915–16. In time, Lloyd George came to see Addison's uses in wider political contexts, as a loyal lieutenant, as a mobilizer of opinion, and as a realistic, untheological exponent of latter-day secular Liberalism. On Addison's side, his admiration for Lloyd George until well after 1918 was almost total. That the Welsh radical, so often accused of the taint of scandal, could enlist the consistent support of one as transparently honest, idealistic, and unselfish as Christopher Addison adds an important dimension to the understanding of this phase of his life.

From the passage of the Insurance Act, Addison's career blossomed in other directions. For instance, after his work on this legislation, Addison was appointed in February 1912 to the Tuberculosis Commission. Its chairman was Waldorf Astor, a lone Unionist sympathetic to the Insurance Act, proprietor of the *Observer*, and later Addison's colleague in the Lloyd George government of 1916–18. This Commission was to advise on a scheme for the treatment and prevention of tuberculosis; it acted with much promptitude. In an interim report in April 1912, it recommended the establishment of machinery for the treatment of the disease, consisting of two units, a dispensary unit and an institutional unit.[51] In July Addison criticized the Insurance Act for postponing the levying of sanatorium benefit for six months so that the whole Act would begin together. In a letter to Lloyd George, he argued that a small number of tuberculosis patients could not be insured during the first six months after the passage of the Act, and urged that payment be made during this period to these patients. Meanwhile he was in touch with Sir Arthur Newsholme of the Local Government Board on the number of beds available and on the appointment of tuberculosis officers in urban districts.[52]

The final report of the Tuberculosis Commission was issued as a White Paper on 10 March; it marked a notable step in the public education on methods to combat the 'white scourge' which caused so much dread in rural communities in Wales and elsewhere.⁵³ But the most hopeful element in relation to tuberculosis lay in the provision under the Insurance Act for one penny per insured person to be set aside for medical research; this was under section 16 (2). It yielded about £57,000 per year, and by its aid was established the Medical Research Council, another notable institution with which Addison was much concerned. He never claimed credit for the idea of establishing a medical research scheme, but it seems highly possible that he was its originator.⁵⁴ It was he who insisted that the money collected for research should be devoted to all diseases, not used solely for research on tuberculosis. This was incorporated in the final report of the Tuberculosis Commission in March 1913. It also recommended the establishment of a committee with executive functions, together with an advisory council in connection with medical research. Lloyd George then asked Addison to serve on this committee in 1913 as one of two members of parliament, Waldorf Astor being the other; there were six additional members with scientific knowledge, and the chairman was the former Liberal MP, Lord Moulton. Addison was closely involved in drawing up the terms of reference for this Medical Research Committee.⁵⁵ A long battle now followed between those who wished to departmentalize the scheme by appropriating the money for the Local Government Board, and those, like himself, who were determined to secure the utmost freedom for the body which had to administer it. There was also much discussion over the establishment of a central institute; Addison took a keen interest in the controversy over whether the Lister Institute should be taken over for this purpose, or whether Mount Vernon Hospital, as originally proposed, should be used. In the end, it was Mount Vernon, in Hampstead, that was to be adapted in 1916–17. Addison urged Moulton that the Medical Research Committee should emphasize that their work had very wide implications: they should avoid the impression that laboratory work was the only method they were to employ, but should encourage medical research throughout the country. A library and information bureaux should be put at the disposal of the researchers whose work fell in line with the plans of the committee. The committee and its staff should have security of tenure for a five-year period, so that research could be planned on an adequate, long-term basis.⁵⁶

Addison was active in meetings of the Medical Research Committee in 1914 when research projects were under discussion. He was one of the committee members who visited several medical and scientific institutions in the provinces and received reports on their work. By November of that year, he was able to record that all the schemes of research proposed by the MRC had been passed and were going ahead.[57] Although the advent of war slowed up its plans, the Committee continued to meet at frequent intervals, producing reports and initiating inquiries. Addison continued to be an active member. He was instrumental in its transformation into a 'council' in 1919. The Medical Research Council has flourished ever since, another memorial to Addison's career of public service.

The passage of the Insurance Act and the part played by Addison in launching medical research must be set against the wider political background of these years. After the passage of the Parliament Act in August 1911, politics were never to be quite the same again. The new social and health programmes were submerged by party conflict. Bonar Law succeeded Balfour as Unionist leader, and saw in Asquith and Lloyd George bitter opponents. Asquith himself commented on 'the new style' emanating from the Opposition benches. The Irish home rule controversy was renewed with the introduction of the third Home Rule Bill in 1912; civil war over Ulster appeared to be looming. The woman suffragettes were also becoming more and more militant in their activities in pursuit of the vote, while organized labour erupted in lengthy and bitter strikes from the Welsh valleys to the London docks.

On each of these issues, Addison had his own views. On the suffragette question, although strongly sympathetic to any extension of the franchise, he did not favour militant activity by advocates of 'votes for women'. The WSPU and the Pankhursts even included him among the Liberal 'Antis'. Certainly he voted against the second reading of Sir George Kemp's Women's Enfranchisement Bill on 5 May 1911, along with such intransigents as 'Lulu' Harcourt.[58] Years later, as Minister of Health, he was attacked by Lady Rhondda for neither appointing women to sit on the Ministry consultative council, nor having a council composed solely of wives and mothers as a link with the ministry. He also refused to put a woman on the Welsh Board of Health, in contrast to Lloyd George's previous policies, and was severely attacked by Lady Rhondda in *Time and Tide*.[59] Undoubtedly Addison was no ardent feminist, though whether this is a flaw in his otherwise impregnable armour of radicalism is open to debate. In fact, he favoured the Labour view which advocated adult suffrage for men and women alike. So, too, did his wife, although she noted the relative apathy of a well-dressed audience of women suffragists in March 1911 contrasted with the passion of the working-class electors of Hoxton when the Lords' veto was being debated.[60] Addison's attitude to women's suffrage proved to be a gradualist one. In 1913, he supported the formation of a joint committee of women who were concerned with social issues as well as with the narrowly political issue of the franchise; they should be associated with MPs of all parties, pro- and anti-suffragist alike, who were concerned to promote the welfare of women and children and who favoured a progressive policy for women but who were tired of the feminist issue being discussed in terms only of the suffrage. He was in contact with the noted anti-suffragette Mrs Humphrey Ward to this effect. Addison joined this new committee, and was instrumental in securing the names of MPs to sit on it, thus adding to his discredit amongst the ranks of militant women.[61]

In addition, there were the labour unrest and violent strikes of the years 1910–14 which also posed a major threat for the Liberal government. From the Cambrian strike in South Wales in the autumn of 1910 to the formation of the Triple Alliance of miners, railwaymen, and transport workers in the spring of 1914, the class-consciousness of the trade unions became more and more pronounced. As a member for a working-class constituency such as Hoxton, Addison inevitably took a keen interest in all matters affecting labour. He worked in the interests of mail drivers, post-office workers, and others who were numerous in his constituency. He also negotiated with Churchill in setting up the Union of City Hawkers.[62] Consistently he declared his support for the establishment of trade unions and free collective bargaining, and spoke in Parliament on behalf of improved conditions of employment and higher wages.[63] He was throughout the period a staunch advocate of close political relations between the Liberals and the Labour party, and struck up friendships with Labour leaders such as MacDonald and Arthur Henderson. In this respect, then, Addison was the very apostle of that 'progressive alliance' so much canvassed in the pre-war years.

The Making of a Politician 27

The most damaging crisis of this period concerned the perennial problems of Ireland. In his memoirs, Addison frequently underlines the dominant role of Irish home rule at this time. He was a strong supporter of the government's Home Rule Bill which passed through the Commons in 1912 and 1913 and seemed destined to become law under the terms of the Parliament Act in the summer of 1914. Intense passions were kindled; there were alarms about a possible mutiny by leading generals at the time of the Curragh crisis in March 1914. Mrs Addison commented in her diary, 'How utterly mad these Tories are getting. They've lost their heads more than ever....' She and her husband poured scorn on Carson's melodramatic departure from the Commons to head for his covenanting friends in Ulster. To their amazement, the Irish seditionist was to become Attorney-General in May 1915.[64] The Liberals were pledged to support the Irish Nationalists' claim for self-government. The Protestant Unionists of Ulster threatened armed rebellion. Addision recorded in his diary that in the event of the failure of the Buckingham Palace conference in July 1914, a forced dissolution of Parliament was the probable consequence. He was contemptuous of what he considered Asquith's feebleness in this crisis.

Few of us could understand how the Government could look on at the organised and open preparations for civil war without making any attempt to put them down.... Most of us certainly were firmly convinced that if the situation had been more firmly handled before it had become thus desparate we should have been spared much distress.[65]

Here was the authentic voice of 'Lloyd George Liberalism', some years before its time.

At the end of July 1914, the Irish impasse seemed as alarmingly insoluble as ever. Meanwhile, a renewed land campaign and a new radical budget in 1914 were intended by Lloyd George as a counter to the government's apparent loss of control in domestic politics. Addison naturally took a close interest in land questions because of his rural background in Lincolnshire. In 1912, for example, he had stressed that a thoroughgoing land reform should involve making the land bear its proper share of those burdens of rates and taxes which fell upon industry and upon citizens of every class. An efficient land valuation could be used to free the land for productive use, for commerce, and for efficient labour. He endorsed the taxation of site values in urban areas. At this period he wrote a pamphlet, typical of its time, on 'how the businessmen, workers and inhabitants of Shoreditch have enriched the ground landlords'.[66] In 1913, he was made chairman of the Land and Housing Council of the new Liberal organization for London. He was also elected to the executive committee of the Central London Housing Council, inaugurated at the National Liberal Council in December 1913 in support of Lloyd George's campaign for land and housing reform. He was closely associated with Lloyd George's new land campaign from the outset and took a leading part in advising speakers on aspects of the land question. 'They had better realise that the poor Londoner was not interested in cabbages and Wat Tyler's rebellion but did want his tenement made decent and habitable. They appear to have been great on Wat Tyler but he has fallen flat.'[67] Undoubtedly much of Addison's later passionate involvement with the nation's housing dated from this time.

Lloyd George also used him in the preparation of the 1914 budget, in planning detailed aspects of new schemes for health and the social services. Addison worked closely with leading civil servants such as Morant and Sir George Newman, chief medical officer of the Board of Education, and also with politicians such as Masterman and Edwin Montagu in preparing schemes for nursing centres, for the treatment of tuberculosis, and for new laboratories.[68] Some of Addison's ideas for preventive medicine, for the instruction of mothers in child hygiene and other aspects of health, were far ahead of their time, and not implemented until after 1945. Undoubtedly Lloyd George viewed the 1914 budget, with its social emphasis and its new site rating of land and taxes on unearned income, as a dramatic new radical initiative, designed to recapture the momentum lost since 1911. In fact, the 1914 budget was hamstrung by procedural difficulties and by dissension in the Cabinet. It proved something of a fiasco and severely damaged Lloyd George's reputation for a time. Even so, it advanced Addison still nearer the centre of Liberal policy-making. More generally, the Liberal party remained intact under Asquith's leadership. It retained the will to govern; compared with the Labour government in 1945, it showed few signs of exhaustion. Men like Masterman, Samuel, and Simon were among a new generation of able politicians rising to political prominence. Addison himself was a symbol of this continued Liberal vitality.

His abilities were finally recognized by Asquith on 8 August 1914

The Making of a Politician

when he was appointed Parliamentary Secretary to the Board of Education. After his distinguished work on behalf of the National Insurance Bill, there had been speculation about other appointments for him over a long period of time. It had been suggested that he might become Herbert Samuel's lieutenant at the Local Government Board.[69] Murray of Elibank, the former Liberal chief whip, had proposed that Addison or Arthur Ponsonby take up a new post as Liberal party organizer in the country; had this come about, Addison would have been strongly placed to assist a bid for party leadership by Lloyd George. He frequently deliberated with his friend, the junior whip and fellow London member, Wedgwood Benn, about aspects of party organization.[70] But an appointment to the Board of Education was a natural one for him. He had been much involved in various aspects of educational work over some years. He had been a distinguished university teacher. He had given evidence on the teaching of anatomy to the Royal Commission on universities in 1912, and had served as member of the standing committee on the Elementary Education (Defective and Epileptic Children) Bill which reported in 1914. He was much concerned in the spring of 1914 with trying to set up schools for mothers, with trying to develop methods of preventing infant mortality, and with securing free milk for children in school. He had also been an active member of the Advisory Committee which negotiated the proposed establishment of a Welsh medical school at Cardiff, an issue complicated by tension between the national Welsh university and the civic aspirations of Cardiff.[71] On all counts, then, Addison was a natural recruit for this department.

But the coming of war on 4 August, just before Addison's appointment, had totally overshadowed all these domestic matters. The war raised issues which were of fundamental concern to him. He was by no means narrowly insular or preoccupied solely with domestic politics. On the contrary, he had been a member of the radical Foreign Affairs Group in Parliament, formed after the Agadir crisis in Morocco in 1911 to keep a stern eye on Grey's foreign policy. This group included nearly eighty Liberal back-benchers; it pressed for reduced armaments, an international settlement of disputes, and the need for parliamentary control over foreign policy.[72] The crisis in the Balkans that followed the assassination of the Archduke Franz Ferdinand at Sarajevo in Bosnia on 28 June 1914 was a bombshell for the Foreign Affairs Group, as was the subsequent Austrian ultimatum to Serbia on

24 July. The parliamentary radicals now felt 'as helpless as rats in a trap'.[73] Addison actually signed the basically neutralist resolution of the Foreign Affairs Group on 30 July. However, after Grey's speech on 3 August, Addison, along with Sir George Scott Robertson, the member for Bradford, significantly voted against a Foreign Affairs Group resolution which claimed that no sufficient reason had been offered for British intervention and that negotiations should continue.[74] Addison was no Little Englander and no pacifist. He believed that Grey's speech showed that the hopes of peace had been crushed, 'that the Kaiser meant to ride rough shod over Belgium' and to reach the channel coast. 'Unless we were prepared to see both France and Belgium wiped out, with no guarantee that we ourselves would not be the next victims, we must join with France and Belgium.' They were 'pledged' now to defend Belgium.[75] Thus Addison, like Lloyd George and the entire Cabinet (save for Morley and John Burns who both resigned), swung decisively towards the resolute acceptance of Britain's entry into war.

Addison's chief concern at the coming of war was that so many of the schemes of social betterment at which the government had laboured for so long had to be arrested. At the time of the outbreak of war, he was himself involved with schemes for providing for the children of the sick and unemployed in the East End of London.[76] However, he took comfort from Lloyd George's pledge that social reform would not be suspended by the war, and that the health centres promised in his 1914 budget, for instance, should be installed.[77] In fact Addison and others were to find that from 1914 onwards warfare and welfare proceeded hand in hand.

Meanwhile he was characteristically active in his new post as Parliamentary Secretary to the Board of Education. The vacancy, indeed, had arisen because the previous holder of the post, C. P. Trevelyan, had resigned along with Morley and Burns. The minister in charge was the amiable J. A. Pease with whom Addison built up a good working relationship while finding him insufficiently pugnacious.[78] One early task was to approach educational and municipal authorities to arrange that the War Office should have additional beds available in what were, at present, educational establishments. Addison had some formidable schemes in mind, including the acquisition of the Imperial Institute in London for this purpose, and moving Winchester School to Oxford so that its buildings could be turned into

The Making of a Politician

a hospital.[79] Needless to say, this effort proved unavailing. Addison was active in building up the links of science and industry through the formation of new technical schools. He also headed a committee which worked out a national research programme for the government and led to the formation of the Council for Scientific and Industrial Research. More generally, the educational proposals included in Lloyd George's budget of April 1915 were largely the product of Addison's energy and inspiration.[80]

This work at the Board of Education won considerable acclaim, not least from the Unionist leader, Bonar Law, a fellow chess enthusiast (indeed, a stronger player than Addison) with whom he became friendly. When he gained Cabinet rank in 1917, it was said that Addison had been 'a great success' while Parliamentary Secretary to the Education Board.[81] More important, he reinforced considerably his already close relationship with Lloyd George. They were in frequent contact over the establishment of technical schools, the state of the health services, and other matters. More generally, they had some significant discussions about the general conduct of the war. In these, Lloyd George unburdened himself pretty freely on such matters as the shortage of shells, the inadequacies of Kitchener as Secretary for War, and the expedition to the Dardanelles. 'A long war is more likely to give us a complete victory than a short one,' Lloyd George declared.[82] Addison's range of contact with Lloyd George was shortly to be rewarded in a most dramatic and unexpected way.

This period of quiet, effective work at the Board of Education was suddenly interrupted by the ministerial crisis of May 1915. It saw the end of the Liberal government that had ruled Britain for almost ten years. In the early months of 1915, growing dissatisfaction on both sides of the House engulfed the Asquith government. On the Liberal side, Lloyd George was the voice for a more vigorous prosecution of the war and a more adventurous 'eastern' strategy as indicated by the ill-fated Dardanelles expedition. The Unionist Business Committee of back-benchers felt more and more unease with the party truce. This unrest came to a head with the dismissal of Sir John Fisher, the First Sea Lord, after a bitter quarrel with Churchill in May. After a complex series of political manœuvres, including the sacrifice of his old friend Haldane to a wave of anti-German phobia (which Addison described in a letter to his wife as 'perfectly wicked'), Asquith remodelled his government. It became a coalition, Unionists and

Labour now being brought in. The critical appointment was that of Lloyd George as Minister of Munitions, a vital new department and, politically, the pivot of the new administration. As his new Under-Secretary for this untried portfolio, he insisted on Christopher Addison. 'A man with a high order of intellectual capacity, full of ideas, resourcefulness and courage', was the description of his lieutenant by the new Minister of Munitions.[83]

Addison described in three long letters to his wife and in his diary the method of his appointment on 26 May.

> I had expected . . . that I was going to be told in a friendly way that I should have to go, to make room for a Tory or someone with longer ministerial claims. I have seldom, however, had a bigger surprise than that which awaited me. L. G. said 'You know I am to be Secretary of State for Munitions, and the Prime Minister and I have decided you must come and be my Under-Secretary and help me to run the show'.[84]

After receiving assurances that his research and educational schemes would not be jeopardized, later that day, Addison transferred to the new offices of the Ministry at 6 Whitehall Gardens, at that time occupied largely by workmen literally hammering the rooms into shape for their new requirements. He then spent some time consoling Pease who was 'simply heart-broken' at being replaced by Arthur Henderson at the Board of Education. Two days later, on 28 May, Asquith sent a note to Lloyd George asking if Addison could be moved back to Education, but the new Minister of Munitions was adamant that Addison must stay with him.[85] This promotion marked a dramatic new stage in Addison's ascent to the first rank in politics. His years of radical campaigning since putting the National Insurance Act on the statute book, his competence as a committee-man and an executive minister, above all his increasingly close relationship with Lloyd George, had given him a stature seldom realized amongst the wider public, to whom he was still relatively obscure. At the crucial new Ministry of Munitions, as Lloyd George's departmental aide and political confidant, Addison was poised to penetrate the highest counsels of the realm, with fateful consequences for the future of his party, his nation, and himself.

2

The Making of a Prime Minister

'The Ministry of Munitions is going to be no sinecure,' Addison wrote in his diary, shortly after taking up his new appointment.[1] Even for so self-effacing a public figure, this was a classic of understatement. The new Ministry was to become a vital pivot in the running of the war. Its ramifications were immense. Not only was it involved with the supply of arms in vast quantities for men at the front, but also in organizing the labour which supplied the work-force in the production of armaments. It had to reconcile the conflicting demands of the state for men for the army and of private factories for industrial production. The state assumed powers of direction hitherto unknown: the familiar *laissez-faire* world over which Asquith had presided now vanished. A new colossus of central collectivism imposed controls over production and supply, raw materials, and manpower in a manner without precedent. There were major changes in society, too, with the new role of trade unions in negotiating with the government over labour supply; the introduction of women workers into arms factories with dramatic results for the advancement of the status of their sex; and the use of government arms establishments as laboratories of social welfare. Men like William Beveridge and Walter Layton, G. M. Booth, and Sir Frederick Black were brought in from outside to promote far-reaching and constructive transformation. Truly, Lloyd George's 'men of push and go' wrenched British history into new directions. Throughout, the association which had developed between Lloyd George and Addison in the years since 1911 was immensely reinforced by their close and intimate contact now, not only in relation to the production of munitions, but also to mainstream politics and public affairs in general. It was a period of his life that left a deep imprint on Addison in many ways. Time and again in later years, as in *Practical Socialism* written in 1926 or in speeches when leader of the Lords, he would cite the 'war socialism' of the period at Munitions as a prime justification for a collectivist approach towards the economy.

The new Ministry began with a core consisting of Lloyd George and Addison, assisted by Lloyd George's Secretary, J. T. Davies, and by Sir Hubert Llewellyn Smith of the Board of Trade with whom Lloyd George's association went back to 1905. It rapidly became apparent to them that the system for the production of munitions was inadequate. There was no head of the Munitions department and positive obstruction from the Director of Munitions Supply, Sir Percy Girouard (whom Lloyd George shortly managed to purge). Addison had thought Girouard 'rather inclined to play the game of the big armaments firms'.[2] There was little co-ordination in the munitions field, and endless delays in the implementation of governmental decisions. It was in this and other areas that Addison at once became a central figure. He was given the role of organizing the supply of raw materials, and also of handling the Finance department. Most important of all, he was allotted the vital task of providing exact statistics on the shortage of munitions. He was assisted here by the new head of the Statistics Department, the economist, Walter Layton. Appalling shortages were soon discovered in rifles, artillery, machine-guns, shells, and mortars, while Addison professed to find himself shocked by the incompetence of the War Office. Soon, in the phrase of the time, 'the goods' were being delivered; there was an enormous increase in the output of ammunition, rifles, grenades, mortars, artillery, and, most significantly of all, the new tanks which were first given a private trial, with Addison amongst those attending, in January 1916.[3] In this vital area of the Ministry's work, Addison and Lloyd George worked in intimate partnership. Addison noted after one discussion (relating to the conscription of labour), 'I am afraid the duty of standing up to him has fallen on me. There is always this gratifying feature about our intercourse, that we know and trust each other.... Indeed, he expects I should stand up to him and tell him when I think he is wrong.'[4]

Addison took steps to promote the use of sources of production hitherto not utilized. Interviews were conducted with representatives of engineering firms and of municipalities to consider the form of organization required. In the event, it was decided to divide the country up into nine engineering districts with officers of the Ministry of Munitions at central locations in each area to assist the local committees and to act as intermediaries.⁵ This system proved to be a great success. Factories were compulsorily taken over by the state, and new National Shell Factories, so called, set up directly by central government, often at Addison's behest. Within a year, the entire scope of domestic munitions production had been transformed, to ensure that arms were produced at home and that imports of raw materials and of finished munitions were severely cut back. There was also, however, an important international dimension. It was Addison who was responsible for arranging for the Welsh coal-owner, D. A. Thomas, to visit the United States and Canada to report on armaments contracts there, and for negotiations with Albert Thomas, the French Minister of Munitions, about international munitions' agreements.⁶ An area in which Addison took especial pride was the introduction of new costing procedures to regulate the prices charged by private arms manufacturers such as Vickers and Armstrong Whitworth. He appointed Sir Hardman Lever as assistant financial secretary to the Ministry to inquire in detail into major contracts and undertakings involving expenditure of upwards of £40,000. In the course of time, this new system, involving the fixing of prices of supplies, produced immense savings in the cost of munitions produced. In later years, when Addison as Minister of Health was being assailed by the 'anti-waste' movement as the model of profligate and uncontrolled expenditure, he delighted to refer back to his experience of costing and contracts at the Ministry of Munitions. He contrasted the real economies he had effected in 1915–16 with the irresponsible vapourings of the right-wing press and the irrelevance of the House of Commons Public Accounts Committees.⁷

The main administrative need of the new Ministry was to try to bring all the facets of organization and production under its own control. Addison had written to his wife, 'I can see that some of these Generals and Colonels don't much relish our intrusion, but they are obviously afraid of us for all that.' A major victory was gained over Kitchener and the War Office when the power in relation to munitions held by the War Office were transferred to the Ministry of Munitions in July–August 1915. But at first neither the Ordnance Factories nor the Ordnance Board was transferred. As Addison recorded, 'The result was that, while people all over the country were bursting with enthusiasm and the capacity to help us, we had to look elsewhere for the supply of things necessary for the very beginning of manufacture, and many were the indignant remonstrances that I had to receive for their not being forthcoming.'[8] He managed to obtain a letter from Asquith to give effect to the decision to transfer the Ordnance Factories to the Ministry of Munitions. The Ordnance Board was finally transferred, following a report on the subject by a Cabinet Committee and a memorandum by Addison himself, on 27 November 1915. After this, the output of munitions speeded up considerably.

But to an ever-increasing degree, Addison's period as under-secretary to the Ministry of Munitions was taken up, not with these technical matters of organization and production, but with an even more complex and controversial area, that of labour. The provision of labour, skilled and unskilled, was vital to the entire armaments programme. For the first time, therefore, Addison found himself involved in the thickets of the trade union world. It was an unfamiliar one to him, less amenable than the world of professional deputations and committees to which he had grown accustomed as a middle-class doctor and politician, but one which he faced with characteristic energy and self-confidence, if not always with total success. The background lay in the so-called Treasury Agreement negotiated between Lloyd George and Runciman, acting for the government, and the Engineers and other trade unions headed by Arthur Henderson, on 19 March 1915. This agreement defined the principles which should underlie the modification of trade union privileges for the duration of the war. The right to strike would be suspended in return for a vague pledge (never carried out, in fact) that wartime profiteering by employers would be curbed. Even more important, traditional workshop regulations were to be suspended by the unions to open factories to 'dilution', that is the introduction of unskilled labour and women into the manufacture of munitions and to cut down the proportion of munitions work undertaken by skilled men and craftsmen. The National Labour Advisory Committee of Trade Unionists was set up under Arthur Henderson's leadership, to implement the terms of the Munitions of War Act. From the outset this Committee, like the Ministry itself, found itself enmeshed in a most complex series of delicate labour questions which plagued the government for years to come.

The Ministry of Munitions engaged in two kinds of operation to overcome the serious shortage of skilled men for the production of munitions; in both, Addison was intimately involved. The first was the obtaining of the release of skilled workers from the colours, allied to the War Munitions Volunteer Scheme. Addison recorded 'We were perpetually engaged in a triangle of forces, with the demands of the armies for supplies at one corner, the demands of the self-same army for men at another, and at the third of a group of trade union and employment issues needing a perpetually changing adjustment.'[9] Despite the assistance of civil servants, such as Llewellyn Smith, who were knowledgeable in labour matters, the task of reconciling these conflicting demands often proved beyond the Ministry. Even so, by the end of July 1915, 80,000 men had enrolled under the Munitions Volunteer Scheme. But the supply of labour for the munitions factories was still inadequate, and a second line of attack from the Ministry now followed. Addison pressed Lloyd George to increase the number of skilled workers in arms factories by transfer, and also to secure the co-operation of the unions in bringing in unskilled labour through 'dilution'. He told the National Advisory Committee on 31 August that it was estimated that 'from 70,000 to 80,000 skilled workmen would eventually be required to man the new factories . . . of whom some 35,000 would be required by October'. They were not getting more than 60 per cent of the possible output of the existing machinery. Addison could 'see no other way out of their present difficulty than to dilute the present supply of skilled labour' and to urge the workers to fulfil their undertakings accepted by the Treasury Agreement.[10]

Dilution, above all, meant the use of women. Addison now actively pressed for the employment of more women workers in factory shops. He produced a major memorandum on 27 August 1915 in which it was suggested that basic conditions as to the wages and hours of women workers be agreed with the unions and with employers, as well as with women's organizations. The assistance of the National Advisory Council should be enlisted to see that women were employed under proper conditions of work and at acceptable wage rates, related to the work of a skilled mechanic.[11] Considerable headway was made after Lloyd George addressed a trade union conference organized by Henderson's National Labour Advisory Committee on the subject of the dilution of skilled labour on 16 September. Addison had prepared detailed notes for Lloyd George for this meeting, and successfully proposed that he broach the subject of setting up a central labour supply committee.¹² The conference duly passed a resolution in favour of establishing such a committee, to advise the Ministry of Munitions on the transfer of skilled labour and the introduction of semi-skilled and unskilled labour for munitions work so as to secure the most productive use of all labour supplies in the manufacture of munitions. Even the Amalgamated Society of Engineers, who had most resolutely opposed the very idea of dilution, now agreed to accept Lloyd George's proposals for a central labour supply committee. By the end of September, with a comprehensive programme for the release of men from the colours now agreed on also, the production of munitions and the intractable problems of labour supply seemed to be making considerable progress.

In the course of the next two years, by methods of 'dilution', some half a million women and men, unsuitable for military service, became employed in the manufacture of munitions. Nevertheless, the principle of dilution caused immense labour difficulties between 1915 and 1917. After all, the privileges and exemptions won after stern struggles by trade unions over generations appeared to have been abruptly swept away with the rapid passage of the Munitions of War Act. The government's 'programme of dilution', officially announced on 13 October, caused immense problems especially the principle that no munitions worker should be employed at any task which required skill of a lesser degree than he possessed.¹³ The introduction of 'dilutees' into tasks previously reserved for skilled workers, for instance through the introduction of machines which took little skill to operate, also involved enormous complications, not least through the process of the 'upgrading' of dilutees. The government now introduced the so-called 'badging system' under which badges were issued to workers engaged upon munitions work or production for war purposes, whose removal from their present employment would prejudice the production, transportation, and supply of munitions of war. This was something close to the dreaded industrial conscription, and caused immense labour unrest. It was the unfortunate Addison who in large measure had to try to deal with it.

The worst labour troubles came in Scotland on the Clyde from October 1915 onwards; this was associated with the rank-and-file shop stewards' movement which here took the form of the Clyde Workers' Committee. It was headed by militant socialists or syndicalists who denounced the Munitions of War Act, of whom William

Gallacher and David Kirkwood were the most prominent.[14] In late October, there was turmoil on the Clyde because of the imprisonment of three shipwrights from the Fairfield yard who refused to pay fines. These related to the notorious Clause Seven of the Munitions of War Act, which made it illegal to engage a workman who had been employed on a government contract unless he possessed a leaving certificate. Without a certificate, a worker was legally unemployable, almost bound in servitude to his employer. The entire Fairfield yard stopped work, and the release of the arrested men was demanded as a condition of the yard resuming production. Addison held conferences with the leaders of the Clyde workers on 26–7 October, and the matter was amicably resolved; the fines were to be paid by the union and the men released.[15] Now and later, Addison was a conciliatory influence in the Ministry in shaping its attitude to the Clyde Workers' Committee. Llewelyn Smith and Beveridge both urged that Gallacher and other leaders should be prosecuted for publishing material which denounced the Munitions of War Act. Addison, however, successfully advised Lloyd George against further action, 'in view of the very qualified opinion of the Lord Advocate, the forthcoming amendment to the Munitions of War Act and the lapse of time since the alleged offence'.[16] His view carried the day, and another crisis was averted.

The Munitions of War (Amendment) Bill was introduced by Addison in December, to try to moderate the unrest of labour.[17] The main principles of the Bill were that profiteering in the arms industry should be limited, that there should be a relaxation of trade practices which were found to stand in the way of increased output, and that there was to be a limitation on both employers and employed as to how they could dispose of their labour. Where a worker was dismissed, he should be given a leaving certificate unless in an exceptional case it could be shown that he had deliberately misbehaved in order to be dismissed. Arbitration tribunals were to be set up, and regulations laid down regarding the wages of women engaged on munitions work. Addison explained, in the debate on the second reading, that, although through the Bill the state made considerable inroads on individual and industrial liberty, the government was trying to adjust differences fairly and to hold the balance evenly between conflicting claims and interests. The Act did indeed somewhat diminish the resentment of the trade unions about the operation of leaving certificates, though the wider problems still remained.

The Amendment Act became law in January 1916, but labour troubles over recruitment and the payment and introduction of unskilled workers continued to plague the government. The Clyde area was again the most troublesome region. Lloyd George, with his popular reputation as an almost hypnotic conciliator of labour, attempted to meet the problem head-on. He addressed a meeting of 3,000 delegates at St. Andrew's Hall on Christmas Day, 1915, in the presence of Arthur Henderson amongst others. On this occasion, the unique Lloyd George brand of charm and persuasiveness signally failed to work; he received a noisy and hostile reception from the Scottish workers. The atmosphere amongst the engineering workers on the Clyde, swayed by the quasi-syndicalist doctrines of men such as Gallacher, Kirkwood, and John Maclean, was now tense: 'every effort will be made to crush us', declared Willie Gallacher.[18] There was a wider background of soaring food prices at a time when the workers' wages were being curbed and union practices undermined. According to one author, the government responded with a planned, concerted strategy to crush the Clyde Workers' Committee, first through the suppression of the Glasgow ILP newspaper, *Forward* (which had reported the Christmas Day meeting with a full account of Lloyd George's unhappy reception), then through the operations of dilution commissioners on the Clyde.[19] The main decisions, of course, rested with Lloyd George. Disentangling Addison's subordinate, though important, role is not easy; but it seems clear that he was in general a moderating force, even if taking the official line on public occasions. He endorsed the dispatch of Labour Commissioners to the Clyde and also to Tyneside, where further labour difficulties had occurred: the government 'ought to be able to count on a firm but conciliatory policy in applying dilution in both places'. One of his consistent aims was to ensure the maximum authority for the Ministry of Munitions itself. When Lloyd George suggested the formation of a separate labour department to provide labour for the Board of Trade, the Admiralty, and the Ministry of Munitions, Addison was instrumental in causing him to change his mind. This department, Addison argued, would mean that Munitions was surrendering a potent instrument in increasing the output of armaments at a time when the Ministry's popularity was now in decline. It would seriously diminish the authority of Lloyd George himself. Instead, the Munitions of War (Amendment) Bill should be invoked and each depart-

The Making of a Prime Minister 41

ment made responsible for the supply of its own labour needs. Lloyd George then dropped this idea, though the broader concept of a separate Ministry of Labour re-emerged after he became Prime Minister.[20]

The trouble on the Clyde came to a head in March 1916. A leading member of the Clyde Workers' Committee, David Kirkwood, claimed rights which were denied by the works' management. Kirkwood, it was said,

insisted that he should be entitled during working hours, without the permission of the management, to leave his work in his own department and go into any other department of the works for the purpose of investigating what was being done with unskilled labour, interviewing the women introduced, and examining their proficiency, rates of wages and other matters.[21]

It was a curious and somewhat mysterious move since, until the end of the previous year, Kirkwood had collaborated privately with the employers in the solution of labour difficulties. The management referred the Kirkwood case to the Clyde Commissioners, but the members of the Workers' Committee refused to negotiate. When Kirkwood was dismissed, strike action began throughout the Clyde yards. On 23 March the chief Clyde Commissioner, Macassey, intervened and wired the Ministry of Munitions that the whole of the Clyde Workers' Committee should be deported. The following day, the Ministry agreed to the deportation of several of the leaders if satisfactory evidence was supplied. As a result, on 28 March eight shop stewards from Weir's works were deported to Aberdeen. On 29 March two further men in Johnstone's works were arrested, and as a result strikes amongst engineering workers spread rapidly.[22]

It was Addison who had the difficult task of disentangling this unhappy situation, as Asquith, Lloyd George, and other ministers were at an Allied conference in Paris. He did so with some success. Certainly his general approach is a counter-argument to the view that the government was engaged in some kind of plot to destroy the Clyde Workers' Committee, a plot that began with the suppression of *Forward*. In fact, the suppression of *Forward* had been almost an accident, and not a decision taken by the Ministry of Munitions at all. The Dilution Commissioners were not, until the end of February 1916, primarily concerned with the Clyde Workers' Committee. They had ignored such provocations as the issue of the *Worker*, a CWC journal which reprinted Lloyd George's speech on Christmas Day.[23]

Addison's speech in the House on 28 March certainly took a strongly critical view of the activities of the Clyde Workers' Committee. He claimed that it repudiated any allegiance to existing trade unions, and had embarked on a policy of disrupting or sabotaging the production of munitions of war in the Clyde region. The Committee sought to compel the government to repeal the Military Service Act and the Munitions of War Act, and to withdraw all limitations on the increase of wages, and governmental control over strike action. The ringleaders had now been deported under Section Fourteen of the Defence of the Realm Act. Their actions had been repudiated by the official trade unions, notably by the Amalgamated Society of Engineers. Addison felt certain that the majority of the workers on the Clyde did not support them.[24]

This speech was not wholly unconciliatory in tone, for all its criticism of the Clyde Workers' Committee, but the total of men on strike continued to rise. In the Commons on 30 March, the Liberal backbencher, W. M. R. Pringle, claimed that negotiations on the Clyde had been near to a settlement, but that further deportations had then taken place and Addison had broken off the talks. In reply, Addison described the mediation efforts of Ramsay MacDonald in trying to get the men on the Clyde back to work. At MacDonald's request, he had seen two leading members of the Clyde Committee, Gallacher and Muir, privately in his room, in the presence of Macassey, the Commissioner. He had refused to agree to the reinstatement of the men deported, and had subsequently written to MacDonald that the proper course for them was to return to the Clyde and use their influence for the workers to go back to work. Lloyd George strongly supported Addison's justification of his actions. He added that to describe a private meeting with two members of the CWC as 'promising negotiations', as Pringle had done, was grossly misleading. In the event, MacDonald's advice had some influence with the deported workers and they agreed to put their case in the hands of union officials.[25]

Addison's version of the circumstances of their meeting was strongly disputed by Gallacher and Muir, the two members of the CWC involved. But their cause was now a losing one. The Clyde Workers were distinctly isolated even from the broader labour movement on the Clyde itself. By 4 April there was a general resumption of work. Shortly afterwards, several strikers were fined for their part in the disputes, while Gallacher and Muir were sentenced to a year in gaol. The Clyde region now became much more peaceful. The extent to which the government's dilution campaign in this area was conciliatory or coercive has provoked lively debate amongst historians. One thing, however, is generally agreed—that Addison's role was that of a moderate throughout. He was far from happy with his own involvement in the Clyde deportations. He told the Engineers' president, Brownlie, a month later 'It was just as objectionable to me as it was to you; we disliked it intensely. I do not think myself I have ever been associated with anything I hated doing more.'[26] However, when work was resumed on the Clyde in early April, he heralded it as 'a triumph for firmness and moderation'. Above all, the authority of the official trade union leadership, as opposed to rank-and-file militants, had been upheld. One legacy was that Addison sanctioned the establishment of an intelligence department to investigate minutely the underground currents of labour unrest and the persons responsible for industrial agitation in different parts of the country, with particular reference to munitions.[27] It would provide a valuable guide in monitoring current industrial feeling as far as the Ministry was concerned, and provide also an early-warning system for dealing with ringleaders in agitation. Clearly, Addison's radical sympathies and attachment to the trade union ideal did not preclude a firm line in handling labour disturbances at a time of national emergency.

The ending of the Clyde strikes in early April marked the end of the long-drawn-out struggle over the principle of dilution. During the summer of 1916, relations between the Ministry of Munitions and organized labour now became more cordial. In August three of the deportees were allowed to return to the Clyde after giving a signed undertaking that they would submit grievances through official trade union channels and abstain from acts likely to prejudice the supply of munitions. In December, Addison, now Minister of Munitions himself, ordered all the deportation orders to be cancelled, on the same conditions.[28] With this improved climate of labour relations, the production of munitions continued to increase impressively under Addison's watchful eye, and the output of such new factories as those at Gretna and Queensferry rose substantially. The expectations aroused by the new Ministry at the time of its creation, amidst the alarm over the 'shell shortage', had been amply fulfilled.

The labour problems that beset the Minister were, however, far from over. There was, for example, new difficulty concerning the inroads that were being made upon the list of exemptions from the army. In the controversy which led to the establishment of the Manpower Board in the autumn of 1916, Edwin Montagu who had succeeded Lloyd George as Addison's departmental head at Munitions in July, on Lloyd George's moving to the War Office, became forthright in his criticisms of the de-badging programmes. These badges had been issued originally by the Ministry of Munitions to people they considered should be exempt from military service; the War Office were now taking some of them away again. The shortage of men in steel works, for instance, had become so acute by July that Addison instructed the badging department not to de-badge any more single men over the age of thirty, or any married men, if they were suitable for work in the steel works or shipyards of the country. Holidays for munitions workers were also postponed. Addison strongly supported the idea of a board to determine the allocation of manpower and to settle the rival claims of the different departments.[29] In August he was amongst those deputed to draw up its terms of reference. He wrote optimistically to Wedgwood Benn in October that 'we are now well up against the Man Power problem and I think the War Office and ourselves are in substantial agreement as to ways and means'.[30] However, he also recorded in his diary how they were subsequently to regret the actions of the Manpower Board in issuing drastic recommendations without sufficient enquiry as to how they would be carried out.[31] Improper enlistment continued to be a growing cause of unrest. An alternative arrangement was made between the Ministry of Munitions and the War Office to the effect that not only unskilled but semi-skilled men up to the age of thirty should be de-badged as quickly as possible. It was ironic that Addison now found Lloyd George, for so long his intimate associate, something of an antagonist in upholding the claims of his new department, the War Office. The Manpower Board's instructions about calling-up continued, and many skilled men were recruited, much to the anger of organized labour.

Matters came to a head in Sheffield where, as on the Clyde, a rank-and-file Workers' Committee had been formed amongst skilled craftsmen in the winter of 1916–17. This was a district with no previous tradition of rank-and-file activism or syndicalist sympathy, unlike its Scottish counterpart. A strike began in Sheffield on 16 November, following the conscription into the army of Leonard Hargreaves, a fitter at Vickers. There appeared to be some evidence of the Vickers firm secretly conniving with the government, not least in failing to provide the papers that would have ensured Hargreaves's discharge. The threat of industrial conscription once again loomed large. The Sheffield strike showed the alienation of rank-and-file workers from both government policy and the edicts of their own union leadership. In mid-November, there were 12,000 men on strike in Sheffield, virtually all the skilled engineers in the town, a remarkable display of class solidarity. They won an impressive and rapid triumph, since Hargreaves was soon reinstated. Addison gloomily commented that 'the escapades of the local recruiting officers have lost us the output of four days in the big armament shops of Sheffield'.[32] It made the case for a rational policy on labour supply all the more irresistible.

The government was now concerned at the apparent undermining of the trade unions' control over their own members, especially in engineering trades. To remedy this, the Trade Card scheme was introduced. Under this, the unions themselves were to issue cards to their skilled members as a surety against enlistment into the armed services. This was on condition that all their members not on war work became War Munition Volunteers, the unions to be responsible for finding, by voluntary means, the requisite number of skilled men required for the army. Addison admitted that the Trade Card scheme was 'a great feather in the cap of the unions', but he did not have much confidence in it. He recorded at the same time, 'it bristles all over with the possibilities of difficulties for the unions, for ourselves and for the recruiting department.'[33] The far more serious May strikes in 1917 were to bear out his forebodings, and to some degree he was to be the political victim of them.

Apart from these interminable labour troubles, the Ministry was in a unique position as a manufacturing and employment agency. Never before had the state assumed such sweeping responsibilities for directing and organizing production in industry. Autarky or war socialism on the German model was firmly installed in Britain, too. But a different kind of obligation was involved, one to which Addison warmed far more readily than to the compulsory direction or coercion of dissident workers. He describes how he agreed with Lloyd George, soon after the formation of the Ministry of Munitions, that the opportunity should be taken in arms factories and shops to ensure better and more humane standards of working conditions. Warfare and welfare fed on each other, and the Munitions Ministry became a pioneer of social change. In September 1915 Lloyd George empowered Addison to appoint specialists to make inquiries and give advice on the health of workers employed in munitions factories. The Health of Munition Workers Committee was formally constituted that month. Its terms of reference were 'to consider and advise on questions of industrial fatigue, hours of labour and other matters affecting the personal health and physical efficiency of workers in munitions factories and workshops'.[34] In *Politics from Within*, Addison gives a full account of the work of this Committee; its chairman was Sir George Newman with whom he had had many dealings over national insurance in the past. It was stipulated, as a result of this Committee's investigations, that there should be a compulsory rest day per week, and that the average weekly hours for men, including overtime, should not exceed sixty-five. Previously, totals of seventy-five or even eighty hours had not been unusual. In October 1915, the Ministry of Munitions also accepted the responsibility for the provision of canteens in national factories and for encouraging their provision in controlled establishments. Addison was again much involved with providing housing accommodation for munitions workers who had to be transferred to work in new armament factories. By the end of the war, more than 11,000 permanent housing units had been set up by the Ministry,[35] a useful contribution towards lessening that shortage of working-class housing with which Addison was to be so much concerned in his later career.

Another important milestone was the third report of the Health of Munitions Workers Committee which elaborated the need for an organized system of welfare for industrial workers. At the end of 1915, the Quaker sociologist, Seebohm Rowntree, famous, for his study of poverty in York and of agricultural problems in pre-war years, was appointed to head a committee responsible for the welfare aspects of the Ministry's work. Addison took great interest in the training of welfare superintendents, although his personal relations with Rowntree were not always good. He also set up, in collaboration with Rowntree, joint committees of employers and workers to deal with labour difficulties and working conditions.[36] Clearly for Addison as for Lloyd George, the war had accelerated rather than suspended the pre-war drive for social welfare.

In a totally different area, Addison was involved in the passage of the Defence of the Realm (Acquisition of Land) Bill in the summer of 1916.[37] Much public money had been spent by the Admiralty, War Office, and Ministry of Munitions in erecting aircraft hangars, factories, and storehouses for war purposes. There had been no time to investigate properly the title and other legal aspects of all this. The Bill's purpose was to place the state as far as possible in a more secure position with respect to expenditure incurred and to safeguard it against avoidable loss. It was necessary to guard against the contingency that at the end of the war, when the Defence of the Realm Act would lapse, the buildings and plant established by various government departments might be forfeited to the owners of the soil. Addison's bill thus enabled the Crown to continue to hold the land for a period of seven years after the war ended.

In all these respects, then, with regard to industrial production, the supply of labour, welfare policy, and compulsory powers exercised by the state, Addison was at the centre of a nexus of decision-making vital to the reshaping of the economy and society, as well as to the running of the war effort. Addison had become a leading practitioner of a degree of collectivism and central planning without precedent in British history. For the rest of his career, he would become the retrospective advocate of state socialism, on grounds both of efficiency and of humanitarianism.

These complex departmental concerns were, however, projected against a wider political background. New forces emerged soon after the formation of the Asquith coalition in May 1915 which were to lead to the eventual breakup of the government and even of the Liberal party itself. Once again, Addison was an important figure in a process of secular, historic change. The provision of manpower for the army was a vital key to these new tensions. This affected not only the army and armed forces, but every workshop and business establishment in the land. It raised fundamental issues of principle with respect to the coercive powers of the state over individual citizens. The traditional Liberal ethic, individualist to the core, was already challenged by the very fact of total war and the policies of collectivism and centralization that flowed from it. From May 1915, the Liberal party at Westminster became riven by internal factions of a serious and fundamental kind. Above all other issues, there arose the question of universal male military conscription, a symbolic divide between a whole-hearted commitment to all-out war, whatever the cost, and respect for the historic faith of individual liberty.

In August 1915, Lloyd George became an open advocate of the principle of conscription, as indeed were almost all the leading Unionists in the government. Addison, like most other Liberals, had always opposed compulsory military service. Voluntary recruitment was far more effective, while there was also the high priority of employing more workers in the munitions factories. Failures on the field, for instance at Suvla Bay, and the neglect of making the best use of the early successes of the British army at Neuve-Chapelle and Festubert were regarded by him as due to deficient staff work and inept leadership, not to a shortage of troops.[38] But he, too, came to recognize the supreme need for supplying men for the front in 1915–16. The Derby scheme of recruiting men from categories, within specific occupations, was not providing nearly enough men for the army, as he now acknowledged. On the other hand, he knew that voluntary recruitment had provided over two million recruits in the first twelve months of the war, and that pressing for general conscription would cause an immense uproar both in the House of Commons and in the country. He was known to be Lloyd George's confidant, and was implored by other Liberal members to 'keep [Lloyd George] straight' on the principle of conscription.[39]

By the autumn of 1915, Lloyd George's known sympathy with conscription and general dissatisfaction with the running of the war were causing more and more criticism from fellow Liberal ministers such as Runciman and McKenna, and from Liberal journalists such as A. G. Gardiner of the *Daily News*. This press campaign made Addison highly indignant, even though he himself supported at the most only a modified form of conscription. Reluctantly, Lloyd George and his Unionist colleagues agreed to give the Derby scheme a fair trial, but by December Lloyd George was threatening to resign unless Asquith gave a pledge to enlist single men. All single men who had not attested should be required to show cause why they should not be enlisted before married men who had attested were called up. Asquith's government now hung in the balance. At the end of

The Making of a Prime Minister 49

December, he was forced to make significant concessions, and the government's Military Service Bill in January 1916 proposed a modified form of conscription dealing with single men only. However, Addison recorded in his diary the traumatic effect of this move upon the minds and consciences of Liberals in the House.[40] Sir John Simon, the Home Secretary, resigned from the government in protest; McKenna and Runciman almost joined him, and others were sorely stricken in conscience. Conversely, there was now formed a backbench movement named the Liberal War Committee, about forty Liberal members including Freddie Guest, Sir Alfred Mond, Sir William Sutherland, and Ellis Griffith, a 'ginger group' who pressed for a more vigorous prosecution of the war. They strongly applauded the first stage of the adoption of male conscription as a prelude to a more effective direction of the war effort, unencumbered by Liberal principles.

Throughout March and April 1916, the arguments over conscription continued to rage fiercely. The Derby recruiting scheme and the compromise bill of January 1916 were held to be inadequate in producing the necessary recruits in sufficient numbers. Asquith's leadership on the whole question seemed more and more indecisive. Meanwhile, Unionist ministers urged Lloyd George to take a strong line. According to Addison, they were prepared to go to the length of supporting him for the premiership. In a characteristically intimate discussion on 7 April, Addison urged his leader not to separate himself from the democratic party. Lloyd George agreed and declared that 'the time had not yet come for action'. Offers from the Unionists of a similar kind were rejected by Lloyd George on the grounds that he could never head the Tory party. He could not identify himself with any new movement if he was not going to have, at the same time, the support of 'a solid and sufficient body of Liberals'. Addison stressed to Lloyd George, now on the verge of resignation, that the basis of his support was still too weak, and that he would alienate himself fatally from the Liberal party if he were to resign with mainly Tory backing. Lloyd George's reply announced his resolve not to break away unless driven to do so by supreme military necessity. As Addison observed in his diary, 'Loyal as I am to L. G., I feel considerable hesitation at this moment in promising to ally' with what would be 'a Carsonite party' and 'a very small section of our own party'.[41]

Matters reached a climax on 13 April when the General Staff put up a document which gave their point of view on the number of men required. This was virtually an ultimatum: they threatened to resign *en masse* if the men were not found. Meanwhile rumours were circulating in sections of the press, notably the *Daily News*, that Lloyd George was actively intriguing against Asquith, though Addison inevitably discounted them. Personally, he remained sceptical as to whether the universal conscription that was being demanded by certain sections of the Cabinet would produce the men required. He believed that men already available were simply not being obtained, and that what was required was 'to put men of brains in command of the War Office recruiting machinery'.[42]

The controversy over conscription had, however, gone too far and too fast. Apart from the genuine crisis over recruitment for the armed forces, conscription had become the very symbol of more decisive methods of waging war. Lloyd George still seemed an isolated, contentious figure, unwilling or unable to take a decisive course of action. At this vital stage, Addison took a highly dramatic and important political initiative. In the first few days of May, along with two colleagues, David Davies, Liberal member for Montgomeryshire and a millionaire coal-owner, and Frederick Kellaway, Liberal member for Bedford, he drew up a list of Liberal members of parliament who would be willing to back Lloyd George in any confrontation with Asquith. They 'might be relied on to support an active policy'.[43] The purpose of this move was clearly to persuade Lloyd George to stay in the Cabinet, especially as he was now winning his point over conscription, and it succeeded. But there is no doubt that the Addison/Davies/Kellaway move was of much longer-term significance. It indicated that Asquith's authority within the Liberal ranks could no longer be taken as axiomatic. The prospect of some profound split within the party was no longer unthinkable. In the event, Lloyd George won all along the line. On 4 May Asquith was forced to introduce a comprehensive Compulsory Military Service Bill for all males between the ages of eighteen and forty-five. This was a complete reversal of policy, and a total triumph for Lloyd George at the cost of a background of seething turmoil in the Liberal party.

Thus were the events of December 1916 foreshadowed during the conscription crisis earlier in the year. In his memoirs, Addison documented the continuing saga of muddle, indecision, and discon-

The Making of a Prime Minister

tent as the Asquith government staggered on. The mishandling of Irish affairs in the summer of 1916 markedly increased disaffection amongst both Unionists and Liberals. Addison himself was more and more disturbed by the political pressures that were obstructing a rational conduct of the war effort. As early as December 1915, he had confessed in his diary, 'Good democrat as I am, I am beginning to change my mind and to think that it would be better for the nation at present if Parliament were not sitting.'[44] From April 1916 he was consciously awaiting some kind of political take-over by Lloyd George, and constantly urged his chief to broaden his basis of political and industrial support. He urged, for instance, the formation of 'Win the War Committees' to direct nation-wide organization in the different regions.[45] Throughout that tense summer, as the war on the western front went from bad to worse, Addison kept in close touch with the Welsh Liberal, David Davies. They both felt that Lloyd George was the sole acceptable leader capable of winning the war. Davies reported that all the officers he had met during a recent visit to the front in France were supporters of Lloyd George. 'There is no pessimism in this crowd, but a pretty average sickness with the way things are being run at home by the government,' Davies wrote to Addison. 'The sooner another crisis comes the better—so long as it serves to provide the country with a new leader and a fresh government which will restore public confidence. . . . Lloyd George is their man.' Addison fully shared these hopes. In late May, he wrote to Davies 'I sincerely hope that it will not be long before we shall want you here to help. It will not be my fault if it is.'[46]

He became more than ever convinced that Lloyd George should replace Asquith. He wrote to his wife in August that Asquith might have to resign over the Irish question and he hoped for 'a reconstruction with L. G. as Prime Minister'.[47] In his memoirs, Addison documents how, until the breakdown of the Irish policy, he had done his utmost to keep Lloyd George in Asquith's government and to prevent its breakup. The disastrous aftermath of the Easter Rising in Dublin was the turning-point. From that time onwards, he felt that he could no longer defend Asquith after the abortive end of the negotiations with the Unionists and Nationalists over an Irish home rule settlement. Asquith, so Addison believed, had thrown away a golden opportunity of granting immediate home rule to a large part of Ireland, with Ulster shortly to follow. There had been a general agreement with Redmond and the Irish Nationalist leaders, which a Cabinet majority had endorsed. Redmond had risked his own political existence, and the survival of a constitutional Irish party, in trying to secure its acceptance. There were only a handful of Unionist reactionaries against it, since the southern Irish Unionists were no longer a stumbling-block—yet the opportunity had been cast aside. Asquith had shown only dilatoriness in handling 'this Irish mess'. Had Lloyd George been in command and in charge of overall policy towards Ireland, he might well have brought off a great settlement and eliminated Ireland as a major problem.[48]

Throughout the summer of 1916, although separated from the War Office by his work at Munitions, Addison maintained his close contact with Lloyd George. He records, 'I had, I think, a considerable measure of influence on L. G.'[49] This seems fair comment, since Addison, of all Lloyd George's close associates at this time, was nearest to that social radicalism from which the Welshman had sprung. Addison helped persuade his colleague not to become Chief Secretary for Ireland in May. He also discussed with him whether or not he should succeed Kitchener at the War Office.[50] Lloyd George was said to have favoured Addison as his successor as Minister of Munitions and it seems somewhat surprising that Edwin Montagu was appointed instead. Lloyd George was also recorded as having favoured Addison for the presidency of the Board of Education when Arthur Henderson resigned in June. This would have been highly appropriate as Henderson had asked Addison in May 1915 to return to the Board of Education as all the departmental staff there were enthusiastic for him.[51] In fact, the colourless Lord Crewe was appointed instead, a typical Asquithian choice. Addison's relations with Edwin Montagu (whose promotion to Minister of Munitions he had originally welcomed) did not improve after July 1916. 'He is too nervy and jumpy for a job like this. He readily gives way if he is opposed and adopts the attitude of throwing up the sponge. Also he is wanting in pluck when he is put into a corner.'[52] Evidently Munitions had lost some of its 'push and go' when Lloyd George left it and his partnership with Addison broke up.

During the autumn of 1916, the war went badly everywhere, with the British catastrophe on the Somme, the French army bottled up in Verdun, U-boat attacks on merchant shipping, and the Grand Fleet severely mauled at Jutland. Lloyd George was more and more critical

The Making of a Prime Minister 53

of the Supreme Command. In particular, he urged that assistance be sent to Romania. After some pressure by Robertson, no troops were sent there, but Lloyd George's fears were amply confirmed when the Germans invaded Romania in November. Addison, too, was deeply disturbed at the conduct of the war, and the procrastination of Asquith on vital matters. On 6 October 1916, he wrote to Wedgwood Benn, 'I am afraid this place absorbs one's energies and thoughts so much that there is little time to keep in touch with "current politics", if there are any such things these days.... One's impression is that so far as constructive capacity and powers are concerned the House has worn a little threadbare during the last eighteen months....'[53] By November he had come to believe that drastic changes were desirable as decision and rapidity of action were essential. Lloyd George needed someone to liberate him from his preconceived notion that he was politically weak and isolated. Addison was to be partly instrumental in doing this.

The important role which Addison played during the days of crisis in the Liberal party of 1–9 December 1916 is fully recorded in his diary. Mr. A. J. P. Taylor has seen him as 'the real maker of the Lloyd George government'.[54] The scepticism that Addison felt in November as to the running of the war was forcibly strengthened during a talk with Bonar Law on 28 November. The latter observed, in his quiet way, 'We cannot go on like this Addison, do you think?'.[55] Addison responded that the public desperately needed 'a strong lead' and that unless a new leader emerged the government would soon be dismissed by Commons and country. For Lloyd George meanwhile, the failure to aid Romania was the last straw: on 9 November he told Hankey, 'We are going to lose this war.'[56] He told Addison that he did not seek to be Prime Minister, but was anxious for a new War Cabinet to run the war on a non-departmental basis and get key decisions rapidly implemented. The idea of such a Cabinet or Committee emerged in his famous meetings with the Unionists, Bonar Law and Edward Carson, from 20 November 1916, under the enigmatic mediation of Max Aitken. Soon, the very existence of the government was in question.

Addison records how Lloyd George, Law, and Carson delivered their ultimatum to Asquith on 1 December.[57] It laid down that a war committee was fundamental for the successful continuance of the war. Unless one were set up, and the Supreme Command radically overhauled, Lloyd George would resign. On Sunday, 3 December, Asquith agreed that there should be a modified War Committee on the lines of Lloyd George's demands. The Prime Minister should retain general responsibility over Cabinet and Parliament and have a veto over the Committee's proposals, but he should not be a member of this Committee. However, allegedly on the basis of an article in *The Times* on 4 December which leaked much of the details and implied that Asquith's role would be reduced to a nullity, Asquith backed down from the agreement of the previous day. Addison himself believed that the real reason for Asquith's withdrawal was that on Monday he saw McKenna, Harcourt, and Simon who turned him against the idea,[58] but this is hard to substantiate by an examination of the chronology of that morning. Lloyd George promptly handed in his resignation. By the evening of the 6th, Asquith realized that he had no hope of retaining Unionist support and he, too, resigned office. Addison remained faithful to Lloyd George throughout this tense period of crisis. On 4 December he and Kellaway 'on our own account' decided to canvass the Liberal MPs to discover how many would support Lloyd George. They went through lists of members drawn up, for much the same purpose, during the summer. By Wednesday, 6 December, this canvass showed that many Liberals definitely would support Lloyd George or might reasonably be expected to do so. Forty-nine were 'out and out' supporters, and 126 others would back a Lloyd George government if it were formed.[59] This information suggested that Lloyd George was assured a substantial degree of support among Liberals, indeed among well over half the Liberals in the House, as well as among Unionists. It was a vital stage in securing broad-based, all-party support for Lloyd George, and was largely Addison's work.

Meanwhile on 5 December Addison had been brought more directly into the crisis, much to his surprise. Lloyd George sent for him to Number Eleven, and the Private Secretary, J. T. Davies, told him that he was to see Bonar Law who had been requested by the King to form a government. From that time onwards, Addison was asked to attend meetings of the party leaders and advisers as 'a Liberal colleague of Lloyd George'.[60] It underlined his role as a key figure in the crisis.

Bonar Law was unable to form a government as the Liberals refused to join him: this was wholly predictable. After a conference with Henderson, Balfour, Bonar Law, Asquith, and Lloyd George at which no agreement was reached, the King sent for Lloyd George on the evening of 6 December and the latter kissed hands as Prime Minister. Earlier that day, Addison had attended a meeting including Lloyd George, Bonar Law, Carson, and Edmund Talbot, the Unionist chief whip, to try to decide on the composition of a Cabinet.[61] It was widely believed among many leading Liberals, including the whips, that Addison was Lloyd George's only 'out and out' supporter of any stature. But he was more than adequate for the task on hand. On the 6th Addison revealed the list of Liberal members willing to support Lloyd George if he became premier. He was also active in negotiating with influential Labour figures such as the railwayman's leader, J. H. Thomas, with whom Addison had some contact at the Ministry of Munitions, and also the Labour MP, John Hodge.[62] At a meeting with Lloyd George on the evening of the 6th, Addison was able to convince Lloyd George that he had now a wide basis of both Liberal and Labour support. He predicted that in a day or two there would be a stampede of support to Lloyd George's side.

At a further meeting with King George V on Thursday, 7 December, Lloyd George was thus able to report his ability to form a government. This was due to Addison in no small measure; significantly, he was the first member of parliament to shake Lloyd George by the hand after he became Prime Minister, and they also dined together at Lloyd George's first dinner as premier. It was a frugal, cheerless affair of cold meat and soup.[63] During the following days, Addison was further involved in the attempts to form a new government. Addison's suggestions to some degree accorded with Lloyd George's views; thus Sir Albert Stanley, a business man, went to the Board of Trade, R. E. Prothero to the Board of Agriculture, and George Cave to the Home Office, as Addison suggested. However, a proposal that insurance be brought under the Local Government Board under the presidency of Milner, with Waldorf Astor as Under-Secretary, did not materialize. Milner had already been appointed to the War Cabinet as Minister without Portfolio, and no substantial reorganization of the Local Government Board took place. Lord Rhondda, another of Addison's suggestions, went to that department.[64] Addison, however, did have the satisfaction of seeing Herbert Fisher the distinguished Liberal historian and principal of his old *alma mater*, Sheffield University, appointed to the Ministry of Education; he and Addison were to be comrades-in-arms on behalf of various Liberal causes over the next few years.

Addison himself became Minister of Munitions. At first Lloyd George wanted him to be chief whip but he declined. 'I should hate the job and I am quite sure I could never manage the horrible touting about honours.'[65] He was happy to be promoted within the familiar department of Munitions, not least because he suspected Edwin Montagu of intriguing against him. Addison and his staff had heard first-hand evidence of Montagu's inadequacy as a minister since the summer. However, Montagu himself responded with much generosity of spirit. 'I am rejoiced to think that Addison succeeds me,' he recorded in his diary on 9 December. 'He is popular, very hard-working and of very good judgement.'[66] It may be noted that Addison was also consulted by Bonar Law as well as by Lloyd George about appointments to the government. He asked Addison to find a Liberal who would be suitable for the post of Financial Secretary of the Treasury. Bonar Law was 'dreadfully afraid of making novel appointments lest he should offend his own people'.[67]

Addison was thus, perhaps, the leading Liberal, other than Lloyd George, to join the new government. The assertion made by A. J. P. Taylor of Lloyd George's supporters that 'their political ability was low . . . none made a serious mark on public affairs . . .'[68] is questionable since they included Fisher, Mond, and shortly Montagu, as well as Addison. The executive ability of Addison himself had long been recognized. It had been noted in December 1915 that he replied to all departmental questions addressed to Lloyd George. The latter was clearly well pleased with his lieutenant's skill in handling the Munitions of War (Amendment) Act in the House. One newspaper commented, accurately enough, 'Dr. Addison is by no means a brilliant speaker but what he says has all the redeeming qualities of absolute clearness and plainness of language.'[69] In speech as in diet, Addison was somewhat austere. *Reynolds Newspaper* noted that

Dr. Addison is a general favourite and he deserves his popularity. I never knew a man less spoiled by promotion to Front Bench rank, there is not even a suspicion of what is called 'side' about him. And in addition to that merit he is one of the most quietly industrious men in the House of Commons, always ready, always well informed, always courteous.[70]

His handling of the labour troubles of 1915–16 it considered to have been an adept blend of decisiveness and diplomacy.

The Making of a Prime Minister

In the political crisis of December 1916, which split the Liberal party so fundamentally and so fatefully, Addison was inevitably drawn into the Lloyd Georgian rather than the Asquithian camp. Of course, his political progress had been linked inexorably with that of Lloyd George, ever since their partnership over the National Insurance Bill in 1911. Until July 1916 Addison had been Lloyd George's intimate assistant at the Ministry of Munitions. But quite apart from the accidents of political association, there can be no doubt that Addison was drawn by temperament, background, and philosophy to the Lloyd Georgian brand of Liberalism. As he himself had observed, both men dreamed dreams but linked them with an existing reality. Michael Bentley ably distinguishes in *The Liberal Mind* between the Lloyd Georgians' empirical-mindedness which identified them with 'the secular and the flexible and the expedient', and the Asquithians' 'quasi-religious view of their commitment to high principle'.[71] This may not be easy to apply to all Liberals in all cases in 1916: classifying H. A. L. Fisher, for instance, would be difficult on this basis. But the distinction is peculiarly apt in Addison's case. By outlook, he was a tough-minded pragmatist, concerned with results rather than with theology. Although he supported Asquith loyally enough until the mishandling of the Irish troubles in the summer of 1916, he had always been irritated, perhaps bored, by the patrician hauteur that marked the Asquithian style. When he met Margot Asquith, this plain Lincolnshire countryman recorded that 'I came away convinced that Mrs. A. had been dreadfully bored, and to tell the truth so had I.'[72] In December 1916 it was inevitably to Lloyd George's dynamic, populistic, opportunist style of leadership rather than to Asquith's 'acidulated church' that he was drawn.

To claim as one authority has done that Addison, along with Aitken and Arthur Henderson, was one of the three 'King-Makers' in December 1916[73] is perhaps to claim a little too much. It was the alliance of Lloyd George with Bonar Law which proved the decisive factor in turning out Asquith. But Mr Taylor is surely right in underlining Addison's key role. A new government desperately needed credible Liberal support in order to survive. If Addison did not create it, he canvassed it, mobilized it, and revealed its existence at a crucial moment on 5–6 December 1916. This made irresistible the triumph of the Lloyd George–Bonar Law partnership on a genuine trans-party basis. It helped transform the supreme wartime command in Britain and began a palace revolution that fatally split the Liberal party. A totally new phase in British political history was thus begun. December 1916 is truly a watershed in the making of modern Britain, in some ways the launching-pad of our contemporary world. The role of the uncharismatic and still comparatively obscure Dr Christopher Addison was amongst its most decisive factors.

3

Munitions and Reconstruction

Addison assumed his new responsibilities at the Ministry of Munitions at a time of profound crisis. It was a dark period for the Western Allies with the fortunes of war having turned against them from Salonika in the eastern Mediterranean to the Somme on the western front. Woodrow Wilson's appeal for peace negotiations in December 1916 had been brusquely rejected by the new British government. It was truly, as Lloyd George had proclaimed to the Welsh national eisteddfod at Aberystwyth in 1916, 'the darkest hour of the night' for the Entente powers.

In addition, it was a critical period in the reconstruction of the British central command, and with this transformation Addison was closely connected. As has been seen, he had played a crucial role in the coming to power of Lloyd George by mustering substantial Liberal support. He was also deeply involved with the reorganization of the central government machinery through the creation of a prime minister's secretariat or 'garden suburb', a new institution which came into existence on 2 January 1917. The Garden Suburb followed pressures from many quarters for a strengthening of the decision-making powers of the Prime Minister, to give him semi-presidential powers over the War Cabinet and the organs of central government generally. The earliest-known discussions on the need for a prime minister's secretariat had taken place on the previous 1 May, just after the main Cabinet crisis over military conscription had been resolved. On that day, Addison saw two influential back-bench MPs. One was David Davies, the Liberal member for Montgomeryshire, who pressed that Lloyd George should resign forthwith and reorganize the government on gaining the premiership. The other was Waldorf Astor, the owner of the *Observer* and another millionaire, a radical, socially-minded Unionist back-bencher with whom Addison had had dealings during the passage of the National Insurance Bill, and on the Tuberculosis Commission. Astor's proposal was that Milner should take over as Prime Minister, with Lloyd George as second-in-command. Addison rejected this suggestion out of hand. Milner, for whom he later conceived a warm admiration, he thought was 'distrusted' at this time as few men in the country were.[1] Nevertheless, contacts began, partly arranged by Addison, between Lloyd George and the Unionist followers of Milner, with the object of fighting the war with more vigour and reorganizing the governmental machine on the basis of 'national efficiency'. Certainly Addison does not seem to have been disconcerted by having these imperialists as his new associates.

    He kept up his contacts with Astor and Davies throughout the summer and autumn of 1916. After Lloyd George became Prime Minister, all three were much involved in the tortuous manœuvres that followed. When the Garden Suburb was formed, two of its five founding members were David Davies and Waldorf Astor. Professor W. G. S. Adams, Joseph Davies, and Philip Kerr, another Milnerite, were the other three. In fact, Addison, while welcoming the new secretariat, was by no means wholly pleased with all its attendant features. He complained that his own Ministry of Munitions had lost several of its most able officials to other departments and to the Garden Suburb itself. He seems to have led an unsuccessful attempt to have Professor Adams of All Souls, who was adviser to the Ministry of Munitions on labour matters, kept out of the Garden Suburb as its organizational head. Only after pressure from Thomas Jones, the new deputy secretary to the Cabinet, and other officials was Adams confirmed in his post. Even so, there is no doubt that here again Addison had played his part in a major constitutional innovation. Many legends later surrounded the Garden Suburb. It was to provide a convenient scapegoat after 1918 for attacking Lloyd George's presidential style of government. The influence of its members, even of the foreign affairs specialist, Philip Kerr, over the formulation and co-ordination of government policy was probably much less great than many contemporaries imagined. The Garden Suburb was basically an administrative instrument, strictly subordinate to the politicians. Nevertheless, there can be no question that the existence of a powerful secretarial aid of this kind reinforced the centralization of the government and the dominance of the Prime Minister over it. Addison, who had helped to propel the new Prime Minister into power, had also helped fashion the central machine through which

Munitions and Reconstruction 61

his power was to some degree projected.

But, of course, his main preoccupation in the critical early months of 1917 was with his departmental responsibilities at the Ministry of Munitions in carrying out the legacy that Lloyd George, and to a lesser degree Montagu, had bequeathed him. As Addison recorded in his diary, it was no great change for him to become Minister since both Lloyd George and Montagu had given him a great deal of responsibility as Under-Secretary.[2] Continuity was also maintained as his old ally, Kellaway, became Under-Secretary at Munitions. Addison enumerated the overshadowing questions of the time:

What success would attend this new and ruthless form of submarine attack. Should we be able to bring in all the supplies necessary for the people at home, as well as for the transport, sustenance and equipment of our armies in the field. The losses to British shipping had already been enormous . . . the most urgent need of the moment was the provision of additional ships to feed this country and our allies before the next harvest.[3]

On the answers to these questions, the winning of the war to a large degree rested.

Addison continued the previous policies for the provision of munitions for the front. The major constructional task was the supply of the new aeroplanes followed by new shipping and tank-building programmes. By April 1917, progress on all three appeared to be impressive. He also worked out a system for anticipating the increased demand for a new eighteen-pounder gun programme, which brought an appreciative letter from the British Commander-in-Chief, Field Marshal Haig.[4] Another of his urgent tasks, as a member of the government committee appointed by Curzon on 21 December 1916, was to try to prepare a scheme to reduce imports of raw materials and to stimulate home production. To this end, Auckland Geddes (another former professor of anatomy) was appointed Controller of Shipping to curtail imports and boost home shipbuilding. By May, Addison could reflect that the savings in imports and the increase of home production had been even greater than anticipated,[5] another triumph for the new 'war socialism'. He was also active in a different area, that of the development of United Kingdom and imperial mineral sources. After a memorandum submitted to the Cabinet by him, it was decided by the imperial Prime Ministers' conference on 23 April 1917 to establish an Imperial Mineral Resources Bureau. Characteristically, Addison urged that this be placed under a public, non-profit-making corporation rather than leaving it to the mercies of private companies.[6] The men that Addison appointed to develop mineral resources at home for war purposes yielded a good harvest. As he recorded, 'they were convinced that we had wasted or insufficiently used immense quantities of materials and that one of the chief causes was the lack of that comprehensive skilled oversight that could only be secured by an authoritative body representing the State'.[7] He, too, had his 'men of push and go'.

As in 1915–16, it was labour that proved to be the thorniest question for the Ministry of Munitions. Since the need for recruits for the army increased, with the appalling losses incurred on the western front in the trenches, the peril of internal disunity in Britain became all the greater. Popular feeling amongst the working class had been deeply stirred by the February revolution in Russia: it released, said Ramsay MacDonald, a 'springtide of joy' all over Europe. Addison kept closely in touch with the influence of developments in Russia as is shown by the reports sent to him by Milner and by Layton, the chief of the intelligence section at the Ministry of Munitions. But there were more immediate causes of labour unrest in Britain in 1917. Chief among them was the troubles that arose from the proposals of the Manpower Board in the autumn of 1916 that the process of dilution of labour should be extended to private, non-war work, and that there should be wholesale volunteer industrial enlistment. A particular source of difficulty was the operation of the Trade Card scheme. This system, launched during the Hargreaves strike in Sheffield in November 1916, and operative from the following February, guaranteed exemption from military service to all members of the craft unions engaged on munitions work. But the essence of the scheme was that, instead of carefully developing a coherent method whereby the recruitment of munitions workers could be avoided, the Manpower Board had committed the country to a scheme under which the trade union executives could administer the law by giving cards of exemption to certain of their own members. This made rank-and-file protest by skilled workers against their own union leadership, as in the shop stewards' movement, all the more probable.

The operation of the Trade Card system brought Addison into still closer contact with the trade unions and the difficult field of collective bargaining. One immediate source of trouble arose in January 1917.

Neville Chamberlain, the new Director of National Service who served as 'the Manpower Board in glorified form', proposed that all men up to the age of twenty-one should go into the army and that a volunteer industrial army should also be enrolled.[8] These proposals caused much friction both with labour and between the Ministry of Munitions and the War Office; Neville Chamberlain thereafter became something of a *bête noire* for both Addison and Lloyd George for the rest of his life. On 16 February, at a conference between the War Office and the Ministry of Munitions, it was agreed that some classification of occupations was necessary as complaints were being made that skilled workers were being called up. The War Office also argued that the Trade Card scheme protected a large number of occupations which it was not designed to protect and that more men were needed for the army than could now be obtained. Addison had always prophesied that the Trade Card system would cause trouble. He now helped draw up a memorandum for the War Cabinet which substituted a well-prepared schedule of exempted occupations for the Trade Card scheme; on 19 March this was agreed to by the Ministry of Munitions, the Admiralty, and the War Office. The assistance of the National Labour Advisory Committee was also sought. On 23 March the Cabinet accepted the schedule of exempted occupations. Addison and Arthur Henderson then addressed a series of meetings of trade unionists to explain and justify the Cabinet's decision to withdraw the recently devised Trade Card scheme and replace it with a different system.[9] As was anticipated, the idea of withdrawing the Trade Card scheme, which had much boosted the status of the unions, met with violent opposition, especially from the Engineers and other unions which had been party to the scheme in the first place. 'We shall have a troublesome time,' Addison gloomily reflected on 1 May.[10]

However, after lengthy negotiations the Engineers' union executive agreed on 5 May to accept the government's proposals for a carefully prepared schedule of exemptions in place of the union-administered Trade Card scheme. There followed a widespread refusal to accept the ASE executive decision by the union's rank and file. Strikes broke out, partly because of the executive's acceptance of the withdrawal of the Trade Card scheme, but mainly on account of the proposals in the new Munitions of War (Amendment) Bill to introduce the dilution of unskilled labour into non-war work. Addison vividly described his reluctance to be responsible for the handling of this Bill and for being blamed for a crisis that was really instigated by Neville Chamberlain, who was eventually dismissed.[11]

The executive of the Amalgamated Society of Engineers now tried to persuade Addison to withdraw the Bill, but in vain. An unofficial strike committee came into existence with whom the Minister refused to negotiate. There followed the strike of May 1917, the largest of the war, involving 200,000 engineering workers all over the country for a period of more than three weeks. Addison flatly declined to bargain with the shop stewards of the unofficial strike committee on 16 May on the grounds that the War Cabinet's decision had been that 'the Government should adhere to its policy of recognising only the constitutional authority of the trade unions and that no deputation of shop stewards could be received except at the request of the executive of the union'.[12] Meanwhile, a press campaign built up in journals such as the Liberal *Daily News* against the Ministry of Munitions, blaming it for these labour troubles. Much of the onslaught was directed against Addison personally.[13]

On 19 May he met the executive of the Engineers and of the strike delegates jointly. The latter now agreed to allow the ASE executive to do their negotiating for them. An agreement was reached that they would discuss the implications of the Munitions of War (Amendment) Bill with the Ministry of Munitions, that no more workers would be arrested, that the arrested men would be released pending their trial, and that the ASE executive and the strike committee would jointly recommend a return to work.[14] As Addison wrote to Lloyd George two days later, he felt, as did Worthington-Evans, Kellaway, and the Ministry of Labour permanent official, Sir David Shackleton, that the best policy, 'in view of the fact that we have got both the Schedule accepted and the principle of the Bill, and the shop stewards hopelessly discredited, is to announce immediately the abandonment of the prosecutions as an act of grace'.[15] W. C. Bridgeman, the Parliamentary Secretary at the Ministry of Labour, thought it far too generous a settlement.[16] At a meeting with Lloyd George, Henderson, and John Hodge later the same day, the agreement concluded between Addison and the executive of the ASE was confirmed. A major industrial crisis seemed to be over, and Addison appeared to have achieved a notable diplomatic success.

But then events took a most curious turn, politically. It was widely reported in the press that Addison had been unable to get an agreement with the unions and that Lloyd George had had to be called in at the last moment to clear up the mess. This was a bombshell; Addison called it 'as horrible an experience as ever I have had in my life'.[17] The sentences in the government statement which referred to Addison and which showed how he had obtained a settlement had been deliberately cut out when the statement was sent to the press. It was clearly intended to convey the impression that no agreement with the unions had been reached before the minister went to see Lloyd George. This was certainly not the case. In addition, the signatures of Addison and of Brownlie, the president of the ASE, had been removed and the agreement appeared in the newspapers unsigned. Addison insisted that Lloyd George make a factual statement to the House of Commons in order to redeem the reputation of the Ministry of Munitions as well as of himself. He refused to believe that Lloyd George, with whom he had enjoyed so intimate a relationship, had had anything to do with this plot. The original statement issued to the press was now retrieved and it became clear that Sir William Sutherland, Lloyd George's press secretary, was responsible for the alterations. Sutherland's own written denial about this episode is equivocal,[18] but Addison satisfied himself that Sutherland had amended the statement and had 'lied pretty freely to Lloyd George and myself to conceal the fact'.[19] Lloyd George expressed his regrets to Addison privately and later made a statement in the House of Commons which corrected the press release. Even so, this somewhat mysterious affair, which surely cannot have been the initiative of Sutherland alone, temporarily soured relations between the Prime Minister and his most loyal Liberal lieutenant. One consequence was that it was decided to set up a Ministry of Munitions press agency to improve communication with munitions workers up and down the country.[20]

As labour discontent continued to seethe, not only in the engineering trades, over the coming of dilution and the operation of the Military Service Acts, Addison supported the government's decision to set up a Commission to inquire into Industrial Unrest in the different regions of Britain. Dilution and the Military Service provisions had both contributed to the Engineers' national strike in May 1917 and, more fundamentally, to the rise of the shop stewards' movement which was threatening to wrest the leadership of labour from the nationally elected officials of the trade unions.[21] Addison attended a preliminary meeting on 30 May and reported to Lloyd George that eight panels of the Commission had been set up to cover the whole of England, Wales, and Scotland.

Meanwhile he continued his task of ploughing the sands in his negotiations with the ASE and other trade unions on the amended scheme for dilution. It was now proposed that, before the principle of dilution was applied to private work of any particular class, notice should be given and opportunity afforded for consultation with the parties concerned.[22] The employers meanwhile agreed to set up a joint committee to consider the Munitions of War (Amendment) Bill and negotiations went on. But on 13 August 1917, under a new minister, the government finally gave up plans for dilution on private work.[23] Addison was now anxious that action should be taken to implement the new Munitions of War (Amendment) Act after it became law in August 1917; this was, in fact, not done when Churchill succeeded him as Minister. The following spring Addison wrote to Churchill to remind him that no date had been fixed for its implementation.[24]

The major troubles that Addison faced in regard to labour during his period at the Ministry of Munitions in 1915–17, both as Under-Secretary and then as Minister, were the results of policies which he personally had strongly condemned—dilution on private work and the Trade Card scheme. As he recorded, 'They have provided the two big messes we have had to try to clean up as well as bear all the odium that was bound to fall on any man that had the job to do. However, this kind of thing happens in public life and it is futile as well as stupid to worry about it.'[25] Even so, these crises served to make his reputation amongst the more militant section of the trade unions a somewhat mixed one. Whatever his radical philosophy, Addison was no defender of industrial indiscipline; he had supported the arrest or deportation of unofficial strike leaders. There had also been criticism of these moves in the press. Both in handling the engineers while at Munitions and later the building workers while Minister of Health, Addison found the Sisyphean task of dealing with the unions the most arduous of his career.

In the early summer of 1917, Lloyd George was anxious to introduce changes in the government, in particular to strengthen its Liberal elements. He was especially anxious to bring in Winston Churchill and use his oratorical and executive talents, even though many Unionists regarded Churchill, tainted as he was with the failure of the Dardanelles, as anathema. Addison, too, was anxious to make

Munitions and Reconstruction 67

use of Churchill's great abilities. On 4 June he wrote to Lloyd George about the Air Board. 'I feel that we should get Winston in, and the more it is talked about, the more opportunity there is for opposition to gather. I should advise acting quickly in this so as to get the ice broken.'[26] He was quite willing to hand over the Ministry of Munitions to Churchill whom he felt was worth a wider responsibility than the Air Board.[27] 'Give me three weeks', he wrote to Lloyd George, 'and I could get the estimates over and shape things here through my new Board of Directors so as to pave the way for Winston if you wished him to follow me.' Thus Addison made it absolutely plain that he was prepared to leave Munitions. Meanwhile, the press was full of reports of the proposal, as they put it, to move him or secure his resignation. According to one newspaper, Addison had been marked out for removal by a powerful clique which had been 'working persistently to get Mr. Churchill back into office'. It was widely rumoured also that Addison might move to the Local Government Board.[28]

There was a possibility of further promotion. Addison knew that Milner favoured his entry into the War Cabinet. He believed that Lloyd George might welcome this on wider political grounds, so that he could 'help Milner deal with those inter-departmental questions and be able to devote my mind, without routine administrative work, to problems of future programme and the like'.[29] But he also felt, as an ambitious politician, that to leave Munitions under existing circumstances would look as though he had been moved to a ministry without portfolio because he had been a failure, especially over the handling of the ASE strike. Lloyd George assured him that no impression of that kind would get about but he agreed that it was best for Addison not to leave the Ministry of Munitions until the whole of the ASE affair had blown over. It was thus agreed in principle as early as the end of May 1917 that Addison would soon leave Munitions. He noted, 'I should be delighted to have such a job [an inter-departmental portfolio] and it would be a considerable relief to be free from a big administrative office.' He felt convinced that 'my best place was on the future policy of which a host of important issues needed attention'.[30] The 'dreaming of dreams', interrupted in 1914, could now be resumed.

Meanwhile, the reputation of the Ministry of Munitions rose considerably when the Munitions Estimates were published, with details of the savings effected in costing and the like. Addison noted, 'there is a great change over in opinion and there is a demand that the account should be printed in America as well as at home'.[31] At this time, during the early part of July, he and Lloyd George discussed the formation of a proposed Ministry of Reconstruction to attend to post-war planning. He told the Prime Minister that 'I am quite willing to take on the job.' Thus, when formally asked on 17 July to move to a new Ministry of Reconstruction, Addison was happy to agree; he informed the senior staff at Munitions of Churchill's appointment on 18 July. He noted that they were 'not very friendly to the idea of Winston's coming . . . but there is no more capable chief of a department than he is, as they will soon find out'.[32] Hindsight and the passage of time caused Addison to reflect less happily upon his move from the Ministry of Munitions to the Ministry of Reconstruction in July 1917. When Lloyd George later on, in 1920, asked him to give up the Ministry of Health and become a political adviser to 'help strengthen the Government', Addison replied that he had done this kind of thing at the Ministry of Reconstruction. That Ministry had lacked a specific portfolio and had consequently been a weak one. It had been 'one of the bitterest experiences a man could have'. It was put about and believed that he had only been given the job 'because it enabled you to find a job for a friend who had been a failure elsewhere'. He would rather 'sweep crossings', than repeat such an experience.[33] This was certainly not his immediate reaction, however, in July 1917.

It cannot be claimed, as one critic has maintained, that Addison did not know that a change was in store for him until afterwards, nor that he was reluctant to leave Munitions and did not know, until mid-July, the circumstances of his replacement.[34] Neither can it be said that Addison was transferred 'not for failure but for the reputation of failure'.[35] Of course, Lloyd George was primarily concerned with the immediate conduct of the war, but he fully realized the importance of creating a Ministry of Reconstruction at an early date. Planning for post-war was seldom far from his imaginative mind. The head of Reconstruction should be a person of energy and determination, as Addison was, and one of unimpeachable radical credentials and loyalty to the Prime Minister. *The Times* warmly applauded Addison's appointment: 'it is welcome on several grounds, of which the strongest is his real interest in social reform'.[36] It is also not correct to argue as one authority has done, that Lloyd George moved Addison to

Munitions and Reconstruction 69

get 'another potential rival out of the way'.[37] Addison was in no conceivable sense a rival to Lloyd George, while his standing as a minister was in fact enhanced by his move.

His achievements at the Ministry of Munitions had been far from negligible. For instance, he saved the country thousands of pounds by the introduction of a new costings system for munitions and by using the services of Lever. It has been written that Churchill was later critical of Addison's performance at Munitions,[38] but this is not correct. Certainly, in late 1917, Churchill wrote that when he took over he had found 'the finances of the Ministry in an unsatisfactory state'. But, he went on,

> this was due to the conditions of the emergency under which the whole of our munitions supply was called into being . . . As the emergency was gradually met and output on a gigantic scale was achieved the attention of my predecessor was directed to the financial aspect of the business. He saw with grave anxiety that the practical process of supply had very largely outstripped the regular machinery of finance and contracts.[39]

Addison had authorized the building of government factories to make the country self-sufficient, the first of which, those for the manufacture of TNT, had already more than repaid their capital cost. The output of munitions increased steadily during his regime. Perhaps his most important long-term work at Munitions, however, lay in the field of welfare, notably the Health of Munitions Workers Committee which he set up in the summer of 1916. This Committee performed important work in connection with problems of industrial fatigue and the regulation of working hours, setting up canteens, and building homes for workers. Seebohm Rowntree, later critical of Addison it is true, paid tribute to him at the time. 'Welfare work', he wrote to Addison, 'is largely the outcome of your own concern.'[40]

Addison was, indeed, a highly competent minister at Munitions. He adopted a plan of surrounding himself with men in constant touch with the productive industries and the sources of the supply of raw materials. He placed them in posts of authority and delegated considerable powers to them. By contrast, it was said that Churchill later interfered with the work of the men he had around him and assumed the role of an autocrat. He was entirely ignorant of British trade unions and workmen and was concerned solely with war needs.[41] The press recognized that Addison's departure would be 'regretted at Whitehall Gardens where his considerateness and accessibility have won him the warm regard of his subordinates of all grades'.⁴² On balance, then, Addison may have proved a more capable Minister of Munitions than the overbearing titan, Churchill, who followed him.

When Lloyd George announced his Cabinet reshuffle on 17 July, Addison became Minister of Reconstruction. The conditions on which he had insisted before his appointment were agreed by Lloyd George who sent a letter round the departments giving him the necessary authority. Addison was given powers to appoint committees on reconstruction questions, to call for papers and reports from all committees affecting reconstruction and post-war development, and was entitled to recommend to the War Cabinet that committees or schemes of development should be placed under his control.⁴³ The new Ministry was set up to handle questions affecting major problems belonging to a number of different departments which had previously been referred to individual members of the War Cabinet. It has been described as a 'species of government-supported ideas factory for a post-war party that would evolve under the leadership of Lloyd George', though whether the purely party aspects were in mind in July 1917 is debatable. Addison himself commented that it was difficult to imagine 'a change of work more definite and complete than the change over from the Ministry of Munitions to the Ministry of Reconstruction'.⁴⁴ At Munitions the objects had been immediate, at Reconstruction they were long-term. It was a transition from the mundane to the infinite.

Addison considered that his first priority in his new department was 'to secure that some provision is made for the millions of demobilised soldiers, munition workers and other war workers on the declaration of peace'.⁴⁵ Here he was assisted by the fact that important work had already been started. The original Reconstruction Committee had been set up by Asquith in March 1916, and Addison's Ministry now took over its functions. There had also been sitting Lord Selborne's Committee on policy towards agriculture, Lord Salisbury's on housing, and Haldane's on the conservation of coal. Addison himself had set up a further reconstruction committee while Minister of Munitions in April 1917. The original Reconstruction Committee, under the chairmanship of Edwin Montagu, had made progress in working out plans for demobilization, while the Whitley

Munitions and Reconstruction 71

Committee was well advanced in devising machinery for resolving labour disputes such as councils for joint industrial consultation.[46] But, while all this provided the new Minister with a platform for reforming policies, 'it seemed to consist of a medley of committees without any plan of campaign'. There was also the major issue of getting attention paid to the recommendations these committees eventually produced. 'There is a good deal of difference between getting a report and a Government making up its mind what it is going to do about it and this is where my business is to be as helpful and as pushful as I can.'[47]

Throughout that autumn Addison worked with much zeal to grapple with reconstruction in all its various aspects. The committees set up indicate some of his priorities. They included the Demobilization Committee, Sir James Carmichael's Committee on Building Materials, the Financial Facilities Committee, and the Engineering (New Industries) Committee. Addison also turned to the Standing Priority Committee which he had formed earlier in 1917 under the chairmanship of Sir John Wormold, and which had set up representative bodies in various industries to focus their requirements. He also backed strongly the formation of the Whitley Councils in industry, to include representatives of both employers and employed, as approved by the Cabinet on 9 October 1917.[48] He believed that one priority to emerge from the war was to create a better system of labour organization in industry, and here the Whitley Councils would be indispensable in breaking down the divisions between the two sides. Arthur Greenwood, later a Labour Cabinet minister, and Ernest Benn, recruited from Addison's staff at Munitions, set to work to promote councils in various trades.[49]

There was also a need for a small group of 'first rate men who will give wholetime help as a sort of council' to help get the various tasks co-ordinated. There was appointed, therefore, the Central Reconstruction Council under the chairmanship of Sir Henry Birchenough. In addition, other capable men were enlisted to organize the various tasks of reconstruction—Sir James Carmichael for building materials, Lionel Phillips for mineral development, Sir Arthur Thring, Arthur Greenwood, and Ernest Benn. Under Addison, the Ministry of Reconstruction seemed likely to become a laboratory of new ideas and of social experiment, enlisting the talents of many gifted figures. By the start of 1918 there were as many as 87 committees at work on aspects of reconstruction.⁵⁰ Inevitably, Addison was criticized for setting up an undue number of committees whose existence was said to confuse the clear direction of the Ministry of Reconstruction. In a memorandum to the Cabinet, he rebutted this firmly enough.⁵¹ Addison was not only a backroom organizer in the corridors of Whitehall. He toured the country encouraging the various reconstruction committees to get to work, and addressed meetings to focus public attention on the importance of reconstruction planning for post-war, and the specific need for innovations such as the Whitley Councils. He inaugurated the Industrial Reconstruction Council to popularize the principles of industrial self-government, and in particular to spread knowledge of the recommendations of the Whitley report. The first Joint Industrial Council was set up in the Potteries at the start of 1918 as a pilot scheme, under the chairmanship of one of the Wedgwoods.⁵²

Another crucial area for the new Ministry was the resettlement of ex-servicemen. The general scheme of the Demobilization Committee for the army was approved by the Cabinet in November 1917, and measures to assist the resettlement of officers were amongst its proposals. Plans made for the acquisition of land for smallholdings were agreed to by the Treasury; proposals for the resettlement of workers after the war were well advanced by April 1918. At a meeting of the Cabinet, much headway was made on land questions: it was agreed that the settlement of ex-soldiers, housing, and afforestation were suitable purposes for the acquisition of land but that compulsory powers should be avoided.⁵³ In addition, proposals for 'Post-War Priority' advanced by the Minister were accepted by the Cabinet, while a standing committee on economic questions also performed valuable work. By July, a complete set of reports and recommendations on the use of raw materials had been received. By the end of August schemes for Post-War Priority had been completed: 'after months of work by many willing people, the bulk requirements of a multitude of industries for all sorts of materials from near and far have been worked out, and trade bodies are now in being to act on behalf of their industries'.⁵⁴ By mid-1918, therefore, a post-war priorities programme was in being.

Much of the effort at the Ministry of Reconstruction was spent on commonplace matters of detail. At the same time, Addison's brief was to prepare for the Cabinet and the Prime Minister a far wider scheme

Munitions and Reconstruction 73

of the long-term implications of 'reconstruction' as a theme. He had already appointed committees to consider such vital areas as land policy and housing. The *New Statesman*'s view that the Ministry of Reconstruction was 'a total failure',[55] a kind of laborious irrelevance, may be discounted. Indeed, the Ministry was central to the Coalition government's entire domestic programme. One major new area to concern the Ministry was housing, perhaps the issue to cause Addison the most acute difficulty during his time at Reconstruction. This was in large measure because of the obstructiveness of the president of the Local Government Board, the Unionist, Hayes Fisher; he was, in Beaverbrook's words, 'a regular party hack'. Addison noted, 'It is pitiful, after a man like Rhondda, to have a man with his parochial outlook at the LGB.'[56] It was known that the housing shortage would become acute after the war. It was already a major source of working-class discontent in South Wales and elsewhere, as the Commission on Industrial Unrest had shown. The report of the Housing Advisory Panel, issued in October 1917 and strongly supported by Addison, urged that preparations should begin immediately on the construction of houses so as to avoid delay and the possible inflation of the costs of transport and building materials. It should be the duty of local authorities to act; if they did not, the central government should act in their place and should provide financial assistance in the form of housing subsidies.[57] The fact that this panel was chaired by the deeply conservative Lord Salisbury is in itself testimony to the dramatic impact of the war years in generating a new commitment to radical social change.

But the Local Government Board, under the dead hand of Hayes Fisher, was most reluctant to take positive action on housing. It preferred to let the local authorities act alone. Fisher also had a doctrinaire faith in the ability of private enterprise to build houses. As Seebohm Rowntree wrote to Addison, 'I believe that the Ministry of Reconstruction takes a very much longer view of the advantages which may be taken of the present situation, materially and permanently to raise the standard of houses, than is taken by the Local Government Board.'[58] Addison told Hayes Fisher that he would brook no further delay and would now ask the permission of the War Cabinet, in liaison with the Treasury, to make the necessary preparations for a new public housing programme.[59] In March 1918, a collective memorandum of the various proposals of the Ministry of

Reconstruction was considered by the War Cabinet. The Local Government Board now pressed for the issue of a circular to translate into definite terms the previous offer of financial assistance. The general idea was that the state should contribute 75 per cent of the annual deficit on housing for a period of not less than seven years, with power to increase it up to 100 per cent, less the proceeds of a penny rate, in areas where the local authority was poor. It also proposed that a bill should be introduced to confer powers to provide houses upon county councils. But Addison believed that two other proposals would make this scheme worthless—that financial assistance would be limited; and that the precise date of the execution of the scheme would not be announced. This would mean that there would be no obligation for the Treasury to provide facilities, that the whole plan would be conditional, and that nothing would result from the LGB circular. He noted how curious it was that he, a lifelong radical, should be fighting side by side with Salisbury, a lifelong Tory, in trying to goad the LGB into action.[60]

To his dismay, the Cabinet accepted the main drift of Hayes Fisher's points on 12 March. Considerations of economy seem to have been the decisive factors. The most that Addison and Salisbury could achieve was the deletion of Clause Five relating to the limitation of financial assistance by the Treasury. On 18 March the LGB then announced its terms in Circular 41 to the local authorities. But Addison was determined that Hayes Fisher's hedging proposals should not be adopted in that final form in a bill. On 1 August he produced a counter-memorandum in which he reiterated his views on the action on housing that needed to be taken by the government. Fisher produced a counter-memorandum incorporating the proposals set out in Circular 41.[61] The two rival documents were then considered by the recently created Cabinet Home Affairs Committee on 2 August. As it happened, Addison had to leave this meeting before housing policy was brought up; in his absence the Home Affairs Committee reaffirmed the policy set out by the Local Government Board. Addison's formal dissent was recorded by the Home Affairs Committee later.[62] He kept up his pressure, and his views were generally reinforced in October when the Tudor Walters Committee (Cd. 9191) argued forcefully for state assistance for private builders to meet an estimated need of 500,000 working-class houses. Addison was, therefore, a prime mover in pressing for one of the key social innovations of the war—the

Munitions and Reconstruction

principle of state subsidies for public housing and for treating housing as a kind of social service. But, as has been seen, his reforming efforts were blunted by the Local Government Board, and the government's response was less than whole-hearted. Housing would be very much 'unfinished business' for the post-war government to confront.

Another prime concern for Addison during his time at the Ministry of Reconstruction was the idea of the formation of a Ministry of Health. As he recorded in his diary,

> the struggle that went on behind the scenes for nearly two years to secure the establishment of a Ministry of Health is a good example of how difficult it is to secure the passage of an effective reform, even when, as in this case, it is supported by public opinion and by men of all political parties. It was, in short, the struggle of the old Local Government Board with its parochial disposition against an inevitable and much-needed development.[63]

As a medical doctor, Addison had always been a strong supporter of a central agency for public health. The social changes wrought by the war strengthened his convictions. The appointment of Lord Rhondda to the Local Government Board in December 1916—an appointment for which Addison claimed the credit[64]—marked the beginning of a long campaign that eventually gave Britain a Ministry of Health in 1918. Within a few days of his appointment Addison had sent Rhondda a memorandum that he, Morant, and Sir George Newman had drawn up in the summer of 1914, arguing the case for a consolidation of governmental health activity into a single ministry. Addison suggested to Rhondda that Newman be appointed chief medical officer, and that infant nurseries, schools for mothers, and health insurance be brought in. He seems to have convinced Rhondda, as the latter took up the suggestion and sent a memorandum to the War Cabinet on the urgent necessity for a Ministry of Health. This was forwarded to a Cabinet Committee, which included Addison who was quick to suggest that the new Ministry should have both a health side and a local administrative side. He hoped that Lloyd George would support it, and again proposed the name of Newman as chief medical officer.[65]

This memorandum passed on through the Cabinet Committee to a Sub-Committee of Reconstruction, again including Addison. Its proposals were endorsed by Milner and then forwarded to the War Cabinet, notwithstanding the objections of the Approved Societies who were determined to maintain their independent status.[66] There, however, the matter stuck. The disapproval of the Approved Societies carried weight with the Cabinet, while there was a political set-back when Rhondda moved from the LGB to become Food Controller on 14 June 1917. As a result, no Ministry of Health was set up during the war, a principal cause in the view of Paul Barton Johnson of the failure of the Lloyd George government to provide that 'land fit for heroes' which the Prime Minister had promised the nation.

Addison continued to attend meetings on the proposed Ministry of Health Bill, while at Reconstruction. But there was great controversy about the focus or core of such a bill. Should the new Ministry be simply an expansion of the Local Government Board? In fact, any attempt to build a new department on the old, hidebound traditions of the LGB was anathema to most of the enthusiastic advocates of a Ministry of Health, both in the medical profession and in the political parties. They believed that the Ministry of Health should be concerned with health above all. It should be scientific, experimental, and free from the parochialism that stifled initiative within the administration of the LGB. The issue had very wide ramifications since it involved both the system of health insurance and the future of the old Poor Law. In October 1917, Lloyd George found time, despite the pressures of the war, to meet a deputation from the Approved Societies, along with Addison, Hayes Fisher, Milner, and Lord Rhondda. Here, an important agreement was reached between Addison and Kingsley Wood, the spokesman for the industrial insurance societies, to begin negotiations for a compromise plan which the government could then submit to Parliament.[67] These negotiations began on 5 November with the blessing of the Prime Minister who announced that government sanction for any bill would be withheld until all the parties concerned were satisfied. The avenue to compromise with the insurance societies opened up with the report of the Maclean Committee published early in January 1918. This Committee recommended that the Poor Law Guardians be abolished, and that the various functions of the Poor Law be distributed among the appropriate branches of the major local authorities. Its report gained Cabinet approval on 21 March 1918 and Addison was then, shortly afterwards, able to reach agreement with the Approved Societies on a draft of the Ministry of Health Bill.

But there remained the perennial obstacle of the Local Government Board under Hayes Fisher. Addison found him 'not big enough mentally to realise what a proper Ministry of Health might achieve in the long run in preventing sickness and improving the vigour of the people'.⁶⁸ The Poor Law division of the Board insisted that if there were to be a Ministry of Health, it should be no more than the old LGB expanded to take in the insurance commissioners. However, defenders of the LGB and the old Poor Law system were stunned on 10 January 1918 by the appearance of the first of two letters in *The Times*, signed by a group of leading back-bench Unionists headed by Waldorf Astor. It called for a Ministry of Health essentially along the lines of the Rhondda–Addison plan and attacked Hayes Fisher for holding up action on it. The Ministry of Health controversy thus came right out into the open.

The government had accepted in principle the recommendations of the Maclean report, so that the concentration of health powers under the new Ministry of Health would not become entangled with the Poor Law.⁶⁹ In fact, this report was not carried out: the Ministry of Health was to be hampered by the Poor Law system from 1919 until the Local Government Act of 1929 which abolished the old Poor Law. Addison now circulated a draft of a proposed Ministry of Health Bill in the Cabinet. He reported the general agreement between the insurance societies and the local authorities, and the tacit approval of the Local Government Board.⁷⁰ The Labour party's annual conference had also passed a resolution which demanded the immediate establishment of a Ministry of Health. Addison urged that the bill be introduced at once, and that he should be authorized to say that the government 'regarded as a matter of urgency' that the recommendations of the Maclean Committee be given effect as soon as possible. But still there was difficulty and delay, mainly the result of the obstruction of Hayes Fisher and the LGB. Until the middle of July, no further action was taken over a Ministry of Health Bill.

Early in June, after the Ministry of Health question had for the fourth time been removed from the War Cabinet's agenda, Addison threatened resignation. Morant had told him already, 'You will never get it through, they will be too many for you.' He was now extremely irritated at the postponement of key decisions on home affairs, above all over a Ministry of Health Bill. He felt that Lloyd George appeared to be playing up to obstructionists such as Hayes Fisher and Walter Long at the expense of his friends.⁷¹ As he (Addison) was probably 'his best friend in the Government' he ought to be able to rely on the

Prime Minister for backing. After a letter written by him to Lloyd George on 5 June, a Home Affairs Committee of the Cabinet had been set up. Addison recorded that this marked 'the opening of another section of the Ministry of Health story'.[72] The Home Affairs Committee for which he claimed the credit was to be the domestic counterpart of the War Cabinet. Its first chairman was Cave, the Home Secretary, and its members included Addison, H. A. L. Fisher, and, less happily, Hayes Fisher. Of the first five meetings of the Home Affairs Committee, three were devoted to the Ministry of Health Bill. The opponents of such a measure here included not only Hayes Fisher, but also Cave, the chairman, as well. Addison pressed that the Bill at least be read a first time before the House rose for the summer recess, and that a pledge should be given that it would be put through in the autumn. But, according to Addison, Lloyd George was no help. He felt that the Prime Minister had no conception of the degree of strength he had in the country, and was too timid in dealing with the Tory party. At last, on 2 August 1918 the Ministry of Health Bill was approved by the Home Affairs Committee. Writing to his wife from Lloyd George's Criccieth home on 22 August, Addison commented, 'At last L. G. seems to have seized on to it [the Ministry of Health] and it is clear that Hayes Fisher and the L.G.B. must be drastically crushed out. H. F. to be got rid of.' The Bill finally went through on 11 September, on the eve of a major address on social questions at Manchester by the Prime Minister. Many imponderables remained, notably the relationship of the new Ministry to the Poor Law system. The taint of the workhouse and 'less eligibility' still remained. There were doubts about the attitude of the friendly societies and the industrial insurance companies. The story of the Ministry of Health was one of protracted delay and frustration as far as Addison and the Ministry of Reconstruction were concerned. But, with all its limitations, it was to result in victory in the end.

The formation of the Home Affairs Committee marked the opening of another section of the history of the Ministry of Reconstruction. By the summer of 1918, a wide range of plans were ready for execution. In a memorandum he submitted to the Home Affairs Committee, Addison emphasized that the credit of the government depended on their reconstruction policy to a degree second only to their conduct of the war. He urged that adequate steps be taken to ensure the closest co-operation between the Home Affairs Committee and the Ministry

Munitions and Reconstruction

of Reconstruction to avoid duplication of work.[73] But most of the Ministry's plans remained at the drawing-board stage. There was little to suggest that many of them would become law.

Suddenly, in early October, it became apparent that the war would very soon come to an end. Addison was amongst the first at ministerial level to realize that the government had not formulated any plan to cope with the resumption of ordinary economic life after the war. On 19 October 1918 he sent an important memorandum to the Cabinet which urged, in the strongest terms, that something be done immediately to prepare for the transition of civilian workers from wartime to peacetime. There was, in particular, the desperate problem of extending the system of unemployment insurance. In all, 2,400,000 men and women had been covered by the provisions of the National Insurance Act of 1911, and a further 1,364,000 by the Act of 1916. But this still left about ten million workers without any financial support except the Poor Law, in the case of temporary unemployment. At that late stage, it would be impossible to enact a comprehensive unemployment insurance scheme and to make the necessary administrative arrangements. Therefore, he urged the adoption of the principle of an out-of-work donation for civilians as well as for soldiers.[74] This was a dramatic extension of the previously accepted principles underlying policy towards unemployment insurance. The system enacted in 1911 was contributory, and based in theory on orthodox insurance principles. The donation system was non-contributory and would be open to all discharged workers, irrespective of their insurance arrangements, as of right. A little over three weeks later, the government accepted Addison's proposals for a universal civilian out-of-work donation, as a preliminary to a wider scheme for regularized unemployment benefit. It was a major social innovation as for the first time the state recognized that an adult unable to find employment had the right to make a claim upon it, in the same way as could the aged, the sick, and children. The social services were made that degree more comprehensive, as Addison had long insisted.

That same month of October he obtained Cabinet approval for a general scheme of post-war priority;[75] he had frequent consultations on this with General Smuts, the chairman of the Priority Committee. Within a fortnight of the declaration of the armistice on 11 November, an agreement had been reached with the industries concerned.[76] The outcome of this was much less happy in the long term, since it began the precipitate post-war policy of de-control, in the first instance in relation to steel and non-ferrous metals. The wartime system of controls was cumbersome and inefficient in many ways; but a sweeping decision like this to return major industries so soon to uncontrolled private enterprise created many difficulties, and was to prove a grave obstacle to the fulfilment of many of the Reconstruction programmes after 1918. Addison would ruefully recall in later years how the dismantling of the collectivism of the war socialist system had helped undermine the progress of social reform.

One of the problems that concerned Addison in the last weeks of the war was the apparent indecisiveness of Lloyd George in dealing with vital aspects of civilian and military demobilization. Addison refused to be 'a party to drift' and demanded action.[77] With the Prime Minister now in Paris, he saw Bonar Law and urged that if the War Cabinet could not find time to take the urgent decisions required for demobilization, then he could no longer remain in office. He also urged Bonar Law to allow him to make an immediate statement to the Commons on the Ministry of Health and to introduce a bill at once with a pledge that it be carried through in the next session of Parliament. He handed Bonar Law an open letter for Lloyd George which embodied his demands. Addison won all his points. A committee was set up to deal with the demobilization and resettlement of discharged servicemen and rapidly got to work.[78] On 4 November 1918 the redemption of pledges to labour was publicly announced; on the 7th Addison introduced the first reading of the Ministry of Health Bill, which was universally well received.[79] The next day, as anticipated, he was asked by Lloyd George to become the first Minister of Health as soon as the new department was set up. It was agreed that the Ministry of Health Bill would be introduced at once in the next session.[80] After almost two years' delay since he and Rhondda had first broached the idea, after long periods of difficulty with the insurance companies, and of obstruction by Hayes Fisher and the Local Government Board, the battle had been won, a notable milestone in the road towards a welfare state.

The achievement of the new Ministry of Health, one so dear to Addison's heart, marked the climax of his period as Minister of Reconstruction. It was a period of his political career peculiarly difficult to assess. Some have considered that the Ministry was ultimately ineffective; as will be seen,[81] Addison himself took that

Munitions and Reconstruction   81

view in 1920 at a time of some personal disillusionment over the difficulties encountered by his housing schemes. The Ministry set up innumerable committees, it gushed forth streams of policy documents and Cabinet papers, but yielded relatively little of immediate substance. Paul Barton Johnson's conclusion appears to be that the administrative structure of the Ministry of Reconstruction suffered from discontinuities and from bureaucratic confusion.[82] This was to some degree the contemporary verdict of W. C. Bridgeman at the Ministry of Labour, who saw Addison wielding 'power which no-one but a Prime Minister should wield, of interference with other departments' and 'embarking on works which were already being done by one department or another'.[83] Philip Abrams has seen the ineffectiveness of Reconstruction in terms of the failure to perpetuate wartime controls and planning mechanisms, and to retain the involvement of social groups in post-war planning in proportion to their social participation in the war effort. Surprisingly, an American author, H. Eckstein, has attributed the founding of the Ministry of Health ultimately to the influenza epidemic of the autumn of 1918. Addison himself often wrote in his diary of his disillusion at the Ministry of Reconstruction, of the way in which his plans for the resettlement of ex-servicemen, the Ministry of Health, and the dismantling of the old Poor Law were frustrated in the Cabinet.[85] But these verdicts are coloured by hindsight and tend to ignore the immense practical difficulties facing a co-ordinated scheme for reconstruction in 1918. Abrams in particular vastly exaggerates the effectiveness of the wartime system of physical controls on production and supply. Addison's own retrospective judgement was soured by the bitterness of his defeat over social reform in 1921.

At the time, Addison's work at Reconstruction assumed major significance. It dealt, uniquely within the Coalition government, with major areas of post-war planning—health, the Poor Law, industrial insurance, unemployment policies, resettlement, and, most important of all in some ways, subsidized housing. It opened up areas for debate hitherto totally neglected. Addison noted, too, that as the essentials of a post-war programme began to crystallize, there would be on many of these issues a good measure of common inter-party agreement.[86] By November 1918, his energy and determination had raised the untested Ministry of Reconstruction to the stature of a major department of state, a unique ideas factory and planning unit. It achieved this without the administrative apparatus and techniques of macro-economic planning which underlay the growth of the welfare state after 1945. The heavy emphasis placed upon social reform and reconstruction in the election manifesto issued by the Coalition in November 1918, the central role played by housing, health, and other social policies in the Coalition's strategies in 1919 and 1920, showed how Addison's new Ministry had helped transform the political and social priorities. This was too easily forgotten later, when the onset of economic slump from mid-1920 onwards swept many of these reform programmes aside. As he faced his colleagues at Reconstruction for the last time, Addison spoke of success, not of failure.[87] American observers, too, wrote enthusiastically about the impact made on transatlantic opinion.[88] The later disillusion that followed the application of the axe of Geddes after 1922, the criteria adopted by later historians (also often Americans) which would not have been feasible in the actual world of 1918, should not obscure the creative and fertile period of work that Addison put in at Reconstruction. It further enhanced his standing as a vigorous and dynamic departmental minister.

Throughout his period as a minister, first at Munitions, then at Reconstruction, Addison was always acutely sensitive of the pressures and requirements of party politics. He was, for instance, much involved with the expansion of the franchise that would result from the Representation of the People Bill in early 1918. This would give the vote to virtually all adult males and to all females over thirty; Addison himself actually voted for proportional representation as well.[89] In particular, far more than any other member of the government, he was much involved in facing the divisions within the Liberal party that resulted from Lloyd George's supplanting Asquith as Prime Minister in December 1916. In theory there was a truce between the parties, renewed until January 1918 on the advice of a committee of which Addison was a member.[90] In theory again, the split between Asquith and Lloyd George was only a temporary one. Asquith was still the titular head of the Liberal party, the machinery of the party was still under his control, and Lloyd George's Liberal followers were supposed to unite harmoniously with those of Asquith as soon as peace returned. Addison knew that this was a hopeless illusion; something much too fundamental had happened to his party in December 1916. He was himself Lloyd George's key political adviser on the Liberal side—and therefore, according to the Tory Bridgeman, 'a man who was not to be trusted'.[91] He was well aware of the profundity of the crisis that had struck the Liberals in December 1916 and the revolution it had effected in British politics. He understood how unreal Lloyd George's position really was—that he was a prime minister on a purely personal basis, with no electoral machinery, organization, or party funds to back him up. Addison further believed that the split between Asquith and Lloyd George was a permanent one, a division not merely between individual leaders but also between rival ideologies and visions of the Liberal ethic. To a radical like Addison, hitching his wagon to the shooting star of Lloyd George, it meant that the crucial problem was trying to perpetuate Lloyd George's leadership, to transform the wartime leader into the president of a new social and political order when peace was restored.

Intermittently throughout 1917, he took part in meetings to try to formulate a programme and a political base for the Prime Minister. For example, on 21 December 1917, a meeting was held at the home of Waldorf Astor, with Lloyd George, Addison, Milner, and Victor Fisher of the British Workers' League present—representing imperialists and social reformers between them. Here they discussed Lloyd George administration. It was agreed that 'L.G.'s chief for devising a radical social programme to frustrate the challenge of the Labour party, the most probable major opponent of a post-war Lloyd George administration. It was agreed that 'L. G.'s chief weakness at present is that he had no organization.'[92] Addison felt that there would be no problem in devising a really far-reaching and comprehensive programme that would carry a large majority of the Tory party as well as Liberals and many Labour men. He felt the country was ready for 'a bold move forward under State inspiration'. The government chief Liberal whip, Freddie Guest, still spoke of a reunion with the Asquithians. In Addison's judgement, this was past praying for. He felt that the Asquithian Liberals 'have the pre-war mind unchanged'.[93] To some Liberal supporters of the government, it seemed as if the Tories were making all the running at this period. Addison, who was in the view of Glyn-Jones, the member for Stepney, 'the best Liberal, next to the Prime Minister', should be more in evidence in the House to assert himself and his radical beliefs.

Still by the early months of 1918, nothing had been resolved. Lloyd George's (and, by implication, Addison's) political future still seemed quite impenetrable. Addison had in December 1917 been placed in charge of a committee to promote the formation of some kind of Lloyd George Liberal organization. At the same time, the system established by Lloyd George for weekly breakfasts with his Liberal and Labour colleagues continued: in January, Guest produced at one of these a list of about a hundred Liberal members on whom it was felt Lloyd George could rely.[94] Addison believed these meetings were specially useful; meanwhile after he went to Reconstruction he was more and more concerned with the planning of future long-term policy. He now felt that it was all the more urgent to create some kind of Lloyd George Liberal party. He was impatient with those of the government's Liberal followers who still talked in terms of a reunion with Asquith and his friends. Addison's strong views were reinforced by the critical situation which arose in Ireland in April 1918 after the breakdown of an all-party Irish convention. He believed that Asquith's failure to endorse Lloyd George's scheme for linking Irish home rule with the introduction of conscription merely underlined the former premier's inadequacy as a Liberal leader. Events, however, were to show that it was Asquith who was right and Addison wrong here; the threat to introduce conscription inflamed Irish nationalist opinion and materially helped on the causes of republicanism and of Sinn Fein.

These matters were shortly brought to a final resolution by the crisis of the Maurice debate. Addison had always taken a keen interest in the running of the war. He had fully supported the creation of an Inter-Allied military council at Versailles at the end of 1917: 'the case for more brains on the staff' had been abundantly justified and had to be forced through. In December 1917 he had prepared a memorandum for the War Cabinet setting out his dissatisfaction with the conduct of the higher command and the Allies' inadequate propaganda work in enemy countries.[95] Along with Churchill, Addison constantly pressed Lloyd George to make room for new men in the higher military commands. During mid-February there was a desperate crisis between Haig and Robertson, the Commander-in-Chief and Chief of the Imperial General Staff respectively, on the one hand, and Lloyd George on the other. Nominally over the appointments to the new military council set up at Versailles, it was basically a bitter struggle for domination between the military and civilian authorities.

Much to Addison's relief, Lloyd George got the upper hand; Robertson was moved to a subordinate post and replaced by the more congenial General Sir Henry Wilson; the government carried the day in a debate on 19 February. Asquith's intervention in this debate, wrote Addison, was 'the worst show I have ever heard him make'.[96]

The struggle between the civilian and military authorities, however, did not end with the defeat of Robertson in February. It took a different turn on 7 May when General Maurice, until recently the head of military intelligence, alleged in the press that the government had denied Haig reinforcements on the western front. He accused Lloyd George and Bonar Law of lying to the House of Commons about the totals of men under arms. Since Asquith put down a motion for a committee of inquiry, the whole affair became in effect a vote of confidence in the government. Lloyd George won a brilliant oratorical triumph in the debate on 9 May, but the fact that 98 Liberals voted against the government on this motion showed that the split in the Liberal ranks was now past healing. A week later, on 15 May, Addison, who had been incensed by Maurice's intervention and by Asquith's attitude ('the most miserable thing'[97]) took a leading part in the formation of what turned out to be a kind of Lloyd George party, the Coalition Liberals. He argued successfully, in the face of the doubts of some fellow Liberals including Churchill and Guest, that the creation of a new party was essential. 'Future progress depends either upon the co-operative action of a group of men who are prepared to apply the lessons of the war courageously and seriously or upon a reinforced and more instructed Labour party.'[98] An organization was therefore set in motion to co-ordinate the Coalition supporters within the Liberal party. By July, a Coalition Liberal party, complete with its own whips headed by Guest, clearly existed at Westminster. It was this body that negotiated, through Freddie Guest, the fateful electoral arrangements—the notorious 'coupon'—with the Unionists in July and August.

Addison had already been in consultation with Beaverbrook about the political tactics underlying the formulation of a Coalition programme. He acted now as chairman of the Coalition Liberal Committee which drew up the proposed Liberal programme to be offered to their Unionist allies.[99] In August, after several meetings with Guest to discuss the content of a programme, it was accepted that an electoral agreement must be reached with the Unionists, and this was endorsed by Lloyd George. The 'coupon' arrangements were thus finally decided.

For a few days (20-3 August) Addison and several other members of the Coalition government stayed with Lloyd George in Criccieth, in such numbers that it was feared that the food suppliers of Caernarvonshire would be unable to cope. In glorious sunny weather, and with diversions like paddling expeditions in the river Dwyfor, the future political strategy was discussed in detail. The presence of Sir Bertrand Dawson showed the centrality of the Ministry of Health question.[100] It was clear now that the next general election was likely to be a peacetime one as the German armies were in steady retreat in eastern France. Addison prepared notes, at Guest's Manchester speech of 15 September which set the scene for the forthcoming electoral campaign. Inevitably, he laid the main stress on the government's concern for health, housing, and social reform in general. He also discussed with Lloyd George the government's programme that might be pursued prior to the holding of an election. A list of six conditions was drawn up on which Lloyd George should insist from the Unionists with regard to the claim for seats. He anticipated that Lloyd George would have a Liberal following of nearly two hundred in the House after the polls.[101]

By the end of October, it was clear that the war was nearly over. Lloyd George and Bonar Law now formally concluded an alliance with which to fight the election. A joint manifesto was also worked out. Lloyd George had now to ensure the support of a large number of his own party, so as to give himself an adequate bargaining position within the Coalition. After two important meetings of Lloyd George's Liberal supporters in the House on 6 and 12 November, this support was ensured, and the Coalition manifesto, improved by literary embellishments from H. A. L. Fisher, was carried with acclamation. At a meeting of the party whips on the 14th, at which Addison represented the Liberal ministers and Laming Worthington-Evans the Unionists, it was agreed to have the first joint declaration made at Central Hall, Westminster, on 16 November to express confidence in the Prime Minister and the Coalition government, and to pledge support for the recognized Coalition candidates in the election. At this meeting, the proposals for a Coalition manifesto were agreed; it was noted that they contained a strong Liberal emphasis, especially with regard to social reform.[102]

As the election drew near, and the campaign got under way, concern with home affairs and reconstruction was mingled with anxiety about retribution and reparations, war guilt, and the exaction of war indemnities from Germany. Addison was certainly not immune to the passions of the hour. *The Times* noted,

> The nature of the peace which is about to be made is a very burning question to the great mass of men and women in this country and candidates are finding it necessary to stress it . . . . Dr. Addison is quoted as saying that he had been struck with the absolute determination of the people that the Kaiser and others responsible must be brought to trial.[103]

Keynes was later, in the *Economic Consequences of the Peace*, to find the atmosphere of the 'coupon election' hysterical and jingoistic, permeated by cries of squeezing Germany until the pips squeaked. But to Addison, like most contemporaries, the election appeared 'apathetic'. He believed that the people had, in the main, made up their minds that the Coalition had pursued wise policies and should at all events be given a chance to deal with the problems of post-war and to carry through a peace settlement. His constituency had been redrawn under the redistribution provisions of the 1918 Reform Act and was now renamed the Shoreditch Division. It had no less than five candidates for its one parliamentary seat. Addison believed that, with one exception, they all made the mistake of advertising himself which helped to boost his chances.[104] Like Lloyd George, he laid stress on social matters and reconstruction in his speeches; but he took a nationalist line as well. 'The Germans, although beaten, were very crafty fellows at the conference table and he did not want to see our representatives there wondering if the people at home were going to back them up. He wanted them to be there knowing they were backed up. The biggest cheer came when he demanded that the Kaiser be delivered to justice.'[105]

Addison was elected with a record majority of 6,118, victorious over an 'uncouponed' Unionist, Independent Liberal, Labour, and National Party opponents. He was thus the first parliamentary candidate to contest successfully a seat in the East End of London on three consecutive occasions.[106] The election results as a whole reflected the verdict of Shoreditch. Fought on a much enlarged electoral register, they marked an overwhelming victory for the Coalition government. In all, 526 supporters of the government were returned, over 470 of them possessing the 'coupon'. In opposition were a mere 57 Labour members and about two dozen Asquithian Liberals (the total here is hard to calculate precisely). It was one of the most shattering electoral landslides in British history. Addison shrewdly noted the high vote gained by Labour. Indeed, he welcomed the fact that Labour candidates had polled so strongly as a guarantee that social reform would be pursued.

In the allocation of posts in the new government, eight Liberals were given Cabinet rank. Addison himself had insisted that the administration should not be swamped by reactionary Unionists and that the Liberal element be strongly represented. On 30 December he told Lloyd George that the people wanted reforms. 'They are set on having them done and unless they are done there will be trouble.'[107] The new government in fact was far from being a 'die-hard' administration. Among its leading symbols was Addison himself who on 14 January 1919 went to the Local Government Board, as a preliminary to becoming the first Minister of Health. His appointment was generally welcomed. Waldorf Astor, who found the government 'on the whole disappointing' and 'an old gang Ministry', described Addison as a good appointment, 'sympathetic to progress on housing, maternity and health'.[108]

So ended a period of dramatic upheaval for Addison. Almost more than anyone in political life the war years had raised him from back-bench obscurity to high office. His connection with Lloyd George from December 1916 had made him a politician of major influence. He had been a leading architect of the newly created Coalition Liberal party and of the political revolution that the 'coupon election' represented. Above all, he had shown himself to be, both at Munitions and Reconstruction, a vigorous and effective minister. At Munitions he had handled complex aspects of industrial production and labour relations with much success. At Reconstruction he had drafted a new agenda for the social policies on post-war housing, insurance, land settlement, a Ministry of Health, Whitley councils, education, and an end to the Poor Law. The reforming and radical aspects of the new Coalition's programme were in large measure his work. Many politicians had their reputations shattered by the pressures of total war: from Asquith to Neville Chamberlain, countless examples can be cited. Addison, by contrast, was made by the opportunities of wartime. Indeed, the war reinforced his basic radicalism and collectivist outlook in social and economic policy. For the rest of his career, including service in the Cabinet of Attlee after 1945, he was repeatedly to cite the collectivism of 1914–18 as a major argument for planning, for social innovation, and for socialism. 'We have been socialists enough in war matters,' he commented in January 1919.[109] As the new Lloyd George government confronted the chaotic postwar scene with its urgent challenges for peace and reconstruction, Addison took his major place within it, as one of its pivotal and influential figures.

4
The Heyday of the Coalition

On 10 January 1919 Addison succeeded Auckland Geddes as president of the Local Government Board, with the promise of becoming the first Minister of Health later in the year. His position in the government was, by this time, a significant one. He was not, of course, a member of the War Cabinet which Lloyd George retained after the armistice, but of the second-ranking members of the administration Addison was clearly amongst the more influential. Relatively ineffective as a speaker in the House of Commons, not yet widely known to the political public at large, he typified that new breed of politician which had risen to the summit through the centralization of government and collectivization of power that total war had brought with it. It was above all as an executive minister that Addison had risen to a position of influence.

His main, and most intimate, associates in the government were, naturally, his fellow Coalition Liberals. They were by no means the negligible ciphers that hostile Tory propaganda or Asquithian commentators of the A. G. Gardiner–J. A. Spender school depicted. On the contrary, they were a formidable element in the government with eight ministers of Cabinet rank and, of course, their status was enormously enhanced by their identification with the ascendant figure of Lloyd George. Of these Coalition Liberal ministers, Addison's closest relations were with H. A. L. Fisher, president of the Board of Education, and Edwin Montagu, Secretary of State for India. They shared his passion for social reform and his belief that the political and social priorities of the nation had been transformed by the war. Another Liberal minister with whom Addison was often in agreement or partnership was Winston Churchill. He also believed that the war had brought new opportunities for social welfare, he had a personal commitment to social reform that went back to 1908, and he advocated at this time such radical policies as the nationalization of

The Heyday of the Coalition

the railways and a levy on capital. Even though Churchill's belligerent anti-Bolshevism and his zeal for assisting the White Russians drove him and Addison further apart, they remained, nevertheless, on friendly terms even after Addison's enforced departure from the government in July 1921. Churchill fought Addison's battle for him, posthumously as it were, against the Geddes 'axe'. With the dominant Unionists, Addison's relations were inevitably less cordial. They came to suspect him as a profligate spender, and perhaps a crypto-socialist. Even so, Bonar Law, the Unionist leader, had a warm personal regard for Addison as a vigorous and competent minister, and frequently defended him against criticism. He and Addison shared a common passion for chess, and often took time off in the Commons to play one another, with Baldwin as an intent spectator.[1] Addison also worked well with Unionists such as Horne and Worthington-Evans on social issues. Milner he now thought 'a grand man' and 'second to none in constructive statesmanship'.[2] Austen Chamberlain, on the other hand, as an orthodox and conservative Chancellor of the Exchequer, viewed Addison with suspicion and they never enjoyed a warm relationship. Overall, however, Addison's position in the government was a strong one, especially as it was believed that he would have the ear of the Prime Minister when he returned from the Peace Conference in Paris.

Addison's importance, above all, was as a symbol of the government's radicalism at home. His policies and programmes at the Ministry of Reconstruction had loomed large in the outlook and manifesto of the Coalition. If the government stood for a new order of society, a 'land fit for heroes' as Lloyd George had rhetorically proclaimed during the election campaign, Addison was one of its key representatives. In fact, during the spring and summer of 1919 the government's commitment towards social reform was most pronounced. This was a time of considerable industrial turbulence. The vision of a new order, of more harmonious relations between capital and labour reflected in the formation of the Whitley councils and the calling of the National Industrial Conference of both sides of industry, soon evaporated. There was a series of damaging strikes from February onwards, including a strike by the police, and a situation of grave disorder in Glasgow. Worse still, there was the threat of a national miners' strike, narrowly averted by the appointment of the Sankey Commission on the coal mines. When its majority recommendation in favour of the nationalization of the mines was rejected by Lloyd George, it merely fuelled the militancy of the Miners' Federation and their commitment to a socialist programme for controlling the commanding heights of the economy. Finally at the end of September, there was a national strike by the railwaymen, and alarm that it might escalate into a general strike. Passions ran high in these months with fears of a revolution by militant labour. Both the Ministry of Labour and the Special Intelligence department claimed that Bolshevik subversion was a prime cause of this unrest. Britain appeared to be torn apart by class war in its most savage form.

Nevertheless, Lloyd George and his leading ministers kept their heads. They insisted that the answer to the militancy of labour lay not in 'die-hard' repression but in an imaginative and bold programme of social reform to meet the practical grievances of the workers. Lloyd George told his colleagues bluntly enough that they had been elected basically to fulfil pledges of social reconstruction, that blind reaction had led to the victory of the Bolsheviks in Russia, and that in dealing with key areas such as housing and health, social insurance, employment, poverty, education, and resettlement, the government's energies must be unabated.[3] In this respect, Addison was the custodian of many of the government's promises and hopes.

To Addison, then, this was a serious, even sombre world in which he had a variety of immensely important constructive tasks to fulfil. To him, the era of the Coalition government after the armistice was an exciting, historic period in British history, one that offered stimulating challenges to honourable, dedicated public servants such as himself. It was certainly far removed from the manic-depressive atmosphere with which, for example Arnold Bennett's *Lord Raingo* invested the period of Coalition government after 1918-22. Mrs Addison, however, responded very differently to the mood of 1919. Always somewhat uncomfortable in the high politics and social whirl of London, her distaste for the pomp and circumstance of political society became more pronounced. When she attended a reception at 10 Downing Street for ministers' wives in July 1919, an occasion to mark Lloyd George's return from the signing of the Versailles peace treaty, her contempt for the proceedings knew no bounds. The wives literally exposed on display there were particular targets for her scorn. Mrs Winston Churchill's 'tall willowy frame, some parts of which were slightly hidden by a light material' was bathed in 'an overpowering scent', to the pleasure of her pink, perspiring husband. Of Mrs Hamar Greenwood, she wrote that 'her complexion was so cleverly made up . . . she was of the "porkier" kind though very unclothed and not thin'. Of Lady Mond,

> she had exposed to the public view at least two square feet of bare flesh, back and front, and not only did she expose it but she gently and firmly pummelled it with her doubled fist while Sir A. stood by smiling in proud ownership and lightly adjusted one of the many diamond pendants on his lady's plump neck . . . . These underdressed and over bejewelled women were the wives of the men who are supposed to be leading and governing the country at a time of unparalleled stress and crisis. Many of them judging from snatches of overheard conversations appeared to imagine themselves interested in such things as Housing, Infant Welfare & other wrongs that are crying out to be righted. Is it possible that women so utterly devoid of the sense of decency and so barbarously decorated with jewels can have their hearts sincerely in any serious subject of civilization?

She herself wore a plain dress, 'high to the neck', bought at a ready-to-wear store two years earlier.[4]

These judgements were no doubt as revealing of Mrs Addison's stern puritanism and social commitment as of the realities of political decision-making in 1919. The following year, she and her children moved from 'Pretty Corner' in Buckinghamshire, where they had lived for fifteen years, to a house, Murley Grange, at Bishopsteignton in Devon. This decision, which obviously meant that Addison's daily contacts with his family were somewhat reduced, was taken because of the severely asthmatic condition of Christopher, the eldest son. It meant that his wife was for some years geographically removed from Addison's political activities. But the family remained a happy and close-knit one. Addison's determined commitment to social reform constantly received the moral support of his radical wife.

Addison began work at the Local Government Board in January 1919. It is not clear why he had not been appointed immediately upon the resignation (or dismissal) of his old enemy, Hayes Fisher, on 4 November. However, he had been enthusiastic in his support for the initial appointment of Auckland Geddes in Fisher's place. 'It is an excellent one and I rejoice to think that we have got a man of vigour at the L.G.B. as it is badly needed.'[5] He himself had already accepted the prior appointment of Minister of Health, and was authorized to introduce the new Ministry of Health Bill in the 1919 session. During the general election he had undertaken a wide range of political duties for Lloyd George, as a leading Coalition Liberal minister, but he also kept a watchful eye on the Local Government Board during this period. For example he protested to Lloyd George when Auckland Geddes appeared to be interfering by trying to reorganize the health services of the department during his temporary period there.[6]

As soon as he took over the Local Government Board on 10 January, Addison began to consolidate a formidable administrative team. His chief assistants were two of the outstanding civil servants of the day—Sir Robert Morant, earlier the architect of the National Insurance administration, and Sir George Newman, shortly to become principal medical officer to the Local Government Board. As second secretary, Addison had appointed John Anderson, formerly secretary of the Health Insurance Commission in 1913 and soon to emerge as the outstanding younger administrator within the central government. Addison's assistant secretary was the capable Michael Heseltine. With this outstanding team at his disposal, Addison began his task of implementing the government's ambitious social programme.

His first task was the reintroduction of the Ministry of Health Bill. After the long struggles during his period at Reconstruction, this had become his personal crusade. Beatrice Webb commented at this time, 'If the P.M.'s new Party is to have any kind of success it will have to build itself up on National Health as an alternative to the more thorough policy of Socialism.'[7] Addison had first introduced it on 7 November, just before the armistice, but it was withdrawn shortly afterwards. By the time the new House of Commons had assembled, the case for a Ministry of Health had received further support from the report of the Machinery of Government Committee under the chairmanship of Lord Haldane.[8] This had discussed the problems of the administration of health at some length and had concluded that 'the exercise of the functions of central government in this sphere could be improved by the further concentration of health services under a Minister of Health who should be charged with the surveillance of all matters of health'. Addison now pressed for the swift establishment of this ministry, and argued the case at several Cabinet meetings.[9] He also helped whip up popular support. At a demonstration at the Kingsway Hall, London, with those present including such enthusiasts for a Ministry of Health as Kingsley Wood and Lady Rhondda, Addison confirmed that when he became president of the

The Heyday of the Coalition

Local Government Board he had done so on the firm understanding that the government were going to pass a bill through parliament. At present, twenty-one government departments were doing the odds and ends of health work, as he put it. The first step should be to create a centralizing ministry. The goodwill and help of the local authorities, the insurance committees, and the organizations of the medical, nursing, midwifery, and other services would also be vital. Machinery had to be devised whereby the great professions outside parliament, and, above all, public opinion, could make their influence felt on the modelling of policy before it was made public. A massive development of the maternity and nursing services and provision for infant welfare was needed. The great keynote of the Ministry of Health should be the prevention of illness. But it was clear that the responsibility for housing must also attach to the Ministry, since inadequate housing and disease were so intimately connected.[10]

On 28 February, Addison moved the second reading of the Ministry of Health Bill. This spelt out the proposals to bring together government departments concerned with health and the proposals for their nation-wide organization. The new Ministry would have transferred to it the health and Poor Law powers and duties of the LGB and the Registrar-General, the duties of the Insurance Commissioners, the medical powers of the Board of Education, and the powers of the Privy Council under the Midwives Acts. As Sir Arthur MacNalty was to reflect years later in 1948, its aims were 'to bring every advance in medical science, every measure calculated to maintain health and to prevent disease to the service of the people.'[11] It existed above all to consolidate and develop the nation's health services. The Ministry would have both a central and a local organizational base. Although the present bill related only to the central organization, there were changes in comparison with the scheme of 1918 in relation to the Poor Law regulations; indeed, many contemporaries believed that a far more radical overhaul of the old Poor Law system was being envisaged.

An important amendment to the bill came in March with a memorandum issued on the work of the Medical Research Committee, with a preface by Addison himself. He had been one of the main founders of this Committee and had maintained a keen interest in its work during the war. This memorandum dealt with the reorganization of medical research work, and had a close bearing on the Ministry of Health Bill. The Medical Research Committee, it was proposed, should come under the direction of a committee of the Privy Council, and not under the new Ministry of Health. In the preface to this memorandum, Addison argued that the MRC should not be associated with a single, strong administrative department as this would undermine the confidence felt in the Committee by the large number of departments which had, from time to time, made demands on the Committee's services. The MRC should be brought into an analogous relation to a committee of the Privy Council under the Lord President, who would become the minister responsible for its activities to Parliament.[12]

The most important new clause which Addison moved during the Committee stage of the Bill related to the provision for Wales. 'The minister shall, subject to the provisions of this Act, appoint such officers as he may think fit to constitute a Board of Health in Wales, through whom he may exercise and perform in Wales.'[13] This major concession to administrative devolution was added to the Bill, with the blessing of Lloyd George. Subsequently Addison consulted such prominent Welsh figures as Sir Herbert Lewis, Parliamentary Secretary to the Board of Education, and Thomas Jones, Deputy Secretary to the Cabinet, about Welsh appointments. Sir Percy Watkins, the very model of the Welsh *apparatchik* and yet another product of the National Health Insurance Commissions, was selected as the first secretary where he proved a great success.[14] On 3 June 1919, the Ministry of Health Bill received the royal assent after an easy passage through Parliament. In the view of the frequently hostile Professor Bentley Gilbert, it was perhaps Addison's 'only triumph in public life', but this judgement may be discounted. Addison was appointed the first Minister of Health on 26 June, with the Local Government Board left with the more narrowly defined affairs of local government.[15]

There was another major aspect of Addison's brief tenure of the Local Government Board, one equally momentous, that of housing. As has been seen, housing was a major priority for him at the Ministry of Reconstruction. The proposals of Treasury assistance made by the Salisbury Committee in 1917, which Addison warmly supported, had been persistently restricted and obstructed by Hayes Fisher and the LGB. Between the summer of 1917 and the late spring of 1918, Addison had fought for a Cabinet statement saying, in effect, that

The Heyday of the Coalition

either the local authorities should undertake to build houses themselves, or that the government would appoint housing commissioners to do so in their place.[16] Addison gained approval for neither policy. As he was not president of the Local Government Board, he was in no position to give orders to the local authorities himself. However, he expected in the near future to see the creation of a Ministry of Health, with himself as Minister. He was, therefore, content to wait upon post-war developments.

Some attempt had been made during the war to supply the infrastructure for a housing programme. The Building Materials Supply Committee had been set up in September 1917 under the chairmanship of Sir James Carmichael to make arrangements for ensuring a supply of labour and of building materials for house construction when the armistice came. The report of the Salisbury Committee had shown that, if disaster on the housing front were to be avoided, a full and free supply of building materials such as timber and bricks was essential. Carmichael's Committee was an efficient one and had by the middle of 1918 secured promises from building suppliers. It had, in conjunction with the Demobilization Committee of the Ministry of Reconstruction, obtained priority for the release of brickmakers from the army, and had promised to finance new brickyards. It had also made provisional legal arrangements to ease the shortage which would be inevitable on the transition from a wartime to peacetime economy. But Addison was unable to put these plans into effect because of the continued postponement of a Ministry of Health. In addition, the committee appointed by the Ministry of Reconstruction to consider the position of the building industry and which reported in November 1918, was not optimistic about the supply of building materials.[17] At a meeting held between the Local Government Board and representatives of the building trades on 2 December 1918, the proposals of Carmichael's Building Materials Committee were jettisoned, in spite of the protests of Addison and Carmichael. The government proposed to control the price of building materials, without rationing and without physical controls; but Addison realized that price control alone was quite inadequate. The industrial building boom of 1919–20, which hamstrung the building of houses, had been made possible. He recorded bitterly in his diary, 'The difficulty is that, apart from the trade, the L.G.B. had been sadly against us . . . and as I am not yet Minister I can do little with them. Their defeat over the Ministry of

Health makes them hostile to anything with the word "Addison" attached to it.' Apparently the building industry had succeeded in convincing Auckland Geddes that there was no need for controls. The criticism was widely made—and in Addison's view there was no reply to it—'We are ready to use the materials, the Government is not.'[18]

Thus when Addison became president of the Local Government Board in January 1919 he had to report to the Cabinet that, for practical purposes, no planning machinery for the building industry had been set up. Despite eighteen months of argument, the situation was virtually unchanged from that in mid-1917. Referring later to the state of the Local Government Board rehousing plans when he was first appointed to it, Addison wrote to Lloyd George that

> it seemed to be an office which had failed to function . . . . Looking back on my first three months there, I feel that it was rather as if I was punching a dough pudding . . . . There seemed to be no coherent organisation. There was no machinery for securing that orders were followed or effected . . . not a single house plan or a single acre of land for the purpose of housing appear to have been sanctioned in any part of the country . . . . The legal powers of the Department and the Local Authorities were quite inadequate.[19]

Yet it was vital that hundreds of thousands of working-class houses should be built. There was a threat of social upheaval, even of revolution. By the spring of 1919, the severe housing shortage, high rents, and a vast range of slum property were acknowledged as major causes of working-class discontent in Scotland, Wales, Yorkshire, and elsewhere. Lloyd George himself was fired by the need for social reform. He strongly backed up Addison in Cabinet discussions while the measure that was to become the Housing and Town Planning Act of 1919 was in preparation.

In January Lloyd George had written from Paris to Addison asking him for his proposals with regard to the purchase of land for housing. Everything depended on the character of the valuation, wrote Lloyd George no doubt with memories of the Budget of 1909 in mind. If the principles involved in this were of the kind which would compel the state to pay more for the valuation of land than was equitable, then both housing and land settlement would fail.[20] Encouraged by the Prime Minister's letter, Addison sent detailed plans of his housing proposals; he confessed that the housing situation was even worse than he had anticipated. He told Lloyd George that Carmichael had been appointed head of the Housing Department, that housing commissioners were about to be appointed, that plans were ready for the financing of the housing schemes, and for the acquisition of land and building materials. An Intelligence Section for the Housing Department would prepare material for weekly or monthly statements of progress as vigorous publicity was necessary for the housing drive. Although the Prime Minister was in Paris, Addison would appreciate 'a frank talk' with him and felt that the premier should hold a major meeting with the local authorities to give housing 'a vigorous send-off'.[21] The Cabinet meanwhile requested Addison to outline all current housing needs on 22 January.[22]

Finance was a crucial aspect of the policy. Under the approved scheme in the Bill for the building of 300,000 houses by the local authorities, the Treasury had agreed to bear 75 per cent of the cost. Addison, however, felt that this was unsatisfactory as it left uncertainty as to the ultimate liability of the local authorities.[23] Lloyd George himself had declared that the government must be prepared to meet the charges that the housing programme would inevitably make: he estimated that the cost would not be more than £71 million. However, to encourage the local authorities to build without delay, the Local Government Board announced that more liberal assistance was to be offered by the state, and issued a circular to this effect. This was the more urgent as, by February, plans for only about 12,000 of the 300,000 initially contemplated had been made; already the inadequacy of the local authorities for the purpose was being underlined. Addison himself felt that, even though the Housing Bill had not yet been introduced, the existing powers were now sufficient for immediate action, with the responsibility of the local authorities limited to the product of a penny rate. There was no justification for any further delay in building houses that were so urgently required.[24]

When he explained the principles underlying his Housing Bill both to the Commons and to the representatives of local and municipal authorities, he promised that the full cost of the scheme would be met in the first instance by loans raised by the local authorities. Future loans would be on ordinary market terms but the local authorities would not suffer because the government would make good any loss on a housing scheme beyond a penny rate. This provision was especially well received. Hitherto the government had not promised any financial assistance in dealing with slum areas, but new housing here was a crying need. Addison promised that exactly the same subsidy would be given by the state for any losses incurred by the local authorities, in any new scheme for the clearance or improvement of insanitary areas where the LGB were satisfied that the requirements would not be met simply by the provision of new houses.[25] The Bill would place an obligation upon the local authorities to survey the housing needs of their districts. If they failed to do so, the LGB would have power to act in their place. The Bill would compel local authorities, within three months after the passage of the Act, to submit to the LGB a scheme for the provision of new houses; when such a scheme was approved, it became binding on the local authority in question to carry it out. The country was to be divided into eleven housing areas and housing commissioners would be appointed.

Addison's bold schemes were well received. According to one newspaper, 'the prevailing feeling is that the Government have met the views of the local authorities wisely and well, and Dr Addison can be assured of the strong satisfaction and support of the municipal bodies throughout the country'.[27] During the latter part of February, details on housing progress were sent to the Cabinet. It was shown that 1,026 local authorities had indicated readiness to build, a special new housing department had been set up, the supply of building materials was being tackled, financial aid for Public Utility Societies and housing associations was being approved, and a manual had been prepared to deal with layout and design.[28] The seriousness of the problem of post-war unemployment helped Addison's schemes as the government saw in house-building a major remedial policy. On 1 March the Housing Bill reached the Cabinet and was warmly welcomed there. Even Austen Chamberlain, the Chancellor of the Exchequer and usually the advocate of economy, entirely concurred. On two occasions, the Cabinet actually outdid Addison in enterprise. The Cabinet conferred full powers on the Local Government Board to compel local authorities to prepare adequate plans in cases of possible default. The Bill was accepted in principle and referred to a committee under Addison's chairmanship. It now had the seal of governmental sanction and need not go back to the Cabinet again.[29]

Addison's momentous Housing and Town Planning Bill was introduced on 18 March; in April it obtained its second reading.[30] It was warmly applauded even by anti-government journals such as the Independent Liberal *The Nation* and the Labour *New Statesman*. It became law on 31 July. Basically, it accomplished two things.[31] First, it laid upon local authorities the duty of providing houses where they were needed. To this end, it required them to make a detailed survey of their areas and report to the Minister of Health upon housing requirements. Secondly, it gave sanction to the historic principle of a state subsidy towards the requirements of the housing loans which the local authorities would contract for the building of houses. In effect, the difference between the capital cost of the houses, spread over a period of years, and the amount of income the houses earned, when let at rents which the working classes could afford, would be made up by the Treasury. This provision meant that local authorities, although having the cost of their loans guaranteed by the state, had to borrow on their own credit. On the one hand, there was no obligation or pressure for any individual authority to hold down the cost of houses. On the other, the Treasury lost the advantage of centralized borrowing. In the end, a major cause of the destruction of the Addison housing programme lay in the high cost of borrowing which this aspect of his bill entailed.

When he moved the second reading of his Housing Bill, Addison stressed that he was dealing not only with the actual shortage of houses, but what he described as a further 'concealed' shortage. There were, in all, arrears amounting to 350,000 working-class houses which would have been built had it not been for the interruption of the war. More serious, there were a large number of occupied houses that were unfit for human habitation. It was proposed in the Bill, under Section Five, to make it the duty of the local authority, in such cases, to undertake a survey and provide a scheme for dealing with rehousing. If it failed to do so, the Ministry would step in.[32]

The supply of skilled labour and building materials remained highly problematical. Addison declared that, within the next twelve months, the shortage of both would be so pronounced that there would be little chance of more than a small part of the forthcoming housing scheme being put into operation.[33] *The Nation* noted, accurately enough,

Despite the production of a Housing Bill by the Government, housing still languishes. Hardly one local authority has begun to build and no real preparation has been made to make building possible. There is a beautiful paper provision for bricks; but as far as it is possible to ascertain these bricks do not exist outside the imagination of Government Departments. The Master Builders have their plant standing idle and are unable to begin operations at present costs until the Local Authorities and the Government give the word.³⁴

These fundamental difficulties were to dog the housing programme of the Lloyd George Coalition government throughout.

As has been seen, the Ministry of Health Bill passed through parliament in June, and Addison became the first Minister of Health and Housing at the end of that month. It was an important watershed in the fortunes of the Coalition government. With the Peace Conference at Paris almost over, Lloyd George was shortly to return to the domestic scene. The government urgently needed his presence and prestige, partly to compensate for recent losses in by-elections to Wee Free and Labour, partly to placate the unrest of the trade unionists, newly inflamed by the impasse of the Sankey Commission's recommendation in favour of the nationalization of the coal mines. Addison's role was now a crucial one. More than any other member of the government, he was in a position to carry through a purposive programme of social reform that would pacify militant labour. He had an indirect involvement with the industrial confrontations of that summer. For instance, he took a close interest in the deliberations of the Sankey Commission on the coal industry and circulated a memorandum in August on the Duckham compromise scheme for reorganization of the mines.³⁵ His authority was further enhanced in October when he became a fully ranking member of the reconstituted Cabinet after Lloyd George reluctantly replaced the old War Cabinet with the traditional peacetime form of Cabinet government.

Over the next two years, Addison's work as Minister of Health and Housing was to arouse passionate controversy. Almost more than any other member of the government, he seemed to be dogged by conflict and crisis. He suffered an immediate blow at the new Ministry when Sir John Anderson, the outstanding civil servant in his new department, was, without warning, removed to the headship of the Inland Revenue. Beatrice Webb and Violet Markham had both wanted Anderson as permanent head of the Ministry of Health in succession to Morant who had just died.³⁶ In fact, the post went to the less imposing Sir Arthur Robinson. Addison, who had won a reputation for concern for the financial and working conditions of his departmental staff, protested bitterly to Bonar Law about the loss of Anderson, but in vain. He felt that it was unlikely to promote good team-work and solidarity in the new department.[37] Still, he rose to the challenge presented by the new Ministry of Health, undismayed, and with all his accustomed energy and pugnacity. His work as Minister may be summarized under the main headings of health and hospital services, national insurance, and, much the most crucial and controversial of all, housing. His ministerial tasks included other incidental aspects, but it was to these three areas of social welfare that his main efforts were devoted. Fortified by an encouraging speech by Lloyd George at the Mansion House, to launch the new Department, the new Minister set to work. As he told the Prime Minister, 'Health and Housing are the two things in the social sphere which are the most popular we have in the country just now and I want you to show that you are our leader in these matters just as much as in the peace negotiations.'[38]

The first area of his departmental concerns was the familiar one of the extension of health and hospital services. He was anxious to increase the provision made for the treatment of such diseases as venereal disease, tuberculosis, and rabies under the new Ministry. The root cause of some of them, he felt, lay in inadequate housing and environmental planning. Unless new houses were built, it was useless to expect disease to be successfully coped with.[39] He often complained in the Cabinet that too much money was being spent on foreign adventures in the Middle East, Russia, and elsewhere while health programmes were being cut back.[40] When circularized, along with other departmental heads in August 1919, on the need for economy,[41] he replied with reasons why this was impossible in relation to health. If anything, he would be applying for increased grants for the Ministry of Health, for the reconstruction of the Poor Law, for research into tuberculosis and venereal disease, and for improved facilities for maternity, child welfare, nursing provisions, and the early diagnosis and treatment of disease. As a doctor as well as a minister, Addison spoke with unmatched authority in these areas. These matters should be dealt with as part of a comprehensive, integrated scheme for improved health services for the community.[42]

Much of this was indeed carried out during Addison's twenty months at the Ministry of Health. In particular, his period in office saw a dramatic improvement in the services for infant welfare, with a 50 per cent grant-in-aid to support medico-social schemes for the prevention of mortality and morbidity in infancy and early childhood. The Ministry's approach to infant health was preventive and educative rather than curative. Supervision of the infant was extended to the supervision of the pre-school child partly by means of home visiting, partly through the extension of day nurseries, while the treatment of more specialized health defects was provided by an extension of the school medical services. Maternal welfare was also to benefit from Addison's period as a Minister of Health. Maternity schemes were undertaken to provide for the further training of midwives, and to ensure that midwives should have the assistance of specialist medical advice in the antenatal and postnatal periods. They were reinforced by the recommendations of the Royal Commission on Health Insurance in 1920. Later Ministers of Health were to build on the foundations laid in 1919–21. Certainly, undernourished, unhealthy children and expectant mothers were two important classes of beneficiary of Addison's energetic and dedicated work on behalf of the nation's health.

To advise on questions relating to medical and allied services, a consultative council was appointed by Order in Council in October 1919 to keep in touch with medical opinion throughout the country and to help Addison carry the profession with him. This was one of four set up to cover all aspects of health in England and Wales. The medical service. Also it was necessary to reform general conditions of hostilities ended they would be offered revised terms in regard to medical service. Also it was necessary to revise general conditions of service: this was to be carried out in the National Health Insurance (Amendment) Bill, introduced in March 1920, with which Addison was closely connected.[43] As in the past, his background as a doctor was a valuable political attribute and he was able to reach rapid agreement with a medical deputation about the need for improved medical services and treatment for insured persons. There remained the question of doctors' remuneration. Addison had warned Lloyd George and the Cabinet on this in December 1919. 'The question of doctors' remuneration has still not been settled whereas Old Age Pensions and Unemployment have.' Doctors should receive a capitation fee of not less than 11s. plus mileage. It would be fatal now to antagonize the doctors and the Approved Societies.[44] He produced evidence to show that 75 per cent of medical practitioners working for national health insurance received less than £500 a year from the scheme. As a result of his efforts, the government's revised scheme for doctors' pay was announced on 14 January 1920. Addison was able to tell a deputation from the British Medical Association that the government were prepared to provide the funds to pay insurance doctors on the basis of an increased yearly capitation fee of 11*s*. together with a mileage fund of £300,000 a year for rural doctors in England and Wales.[45] The new Medical Benefit regulations in the National Health Insurance (Amendment) Bill aimed at improving terms of service. The government would give approval for medical attendance at 11*s*. per head, even though the BMA had sent it to arbitration. One major grievance was thus removed.

Addison was also active in improving the nation's nursing services. His Nurses Registration Bill in 1919 set up a register of those entitled to be enrolled as nurses. The Bill set up the authority to compile the register and to prescribe the conditions of training necessary for admission. After piloting this Bill through the Commons, Addison received the warm thanks of the nurses for a marked enhancement of their professional status.[46]

A second crucial area of Addison's departmental work was national insurance. As has been seen, his proposal for a universal civilian out-of-work donation and the government's acceptance of it in the autumn of 1918 marked a major step forward in the progress of post-war welfare history. The announcement of the scheme, however, emphasized that it was purely an emergency measure, that contributions would continue to be collected under the regular unemployment insurance system, and that in the meantime 'the government were pressing forward with their scheme for general contributory insurance'. Addison also urged that health and unemployment insurance contributions should be linked together. In a somewhat erratic fashion, a new principle had been established. An unemployed man was agreed to have a claim to make upon society as of right. When the Civilian Donation came to an end, the government was forced now to couple the disappearance of the 'dole' with a positive announcement of a scheme for universal unemployment insurance.[47] The provision for 'contracting out' on which Addison had insisted in November 1918 despite the objections of William Beveridge, was now dropped.[48] In early 1920, it fell to Sir Robert Horne, the Minister of Labour, to introduce a bill for Unemployment Insurance. The comprehensive scheme that this measure introduced was to form one of the social legacies of the Coalition government. The notorious 'dole' had come into being, means test and all.

The most crucial, third area of policy was housing. Throughout that summer of 1919, Addison campaigned for the speedy construction of houses. He addressed representatives of local authorities at Nottingham, Manchester, and Leeds, trying to whip them into action.[49] He felt that the difficulties relating to the supply of building materials were now being slowly overcome, and he urged the authorities to speed up building while the weather remained fine. There were still difficulties over bricklayers, carpenters, and other skilled labour; but there were now available materials to build far more houses than were covered in plans already submitted to the LGB. He set up the Housing Advisory Council, under the chairmanship of Sir Tudor Walters, a Liberal MP, to advise on housing problems. There were now three main links between the Ministry of Health and the local authorities—the Parliamentary Housing Group, the circulars and memoranda gushing forth from Whitehall, and the Regional Commissioners. The Parliamentary Housing Group of nearly 200 members was formed with the Unionist solicitor, Kingsley Wood, an old associate of Addison's since 1911, as its secretary. Wood also headed a Housing Bureau to deal with technical questions concerning housing schemes.[50] Addison displayed great optimism when addressing the Housing Group in June. He hoped that the Council of the Building Trades Federation would be able to draw up a comprehensive scheme for skilled labour which would receive the approval of the employers and the unions.[51] In reply to criticism from Asquith that difficulties in the acquisition of land and the price of it were likely to delay the progress of housing, Addison pointed out that, starting from nothing in January 1919, there had been surveyed, valued, and planned for housing purposes by local authorities up to the end of June no less than 28,214 acres of land, of which 14,392 had been approved for building. The cost of the whole would average at £170 per acre.[52] Meanwhile, to encourage local authorities to contribute housing schemes and build more houses, the Ministry of Health started a new journal, *Housing*, to serve as a means of communication between the Housing Department and the local authorities up and down the country: for two years it was published fortnightly.[53]

During the later part of 1919, the Ministry of Health continued to make optimistic statements about the progress of housing. In September, its staff received applications for 582 sites, which brought the total to 5,105; on the 46,000 acres involved, 460,000 houses could and would be built.[54] 'We may safely claim to have mastered our first great difficulty of securing and approving sites,' Addison declared.[55] The provision of additional housing was already making much more progress than could have been expected. A large number of vacant houses in London, suitable for conversion into tenements and flats, were being acquired under the compulsory powers given by the Housing Acts. As a result of the activities of the municipal authorities in London alone, a thousand of these had been obtained; steps were being undertaken to double the total.[56]

But Addison's colleagues did not share his blithe optimism. By the end of November he was forced to acknowledge himself that the housing position was far from satisfactory. Mond, Macnamara, and other ministers protested that 'the position is a very grave one'.[57] Addison remained buoyant in refuting press criticisms about delays and broken promises on housing. A scheme as ambitious as that proposed under the Housing Act could hardly be carried out in only a few months. They were dealing with 1,800 local authorities with varying degrees of competence, determination, and financial resources. Their difficulties had been compounded by the war. In a White Paper, he showed that many building firms were prepared to supply houses of new types and construction. He admitted that the actual amount of building by the end of November was insignificant, but after all the Act had become law only five months previously. In the interim, 24,000 acres of land had been approved, surveyed, and planned for houses, and a further 24,000 acres had been surveyed by the authorities. These 48,000 acres would be more than enough for the 50,000 houses of the programme.

But he was forced to admit that there had been mistakes. There were also structural problems inherent in the nature of the building industry. There had been difficulties with the transport of building materials and the cost here had risen by 150 per cent in the post-war inflation. Again, the war had depleted the building trade of 200,000 men—carpenters, joiners, masons, and, above all, bricklayers were in short supply. The high cost of building materials caused local authorities to be hesitant, and although many had put tenders in, they had refused to go further. Again, many local authorities were innocent of knowledge of house-building, yet they were suddenly given the awesome responsibility of carrying out the most important, expensive, and perhaps the most complicated of the government's reconstruction promises.[58]

Another set of difficulties arose out of the state of the private-enterprise building trade itself. With regard to house-building, there were two sets of builders with little relationship with each other—the private builders and the publicly employed builders. There were also restrictive practices operated by the building trade unions who resisted 'dilution' in their ranks, understandably so in some ways in view of the seasonal nature of the building trade. To try to increase the supply of labour, Addison proposed that a conference of all those employed in the building trade be called by the Minister of Labour.[59] But the unions remained suspicious of any such initiatives. In an attempt to increase the number of houses built, after long negotiations with the Joint Industrial Council of the Federated Builders Addison gained their agreement that if houses of the appropriate type were built, the government would provide a subsidy of £150 per house.[60]

This was embodied in the Housing (Additional Powers) Bill which received its second reading in December 1919. The Bill also included a provision for the issue of housing bonds by the local authorities to help finance their housing drives, and also the stipulation that all luxury building should be stopped. This Bill, inevitably, attracted criticism. The attractiveness of the housing bonds to the investor was not clear: Addison had failed to persuade the Cabinet's Finance Committee to attach a rate of 6 per cent to them.[61] The housing subsidy gave rise to hostile criticism. Labour members and radicals generally declared that the £150 subsidy for private builders would succeed only in stimulating building for well-to-do people and to that extent actually withdraw labour and capital from working-class housing. The private builder who put up houses with the aid of the subsidy would find it impossible, so it was claimed, to let houses at the same rent as the municipality. The presumption was that he would avoid competition, which would involve him in serious loss, and would devote himself instead to meeting a rapid and growing demand for middle-class housing which could be sold at from £1,000 to £1,400. Unless the government assumed full financial responsibility, broke the power of price-fixing 'rings', pegged builders' profits at a reasonable rate, and devoted much effort to solving unemployment or underemployment in the building industry, the housing famine would continue.[62]

These were serious criticisms, although Addison did his best to refute them. It was not a paying proposition, he argued, for private persons to build houses of the type required without some kind of subsidy. The local authorities, with the assistance of the Treasury behind them, were failing to meet the housing needs and therefore some new policy needed to be tried. He had, during the past two months, reached agreement with the whole of the building trade. The builders had agreed to co-operate on the understanding that they would share among themselves, in addition to whatever other work they may have had, a minimum number of houses for the local authority as part of the housing scheme. In return they would receive £150 per house subsidy on condition that the house was begun within twelve months. The Minister's view was warmly defended in the Commons by the housing expert, Tudor Walters, who declared that Addison had shown 'great prescience and wisdom' in his handling of the housing situation.[63]

Strenuous efforts were made meanwhile to reduce the highly inflated cost of building materials or, at least, to prevent them rising still further. He appointed a committee under Tudor Walters to investigate this problem, while his Under-Secretary, Waldorf Astor, arranged with Auckland Geddes to have the cost of materials that were used in building examined by the accounting branch of the committee set up by the Board of Trade under the Profiteering Act. The Ministry achieved some success in this direction: Pigou later showed that down to the end of 1920 the rise in the price of building materials was less than that of materials in general.[64]

There was also the question of finance, especially with reference to the new housing bonds. In the Housing (Additional Powers) Act in December 1919 Addison had supported the principle of encouraging local authorities not to rely on the Treasury in the issue of these bonds. He also asked Herbert Samuel (without success) if he would be willing to lead the campaign to popularize the housing bonds and to induce local authorities to issue them.[65] But there were many problems, mostly located at the Treasury. Addison had failed to agree on matters vitally connected with housing finance with Austen Chamberlain, the Chancellor. Since the end of 1919, the Treasury was committed to a dear money policy, based on high interest rates, as a preliminary to a return to gold. This was supported, even by economists such as Keynes, to redress the post-war speculative boom. Lloyd George and

Bonar Law had tried in vain to promote a policy of cheaper money to help with housing bonds and to reduce the cost of government borrowing.[66] In a memorandum circulated to the Cabinet, Addison wrote that although local authorities were empowered to issue bonds to finance their housing schemes and although a vigorous publicity campaign in the country had been prepared, two questions were still outstanding. These were the rate of interest to be offered and the date of issue of the bonds. He had failed to reach agreement with Austen Chamberlain on either point. Addison had urged that the rate should be 6 per cent, and that the bonds should be issued as a matter of urgency. Chamberlain, however, believed that the bonds should not be floated at present 'to keep the field clear for the new exchange bonds', and he successfully insisted that the rate of interest be kept at $5\frac{1}{2}$ per cent.[67] Meanwhile the steady rise of bank rate made the problems of housing finance all the more difficult. Chamberlain's view was hard for a departmental minister to resist, especially given the reinforced ascendancy of the Treasury over the civil service: Warren Fisher, its permanent head, was now recognized as head of the civil service as a whole.

The obstructive tactics of the Treasury were thus one major reason for the holding up of the housing schemes. Addison himself still favoured a National Housing Loan as the only solution to the financial problems of the local authorities, but the Treasury objected and the Cabinet decided against him.[68] The issue of housing bonds was decided upon as an alternative. But many local authorities refused to raise money by the issue of bonds. The Housing and Town Planning Association, which had rendered valuable assistance to the Ministry in dealing with housing problems, now supported the defeated scheme for a National Housing Loan, while it complicated matters still further by refusing to support the principle of the £150 subsidy to private builders.[69]

Apart from finance, there remained the continuing difficulty of getting the building trade unions to accept new recruits to apprenticeships or to widen their ranks to include semi-skilled workers. The Addison Housing Act of 1919 had been regarded, by the Coles for example, as a great opportunity for the building workers. It was 'almost ideal' for a real step towards Guild Socialism; the public authority could provide the capital and own the houses, while the workers' organizations could contract to produce them by 'self-governing' guilds. The Manchester Federation of Building Trade Operatives formed themselves into a 'Guild Committee' and offered to undertake house building for the local authority on a 'non-profit-making' basis. Their example was followed by at least sixty-three authorities by 1922. But labour problems formed an insuperable obstacle to this as to every other aspect of the housing campaign. In February 1920, Lloyd George strongly attacked the building trade unions in the House of Commons because of their refusal to accept the 'dilution' proposals made by the Ministry of Health. The result of this refusal was twofold—the work of building houses was denied to 350,000 discharged soldiers who were anxious to offer their labour, and the municipalities could not build because they could not obtain labour.[70] Lloyd George tended to use the building workers, too, in a wider context, as a convenient anti-labour argument to spur on moves for 'fusion' between Unionists and Coalition Liberals.

On the other hand, critics of the government maintained that many bricklayers were in reality available. The fact that they were employed, not on building working-class houses but on warehouses, departmental stores, and cinemas called for some explanation other than that given by Lloyd George. They agreed that finance was an important stumbling-block, and that the rapid inflation in the price of building materials made it impossible for builders or local authorities to erect small houses except at exorbitant cost. But Lloyd George ignored, or misunderstood, the point of view of the unions who resisted dilution. The building trade was always seasonal; there were long periods of enforced unemployment. The trade unions had said that they would agree to dilution, and to raise output to the highest possible limit, if a worker could be guaranteed reasonable maintenance during his period of enforced idleness, if the community could be safeguarded against profiteering by the master builders, and if the power of the building material 'rings' could be curbed. No attempt, they maintained, had been made to meet these points.[71]

Even though criticism of the lack of progress on housing was mounting by February 1920, Addison remained optimistic as to the over-all situation. As he explained to the Commons, the past year had been spent in building up organization and resources. More and more responsibility had been given to the Housing Commissioners who, by February 1920, had complete authority with regard to sites, house plans, and tenders. There was a shortage of men, money, and material still but this lay beyond the government's control. Only now were they reaping the results of the Housing Act passed in June. He believed that the approval for tenders for 200,000 houses in the 1920 programme would be made good. During the past seven weeks, as he argued on 17 February, more than twice as many houses had passed into the 'accepted tender' stage than in the previous twelve months. Since the passing of the Amendment Act, they had the proposals from thirty new public utility societies before them. He remained convinced that the local bond issue, if it received support, would be a great success. The Builders' Federation had agreed to limit their profits, which would reduce high costs, although a shortage of bricklayers remained a grave problem.[72]

In a speech in Scotland, he rebutted, with much force, Asquith's hostile comments about the 1919 Housing Act and its administration. The ex-Prime Minister's own record in dealing with housing problems under conditions much less difficult than those prevailing in 1920 was a poor one. In acid comments which underlined Addison's intuitive distaste for the patrician Asquithian style, he went on:

I have never looked to Mr. Asquith for useful, constructive suggestions. I am not aware that he has ever made any that were calculated to remedy the evils arising out of bad housing . . . but I confess that when he set out to criticise the Housing Act and our efforts in that connection, I did look for something a little more substantial than the tenuous stuff which he supplied to his audience at Paisley.

Asquith had described the Housing Act at Paisley as 'an admirable piece of paper'. He had expressed surprise that within six months of its passage into law it had had 'little practical effect' in eliminating the arrears of 100,000 houses required to be provided. Addison now compared the facts of the six months' existence of the Housing Act of the Coalition government with the six or more years of Asquith's premiership before the war. From 1906 to the start of war in 1914, the total number of houses built in England and Wales had been 8,381. Under Addison's Act, 105,758 plans for houses had already been submitted, of which 90,491 had been approved and passed. Of those, 30,600 had been tendered for, and the tenders of 26,180 finally approved.[73]

This was useful debating material, and certainly the priority accorded to social reform by the Asquithian Liberals was not impressive. But the fact remained that, by the spring of 1920 the houses

The Heyday of the Coalition

hoped for had not been forthcoming, in spite of all Addison's optimism. Labour was still in short supply; the trade unions were still suspicious and hostile to dilution; the price of building materials remained high; and local authorities were remarkably slow in pushing on with their housing schemes. The forces which would eventually bring an end to the Addison housing programme were beginning to crystallize. The most powerful of all was now looming up. In August 1918 a committee headed by Lord Cunliffe, the Governor of the Bank of England, had given its recommendations for government financial policy after the war; they were headed by the return to gold. The Bank of England now began to take steps to put them into operation, by contracting the note issue and raising interest rates. The increase in bank rate to 6 per cent in November 1919 brought Addison into angry collision with other members of the Cabinet.[74] In a series of tense ministerial meetings in the latter part of 1919 he admitted that only 43,299 houses had actually been approved out of the 500,000 needed; virtually none had been completed of those mythical 'homes for heroes'. Only 715 houses had been completed in England and Wales by 31 March 1920, according to the Ministry's own annual report.[75] This was chiefly because the local authorities were unable to borrow money. Austen Chamberlain refused Addison's demand for Treasury assistance to the local authorities, beyond what was already committed, and his view inevitably prevailed in the Cabinet. By March 1920, Addison's main initiative and social priority, the housing programme, was running into the sands. The local authorities were hamstrung, the unions fearful of dilution, the building trades inefficient. Meanwhile the government had handicapped itself by the ending of wartime controls over the price of raw materials. The overall finance of Addison's programme seemed to be getting out of control, as the vocal 'anti-waste' lobby pointed out. His whole reputation as an effective minister was now thrown into the balance.

Addison's role in the wider field of national politics went through profound changes in these years. At first, he was something of a radical critic of the Prime Minister, notably over foreign and Irish policy. He was also interested in the coal industry and attended Cabinet meetings in August 1919 to discuss the question of possible nationalization. He told Bonar Law angrily in July that his not being summoned to a Cabinet to discuss miners' claims on profiteering by the coal-owners was 'a little less than insulting'.[76] As a Cabinet minister, Addison was noted for his occasional over-sensitive prickliness, though he was generally popular with his colleagues. As has been seen, in August 1919 he prepared a memorandum on the Duckham scheme for the reorganization and rationalization of the mines. He acknowledged that the objections held by many to the nationalization of the mines related to state management. At the same time, under the system of private ownership, bad accounting, insensitive management, and inefficient methods of production prevailed. The existing conditions in the various coalfields provided a serious indictment of the present system. At the very least, state ownership of minerals and royalties should be accepted and extended, not only for coal but for other minerals. He generally endorsed Sankey's proposals for the compensation of the mineral owners. After study of the various schemes of Sir Arthur Duckham, Llewellyn Smith, and George Barnes, a Labour minister, Addison came down in favour of state ownership of the mines, though not state management. Direct management by the state would, he felt, be uneconomical, stereotyped, and liable to lead to undesirable parliamentary interference with the running of the pits. Addison's views, though, were those of the extreme left in the Cabinet. He was one of a minority of just five (Barnes and Roberts, two Labour men, Montagu, a Liberal, and the imperialist, Milner, being the others) who voted in Cabinet for the nationalization of the mines on 7 August 1919.[77] Lloyd George, Bonar Law, and the main strength of the Cabinet strongly took the opposite line; conflict between the government and the Miners' Federation inevitably continued.

Addison also found time to reflect on foreign affairs. Even before the start of the Paris Peace Conference, he was pressing Lloyd George to take a positive line on the League of Nations and on proposals for disarmament; he criticized Churchill's proposals to impose a fresh Military Service Act.[78] While in general sympathetic to Lloyd George's attempts to moderate the peace terms imposed on Germany in Paris, he was very critical of intervention in Russia. With his Liberal colleagues, H. A. L. Fisher and Edwin Montagu, he repeatedly urged that Britain should cease to assist the White Russians in the civil war in the East.[79] He played a vigorous part in inducing that change of view in the Cabinet which resulted in the almost complete withdrawal of British troops from Russia by the end of 1919. He had reminded the Cabinet on 25 July of the strength of popular feeling in Britain against any intervention in Russia on behalf of the Denikin 'White' forces.[80] On imperial and colonial issues, Addison took a consistently liberal stand. Over India, he strongly backed up Edwin Montagu after his dismissal of General Dyer for perpetrating the massacre of several hundred Indians at Amritsar, while he endorsed the Milner report which called for a strong degree of internal self-government for Egypt.[81] On the other hand, Addison did tend to support Lloyd George in his belligerent anti-Turkish policy in the Near East. For Addison, as for many Liberals, the Turk was truly 'unspeakable' while support for liberal Greece was imperative in the eastern Mediterranean. Addison, Curzon, and Auckland Geddes were the only Ministers to back up Lloyd George in his extreme view that the Sultan should be removed from Constantinople.[82] For Addison as for Lloyd George, Turkey was a blind spot in an otherwise pacific and liberal approach to overseas affairs.

Addison was also an effective and persistent critic of the government's policy towards Ireland. He argued that, with the Home Rule Act now on the statute book, proposals must be put to parliament for self-government; if the government waited until Irishmen reached a united view, then they would wait for an eternity.[83] In practice, the worsening climate in Ireland with the government employing the Black and Tans and the 'Auxis' to reinforce the regular troops in retaliation against the IRA and Sinn Fein merely reinforced the anxiety of Addison, Fisher, Montagu, and other Liberal ministers during the era of the 'troubles'.

In a wider sense, however, Addison was intimately involved in Lloyd George's basic political strategy in the autumn and winter of 1919–20. This was the idea of 'fusion' between the Coalition Liberals and the Unionist supporters of the government. The party system that unfolded in the months following the 'coupon election' was largely unrecognizable in terms of pre-war politics, with an immense government majority and a miniscule opposition of Labour and Wee Free Liberals. The absence of the Prime Minister at the Paris Peace Conference until July merely added to the air of unreality. Addison had little contact with his chief until mid-summer when he returned from Paris. In July he wrote to the Prime Minister asking for a talk in which they could discuss broad policy 'in a considered and methodical way'.

He believed that the failure to consider big questions of policy beforehand had partially contributed to the present unpopularity of the government as shown in by-elections. Lloyd George had a unique opportunity for remoulding and it would be a tragedy if it were not used.[84]

On Lloyd George's return home, he felt that now was the time to translate his semi-presidential ascendancy of the wartime years into something more permanent. The war had increased his impatience with the old politics and with the tattered remnants of the Old Liberalism. Supporters such as Addison now sought to perpetuate the Coalition on a more permanent basis. Bonar Law, at the outset of the new parliament, had urged that all Coalitionists, irrespective of party, should sit together as a homogeneous whole. But as long as separate Unionist and Liberal organizations continued, the Coalition would remain fragmented. In 1919–20 this idea of a 'fusion' of the two parties was foremost in Lloyd George's mind. He wanted a union of the two at all levels, and thereby to provide himself with a permanent base from which to fight off the challenge of the Labour party. He broached the idea with Fisher and Addison as early as 23 September.[85]

In October, Lloyd George had been forced to restore the pre-war Cabinet. As the wartime Cabinet had disappeared, so had the wartime party truce. The fierce fight being put up by Labour in by-elections in 1919 and early 1920, with as the climax the party's victory in a three-cornered contest at Spen Valley in December 1919, confirmed this. 'Fusion' now appeared to supporters of the Coalition as the sole method of welding the administration into a united front against Labour. Addison and Churchill were the chief Cabinet ministers in favour of fusion—but for very different reasons. Churchill wanted fusion so that the forces of private capitalism and 'law and order' could be united to combat the menace of socialism. Addison, by contrast, wanted to perpetuate the Coalition for positive reasons, to press on with a massive programme of radical and social reform. He wanted 'fusion' at the constituency level first; 'At the first opportune moment, the Party fusion that we have so often discussed should be pressed with a proper declaration of policy. I think, however, it should be possible even before this to form a Central Coalition Whips' Organization.'[86]

Addison was unrepentant about the social achievements of the Lloyd George Coalition. He was angered by Asquith's sneers at the Coalition

The Heyday of the Coalition

Liberals as 'little better than hewers of wood and drawers of water for an all-powerful Tory majority'. He compared the 'so-called Liberalism' of Asquith's pre-war regime with the real Liberalism of Lloyd George's governments. The latter had passed the Franchise, Education, and Housing Acts which were notable landmarks in social, progressive legislation, whereas Asquith's speeches were devoid of constructive content on the social front. There were no measures passed by Asquith except the Parliament Act and those pioneered by Lloyd George which could compare in courage and comprehensiveness with those of 1916–20.[87] Like other Coalitionists, Addison insisted that he remained a good radical, anxious to promote reform within a more hopeful setting than the sterile partisanship of pre-war politics.

After the Labour victory at the by-election at Spen Valley in Yorkshire in December 1919, it became all the more urgent, in the view of Lloyd George and Addison, to secure the agreement of the Coalition Liberals to 'fusion'. In January and February, Lloyd George devoted much effort in trying to convert the Liberal ministers to the idea of 'fusion'. On 4 February, he met Addison, Fisher, Kellaway, Macnamara, Hewart, Thompson, and Munro at Cobham where they discussed the formation of a new 'national' party. Lloyd George urged that 'Liberal labels would lead nowhere, we must be prepared to burn them.'[88] In a long letter soon after, Addison sent Lloyd George some reflections as to why he and his government were losing popularity. This was mainly due to the Prime Minister's being withdrawn from domestic affairs, to post-war reaction in the social and industrial field, to the lack of a central organization to direct government propaganda (always a favourite theme of Addison's), to a hostile press, and to the management of affairs at home being left partially to men of little political experience (for example, no doubt, the Geddes brothers).

Lloyd George's response to Addison's overtures had been the unexpected one that he move from the Ministry of Health and become Minister without Portfolio in place of George Barnes who had just resigned. Addison was hurt by this suggestion. He felt that his experience on his removal from the Ministry of Munitions to the Reconstruction department would be repeated. He would be marked down as a failure, notably over housing, as he had been on his departure from the Ministry of Munitions. He offered instead some more constructive suggestions. A central Coalition Whips' Office should be formed and 'a good policy section' set up to take note of public opinion. Addison suggested that a small committee be created to work out these proposals, and that Lloyd George appoint a small group of his colleagues to consider affairs regularly and present the Prime Minister with frequent reviews of the political situation. Addison himself offered to take charge of this.[89] Lloyd George did not immediately respond. The loyal lieutenant of 1911, 1916, and 1918 was already becoming expendable.

In March the fusion of the Unionists and Coalition Liberals was generally anticipated. The Unionists supported the idea although with much reluctance. While they comprised much the largest element in the Coalition, they could not afford to lose Lloyd George's leadership. Then there were the Coalition Liberals. On 16 and 18 March Lloyd George tried to persuade his fellow Liberals to 'fuse' but the idea fell flat. The Coalition Liberals, quite unexpectedly, proved to be a crucial stumbling-block. Many of them were anxious to keep the way open for reunion with their Asquithian comrades rather than to unite with the Tory enemy. On 16 March it was the Coalition Ministers who demurred, notably Montagu, Fisher, Mond, and Shortt. On 18 March when Lloyd George met his Liberal back-bench members, there was so much opposition voiced in advance that, instead of appealing for fusion, he made only a vague plea for 'closer co-operation' in the constituencies.[90] The Coalition Liberals remained Liberals still—and so, in spite of himself, did Lloyd George. This meant that the whole idea of 'fusion' was exploded. If the Coalition Liberals were not willing to merge, the Unionists, with much right-wing discontent voiced in constituency parties about the Coalition, would not give fusion any more encouragement.

The Liberal back-benchers who expressed their anxiety on 18 March about 'fusion' did so for many reasons. Mostly their concern was traditional—concern about their historic name, concern about historic Liberal principles such as free trade and Irish home rule. Addison shared few of these worries. As a pragmatist and a realist, he cared little for the historic name of Liberal; he entertained a profound contempt for Asquith. As for a traditional policy like free trade, Addison's view, like that of Lloyd George himself, was highly flexible. Like the Prime Minister, he was never a doctrinaire free trader. He welcomed the inroads into traditional tariff policies introduced during the war years; he had worked closely with an arch-imperialist like Milner. He felt scant concern about the threats to free trade contained in the Anti-Dumping Bill of 1919, the proposals to protect 'key industries' from foreign competition with import duties, and the imperial preference proposals contained in Austen Chamberlain's budget of 1919. Years later, he was to be a markedly protectionist Minister of Agriculture under Ramsay MacDonald. Events proved, however, that in this respect, he and Lloyd George were out of touch with many of their parliamentary supporters. The Coalition Liberals believed that they were still Liberals, and this was invariably related to the shibboleth of free trade. As a result, 'fusion' as an idea collapsed for ever.

The events of March 1920 marked a great divide in the history of the Coalition government. Henceforth, Lloyd George's political future was uncertain with the prospect always before him of the dominant Unionists breaking away from the Coalition Liberal minority. His future as Prime Minister was henceforth permanently at risk. But, at a less elevated level, the failure of fusion marked a watershed for Addison also. Henceforth his brand of social radicalism was threatened within a Tory-dominated coalition and was increasingly under fire in the country. If the future of the Coalition was uncertain, this was even more true of Addison, its most left-wing member. He was now a more and more isolated figure. He was remote from Labour, hostile to the Asquithians, despite his friendship with individuals such as Wedgwood Benn. More than ever before, Addison's political future seemed to rest on his retaining a close relationship with Lloyd George, his old hero and patron. This, in turn, depended on the Prime Minister supporting his free-spending housing and health programmes against growing Unionist attacks. If Addison were to break with Lloyd George, then his prospects would be vulnerable indeed.

5
The Break with Lloyd George

After the failure of 'fusion', the position of Coalition Liberal ministers such as Addison became increasingly vulnerable. Apart from their difficulties with their more right-wing Unionist colleagues, the prospect of any kind of reunion with the Independent Liberals now finally disappeared. The Wee Frees were fired with new enthusiasm by Asquith's return for Paisley followed by a by-election victory at Louth later in the year. This reinforced their determination to sever any remaining links with the Coalitionists. The occasion of the final breach was the stormy meeting of the National Liberal Federation on 7 May 1920, and Addison played a prominent and pugnacious role in the disturbances that ensued. The Coalition Liberal ministers, headed by Addison, Hewart, Macnamara, and Kellaway, decided to provoke a confrontation with the Asquithians by attending the meeting. Dudley Ward and Captain William Edge, the Coalition Liberal junior whips who arranged this at forty-eight hours' notice, were greeted with violent abuse. Amidst great uproar Addison's own speech was shouted down. He was never one to shrink from a fight: beneath a placid, countryman's exterior, he was a passionate man with a strong temper not always kept under control. He managed to shout out a few sentences defending the Coalition's record and denouncing the 'sentence of excommunication' now passed upon them. Then he and the other Coalitionists left the meeting *en bloc*.[1] He wrote cheerfully to Lloyd George afterwards, 'We had a lovely, indeed enjoyable time at Leamington.' The 'machine minders of Abingdon Street' had given the Coalitionists 'the very opportunity we wanted.'[2] It was a spectacular occasion, but it merely confirmed the events of March and made even more unbridgeable the gulf between the Lloyd Georgian and Asquithian forces. A year earlier, Addison had been removed from the presidency of the Horncastle Liberal Association on the grounds that his conduct in the 'coupon election' was 'hostile to

The Break with Lloyd George 121

Liberalism'—a minor brickbat from his native country of Lincolnshire.[3]

At this time, he appeared as the most emphatic champion of the government and of Lloyd George's social policies and political strategy. Yet in fact, from the spring of 1920 onwards, his relations with the Prime Minister became increasingly difficult. There were many facets of the government's policy now which a radical like Addison found hard to swallow. Some aspects of the government's foreign policy alarmed him, notably the maintenance of large British forces in bases in Mesopotamia, Persia, and Egypt. On 31 December he protested vehemently in the Cabinet about expenditure in Mesopotamia.[4] Although he was strongly anti-Turk as has been seen, like other ministers he became alarmed as to the extent to which the government was forcing through a belligerently pro-Greek policy in the Near East, with the possible threat of war with Turkey. A minority in the Cabinet, headed by Curzon, Balfour, and the Prime Minister, favoured the 'bag and baggage' policy of evicting the Turks from the whole of Thrace on the European mainland, and even from Constantinople itself, with all its religious associations for the Muslim world.[5]

The 'troubles' in Ireland caused Addison even more agony of conscience. The atrocities of the IRA were being met by counter-violence and 'retaliation' from the Black and Tans and the 'Auxis', supported by the British government. Addison and Fisher, often backed up by Munro, Shortt, and Montagu, all Liberals, were active in the Cabinet in trying to reverse Hamar Greenwood's policy of 'retaliation'.[6] They wished to explore the prospect of negotiation. 'You must bargain with Sinn Fein,' H. A. L. Fisher observed.[7] But Addison's efforts seemed to lead nowhere. Speeches such as that by Lloyd George in Caernarvon on 9 October 1920, declaring that Britain had 'murder by the throat' in Ireland, seemed to show that the government was committed to a policy of bloody repression of foreign nationalism in the most unenlightened and reactionary fashion.

The major reason for Addison's disenchantment with the government and with his old leader, however, lay in the growing difficulties that confronted his housing programme. Indeed, it was largely the political and financial problems facing Addison's housing schemes that dictated his circumstances for the remaining period he spent as a minister under Lloyd George. By the summer of 1920 the Minister of

Health had become the most controversial member of the government, particularly with the swelling and noisy chorus of Unionist critics in the country. Some months earlier, J. C. C. Davidson had told the King's private secretary, Lord Stamfordham, that the Minister of Health 'generally fails to inspire confidence,'[8] a standard Tory judgement. Above all, Addison was under fire for his housing programmes from the variegated protagonists of 'anti-waste'. In by-election campaigns, in the newspapers of Northcliffe and of Rothermere, in the outpourings of irresponsible demagogues like Horatio Bottomley who sat in the House as an Independent, it was alleged that Addison had a prime responsibility for the heavy expenditure that underlay the country's financial difficulties. 'Eddy' Hartington, as an old-fashioned Tory of the shires, attacked the Prime Minister for 'giving in to extreme Labour and rotten Socialists like Addison'.[9] It was argued that the country suffered from a huge post-war debt, that this was the result of extravagant public expenditure. A severe curtailment of the government's free-spending programmes, such as Addison's at the Ministry of Health and Fisher's at the Ministry of Education, was essential. This criticism was vocal enough in 1919 when the country was enjoying a brief post-war speculative boom. By the late summer of 1920 it was obvious that the bubble had burst, with trade depressed, major industries idle or working far below capacity, and unemployment soaring to well over a million and a half. The 'anti-waste' campaign now became all the more strident in the press and in by-elections. It was the major campaign platform for independent Unionist candidates, who repeatedly defeated Coalitionists in by-elections up and down the country. In 1921 Lord Rothermere formed a new Anti-Waste League which won three by-elections between January and June at Dover, St. George's, Westminster, and Hertford, and polled strongly in others. For all of them, Addison was a prime target for attack. This formed the background to the agitated debates in the Cabinet about salvaging or sacrificing Addison's housing programmes with all the expenditure that their subsidized schemes involved.

The housing programme had not gone well from the start. In spite of Addison's optimism and grandiose plans, the 'homes for heroes' drive had hardly taken off the ground by the spring of 1920. As has been seen, the high and increasing cost of building materials, the reluctance of the building trade unions to admit semi- and unskilled

The Break with Lloyd George 123

labour into their ranks, the inadequacies of the local authorities and the financial problems they faced, and the disorganization of the private enterprise building industry were major causes of the failure to build the houses planned. In addition, Pigou noted the special nature of demand in the building industry. Since working-class people could not afford the large increase in rents for private housing, subsidies from the state, with the open-ended expenditure that resulted, were inevitable. The consequence could only be more inflation.[10] The housing bonds which the Housing (Additional Powers) Bill had sanctioned the local authorities to issue to help them finance their schemes were not generally a success.[11] Addison encouraged local councils to carry out a vigorous campaign to attract money for their housing schemes: for instance, he persuaded H. A. L. Fisher to accept the invitation to speak on behalf of the housing bonds given by the Wood Green UDC.[12] But the drive for housing bonds coincided with the Chancellor of the Exchequer's demand for subscriptions to the new Treasury loan to pay off the floating debt, and this siphoned off much possible investment. As an alternative, the government offered a more attractive security in the form of Housing Loans.

At the end of 1919 the government had changed the emphasis of its housing policy by offering a £150 subsidy to private builders. This caused controversy at the time and much criticism from the left; it had little immediate effect on the number of houses actually produced.[13] As Addison had recognized, private individuals would not build if they had to do so at a loss; industrial and commercial construction was far more profitable. Hence the need for a direct subsidy to the builders. It was also vital that the existing stock of houses be kept in repair. This could not be done without the unfreezing of rents. In June 1920, therefore, Addison introduced the second reading of the Increase of Rent and Mortgage (Restrictions) Bill. Its main provisions were that security of tenure should exist for occupiers for three years, but that the limit of rent for a dwelling house could now be raised.[14] He knew that the latter proviso would be unpopular, but he had always emphasized that it was not sound policy to subsidize wages by underrenting houses. Instead, the workers should be secured incomes which enabled them to pay adequate rents.[15] This philosophy appeared sound in 1919–20 when wage rates were rising appreciably. In the depression, unemployment, and enforced wage cuts that followed from the end of 1920, Addison's policy of raising rents appeared to be another burden for the wage-earning occupier.

By April 1920, the Housing Department had approved tenders for nearly 100,000 houses. As Addison stated, when addressing the International Building Trades Exhibition at Olympia, there was nothing to prevent the work being pressed on with, so far as the Housing Department was concerned, and the number being increased to 200,000 by the end of June. There remained a scarcity of labour, materials, and of finance, but he appealed to the trades involved to provide materials for housing at a cost which was not exorbitant. To facilitate the supply of materials, in June the Housing Department took over the Building Materials Supply Department formerly in the Ministry of Munitions.[16] On the labour side, the negotiations over the matter of dilution in the building trade and the guaranteed week for building trade operatives were now in the hands of a committee representing the National Federation of Building Trade Employers and the Operatives Federation.[17] By July 1920 Addison was able to report to the Commons that the Housing Department was now past the final stage with regard to a target for over 200,000 houses. Tenders had now been approved and finally settled for 126,000 houses, and there was nothing to prevent the work from proceeding apart from the two conditions of finance and labour.[18] But these two conditions were, of course, fundamental, and were to prove the decisive stumbling-blocks as far as provision for housing was concerned.

Throughout the summer and autumn of 1920, Addison persevered with efforts with the local authorities and the builders' trade unions to try to reduce the cost of house construction, and to speed up progress generally. He also pressed Austen Chamberlain and the Bank of England to reduce the high cost of borrowing money. He emphasized time after time that if the work of house building was to proceed at the necessary speed, a great many more builders must be brought into the industry. This meant cheaper credit. Chamberlain blankly repeated the point of view of the Treasury and, to some degree the Governor of the Bank of England, that the demands of the local authorities were wasteful. Sir Montague Norman, the Governor, however, also assured Addison that the Bank was striving to give every assistance to housing finance.[19] Addison claimed that he was anxious to co-operate with the Chancellor in reducing government expenditure. 'I have given careful consideration to your communication of 10 October

The Break with Lloyd George 125

1920 re the estimates for next year. I am extremely anxious to do all in my power to reduce the proposals of the department to the strictest minimum and shall certainly have every item of proposed expenditure most critically examined.' But of the four main headings of Health Service Expenditure, Health Services, Insurance, and Housing, it was the last which presented by far the greatest difficulties since so many of the key factors were largely beyond the government's control.[20] Chamberlain replied that the answer to the problem of expenditure was not to make borrowing easier but to bring pressure to bear on the builders' trade unions to accept dilution of labour, to abolish the awkward and exclusive apprenticeship regulations, and to bring large numbers of unskilled workers, notably ex-servicemen, into the building industry.[21] This, however, was infinitely easier to state as a general proposition than to bring about.

Addison had been urging 'dilution' on the building trade unions since 1919, as had Lloyd George.[22] But negotiations between the building trade unions and the government had dragged on inconclusively throughout the summer of 1920. Addison publicly expressed his discontent in October about what he considered to be the obstructive policy being pursued by the unions towards dilution.[23] The government's considered proposals for a dilution scheme were put before the Federation of Building Trade Operatives at Manchester, where a paper submitted by Addison was considered at length. The government would select certain housing schemes which were being held up because of lack of labour and would set them aside as schemes to be carried through by ex-servicemen who would be trained in the various trades. They would receive rates of pay based on local district rates, rising to full rates as the men qualified in their work. The government would ask the building trade unions to help especially by encouraging their members to take on the job of training the ex-servicemen.[24] In November, in the company of T. J. Macnamara, the new Minister of Labour, Addison met the representatives of the Builders' Trade Union Federation, and it was reported that good progress was made. The general principles of Addison's draft paper were not rejected by the unions but were accepted as a basis for discussion. In December, Addison then met representatives of the Building Craft Unions and placed before them the government's plans for dilution.[25] A concordat with labour over the building of houses for the workers still seemed possible.

But at the start of 1921, the prospects of a settlement of the dilution question did not appear very hopeful. Macnamara was anxious that the government's pledge given to 500,000 ex-servicemen that they should be given employment on housing schemes should be redeemed. He raised the question at a conference of ministers on 25 January 1921, where Addison was one of the committee appointed to take steps to secure the redemption of pledges if the building trade unions gave a negative reply.[26] At the end of January, a ballot was held by the building unions to see whether its members would agree to absorb the ex-servicemen proposed by the government. But it was to produce a negative result. So the problem of a shortage of labour dragged on, with the government helpless.

In addition to these intractable industrial reasons for the failure to build houses, Addison felt that the government's attitude towards his own department was a contributory factor. In the autumn of 1920, he produced a memorandum in which he complained that the urgency and complexity of the housing problem might have justified the responsible Minister in hoping that he would have the ready support of the Cabinet. Since the autumn of 1919, the freedom of action of the Ministry of Health had been progressively circumscribed by a succession of committees who thought it necessary to review in minute detail the activities of the Housing Department, and to scrutinize every proposal by the Minister. Thus for nearly twelve months, the policy of the Minister and the work of the Department had been almost constantly under the review of Cabinet committees which had, in many vital respects, modified or rejected proposals which the Minister of Health put before them. This procedure caused grave delays in the taking of positive measures.[27] In addition, the appointment of Tudor Walters as Paymaster General had led to comments in the press that he was supplanting Addison by becoming a *de facto* Minister of Housing.[28] All this undermined the prestige of the Minister and his new department. In this memorandum, Addison was echoing a widely expressed criticism of Lloyd George's methods of government through which a maze of committees and 'conferences of ministers' were undermining both departmental initiative and the collective responsibility of the Cabinet.

By the winter of 1920–1, with some members of the Cabinet already speaking out freely against both building trade employers and the unions, Addison was beginning to urge upon the government a still more costly form of expenditure on house building—the direct employment of labour by the local authorities themselves.[29] At the same time, in November he moved the second reading of the Ministry of Health (Miscellaneous Provisions) Bill, which contained a number of unrelated provisions, mainly with regard to what Addison conceived to be the facilitating of house building. For example, local authorities were to be empowered to hire compulsorily any empty houses in a locality suitable for the housing of the working class. They were also to be authorized to contribute to the voluntary hospitals. In addition, the Bill proposed to extend the period of granting subsidies to private builders, as it had been found that a number of builders would not be able to build within the specified time. Addison categorically denied that his department would impose any new burdens on the ratepayers by this Bill, and that any higher rates were due to higher wages and more costly materials. But the tide of public opinion was running hard against him. The general feeling of the House of Commons was that Addison was heaping new and heavy burdens on the rates, whether the local authorities liked it or not, in connection with housing, hospitals, and other matters. The *Daily Mail* noted, 'This is a Bill to enable Dr. Addison to thrust the cost of his policy upon the rates over which Parliament would have no control after the Bill was passed.' *The Times* dismissed it as 'a misguided Bill'. It added, 'Dr. Addison's craze for legislation required a wholesome check.'[30]

That check was soon to come, and from a familiar source. The Bill had focused once again the attention of the 'anti-waste' campaign upon Addison and his policies, in by-elections, in the columns of the press, and among Tory back-benchers. No forum was more exquisitely sensitive to these cries for cuts in social expenditure than was the House of Lords. The rejection of the Bill by the Upper House on 15 December was the work not of traditional Conservatives such as Salisbury or Selborne, but of 'backwoodsmen stimulated by the Harmsworth press'. In Dr Cowling's words, the government's passive response to this defeat was 'the slow withdrawal from radical positions which characterized Lloyd George's last two years in office.'[31] Addison's beleaguered position symbolized this reversal of policy.

After the rejection of his Bill, some felt it possible that Addison might resign.[32] *The Times*, always an organ particularly critical of him and his policies, wrote on 16 December, in the aftermath of the Lords' vote, that

> the real stumbling block in the matter of housing has been Dr. Addison himself together with his cohorts of bureaucrats . . . . The Minister of Health has gradually got the question of housing into confusion. For the muddle in which he is now placed upon the subsidy to private builders, Dr. Addison is alone to blame. He began by a serious breach of Parliamentary convention, for he increased the subsidy and extended its duration without obtaining leave from the House of Commons. When he sought to regularise his position by a Bill, he dragged over twenty other subjects into his measure.[33]

There can be no doubt that Addison and his policies were unpopular. There can be no doubt, too, that the Miscellaneous Provisions Bill was truly a miscellany of a singularly uncoordinated kind. But the *North-Eastern Daily Gazette* was far nearer the truth when it argued that, for the politicians, 'the Ministry of Health is a battlefield where the reactionaries struggle to assert against the progressives a final full control of Government policy. The men who resist Dr. Addison and regard Mr. Fisher at education with animosity have never lifted a finger to check the Cabinet's worst extravagances.'[34]

Addison now did try to scrutinize his expenditure more carefully. In January 1921 he appointed a committee to inquire into the high cost of building materials and to make recommendations for reducing costs. It was to report in July, recommending that a limit be set on the number of houses built on a penny rate basis, and that any future grant of aid from the Exchequer should be limited to a percentage of the total deficit.[35] These seriously modified Addison's financial arrangements. Addison was also involved in negotiations which took place amongst Ministers in January 1921 to try to halt the severe rise in unemployment. Along with Horne and Macnamara, he sent out letters to Chambers of Commerce, employers' organizations, local authorities, and trade unions, asking them to extend short-time working so as to prevent further dismissals and inviting them to re-absorb some of the workers now unemployed, for instance on house construction.[36]

However, the decision which would bring Addison's housing programme to an abrupt end had been made in November 1920. Chamberlain, the Chancellor of the Exchequer, was anxious to reduce the government's short-term borrowing; he hoped in the next budget to apply at least £250 millions to reduce the floating debt. To this end, he intended to ask for a cut of at least 20 per cent in the spending of all departments with particular reference to health, education, and transport. In the case of the Ministry of Health, he suggested that some limit—Chamberlain proposed 160,000—be placed on the number of houses for which the state would be responsible. The annual loss on every 100,000 houses could be as high as £7,500,000.[37] Addison's retort indicated that he could not agree to the reduction of housing commitments; where Chamberlain spoke of 160,000 houses, Addison mentioned 300,000 to cost £15 million up to 1923. He would probably have to ask for an increase in expenditure, not a reduction. But the weight of the government was against him. The Finance Committee of the Cabinet which met on 30 January reported that 'there was no alternative open to the Government but to decide housing questions not on merit, but on financial considerations only'.[38] Addison reluctantly agreed in February to accept drastic new limits on expenditure, with a total of 300,000 houses accepted as the extreme upper limit. Meanwhile the rejection by the Lords of the Miscellaneous Provisions Bill meant that the subsidy to private builders would end on 23 December 1920. In addition to the 4,495 already constructed by private builders under this scheme, there were about 27,000 additional houses proposed in respect of which certificates had been granted.[39] Addison was concerned that at least the government's pledge to those to whom it had agreed to give subsidies would be honoured.[40] In early March, just before he left the Ministry of Health, he reached an agreement with Chamberlain that a total of 250,000 houses would be sanctioned by June 1922, while Chamberlain agreed to ask parliament to extend the housing subsidies to 30 June 1922.[41]

The constructive work undertaken by Addison as Minister of Health has tended to be overshadowed by his alleged failure to provide 'homes for heroes'. His anxiety to provide houses stemmed from his long-standing belief that the health of the people was intimately connected with decent houses. But alongside his persistent battles on housing, there were other campaigns to improve the nation's health. If statistics may be relied on, he achieved his objectives more successfully in this latter area than in the former. On the other hand, as Sir Arthur Newsholme was later to reflect, the powers of the Ministry of Health in co-ordinating the health services of the nation were seriously handicapped from the outset by the contraction of the Ministry's powers and the failure to reorganize local administration. On the medical side, there was a serious shortage of trained personnel, while much more investment was needed in medical research. Addison took the lead in agitating for an increased grant for the Medical Research Council in which he had always been a firm believer.[42] He continued to take a most active part in promoting work for the prevention of tuberculosis and venereal disease, in promoting child welfare, and improving maternity services and the training of midwives. By July 1920, he could report, for instance, that over 700 women were being prepared as midwives, under training schemes, and that there had been a considerable reduction in the rate of infant mortality.[43]

It was inevitable that Addison's schemes should cost more money, and that in the sphere of the health services also he should lock horns in conflict with Austen Chamberlain and the Treasury. For example, in reply to one of the Chancellor's many circulars calling for economies, Addison characteristically proposed to remodel the Poor Law and to extend the health services at the same time. He put forward the idea that both the Poor Law and the health services should be financed by a single consolidated grant, independent of local expenditure. The scheme could be brought forward in the financial year, 1922–3.[44] Inevitably, nothing came of this. Addison's great project of unifying the Poor Law and public health work with local administrative bodies generally was not effected until Neville Chamberlain's Local Government Act of 1929. When Austen Chamberlain proposed cuts in expenditure upon hospitals also in 1921, Addison again was resistant. He accepted his suggestions for limiting the number of extra beds required for sanatoria and for child welfare, but argued that the proposed cuts in the number of maternity beds were too severe. 'No service is more vital to the nation . . . . None has been so successful or so cheap.'[45]

One of the most dramatic reforms that Addison aimed to push forward was totally frustrated by the Treasury and by considerations of economy. This was the so-called Dawson report, issued in 1920, for the total reorganization and regionalization of the nation's hospital services.[46] This report, technically the interim report of Addison's consultative council on medical and allied services, proposed an integration of the medical services. It acknowledged that general medical practitioners were not adequately associated with the clinics and public health services, and that the National Health Insurance Act did not provide at all for specialist hospital treatment. The report proposed that primary health centres would be set up in areas of small population, mainly under the control of general practitioners. Secondary health centres served by consultants would be set up in more populous areas with links with the nearest teaching hospital centres. The Dawson scheme had serious drawbacks. The Socialist Medical Association later criticized it for having no concept of group practice: the primary health centres proposed were a network of cottage hospitals, with plenty of private pay beds. Nevertheless, it foreshadowed many later ideas for regional health services and for that reorganization of the hospital system finally undertaken in the National Health Service of 1948. Addison was passionately enthusiastic about this scheme; the British Medical Association, equally predictably, was suspicious. More to the point, the Treasury saw it as merely another source of profligate expenditure. Addison's farsighted schemes for a remodelled hospital service, adapted to the needs and population movements of the twentieth century, had to wait another quarter of a century for fulfilment.

His removal from the Ministry of Health in March was popularly taken to be a sign of the failure of his housing programmes. But an important latent factor was his personal loss of power within the Coalition since the failure of the 'fusion' attempts, and also the more general discontent with the government in the country at large. Despite intensive government propaganda through Freddie Guest and 'Bronco Bill' Sutherland, despite the publication of the *Lloyd George Liberal Magazine* on a monthly basis from October 1920, the electorate remained thoroughly discontented with its governors. Defeats in by-elections and attacks in the press reflected this disillusion. The pressure for 'anti-waste' and 'economy' reached a crescendo. 'Our difficulties have arisen out of the absence of Cabinet Government . . . . Each minister goes his own way . . . . Dr. Addison, Mr. Fisher, Sir Eric Geddes spend what they please,' noted one organ of the press.[47] Lancashire Unionists, so Bonar Law was told by Lord Derby, regarded Addison as 'unbusinesslike' and, worse, as 'socialistic'; they deplored his and Fisher's wild schemes.[48] In January Curzon could contemptuously include Addison, along with Geddes, Munro, Horne, Lee of Fareham, Shortt, and Macnamara, in Lloyd George's 'family' in the Cabinet. But by March Lloyd George was becoming increasingly aware that people would soon refuse to accept Addison as among 'the inevitable natural catastrophes' or allow the Prime Minister to attribute all the grievances ventilated in press, parliament, and country to 'conditions over which neither governments nor parliament have any control'.[49] Hankey recorded him in January 1921 as considering the removal of 'duds' like Addison and Illingworth from the government.[50] The standing of both Lloyd George and of his government was in jeopardy. By March the split of the Coalition was being widely predicted, as Unionist pressure for independence built up. Clearly, action by the Prime Minister was urgently needed.

So Lloyd George asked Addison on 31 March to resign from the Ministry of Health. He used as an excuse Bonar Law's resignation as Lord Privy Seal, through ill health; this had made 'considerable changes' in the government essential.[51] He asked Addison to move from Health to take instead a Ministry without Portfolio. He reminded Addison that he had suggested this almost a year earlier in April 1920, so that Addison would be free to help the Liberal leadership with 'general practical work'. His task now would be 'co-ordinating the political effort of the Government and adjusting it to the needs and sympathies of the new electorate'.[52] It was a vague enough brief; obviously, Addison was being demoted. He, too, had been shocked by Bonar Law's resignation. It would, he wrote, 'be a great grief . . . to every member of the House, for nobody is more truly respected'. He felt that Austen Chamberlain was a 'poor choice' as Law's replacement as Unionist leader and leader of the House, but 'the only one open to the Unionists . . . . Unless he becomes less reactionary than at present it must mean a separation before long.'[53] But his reply to the request to him to resign showed that Lloyd George's letter came as a complete surprise. Before moving to the Ministry without Portfolio he demanded to know whether the improvements in the health services and in the reform of the Poor Law would be carried, as promised, and whether the proposals of his Valuation and Rating Committee would be carried out.[54]

He also discussed the matter of his transfer from the Ministry of Health with two senior Coalition Liberals, Sir William Glyn-Jones, another medical man, and Sir Thomas Robinson, member for Stretford. It was agreed that if Lloyd George gave assurances that there would be no change in policy, then Addison would accept the post of Minister without Portfolio. On 1 April Lloyd George telephoned through to say that there would be no change. Addison was understandably bitter about the whole procedure.

The Break with Lloyd George 133

On the whole this shows the Prime Minister at his worst . . . . He wrote—for his letter was the first intimation I had—because he could not face me upon it after our long association, for the same reason he telephoned. These things will be difficult to forget, but they sadly illumine the big defect in a great man's character.

Even the Carlton Club, 'that high place of orthodox Toryism', considered Lloyd George's treatment of Addison to be 'the base letting down of a good friend'.[55]

Addison's departure from the Ministry of Health received a mixed reception from the press. *The Times*, so often hostile, criticized him as a Minister for giving 'the impression of playing second fiddle all the time to his Chief Medical Officer, Sir George Newman'. It rejoiced at Addison's dismissal as it would 'mark the end of the Newman policy' which it believed was 'the policy of having special departments centralised at Whitehall'.[56] By contrast, the medical members of parliament passed a resolution which expressed cordial appreciation of his services as Minister of Health. They expressed 'admiration of his zeal and devotion to duty and untiring work in the interests of public health'.[57] The chief organs of the medical profession were notably sympathetic to Addison on his departure. This applied to the *Medical Press* which had been markedly hostile to his appointment. *The Hospital* commented 'His fault was not that he did too little but he tried to do too much. His task in health and housing was gigantic . . . . Dr. Addison is entitled to the gratification of the public for the courage and tenacity with which he faced his task.' *The Medical Officer*, which had criticized him for paying too little heed to the views of local authority medical officers when forming his consultative councils, nevertheless saw his removal as a grave blow to the public health services and regarded him 'as a victim of foul play'.[58] The *British Medical Journal*, not always friendly, observed 'We should have preferred to see Dr. Addison still at the Ministry of Health because he is of great advantage to the medical profession.'[59] Perhaps the most balanced judgement at the time came from Sir George Newman, appointed chief medical officer of the Ministry of Health in 1919. The Ministry, he wrote,

has suffered from some of its friends as well as from its enemies. Some of its friends and supporters hailed it as an end in itself . . . as a species of millennium. They expected too much of it, as its enemies expected too little. It represented a reform in central health government, the establishment of a means rather than an end, an improvement of the machinery of government. It cannot be a substitute for medical science or for that impulse without which all instruments of government are useless or for an enlightened public opinion and a national health conscience.[60]

Newman is surely correct in seeing the period 1919–21 as a launching phase for a new department, and in emphasizing the constraints on any new minister, however energetic or determined. Subject to these qualifications, both for his achievements in relation to health and housing and for his unfulfilled projects such as the hospital reorganization proposed in the Dawson report, Addison's period as Minister of Health may be taken as an important first step in the creation of the modern welfare state, and a national health service.

In the past, Addison had been the most ardent Liberal supporter of the Coalition and of Lloyd George. But as 1921 progressed he was becoming increasingly disillusioned with both. This discontent became far more pronounced when he was moved from the Ministry of Health. Some MPs believed that, however regrettable his transfer to a Ministry without Portfolio might be, he still might be genuinely required for important tasks in his new post.[61] It was well known that Addison had been turned out of the Ministry of Health because of Tory pressure. Lord Edmund Talbot, the Unionist chief whip, admitted openly to Addison in a letter of 7 April, that it was probably due more to him than anyone else that Addison had been removed. When discussing his position with Lloyd George and Bonar Law, he 'always had to say in my opinion you were not effective in the House and did not carry enough weight in debate'. He claimed that this view was not confined to the Unionist section of the Coalition.[62] No one could dispute that Addison was far from commanding as a parliamentary speaker. But he himself felt that Talbot's view was destructive of the solidarity of the Coalition and that the government could not survive for long on this basis.[63]

Misgivings about the government's policy became more profound that spring. His breach with Lloyd George widened perceptibly, despite the useful work he was called upon to perform whilst Minister without Portfolio. He continued to be a member of the Cabinet Home Affairs Committee, he was a member of the Committee on the Water Power Bill amongst others, he was chairman of the Cabinet Committees on Valuation and Rating Reform, and on Unemployment Insurance.[64] All this was useful and a constructive outlet for his energies.

But his criticism of the government became more vocal. He was especially hostile to the drift of the policy in Ireland. In April 1921 he produced a memorandum for circulation in the Cabinet on 'The Irish Elections and an offer of a Truce'.⁶⁵ In this, he advocated the offer of a truce to Sinn Fein and the IRA. Should it be accepted, it would afford the opportunity of holding the elections under quieter and more practical conditions. It might also offer a chance for rallying those moderate influences which alone could make for a more lasting settlement. Full-scale negotiations could then be reopened with the Sinn Fein leaders. On 2 June he raised the matter of a policy of military reprisals. 'Cabinet decided *nem. con.* against reprisals and even Austen strongly backed me on this.'⁶⁶ It would be wrong to exaggerate the extent of Addison's impact on Cabinet discussions, but clearly he was amongst those still trying to influence policy in a more liberal direction. He played an honourable part in the early summer of 1921 in that reversal of policy which ultimately led to Lloyd George embarking on face-to-face negotiations with Eamon de Valera in August.

Elsewhere, the general tendency of government policy was to swing to the right in the spring of 1921. This was shown in its confrontation with the miners in April and in the severe cut-back in government spending on social welfare. As a man with wide experience of labour relations during the war, Addison was much concerned with the miners' national strike, though from a somewhat uncommitted standpoint. He was concerned that 'revolutionaries have seized control' of the railways and other transportation.⁶⁷ After listening to a Commons debate on coal on 5 April, he wrote to Lloyd George,

> the Labour people are clearly conscious of the weakness of their case as it has been put forward (with regard to subsidy and non-pumping) but for all that I think such figures as Hartshorn gave cannot, if correct, stand. I don't think any of us understood that such results arose at a fortnight's notice. I suggest you offer to call a conference of the two parties tomorrow, with a view, say, to considering what further time should be given for a settlement of a wage basis with no subsidy on the understanding, say, that it is not more than six weeks.⁶⁸

He felt that Horne, the new Chancellor of the Exchequer, was anxious for an open fight with labour, and that his unsympathetic attitude was responsible for the strong reaction of the miners' executive.⁶⁹ Lloyd George 'went some distance in his reply. At the Cabinet this morning it was agreed to send a letter to both parties tendering our good offices. So far as it goes it is promising.'[70] He regularly attended meetings and conferences of ministers called to discuss the miners' strike and the possibility of a general strike by the Triple Alliance. He also tried to persuade Frank Hodges, the General Secretary of the Miners' Federation, to help in securing the preservation and safety of the mines, in other words to avoid the flooding of pits.[71] The threat of a wider general strike by the Triple Alliance, backed by the TUC, was removed largely through the initiative of back-bench members of parliament. On 14 April, Addison still felt it might be possible to get a settlement of the coal dispute, and circulated a memorandum containing his ideas. He felt he could collaborate with the Labour party if they were 'less led by extremists'.[72] But the complete collapse of the Triple Alliance, on 'Black Friday' after the alleged 'betrayal' of the miners by Hodges when addressing the members of parliament, in fact removed the possibility of any general strike, even though the miners' national strike was to drag on until July amidst great suffering in mining communities.

Many Unionists in the country were now deeply discontented with the government and with their party's standing in the Coalition. In December 1920, Sir William Joynson-Hicks, a die-hard backbencher, had called for the dissolution of the Coalition.[73] Dissension continued to mount in the spring of 1921. The *New Statesman* listed some of the causes of friction—'the coal dispute, the recurring clash between the Prime Minister's international activities and the competitive activities of the Foreign Office, the difficulties of reconciling Mr. Chamberlain's tariff obsessions with what Mr. Lloyd George regards as the Coalition's electioneering interests, keeping peace between the two factions in Ireland'. Friction had been aggravated by the 'dead set made by the general body of Unionists against Lloyd George's fellow Liberals in government, Macnamara, Fisher, Addison and Kellaway'.[74] None of these ranked with Addison as a target for right-wing abuse. As he noted in his diary at that time, 'The appointment of myself as Minister without Portfolio on 1 April, after that office had been allowed to lapse, naturally filled the "economists" with apprehension and gave the malcontents in the Coalition Unionist Party a useful target for their opposition.'[75]

A convenient theme for these critics was Addison's salary in his new post. Anger was aroused by the fact that the vote, required to

The Break with Lloyd George

authorize his salary as Minister without Portfolio, was postponed on two occasions. At a time when there was an outcry for cutting government expenditure, there were doubts as to whether the new Ministry was giving value for money. Addison himself shared these doubts. He complained that Lloyd George was slow to delegate him duties in his new office.[76] After years of frenetic activity, he suddenly found himself with little to do. 'After the strenuous work of the last five years it is a slack business and were it not that I had promised a few of my faithful friends in the Cabinet and outside that I would hang on for a bit and give it a fair trial . . . it has been a thoroughly disheartening and unsatisfactory experience.'[77] Thomas Jones, Deputy Secretary to the Cabinet, was led to observe shortly that 'the Secretariat are trying to invent committees for him'.[78] This all lent fuel to Unionist cries that the new office was an expensive redundancy. Bonar Law, writing to Thomas Jones in May, commented: 'Poor Addison! He must feel pretty wretched and his Ministry without Portfolio cannot last very long, I fear.'[79]

Soon after his appointment as Minister without Portfolio, therefore, pressure mounted to reduce Addison's new salary of £5,000 a year and thus cut expenditure. The West Ham Board of Guardians, by eighteen votes to one, passed a resolution emphatically protesting against 'the payment of £5,000 to Dr. Addison as Minister without Portfolio'.[80] *The Times*, hostile as ever, commented, 'It is a puzzle why a man with so many failures to his credit should be comfortably settled again in office as Minister without Portfolio.'[81] By June the revolt among dissident Unionists of the 'die-hard' persuasion, 'stirred up by the "anti-Waste" and the Northcliffe Press',[82] had reached terrifying proportions. The vote for the payment of Addison's salary had been postponed twice since 14 April. Addison himself felt that the government had paid the penalty for this tactical error, since it now gave a continuing advantage to the 'anti-waste' campaign especially in by-elections where the Anti-Waste League was prominent. He believed that it was Chamberlain's fear of Edward Carson which caused the vote to be postponed. For Addison's salary was going to be defended by his old wartime colleague, the Irish Unionist, Carson, who was incensed by Lloyd George's treatment of an old lieutenant and supporter. 'The reactionary Tories are more afraid of Carson than anyone.'[83]

On 15 June, a statement was issued that Addison had actually resigned. In two interviews in the London press, one in the *Evening Standard*, the other in the *Daily News*, he denied this in highly belligerent fashion. He was aware that a body of about 180 Unionists had signed a document supporting 'anti-waste' and that it had been presented to the Prime Minister. The majority of them had no doubt done so for genuine reasons, 'to assert the healthy principle of the parliamentary control of finance'. But there were other Unionists 'with less innocent motives'. They were hostile to the very notion of Coalition; 'if they had their way, they would sweep all active Liberals out of the Government'. Addison was merely a convenient scapegoat for right-wing reaction. 'I do not intend to resign as long as I possess the confidence of the Prime Minister and the Cabinet.'[84]

For the Unionist leadership, already gravely harassed, this was the last straw. Austen Chamberlain chose to interpret Addison's press interviews as a constitutional attack upon the Unionist party in general. He wrote to him, stating that he would now be unable to support Lloyd George, evidently on the Commons' vote on Addison's salary.[85] In his reply, Addison robustly denied that he had launched a general attack on the Unionist party.[86] Some days earlier, Lloyd George and Chamberlain had had an anxious correspondence on the vote for Addison's salary; the victory of the Anti-Waste candidate in the St. George's, Westminster by-election gave their concern a new edge. Lloyd George was evidently morally committed to removing Addison on policy grounds, quite apart from Chamberlain's insistence that the majority of Unionist MPs would vote against the Minister's salary in the lobbies. Lloyd George felt that Addison was trying to turn himself into a martyr over public health. 'Winston can afford these little exhibitions but in Addison they are quite intolerable.'[87] Meanwhile the Coalition Liberal whip, Charles McCurdy, informed the Prime Minister that many Liberal votes could not be relied on either, and that defeat in the vote on Addison's salary was inevitable.

Lloyd George's reply to his whip was ominous indeed. He recalled that he had tried to persuade Addison to move from the Ministry of Health over a year before. 'Whether he was succeeding or not, he was creating the impression of failure. However, he refused to take my advice on that occasion and I am very much afraid that it is now too late to save him.'[88] The retreat from social reform was fast becoming a rout. Chamberlain had suggested to Addison that he might resign

The Break with Lloyd George 139

voluntarily and 'thereby relieve you and the Government of the necessity of meeting an embarrassing situation'. With characteristic tenacity, Addison refused, because it 'would be discreditable all round'.[89] He believed that 'a courageous forcing of the issue on the Vote would result in its being carried by a large majority'.[90] He discussed his situation with several Liberal colleagues including Hewart, Shortt, and Montagu who all offered encouragement; Winston Churchill was also 'keen on my not giving way'. He then sent a letter to the Prime Minister enclosing his correspondence with Austen Chamberlain. All his colleagues, Addison reported, 'were strongly of the opinion that I should stick to my guns'.[91]

On 22 June, the eve of the vote on his salary, Addison wrote to the Prime Minister about the forthcoming debate. Lloyd George had already agreed that 'the Vote must be defended and made a question of confidence in the Government'.[92] Addison's letter stressed that his own appointment as Minister had been entirely the Prime Minister's decision and that 'neither in this nor in any other post have I ever suggested or desired that my office should either be provided or continued for my personal convenience or benefit'.[93] Finally on the morning of 23 June, the day of the debate, Addison breakfasted with the Prime Minister, with the same friendly atmosphere prevailing as so often in the past. Lloyd George was 'all amiability' and 'seemed to have made up his mind to champion me properly'. Addison had urged that the Prime Minister should not 'give way or give his minister away to clamour'. Lloyd George replied that there had been 'a Tory cabal against him lately . . . so it was all the more important not to alienate his Liberal supporters'.[94]

The significance of the vote on Addison's salary for the future of the government may be seen from the accounts of two informed contemporaries. Beaverbrook wrote of how 'preparations for a critical division in parliament went forward in agitated haste . . . . Everything pointed to the defeat of the Government . . . . There were important ministers and others crying "Stand fast, Addison". Churchill was actively supporting him. Birkenhead, though declaring he was no friend of the Minister without Portfolio, would also give support'.[95] Frances Stevenson, Lloyd George's secretary and mistress, gives a different perspective.

[Lloyd George] says he cannot persist in retaining him, especially as Addison has not been too loyal and is intriguing with Winston on Ireland. McCurdy had three hours with Addison this morning and an arrangement was come to whereby Addison is to go at the end of the session and D. [Lloyd George] will defend this in the House on Thursday. McCurdy says Addison has no conception of the real position—says that the whole conspiracy is against him as a Liberal and progressive and to separate D. from his Liberal colleagues. He has no idea how unpopular he is.[96]

On 20 June, three days before the debate, McCurdy had indeed given Lloyd George a memorandum recommending that he should defend Addison in the Commons, though on a modified basis. He should explain the need to retain the Ministry without Portfolio for that session only. But he should also announce that the post was never intended to be permanent and should end with the session. Lloyd George had a high, indeed exaggerated, regard for McCurdy's sense as a political tactician, and paid due heed to these ideas. Leslie Wilson, the Unionist chief whip, had agreed that support from his party would also be given on such terms only. McCurdy, Addison, and Lloyd George had a joint discussion on tactics and principles.[97] But, as Addison himself noted, he was active right up to the debate in trying to persuade Lloyd George to give no date for the abandonment of the Ministry without Portfolio. Beaverbrook noted, 'It is by no means certain that Lloyd George accepted McCurdy's plan.'[98]

But when the debate on the vote for Addison's salary came up on 23 June, there was a great surprise. Lloyd George defended his colleague in 'a lukewarm fashion'. While he made a perfunctory defence of Addison's value as a minister, including a mention of the economies he had been able to effect in the period at Munitions during the war, he commented unkindly that Addison's 'unfortunate interest in public health had excited a good deal of prejudice'. He added that he 'has been rather too anxious to build houses'. Lloyd George beat a tactical retreat and invited the House merely to vote a sum of money to enable the government to retain the services of the Minister until the end of the present session only. Astonishingly, he suggested a more sweeping reduction of the salary from the £3,000 proposed in the motion to only £2,500. The net result of the debate was to give Addison three months' notice and a salary cut by half to £2,500. After this calculated insult, the government won easily on the division by 250 votes with forty abstentions.[99] Addison's reflection was that 'it enabled the opponents to feel that they had won a victory'.[100]

Frances Stevenson recorded after the defeat that 'D. took the ground from under the critics' feet. D. was very pleased with himself last night.'¹⁰¹ Beaverbrook, with much more reliable instinct, wrote that 'for the first time in the years of his downfall Lloyd George had made a fatal mistake'.¹⁰² He even dates the fall of the government from the debate on Addison's salary. Addison himself felt that the original vote could have been carried easily. Then Lloyd George would not have faced any recriminations and the government would have been strengthened instead of being undermined. He personally felt 'beastly indignation' and thought that 'his position was impossible'.¹⁰³ However, he decided to take no action until a dinner that had been arranged in his honour for 29 June by old friends like Carson, Shortt, Illingworth, and Munro had taken place. Some of his Liberal ministerial colleagues, notably Hewart and Macnamara, implored Addison to take no rash action until they had put their view of the case to Lloyd George.¹⁰⁴

But the victim himself wrote that 'it is more than likely that things will be precipitated and one will be relieved of the embarrassment of clearing out on anything that seems to be a personal ground'. This was soon confirmed. Addison was able to challenge the government, courageously and altruistically, on an issue of high principle, and on one of his favourite themes, that of housing. He knew that on 30 June the Finance Committee of the Cabinet had turned down a memorandum on housing drawn up by his successor at the Ministry of Health, Sir Alfred Mond. This had been drawn up as a result of the Cabinet's instruction to all departments to reduce their estimates by 20 per cent for the year 1922–3. Mond's proposals were, briefly, to suspend all housing schemes by the local authorities at the number of houses already contracted for, to reduce the amount of the subsidy to private builders, and to finance slum clearance, starting at a sum of £200,000 for the next year and working up to £1,000,000 per year.¹⁰⁵ These were not wholly illiberal proposals at all, especially in relation to slum housing. But Mond told Addison that Lloyd George's mood was now 'the most reactionary imaginable' and that he had the impression that the Prime Minister was going to pay the 'anti-wasters' with their own coin, while 'his colleagues and promises could go by the board'.¹⁰⁶ There seemed every indication that Mond's diagnosis was correct. Addison himself believed that Lloyd George was now obsessed by 'economy'. He believed that the Prime Minister had deliberately prolonged the coal strike and avoided a settlement, so as to 'fight the wage reduction issue on a big scale and at any cost'. He himself felt that he must take a fundamental stand on the future of the housing programme. 'I would rather be out with all its disadvantages and disappointments than be a party to such a monstrous betrayal.'[107] He well knew that the probable price of challenging the Prime Minister and the Finance Committee was total and permanent political oblivion; but with dogged courage and commitment he was determined to fight for the people's houses and for the remnants of the government's social programme of which he had been in large measure the architect. It was perhaps the most unsordid act in Addison's lengthy public career.

In fact, the Cabinet Finance Committee decided to reject Mond's memorandum on housing policy and to reduce the future housing programme still further. The effect would be that local authorities would be limited to the construction of a final total of only 176,000 houses, unless contracts for them had been approved before 2 July 1921. A maximum sum of £200,000 would be allotted for slum clearance, not for the first year as Mond had requested, but phased over two years. These decisions obviously marked the death-knell for the public housing programme, and Addison asked Hankey, the Secretary to the Cabinet, to circulate them to all ministers.[108] He himself prepared a memorandum which pointed out that the net result would be that, when existing contracts had been carried into effect, house-building in England and Wales would be 'practically at a dead stop'. He sent this to Lloyd George and asked the Prime Minister to call a Cabinet meeting at which it could be discussed. On 5 July he circulated his memorandum to the Cabinet himself.[109]

Of course, his memorandum was almost certain to be rejected, with Lloyd George, Horne, and Chamberlain bound to be hostile. But it would be a good issue on which to take a stand and perhaps to leave the government. On 6 July he had already written the first draft of a resignation letter to be sent to Lloyd George.[110] The next day he wrote to his wife, 'I am packing up papers today and no doubt shall be out on Monday, when at last it seems that the issue will have to be decided.' He knew that Lloyd George would probably adjudicate that only the Finance Committee had authority to decide on the future expenditure on housing; he was looking forward to political freedom even if there was some penury attached.[111] Then, as throughout his career, Addison was never a wealthy man; politics had meant financial sacrifice for the successful anatomist and for his wife and children.

A meeting of the Cabinet was held on 11 July to consider Addison's memorandum and future housing policy in general. At this meeting, Addison spoke out freely and belligerently. He was supported by a number of ministers, the Liberals, Churchill and Macnamara, and 'to my surprise' the Unionists, Lord Birkenhead and Laming Worthington-Evans. It was decided to set up a committee of which Addison would be a member to consider the exact form of the statement to be made to the House on the government's future housing policy. But, against Addison's wishes, it was decided that the Cabinet was not entitled to modify a new statement, drafted by Mond, which incorporated the decisions of 30 June made by the Finance Committee.[112] Mond had surrendered entirely to the 'economists': the total of only 176,000 houses was confirmed as a Cabinet decision. There was but one concession made by the Chancellor of the Exchequer, Sir Robert Horne, whereby the £200,000 per year for slum clearance was made a continuing charge instead of being confined to the next two years, 1921–2. In a further Cabinet meeting on 13 July Addison's memorandum containing revised proposals for housing was rejected, and Mond's proposals in CP 3133 were endorsed. 'L. G. backed up Mond who made rather a hash of his case.' The Finance Committee's decisions about the 176,000 total of houses and the limit of expenditure on the clearance of slums were adhered to. Addison's protests that this was both profoundly uneconomic in view of the expenditure already incurred by the local authorities, and the dishonouring of a fundamental pledge to the nation, were swept aside.[113] The crusade to build 'homes for heroes' was in ruins.

On the evening of 14 July Addison sent an angry letter of resignation from the government to Lloyd George. He declared that he proposed to read it out to the House of Commons, setting forth his reasons for resigning. Thus, technically on the issue of housing finance but more fundamentally because of the government's rightwards swing, Addison left the Coalition government after over four and a half years in high office. He had written to his wife, who backed him solidly throughout, about the housing decisions of the Cabinet on 11–12 July. 'I do not intend to yield at all and on the whole inwardly long that they will stick to the Cabinet Finance Committee's findings and give me a chance of getting out on a good issue, as you say. This is now my clear wish and my only misgiving is that they will all climb down.'[114] A day later he knew that resignation was the only course left to him.

His letter of resignation to Lloyd George was presented in bitter terms.[115] He had, he claimed, come to an agreement with Austen Chamberlain about housing expenditure months ago. Then on 2 July the decisions of the Finance Committee taken on 30 June had become known. They were accepted by the Cabinet, the agreement with Chamberlain was thrown aside, and an end put to the Addison housing programme. This action would rightly be seen as 'breach of faith' on the part of the government. It was a 'betrayal' of the solemn pledges to the people of the country and of a moral obligation to the local authorities who had already incurred so much expenditure. The real reason, he argued, for the change of policy on housing was unwarranted expenditure elsewhere, including military bases overseas. Lloyd George had solemnly promised that the policy of the Ministry of Health would not be altered when Addison moved from that department. He was thus guilty of personal dishonesty. Mond had been refused permission to 'make it plain that the action he will be required to take is based upon the decision that he should cancel contracts for building houses'. While 'in no event must the number of houses built by the local authorities exceed 176,000,' this figure was 'to be reduced to the utmost possible extent'. Lloyd George replied angrily to the effect that he refused to accept Addison's version that the government's decisions meant an abandonment of its housing policy. The financial situation 'has forced us to cry a halt in the development of your housing plans. Meanwhile, time will be given to the Minister of Health to put these schemes on a more businesslike footing.'[116]

This bitter exchange of correspondence was echoed in Addison's speech to the House of Commons justifying his resignation on 14 July. It was a tense and difficult occasion. Addison reported that 'I had a great reception in the House—hearty and prolonged—apart from its merits I think everybody was delighted that anyhow a man would stand up for conviction and challenge L. G. Winston and co. think that L. G. is up against the biggest proposition of his life this time.'[117] *The Nation* and *New Statesman* both were to applaud Addison for resigning so courageously on an issue of high principle.[118] But in the House, Addison's inadequacy as an orator made his cause more difficult. His speech was somewhat disjointed and not very effective. He was almost prevented by the Speaker from referring to private government memoranda and correspondence in the course of it. The intervention of Asquith allowed Addison to develop his case without interruption. Still, for all its inadequacies of presentation, Addison's resignation speech was a powerful indictment of the betrayal of the government's social programme. Instead of half a million new houses being built, barely a third of that number were in progress; the rehabilitation of the slums had been drastically set back.[119] Many shared Addison's proclaimed belief that he was acting as a sacrifice to right-wing 'die-hard' opinion. As *The Nation* observed, 'It was not waste but the success of the Anti-Waste campaign which had brought about the resignation of a capable and energetic minister.'[120]

His removal from the government was a profound watershed for British social policy, for the political balance of the Coalition government, and, of course, for Addison himself. In the first place, the housing programme under Addison's successor, Mond, went into complete reverse. The extent of Addison's success or failure in house building may well be open to debate. In 1921 the housing which he had inaugurated was reaching its peak. In all, 210,237 houses were completed under his programmes between 1 January 1919 and 30 September 1922, including houses built under Mond but negotiated under tenders put in during Addison's period at the Ministry of Health. Philip Abrams's criticism of Addison's 'failures' seems in some respects unhistorical and unrealistic. Abrams assumes an automatic link between wartime controls and group involvement in the governmental processes on the one hand, and post-war social engineering on the other.[121] He pays scant attention to the facts of financial, industrial, and political constraint on Addison's policies. A right-wing critic, Earl Winterton, wrote that 'Addison was a man of both character and talent, but the housing scheme contained in his Bill was a calamitous failure, and was used for the next thirty years as the classic example of what to avoid in schemes of housing with aid of grants of public funds.'[122] This is also much too severe. It ought never to be forgotten that the period during which Addison was battling with the housing problems was one of extraordinary difficulty, as a direct result of the unparalleled dislocation of industrial life during the first world war. As H. R. Aldridge of the National Housing and Town Planning Council was to point out in 1923,

Nothing is easier than to be wise after the event. Nothing is more difficult than to achieve a great national purpose on economical lines in a period such as that through which the nation has recently passed . . . . A great national purpose has undoubtedly been achieved . . . . The 200,000 built provide good homes for quite a million men, women and children.[123]

A reforming Labour government, with Aneurin Bevan at the Health Ministry, was to encounter many of the same problems after 1945.

Professor Bentley Gilbert also concedes that Addison's housing programme was 'by no means an unmitigated failure' as the first experiment in large-scale public housing in Britain.[124] The number of houses built between the summers of 1920 and 1921 was the largest number to be completed under government sponsorship in any subsequent year between the wars, apart from 1928. A recent writer has also reached the conclusion that

the 1919 legislation inaugurated a great experiment in State intervention . . . the most successful in the interwar years. The [Neville] Chamberlain Act of 1923 and the Wheatley Act of 1924 were in part a reaction against the methods adopted in 1919 but both owed a great deal to the fact that the precedent of state aid for housing had been established.[125]

In towns such as Manchester or Swansea, the houses built under the Addison programme were to inaugurate a dramatic new phase in urban planning and development.[126] Often they were semi-detached or detached houses set in pleasant suburban avenues like the Townhill development in Swansea. Whatever conclusions, in fact, one may reach about Addison's period as Minister of Health, which was undeniably controversial, there can be little dispute that after his departure things became very much worse. Mond now became a firm champion of 'economy' as befitted a capitalist millionaire. Then in mid-August 1921 the government appointed the notorious Economy Committee composed of leading business men, under the chairmanship of Sir Eric Geddes, himself recently a free-spending Cabinet minister whose policies had been denounced by 'Anti-Waste'. The purpose of the Economy Committee was obviously to slash expenditure massively in all areas of government, not only in relation to the armed services and overseas policy but also in the social and welfare services at home. As will be seen, the Geddes 'axe' was to show how faithfully this Committee interpreted its brief. It had a shattering impact on the housing and educational policies in which Addison so

The Break with Lloyd George 147

passionately believed. The difference was that he had resigned in protest; the other Liberal ministers were too timid to do so. The very appointment of the Geddes Committee, so soon after Addison's departure, confirmed the profound rightwards shift in the social thinking and policies of the government.

Secondly, Addison's resignation was a notable watershed in the history of the Coalition: as has been seen, Beaverbrook even dated the downfall of Lloyd George from this moment. Addison's removal left the other Coalition Liberals beleaguered, especially as Churchill, in a high fever of anti-Bolshevism, was moving to the right on most issues. After Addison's departure, the other Coalition Liberals were a demoralized, purposeless band, hemmed in and dominated by the Unionist majority. Without Addison, their most radical spokesman, the Coalition Liberals were much enfeebled, and lost much of their credibility. The resignation of the other leading Liberal in the government, Edwin Montagu, over the government's warlike policy in the Near East in March 1922 only confirmed the process that Addison's departure had begun. In short, Addison's resignation pointed the way to the final disintegration of the Coalition and of Lloyd George's vision of a permanent 'government of national unity'.

Finally, Addison's resignation of course marked a profound crisis for the man himself. Ever since 1911, his political career had been intimately linked with that of Lloyd George. Even as recently as the 'fusion' talks of March 1920, he had been Lloyd George's most confidential political adviser in peace as in war. Now his lifeline was abruptly snapped. Indeed, the circumstances of his resignation left a legacy of remarkable bitterness between him and the Prime Minister which lasted for nearly ten years. The view of Lloyd George recorded by Ramsay MacDonald in his diary in 1929 could well have been expressed by Addison in 1921. 'He was a friend who never felt friendship, a colleague who was ever disloyal; he never used a partner but for his own ends and sacrificed everyone who trusted him.'[127] As late as the general election of 1929 accusations between the two men about the record of the Ministry of Health after the war flew freely.[128] In the summer of 1921 it seemed that this breach could have only one ending. For all the unpopularity of his Coalition, Lloyd George still dominated political life. From the renewal of the Anglo-Japanese alliance to the starting of negotiations with Sinn Fein, it was Lloyd George's decisions which dictated British policy and which established the framework for international relations and for domestic alignments. Addison, by contrast, was an Ishmael, a political refugee, dismissed with the shadow of incompetence hanging over him, with not even his own Coalition Liberals to afford him shelter. Truly he might reflect that Lloyd George, above all other Prime Ministers, was indeed a good butcher. It was to prove one of the ironies of British politics that the next decade was to see the fortunes of the two men sharply reversed. Lloyd George was to be cast into the shadows for ever, doomed to a final twenty years of political impotence, while the apparently crushed and humiliated Addison found a new incarnation and a new role. Not for the first or last time, Addison was to prove his remarkable capacity to bounce back in the face of apparently hopeless odds. In reality it was Lloyd George who was almost finished in 1921, and Addison whose career and future were to be dramatically fashioned anew.

6
From Liberalism to Labour

Addison's political role after his resignation from the government was that of a lonely and bitter critic. He declared in the press that he was now going to fight the Coalition vigorously on the failure of its social programme, and he was faithful to his promise.[1] Of course, the breach with Lloyd George in such bitter circumstances caused him much personal distress; over twenty years later he would tell his children how enduring the pain of that period from 1921 had been. It was distressing for him to clash publicly with old colleagues with whom he had been so intimately associated. Nevertheless, for Addison duty and principle always came first. He felt it was his obligation both to condemn the government for its broken promises and to ally with members of any party who took a similar stand.[2]

His main target was the broken pledges of the government on housing—the reversal of the housing drive and the failure to continue the improvement programme for slum property. But in addition he broadened his attack to criticize the government's failures to deal with rapidly rising unemployment. In the winter of 1921–2, the total of unemployed neared two million. The government offered little by way of palliatives. Lloyd George's so-called 'Gairloch' proposals, evolved after meeting the Labour mayors of London in the Scottish Highlands in September 1921, and designed to promote local public works schemes, made no real impression. Addison denounced both the general failure to tackle unemployment and the specific loss of jobs caused in the building trades by the government's scrapping of so many contracts for housing.[3]

Another target for Addison was the government's cuts in educational spending—the slashing of expenditure on school buildings, on medical services, and on school meals that resulted from the report of the Geddes Committee. Also open to attack were the deliberate increases in the size of classes and the levy of new charges on teachers' salaries for their superannuation scheme. These issues brought Addison into conflict with an old comrade-in-arms, H. A. L. Fisher, who remained unhappily at the Board of Education, in an endeavour to resist the axe of Geddes. Addison also severely criticized aspects of the government's foreign and colonial policies, especially the wanton expenditure in such areas as Palestine, Egypt, and Mesopotamia in maintaining Britain's imperial pretensions through military and air bases. As a result of these criticisms over a wide range of domestic and overseas topics, Addison became during the next fifteen months a forceful and knowledgeable critic of the declining Lloyd George Coalition.

At times, even with his naturally sanguine disposition, he gave way to a momentary uncertainty over his future role. For example on 8 March 1922 he had a long heart-to-heart talk with his old friend and fellow London member, the Independent Liberal, Wedgwood Benn. In his diary, Benn noted 'He [Addison] has given himself six months neutrality and now is anxious to attack. He talked of retiring from Parliament and writing on politics. He has no idea of going back to his profession. I strongly advised him not to give up his seat in the House.'[4]

Fortified by Benn's support, and contrary to the prophecies of some newspapers, including the *Manchester Guardian*,[5] Addison stayed on in the House to pursue his attacks on the government. These took a variety of forms. To some degree, his criticisms appeared in the newspaper press. In opposition journals such as the Liberal *Daily News*, he denounced the government's betrayal of its pledges on houses. In the quarterly periodical, *Nineteenth Century*, he launched a vigorous attack on the government's unprincipled methods in dealing with such issues as unemployment.[6] More powerfully he produced in late 1922, just before the fall of the government, a strong indictment, *The Betrayal of the Slums*.[7] Here, with all the authority and knowledge of a former Minister of Health, he described the pledges given by the government to ex-servicemen that slums would gradually be wiped out. He emphasized the precise and detailed nature of the government's commitments, including promises given in the election manifesto in 1918, the specific proposals put forward by the Ministry of Reconstruction during Addison's period there, and the spare capacity in the building industry. Nevertheless, the government had in every case broken its word. Inadequate and insanitary dwellings remained in their hundreds of thousands in major cities and in rural areas, and the Prime Minister, in Addison's judgement, held a prime responsibility for this. He rehearsed again the circumstances of his departure from the government in July 1921 and the government's decision to cut back its grant for slum clearance to a totally inadequate £200,000 a year.

Since then, things had gone from bad to worse. The number of men employed by local authorities on housing schemes and by Public Utility Societies had fallen from 138,334 on 1 October 1921 to 91,175 four months later. The result was mounting unemployment in the building trades, a catastrophic decline in the number of houses being built, the failure to impose controls upon inefficient private builders who sought quick profits elsewhere, and the cutting of the assistance to local authorities to which they were entitled under the Housing Act of 1919. As a former medical doctor, Addison described graphically the effects of these insanitary slum tenements on the health of their occupants—the tuberculosis, the child malnutrition, and the rising death-rate in London, Birmingham, Glasgow, and elsewhere. He concluded with an appeal for a new state housing drive. Addison was not a spectacular writer, any more than he was a commanding orator, but his marshalling of the facts in his clinical, austere fashion was undeniably impressive. The whole pamphlet was a shattering criticism of the government's social failures, and was freely used by the Labour party in attacking the Coalition in the 1922 election.

Finally, Addison also expounded his criticisms in the House of Commons itself. He made a number of forceful, if somewhat dour, speeches attacking government policy. Several of them brought a bitter reaction from Lloyd George and other former colleagues. The first was delivered on 21 July 1921, very soon after his resignation, in a debate on the vote for the Ministry of Health. Addison now repeated at length his criticisms of the government's housing failures, made in his resignation speech, especially the limit set on the building of houses by the local authorities to 176,000 in all. Another attack on the government came on 26 October during a debate on overseas trade. Here he ridiculed Lloyd George's proposals for tackling unemployment, which he dismissed as 'egregiously unworkable'. On the Gairloch proposals of September 1921, he commented, 'You cannot carry on a Government by advertisement as if you were selling a quack medicine . . . . You cannot satisfy the cravings of the unemployed by dishing up stuff like this . . . . You only raise all kinds of expectations you cannot possibly meet.' He dismissed all the government's proposals as regressive or inadequate—the export credit scheme, the raising of new capital loans, the higher national insurance contributions of an additional two pence per head on the unemployed, and the 'monstrous disgrace' of the failure to assist the building programmes of the local authorities.[8]

This attack brought a fierce rebuttal from his successor at the Ministry of Health and former friend, Sir Alfred Mond. He pointed out that Addison had recently chaired a Cabinet committee on unemployment himself and therefore bore a prime responsibility for any governmental failures; he also seemed ignorant of the fact that the Ilford and other housing schemes had had to be terminated because of the astronomic cost of new houses. Mond's reply was thought by the *Spectator* to be particularly effective.[9] If this was so, it probably owed more to Mond's superior oratory and debating skill than to the merits of his case with regard to the reversal of the government's social programme and its surrender to orthodox finance and to deflationary fiscal policies.

In 1922, Addison's parliamentary attacks were set against the background of the Geddes economy proposals. To him, the proposed Geddes economies of £75 millions in public expenditure, including £18 millions on education and £22 millions on health and housing, were a total disaster. On 13 February 1922, in the debate on the King's Speech, he deplored the effect of the Geddes proposals, for example on the training of skilled workers for industry. The Geddes Committee had ignored the need to curtail military expenditure in the Empire, for instance in Egypt and the Middle East, while its suggested economies on the social front were not truly economies at all. 'The poor and needy in our own land have been sacrificed from the start,' Addison declared. He claimed that the Budget would be balanced at the expense of slum dwellers, necessitous mothers, and sick children.[10] On 27 February he returned to the attack on Mond's estimates for the Ministry of Health. He repeated his denunciations on the ending of government assistance to the housing programme. At a time when 40,000 additional men in the building trades were out of work, a sum of £250,000 compensation was being paid to the building contractors.[11]

On 27 April 1922 he turned to education, launching a vigorous attack on the education cuts over which Fisher had miserably to preside. In fact, Fisher had resisted many of the Geddes proposals, notably the demands for cutting teachers' salaries, raising the age of school entry for younger children, and ending the percentage grant system to the local authorities. But there was still ample grist for Addison's whirling mill in the cuts of £730,000 in the school meals service at a time when half a million children were certified as suffering from malnutrition. There was also 'most discreditable' cuts in the special services estimates of nearly 20 per cent: these covered school medical services, mentally retarded children, evening play centres, and nursery schools. In this area, Addison was on his most familiar ground. He also criticized the failure to expand the state secondary schools, and the suspending of the day continuation schools for younger employed people. In Addison's view, these measures nullified the effect of Fisher's Education Act of 1918.[12] On 10 July he repeated his attacks on the educational and housing cuts, and argued once again that the Geddes Committee had usurped the role of the government. In this, he was unconsciously echoing an argument adopted by Winston Churchill in the Cabinet at the time the Committee was appointed in August 1921. Addison now moved the rejection of the Economy (Miscellaneous Provisions) Bill which sought to implement some of the Geddes proposals. The Bill, he claimed, should be named 'a Breach of Pledges Bill'. This brought him into conflict with another old colleague, Sir Robert Horne, the Chancellor. Although Addison's motion for rejection of the Bill was inevitably lost, his attacks aroused a great deal of enthusiasm among the Labour members.[13]

These onslaughts by Addison coincided with a gradual decline in the stability and credibility of the government. Individual resignations like that of Edwin Montagu from the India Office over policy towards Turkey in March 1922, the failures in foreign policy after the débâcle of the Genoa conference in April–May, and the discredit attaching to the sale of honours by Lloyd George made the government's breakup more and more imminent. There was mounting pressure from Unionists in the country to strike out independently of Lloyd George; by August disaffection was widespread amongst junior Unionist ministers in the government. The ultimate occasion for Lloyd George's tumbling from office was the confrontation at Chanak on the Dardanelles with the Turks in September. This threat of war led to a massive rebellion by Unionists, traditionally the pro-Turk party. In the country, on the back-benches in the Commons, in the junior levels of the government itself, revolt was widespread. The famous Carlton Club vote by the Unionist MPs on 19 October, in which they defied Austen Chamberlain and their own party leaders, cast Lloyd George out of power for ever. Bonar Law now became the Unionist Prime Minister and was able to form a plausible government even though the leading Unionist former ministers such as Chamberlain, Horne, and Birkenhead still backed Lloyd George.

The new Prime Minister at once called a general election for November. It was one in which Addison's position as an Independent Liberal and an ex-Lloyd Georgeite was obviously hopeless. As he knew, defeat stared him in the face. However, he fought hard in Shoreditch, the constituency he had represented for the past twelve years. He continued to provide finance for its pro-Coalition constituency party, and to pay most of the salary of its election agent, G. H, Jobson. On 31 May 1922, however, at a meeting of several officers of the reconstituted Shoreditch Liberal and Radical Association, led by Jobson, a resolution was passed that 'consequent upon the changed political attitude of Dr. Addison, he no longer has the confidence of this Association'. They then adopted E. G. Price, a contractor and wharfinger from Ilford, as prospective National Liberal candidate for Shoreditch in his place. At the same time they changed their name to that of the Shoreditch National Liberal and Radical Association to indicate their support for the Coalition, which all the members of the former Association's executive now joined.[14] Addison now determined to stand as an Independent Liberal. As he stated in an interview, 'I have no intention of being driven out of Shoreditch by manœuvres of this kind.'[15] He was adopted as prospective Independent Liberal candidate in July by a meeting of the reconstituted Shoreditch Liberal Association, a predominantly Asquithian body, which Addison himself had sought to suppress in 1918, and which he had now helped re-form, with the aid of a £50 cheque. Here he declared that he would be prepared to answer the Independent Liberal whip, subject to the maintenance of Liberal principles, but added that he must be allowed the right to liberty of conscience. He also stated that if the Labour party were returned to power, he would support them, in so far as he felt he could, because they would be trying to carry out many of the social reforms that he had himself sponsored.[16] His political transition was clearly foreshadowed here. However, his new agent, Richard Childs, was able to inform him that

From Liberalism to Labour

as late as September only 140 of the 500 delegates of the old Shoreditch Liberal party would guarantee to support him in a general election.[17] Clearly the bulk of Shoreditch Liberalism was hostile.

In a fighting election address, Addison emphasized that he had sacrificed office for principle. He had objected to the spending of millions of pounds on foreign adventures when many people in the East End and elsewhere were living in poverty and in grossly inadequate housing or in slums. Since he had become the first Minister of Health, the nation's health had improved, there had been a dramatic decrease in the number of deaths from consumption, as in the infant death-rate, while many new maternity homes and medical centres had been opened. New facilities for treatment of persons suffering from tuberculosis had been opened, and for other major diseases and for the blind. The major necessities of the time were the restoration of trade and employment, the reduction of indirect taxation, and the improvement of the conditions of life for ordinary people. These things could be achieved only by a policy of peace abroad, and by a sensible, compassionate, progressive effort at home. He criticized Lloyd George's 'autocratic methods' of government, his disregarding of pledges to the electors, and his changing from one widely advertised expedient to another. This policy had resulted in heavy burdens being placed upon the people of Great Britain. Lloyd George had 'alienated our friends, failed to reconcile our enemies, and made the recovery of trade and industry impossible'.[18] But the presence of Price, the National Liberal candidate, caused a division in the Liberal vote. There was also a strong Labour candidate, a vocal champion of ex-servicemen, Ernest Thurtle, who further split the radical vote. He was in fact to win Shoreditch for Labour in 1923. Conservatives, such as there were in Shoreditch, presumably backed the National Liberal, following Bonar Law's advice to rank-and-file party members. Addison's defeat in this three-cornered contest could hardly have come as any surprise to him, because of his vulnerability in such an election. In the event, the result was E. G. Price (National Liberal), 9,084 votes, Ernest Thurtle (Labour), 8,834, with Addison receiving only 6,273 and at the bottom of the poll.[19]

Addison's defeat at Shoreditch and the fact that, in effect, he was not attached to any party seemed to signify that his career in politics was over. He possessed the most eminent qualifications within the medical profession and had held important positions as a doctor long before he became a member of parliament. The easiest and most obvious solution for him now was thus to return to the field of medicine after an interval of twelve years. As early as 1921 it had been predicted by some organs of the press that he would return to his former, highly distinguished career.[20] But he had no intention whatever of leaving politics after his defeat at the 1922 election. He was still in excellent health at the age of fifty-three; although his hair was now white, his ruddy, countryman's complexion and spare figure indicated that he was physically as well as intellectually vigorous. Above all, he was passionately committed to furthering great political and social ideals; this was no time for retreat to the shadows. He took encouragement from the defeat of Lloyd George. Indeed, so profound was his disenchantment with his former leader that he was, if anything, pleased that the Conservatives had won the election. He wrote to his old friend, Bonar Law,

> How greatly relieved I am that you had a majority sufficient to keep you independent of Lloyd George's faction and of his tricks. You have never, I am sure, suspected me of a Conservative disposition, nor do I possess it now, but I am sure that an established Conservative administration, under a man who is as honest and respected as you are, is a thousand times better than one influenced by that opportunism and lack of consistency by which Lloyd George had brought the country near to disaster. Good luck to you.[21]

Addison's problem was now to find a suitable haven for himself within the political parties. It was a time of unusual flux, with two parties, Conservatives and Labour, well in contention and the third, the Liberals, potentially powerful but riven in two. Evidently, Addison was finished with the Liberals, not because their policy was inadequate but because they could not be trusted to carry it out. He considered Lloyd George to be too opportunistic and Asquith a spent force. In any case, although he had stood at the election as an Independent Liberal, Walter Isaac in the Liberal central organization had coldly rebuffed Addison's request for assistance in meeting his enormous election expenses which had forced him to turn to his bank for a large loan. Isaac wrote bluntly: 'Our help has been given to men who did not desert the faith and work with our political enemies in the great betrayal of 1918 for mere personal position and profit. Nor do I forget that this betrayal involved the temporary break-up of the Liberal Party at a moment when its help was most needed to secure a proper peace.'[22] Viscount Gladstone, the head of the party organization, was no more forthcoming. Clearly, then, Addison was unlikely to find comradeship here. Nor, despite his warm letter to Bonar Law, could he ever conceivably ally himself with the Conservatives, even though some organs of the press speculated that he might 'ally himself with the constitutional side'. He had been a radical all his life, and this inevitably meant that the Labour party was his only possible destination, especially given its stand on the social issues in which he so fervently believed. Furthermore the Labour party was now rapidly increasing in strength; after the 1922 election it claimed 142 members of parliament, more than both the Asquithian and Lloyd Georgian Liberals combined. It had obviously supplanted the Liberals as the chief voice of the left. For a self-styled 'advanced radical' like Addison, it offered many attractions. He had enjoyed friendly relations with leading Labour figures like Ramsay MacDonald and Arthur Henderson throughout his parliamentary and ministerial career. His wife was always strongly sympathetic to socialism on Christian grounds. In the 1922 election, as has been seen, he openly expressed his sympathy for Labour's approach to domestic and overseas policies. With his continuing commitment to progressive policies on behalf of housing, education, and social welfare, it seemed inevitable that he would join the Labour party in the very near future.

Addison is highly significant in being the only leading Coalition Liberal to move into the Labour party. Most of the others who remained in politics, men like Winston Churchill, Hamar Greenwood, Freddie Guest, Edward Grigg, Hilton Young, and Alfred Mond, were to move to the right; several of them were soon to hold office under Conservative Prime Ministers. The Coalition, especially in its latter period, had adopted a strongly anti-socialist and anti-labour stance that made its supporters natural recruits for the Conservatives after 1922. E. G. Price, the 'National Liberal' victor at Shoreditch, was shortly to join them. Such Liberal recruits as there had been to the Labour party—and they were numerous in the immediate aftermath of the war—were almost wholly from the anti-Coalition section of the party, especially men like Ponsonby, Trevelyan, and Morel who were associated with the Union of Democratic Control during the war. But Addison, almost uniquely for a Coalitionist, retained his commitment to radical reform and to collectivist policies throughout the wartime and post-war periods; indeed he regarded the 'war socialism' of 1914–18 as a major justification for them in practical terms. His activities in 1923, especially after Baldwin succeeded Bonar Law as Prime Minister in May, indicated clearly that this quasi-socialist attitude was continuing to evolve. It was fortified by the circumstances of his resignation from the government in 1921. He wrote Arthur Henderson a letter in November 1923 which he allowed to be published in the press.

I am anxious to do what I can to assist the Labour Party because they stand resolutely for free trade and more unitedly I think than any other political party for a peacemaking policy abroad. These things are of vital importance, but they alone are insufficient and it is because I believe that the Labour Party is more resolutely intent than any other political party on better housing, health and education of the people that I think they ought to be supported.... It would not be honourable of me to conceal the serious misgivings I have entertained on the possible effect of the imposition of the debt redemption levy in a time of depressed trade, and that it might have unfortunate industrial effects, but I offer any help I can give. The immediate and pressing task is to resist the present outrageous attempt to deflect the country from putting its whole power into promoting a European settlement by engaging us in a long-term domestic controversy over proposals that will do nothing to abate the present dislocating turmoil.'[23]

This last reference was to Baldwin's declaration in favour of a tariff to protect the home market, made at Plymouth on 25 October, which aroused the fury of free traders everywhere. For their part, MacDonald and Henderson cordially welcomed the support of so distinguished a radical;[24] the Labour party generally was enthusiastic, even though Addison was a somewhat suspect figure in the trade union world after his difficulties with labour during his period at the Ministry of Munitions in 1915–17. Addison was more explicit in an article written in the Independent Labour party journal, the *New Leader*, in which he spelt out his reasons for leaving the Liberal party and criticized their election manifesto in 1923 for its inadequacies on the social and economic side.[25] The fact that Lloyd George was now reunited with the old Asquithian enemy increased Addison's distaste for the character of his former party. He was actually invited to contest a seat for Labour in the 1923 general election, at Totnes in Devon which would have been convenient in view of the family's home at Bishopsteignton in the constituency, but he felt compelled to refuse on the grounds that his financial circumstances prevented his standing.

Of his straitened financial condition at this time, there can be no doubt. He had realized some capital through the sale of property. 'Pretty Corner' had brought a good price (£6,500) when auctioned in 1920 though the new house in Devon, Murley Grange, was equally spacious. Addison had also sold the family farm at Hogsthorpe in Lincolnshire, now amounting to 144 acres, in July 1921, at a time of booming prices in the English land market. In addition, his wife had sold off to the tenants a few cottages that she owned in Northwood, and continued to sell others until 1928. On the other hand, the demands on the family finances were immense. Apart from the inevitable expenses involved with bringing up four young children, the eldest of whom was consistently unwell, there was the loss of an MPs salary since November 1922. Most disastrous of all, the division in the ranks of Shoreditch Liberalism in 1921–2 had cost Addison a great deal of money, amounting to nearly £2,000. This arose from the curious political situation prevailing in the Shoreditch constituency in 1922. Addison had been financing the Coalition Liberal party machinery there until the summer, and had paid the agent, Jobson, £250 a year until the end of August. Then he gave financial support to his erstwhile Independent Liberal opponents when they organized themselves in July 1922, and helped renew the lease in the old Liberal offices at 184 Kingsland Road. It seems clear that in July and August 1922 Addison was in the unfortunate position of financing both pro- and anti-government Liberal parties in the constituency simultaneously. To make matters worse, his new agent, Richard Childs, had proved completely incompetent in managing the party's finances. Addison had budgeted for expenses running to a maximum of £700. Yet, even though the campaign proper lasted not much more than a fortnight, Childs presented him with bills running to the huge amount of £1,209 15s. 7d. As has been seen, the Independent Liberal central organization coldly refused to offer any assistance. Addison had to take out a massive loan from his bank and faced near bankruptcy. It set the seal on a period as disastrous for him financially as it had been politically. At no time in his life can he have been nearer to total despair.[26]

As ever, he found his solace in public activity. He took a very vigorous part in the general election campaign of November–December 1923, even though not a candidate. He spoke all over the country, often in the wake of Lloyd George, at Rochdale and Leeds in the north, at Swansea and Aberavon in Wales (the last on behalf of MacDonald), at Swindon, Plymouth, and Totnes in the west of England, and at Twickenham and Whitechapel in the London area. Usually, his appeal was to former Liberal voters urging them to move to the left as he had done himself. In letters to his wife, Addison responded excitedly to the high passion of these election meetings. At Rochdale (where his intervention greatly annoyed the Liberal candidate, Ramsay Muir), there was an 'immense' meeting of at least 3,000 people. There was an even larger one of 5,000 at Leicester West where F. W. Pethick-Lawrence stood for Labour and where Winston Churchill was making his last public appearance as a Liberal candidate. 'It is a real religion to them there,' Addison wrote of Leicester. There were also 'tremendous meetings' at Swansea. 'They really seem hopeful of getting Mond out—I hope they will, but he is simply shovelling money out. They put his expenditure this year in the Division at not less than £10,000. . . .'[27]

Addison's interventions did not always coincide with a Labour victory—Ramsay Muir captured Rochdale for the Liberals, for instance—but they were thought in Labour circles to have had considerable effect. His help was especially appreciated by Pethick-Lawrence who won Leicester West. Lawrence also gave some of the credit for Sir Alfred Mond's defeat by Labour at Swansea West to Addison's campaigning.[28] MacDonald, elected for Aberavon, wrote after his return. 'You have placed us all under the deepest obligation to you for the fine way you came out and gave us your assistance. . . . Your appearance on my platform had considerable effect amongst the Liberals and several candidates to whom I have spoken, who received your assistance, expressed equal gratitude.' MacDonald added that he would very much appreciate a talk with Addison about the formation of his first Labour administration, as he knew he was in for a 'hard job'.[29] In reply, Addison made a number of suggestions about policy on unemployment, transport, education, and housing. He also made some proposals about personnel. The most important was that MacDonald should not take on the Foreign Office himself as it would be too taxing to combine this with the premiership as well. Haldane was Addison's proposal, with Arthur Ponsonby as his deputy.[30] Unfortunately MacDonald who believed, with some reason, that he had special talents in international affairs, failed to heed Addison's advice. His decision to combine the Foreign Office with leading the government posed many personal difficulties for the first Labour administration.

Addison was now anxious to stand soon for parliament as a Labour candidate, whatever the financial sacrifice. He did not have long to wait, as the first Labour government lasted only ten months. MacDonald's minority administration was forced out of office in October over its mishandling of the case of a Communist journalist, Campbell. Addison who had formerly joined the Labour party was now adopted prospective Labour candidate for the London constituency of Hammersmith South.[31] He had been previously approached by the Labour party in Swindon, which, in fact, eventually put up R. H. Tawney as candidate.[32] Addison may have felt that he had better prospects in Hammersmith South as the neighbouring division of Hammersmith North had been won by Labour in 1923; the constituency was compact and easy to contest, and the Labour party vote had been over 35 per cent in both 1922 and 1923.[33] Swindon, on the other hand, although the centre of the Great Western Railway works, was in the heart of rural Wiltshire and was represented by a Conservative. However, as will be seen, Addison's contact with the Swindon constituency was by no means over.

He fought a characteristically brisk campaign in Hammersmith South. As *The Times* noted, 'Housing was in the forefront together with unemployment; the Russian [trade] Treaty was nowhere mentioned.'[34] In his speeches, Addison claimed that the Campbell case was an artificial issue, merely a pretext to throw out a socialist government. The Zinoviev letter scandal that arose during the campaign, in which the government was to be falsely accused of links with the Comintern in Moscow, added point to this charge. In foreign policy, especially in the reparations settlement made at the London conference and the arbitration agreement at Geneva, shortly to produce the 'Geneva Protocol', the government, according to Addison, was heading for extraordinary successes in its diplomacy. If the Geneva agreements were ratified, they would be the greatest victory for international peace achieved by the European powers since the war. At home, Addison warmly endorsed Wheatley's Housing Act of 1924 which had resumed his own policy of subsidized local authority house building. For his part, Wheatley had written to Addison at the outset of the Labour government, 'You had no greater admirer than I during your period at the Ministry of Health.'[35]

In Hammersmith South, Addison faced the sitting Conservative (formerly a Coalition Unionist), Sir William Bull, who had represented the constituency for twenty-five years. *The Times* reported that Addison was proving a strong candidate. He had 'renounced his former Liberal faith with a convert's zeal and was running over the full Labour programme in a spirit of large acceptance and little criticism'.[36] This was all the easier for Addison since the capital levy, about which he had reservations as has been seen, had now been quietly dropped from the Labour programme. It was expected that Addison would win over many Liberal voters, while he himself claimed to give the constituency 'the fight of its life'.[37] For all that, the result was a predictable Conservative victory with an increased majority, with Bull polling 12,679, Addison 8,804, and E. D. Wetton (Liberal) 1,393, the last losing his deposit. Addison had been a late arrival in the constituency and had faced the disaffection of the followers of W. M. Reid (his rival for the Labour nomination and a veteran in Hammersmith politics from the days of William Morris). But he had put up an excellent fight in his first contest as a Labour man. He had raised the Labour poll by nearly 2,000, despite the 'red scare' atmosphere generated by the Zinoviev letter affair; Labour's share of the vote rose from 36.9 per cent in 1923 to 38.5 per cent in 1924. What kept Addison out of Parliament was the flight of over 2,000 who had voted Liberal in 1923, mostly to the Tory fold. It is not surprising that the Hammersmith South Labour party was enthusiastic about Addison as a candidate and anxious to fight the seat again.[38]

Although Addison, like the Labour government, was defeated at the 1924 election, there was no prospect that he would withdraw from the political scene. He was more firmly convinced than ever that the Labour party alone could bring about radical reform, and that the Liberals were doomed to extinction. As he wrote in November 1924 to his old friend, Wedgwood Benn, himself still a Liberal though not for much longer, 'Liberalism is a living thing but there is no hope for the Liberal "party" as it is until insincerity is cleared out.' As for the Labour people, 'their zeal is unquenchable and they would sooner anything than be mixed up with your Monds, Fishers and above all L. G.'[39] Addison went further and joined in December the Independent Labour party; this was still a powerful socialist force and one which had enjoyed a considerable surge of membership since 1920. Addison's move was the result of an approach by Fenner Brockway, a

Dr Christopher Addison in 1901
(in the possession of the Dowager Lady Addison)

THE OVERLOADED OMNIBUS
Conductor Addison (to Driver Law): "What, you can't get 'ome by Christmas with all them passengers on top? Well, why didn't you tell me before I took 'em on?"
"Punch", Nov. 24, 1920

THE SACRIFICE
Chamberlain "For heavens sake let them have him."

The Sacrifice: Addison's resignation, July 1921
(in the possession of the Dowager Lady Addison)

The Overloaded Omnibus: the Ministry of Health Bill, 1919
(in the possession of the Dowager Lady Addison)

Lord Addison and Mackenzie King, Ottawa, September 1946
(in the possession of the Dowager Lady Addison)

The Commonwealth Prime Minister's Conference, 1946 (in the possession of the Dowager Lady Addison)

From Liberalism to Labour

leading ILP activist and journalist; it was suggested that Addison join the national branch.[40] His progress from Liberalism to socialism was confirmed.

After his defeat at Hammersmith South, Addison occupied his time writing Labour propaganda and working in the Labour interest. There was also the need to earn some money as he had enjoyed no regular income since his loss of a parliamentary seat (with such painful financial consequences) in 1922. For this reason, in part, he turned to writing. In November 1924, he published two major volumes of reminiscences of his political career between 1910 and 1918, *Politics from Within*: their publication by Herbert Jenkins was delayed from 23 October to 4 November on account of the election.[41] Some newspapers queried the reasons for this delay. One claimed that it was because of the books' damning accounts of the way in which the production of munitions was held up during the war by pacifist revolutionaries, some of whom now occupied prominent positions within the Labour party.[42] Another attributed it to the fact that it contained 'remarkable tributes' to Conservative leaders, for instance Bonar Law and Carson.[43] The books created a considerable stir and aroused much controversy as the reviews indicated. They provided basically a factual account, based on Addison's detailed political diary, of his work between 1910 when he became a member of parliament and 1918 when Lloyd George called the 'coupon election'. They contained an immense amount of information on the politics of the period which had been previously quite unknown; they were, for example, immensely revealing on the circumstances in which Lloyd George became Prime Minister in December 1916 in which Addison himself played such a key role. But the books also showed Addison's success in making friendships and attracting support on a cross-party basis, and this caused some resentment after their publication.

Addison's friendship with the veteran Unionist and former Irish leader, Lord Carson, was established long before he asked Carson to write the foreword to *Politics from Within*. They had been closely associated during the war years, especially in 1917 when Addison was at Munitions and Carson at the Admiralty. Carson, as has been seen, defended Addison at the time of his resignation in 1921. In a letter to Addison in January 1922, Carson had written with great warmth: 'You know how much I value the friendship you and I started in time of stress. . . . After all, political differences are of little importance to those whose main object is to do what is right.'[44] Carson had presided at the dinner in honour of Addison at the end of June 1921 during the crisis that led to the breach with Lloyd George. The foreword to *Politics from Within* contained a warm tribute to Addison, 'an old political opponent', especially for his work at Munitions during the war. Carson mentioned in particular the provision of mines by that Ministry for the Admiralty in 1917.

Others attacked these volumes on other grounds, for example Sir John Simon, the Liberal, who argued that the decreasing cost of shells and other war materials referred to in *Politics from Within* was the result, not of war socialism as Addison claimed, but of emergency organization and of mass production methods.[45] Addison rebutted this in a speech at Dundee where he was speaking on behalf of the Labour candidate in a by-election, along with Bob Smillie, Jimmy Maxton, Tom Johnston, and David Kirkwood of the ILP.[46] The reviewer in the *Daily Mail*, predictably hostile, wondered how 'such a little man became concerned with great affairs'.[47] *The Spectator*, after noting that Addison was always regarded as 'a philosophical radical of the gentle school', commented that in his book Addison was now out to split heads rather than hairs.[48] A more constructive review appeared in a Midlands newspaper. It saw *Politics from Within* as

a historical document of the first importance, a detailed record of some of the most momentous transactions to be found in British annals. It explains how the war was won. It narrates triumphs of organisation which are absolutely without parallel. It removes the veil from a great number of transactions of which the public have hitherto only had an imperfect appreciation.[49]

This last review probably gives a fairer view of Addison's book than do the others cited. At a time when revelatory memoirs by politicians recently active were far more unusual than in the 1970s, Addison's provide a vivid, detailed, and largely accurate record of high politics at a critical time. He was no Crossman; his self-restraint and modesty made him perhaps a more reliable chronicler of great events than the tape-recording diarist of fifty years on. For the historian of British politics during the first world war, Addison's memoirs have always been a quite invaluable source, which retain their high value down to the present time.

Throughout *Politics from Within*, Addison always stressed that much of the central organization and collectivist controls that had won the war should be maintained and developed in peace for social reconstruction. This outlook provided the main thesis for his next book, *Practical Socialism*, published by the Labour Publishing Company in two volumes in 1926. Practicality was indeed the author's keynote. He showed, for example, how state factories had revolutionized wartime production and how the nation had avoided defeat by the adoption of socialist methods for allocating raw materials. The book ranged over the major areas of employment, costs and prices, the control of supply and distribution, the development of mineral resources, scientific and industrial research, and medical research. The constant theme was how in each case the state had assumed new powers during the war years with immense social benefit. Addison drew the conclusion that if socialism had saved the nation during the emergency of war, it could equally serve to further the needs of the civilian population in facing the new challenges of peace. The *New Leader* warmly commended his book. 'Every militant Socialist should have a copy and, if possible, memorise its contents.' It was 'a valuable book for propagandists'.[50] Addison again and again returned to this theme—that the first world war was an age of discovery, the dawn of a halcyon era for socialist principles. The techniques and strategy adopted then should be reasserted to inaugurate a socialist commonwealth for Britain.

Another area which attracted Addison's busy pen in these years was the need for Labour to evolve a sound agricultural programme. He produced two pamphlets at this time, *Why Food is Dear* in 1925 and *The Nation and its Food* in 1929.[51] Agriculture was a subject in which Addison, with his rural background in Lincolnshire, had always taken a close interest. He lived in the country, first in Buckinghamshire, then in Devon. For nineteen years, before, during, and after the first world war, he had administered his father's farm at Stallingborough, and could claim to have 'gained practical experience of farming in both good and bad times'.[52] He was now to become Labour's leading authority on agricultural problems. Indeed, agriculture was now to transcend health and housing as Addison's leading political priority. This was the more significant as there had been complaints for some time that Labour, based on its strength amongst industrial workers, had largely ignored the problems of small farmers and agricultural workers. Addison's voluminous writings mark a notable shift in Labour's emphasis on rural problems. As Dr McKibbin has shown, Labour's Head Office had devoted a surprising amount of attention to rural constituencies following the by-election in South Norfolk in August 1920; but this did not lead to any rethinking on policy.[53] Only in the ILP was there any sign of original ideas. E. F. Wise and J. A. Hobson became involved in drafting its economic proposals in the mid-twenties and placed a fresh emphasis on new capitalization of the land and new security for tenant farmers as a way of boosting production. Addison's new concern with agricultural questions thus marked a real breakthrough in Labour party policy. It also, as has been seen, marked a considerable shift in Addison's own political interests. It was, perhaps, an opportune shift as well, since the Labour party was fully stocked with experts on housing and the social services, whereas on agriculture, apart from Noel Buxton who had served in the 1924 Cabinet, Addison had few rivals.

In *Why Food is Dear* in 1925, Addison drew attention to the report of the Royal Commission on Food Prices which exposed the menacing control of a few large corporations over the bulk of the nation's food; this caused the prices of essential commodities to be high. In the period of the first world war, to which he constantly returned, the state had replaced the food corporations and there had been control over prices. There had been guaranteed prices for wheat and oats farmers, and minimum wages for farm labourers. The state had acted in the interest of the community against the few. Once again, he argued that, if the national and socialistic methods for which the Labour party stood had succeeded in wartime, they could justifiably be applied further in peacetime. In *The Nation and its Food* in 1929 he referred yet again to the war period as a model to follow. He showed the necessity for the elimination of middlemen in industry and agriculture, and the need for establishment of national boards for distribution. Most originally, he elaborated a scheme for the setting-up of marketing boards for basic foodstuffs such as corn, meat, and milk. Agricultural marketing through boards of producers was a scheme which he was to make very much his own over the next six years. The Fabians and others had advocated co-operative marketing arrangements for farmers on the lines of those flourishing in Denmark, but little detailed work had been done on the idea. Addison's contribution to policy here was as original and creative as in housing and health. The pamphlets struck a bold note. 'Are we prepared to apply our experience and capacity in an endeavour to

From Liberalism to Labour 167

administer to an obvious national need or shall we look on whilst others see the vast opportunities and are enabled to use them for the reaping of countless riches for a few?' By the end of the twenties, Labour had a constructive and progressive agricultural policy for the first time.

Agriculture, however, absorbed only a part of Addison's attention at this time. He was far from oblivious to the industrial tension of the mid-twenties. 'Red Friday' which saw the confirmation of a temporary subsidy to the coal industry in 1925 was followed by the breakdown of negotiations between Baldwin's government and the miners and the traumatic experience of a general strike called by the TUC in May 1926. Addison plunged into these battles boldly. At a Labour meeting in Dorset in August 1925, he expounded the advantages of a nationalization of industry both in terms of productive efficiency and in terms of better labour relations.[54] He poured scorn on claims that Baldwin's capitulation to the miners on 'Red Friday' was a surrender to Bolshevism. It was really a surrender to the solid common sense of any trade unionist and right-thinking citizen. Every Royal Commission on the coal industry had reported that the mining industry was inefficient and badly managed. Public ownership was the only remedy. The Liberals had recently put forward two reports outlining their policy on the coal question. Addison claimed that they were both based on his own recommendations to the government in 1918 in the form of the Coal Conservation Report and the Report on Electricity. How could the Liberals be taken seriously if they waited for seven years before demanding action? Labour called for national direction of the coal industry, to protect consumer and workers alike. He took pride in the fact that he had issued the first order in the country to control the costs of coal while a minister. The country would never get action from a Tory government as Baldwin's deliberate ignoring of the recommendations of the Sankey Commission on the mines served to illustrate.

He was also much concerned with the Trade Union Bill passed by Baldwin's administration in 1927 after the total defeat of the general strike. Its main provisions were to define certain categories of 'illegal' strikes and to substitute 'contracting in' for 'contracting out' with regard to the unions' political levy to the Labour party. In *An Exposure of the Government's Trade Union Bill*, Addison denounced this measure with great passion. He claimed that it made effective workmen's combinations impossible, rewarded treachery to one's fellow workers by law, and drained the funds of the Labour party, which depended on the pence of working people rather than the contributions of the rich. The Bill provided modern employers' associations or hostile governments with a legal apparatus for the oppression of working people, at a time of severe trade depression. Addison's long acquaintance with trade union practices after his years as a minister added depth to his argument.

These years in the wilderness, then, saw Addison emerge with increasing prominence as a Labour planner and publicist. Apart from agriculture and the Trade Union Bill, he retained his keen interest in the housing question. He kept in close touch with George Hicks, secretary of the building trade workers, on the subject of the building trade after 1922. In late 1923, Hicks consulted Addison for advice before making proposals on dilution in the building trade to the incoming Labour government.[55] In reply, Addison wrote 'I am really keen to leave no stone unturned to get the country committed to a comprehensive housing policy and I do not think myself that we shall get it from any party except the Labour Party.'[56] It was impossible to overcome the housing difficulties, Addison argued, through private enterprise methods. With regard to building materials, he advocated that action be taken on the lines adopted by the Ministry of Munitions when there was a shortage of munitions during the war—that is, the use of physical controls.[57] He often cited the failure of the Liberals to keep their promises on housing as his ostensible reason for leaving the Liberal party. Addison's private papers also reveal a continuing concern for information on housing statistics throughout the twenties.[58]

He was much involved at this time in speaking tours to propagate Labour party policy, notably in rural areas where he could expound on agricultural policies. In late 1925, at the request of Arthur Henderson and the Labour party national agent, he addressed a series of Labour party meetings in south-west England where the party was comparatively feeble.[59] At a meeting of the Tiverton divisional Labour party in September, he advocated the nationalization of the land as the only way for tenant farmers to gain security of tenure. He also took the opportunity to reopen some old personal battles. He maintained that the agricultural proposals made by Lloyd George in launching a land campaign in a recent speech at Killerton Park in

Devon were merely a repetition of those made by himself in 1918 when he had advocated a scheme for giving smallholdings to ex-servicemen and setting up training grounds for them to acquire agricultural skills. The rent which he had proposed was to be paid not by entering the market and buying up the holdings, but by a system of perpetual tenure, which would avoid a large outlay of capital. On the eve of the 1918 general election, according to Addison, Lloyd George had authorized the then Minister of Agriculture, Lord Ernle, to ignore the recommendations of his colleagues and to earmark only £20 millions for the creation of smallholdings. By 1921 this £20 millions was exhausted. There was thus no man more responsible for the present scarcity of smallholdings and insecurity of tenure than Lloyd George. Addison had also proposed £200,000 for afforestation schemes, while Minister of Reconstruction. This had been axed by Lloyd George to just £20,000.[60]

That summer Lloyd George had launched his new agricultural policy encapsulated in the 'green book', *The Land and the Nation*. In this, he urged a vast new programme of food production; Britain imported well over £400 million of food and timber which could easily be produced at home. He also advocated a new system of 'cultivating tenure', a kind of state ownership of cultivated land. Addison was anxious that this attractive programme might revive the fortunes of Liberalism in rural areas. Labour badly needed a policy 'easy to be understood, definite and with some beef in it'. He badgered both MacDonald and Henderson about formulating a new Labour agricultural policy. Both were responsive, as the extinction of any prospect of a Liberal revival anywhere was a vital part of Labour's long-term strategy. Meanwhile, Addison wrote two vigorous articles for *The Times* either criticizing Lloyd George's land proposals for having been advocated by himself in 1918 or, alternatively, for simply being impractical. He himself believed that the only solution was the complete national ownership of all cultivable land, as Labour demanded.[61]

From now on Addison was an intense evangelist for Labour's agricultural policies. In 1926 he addressed the Labour party conference for the first time, and spoke in strong support of 'A Labour Policy for Agriculture'. This policy document advocated the control of land by the state, which should set new standards for cultivation.[62] In 1927 he spoke to the Labour party Easter Week-end School at

Oxford on agriculture again. He called for security of tenure for the farmer, more efficient, co-operative methods of production, and a system of marketing for basic foodstuffs. For the agricultural labourer, there should be the freedom of his home, freedom of access to the land, and above all a living wage. Again, the war years, with the 1917 Corn Production Act, provided a model. He was realist enough to believe that profoundly independent farmers would never volunteer to engage in co-operative schemes; therefore the machinery of co-operation must be provided for them.[63] In early 1928 he was in touch with Alfred Barnes, the Labour Co-operative MP for East Ham (South) and later Minister of Transport, about Labour's agricultural policy. Barnes forwarded to Addison a draft for a co-operative system as part of a national plan for the organization of the production and distribution of food. This had been embodied by Lloyd George's adviser, E. F. Wise, now active in the ILP, as part of his scheme for the establishment of import boards for foodstuffs. This idea was developed further in a memorandum by Addison which concentrated on the marketing side of the distribution of food.[64] As his pamphlet, *The Nation and its Food*, had shown, Addison was anxious for a totally new approach towards agriculture, especially on the marketing side. The provision of import boards as part of a wider scheme for improved home agriculture was seen by many as the socialist answer. It would have meant taking over the importing of foodstuffs as the country's largest nationalized industry, and would have led inevitably to the state control of many subsidiary industries connected with agriculture. These proposals were supported by a strong group within the ILP including men such as E. F. Wise and George Dallas, a leading representative of the agricultural labourers.

Although one contemporary author claimed that 'it was clear that it was never likely to be more than a plank in the party platform',[65] the proposal for import boards found its way into the collection of policies embodied in *Labour and the Nation*, the party's new national programme published in 1928. It represented an important advance on *Labour and the New Social Order* (1918) in several respects, of which agriculture was one. Labour's proposals for agriculture in 1923 and 1924 had been vague and unoriginal. But its manifesto in 1929, while still couched in general terms, called for 'a system of organized marketing and stability in the prices of main crops and products' for farmers, as well as for a minimum wage for farm labourers and the public

From Liberalism to Labour   171

control, (the concept of ownership was omitted), of the land. As Clement Attlee later wrote of the Labour party at this time, the manifesto was 'a bid for power by a party which expected in the normal course of events to attain it.[66] The new agricultural policy, of which Addison was perhaps the chief architect, was among the programme's most novel features.

Addison was now seeking a winnable seat for which to stand again as a Labour candidate. Encouraged whole-heartedly by his wife, he began his search as early as the beginning of 1925.[67] In October 1925, he was selected as a prospective Labour candidate for Swindon in Wiltshire, the seat which he had turned down in favour of Hammersmith South in 1924.[68] Swindon was a constituency long coveted by the Labour party. It was the centre of the Great Western Railway works which employed 12,000 men as well as Garrards engineering and Messrs Wills; it contained, therefore, many working people.[69] It included the seat of Lord Faringdon, a businessman peer who had served on the Geddes Committee. When he died in 1934, his grandson and heir proved to be an ardent supporter of the Labour party and of Dr Addison. His Georgian home at Buscot Park near Faringdon still (in 1979) contained frescoes which depict the Faringdon Labour party and the history of international socialism. In 1923, Swindon had been retained by the Conservative, Sir Reginald Mitchell-Banks, with a majority of 3,504 over the Labour candidate. In the 1924 election in a straight fight with the highly eminent Labour representative, R. H. Tawney, his majority fell to 2,904. A swing of 5.2 per cent was needed to turn it over to Labour. Addison was advised by the National Labour party agent to accept the offer from Swindon in preference to Crewe or York, constituencies which he also considered (and which were both, in fact, to be won by Labour in the 1929 election). He was told that the Labour party in Swindon would take the financial responsibility for the contest, and raise the money.[70] 'It is a good division and there is a very healthy movement and the constituency ought to yield a Labour victory. It will require a special type of candidate as the ordinary industrial nominee will never lift it.'[71] This undoubtedly referred to the fact that the Swindon constituency included a substantial agricultural perimeter in addition to the town itself, and here Addison would come into his own. At his nomination meeting on 5 October 1925, he advocated a comprehensive programme including the nationalization of the land, and also of the mines and the railways. He also declared that the national control of banks and credit was urgently necessary, especially in view of the stern deflation of government finance since the war.

He campaigned hard in Swindon in the few years prior to the 1929 general election.[72] Indeed 'the doctor' was to become a part of political legend there for thirty years to come. He frequently appeared in the constituency, and invited such Labour notables as MacDonald, Philip Snowden, George Lansbury, and Ellen Wilkinson to speak there on his behalf. In his immediate pre-election campaign, he concentrated on the government's priorities in spending freely on overseas adventures, notably in Palestine and Iraq, while economies were achieved at home in closing rural schools, enlarging the size of classes in schools, and trying to cut off free milk to nursing mothers. He responded angrily to an attack from Lloyd George, made while he was answering a question at a meeting at Pwllheli in his Caernarvonshire constituency, about the reasons for Addison's leaving the Liberal party. Lloyd George was reported as having said, 'He did not make a success of it [housing]. He got the sack because he was no good and he has now joined the Labour Party.' Addison defended himself pugnaciously, and received the support of Lieutenant-Colonel E. H. Mosley, one of the housing commissioners he had appointed in 1919.[73] The bitterness between the two old Liberal colleagues continued to fester. Addison declared during the campaign, 'I say deliberately that anyone who relies on Mr. Lloyd George to be steadfast in giving effect to his promises, if he ever comes to have the opportunity again, is a fool.'[74]

In the general election held in May–June 1929, Addison's efforts in Swindon received their reward when he was returned as Labour member with a majority of over 2,000 over Banks. The result was Addison (Labour) 16,885, Banks (Conservative) 14,724, and E. Thornborough (Liberal) 7,060. Addison had achieved a swing to Labour of nearly 9 per cent compared with 1924. The results as a whole saw Labour successful in the election. In all, 289 Labour candidates were returned, Labour became the largest party in the House for the first time, and was able to form a government for the second time. The new administration would still depend on the Liberals for a majority—only 59 in number, despite Lloyd George's vigorous campaign and programmes to combat unemployment, but its prospects appeared far more stable than in 1924.

From Liberalism to Labour 173

There was some surprise when Addison received the post only of Parliamentary Secretary to the Ministry of Agriculture: it was wondered by *The Times* whether Lloyd George's attacks had damaged Addison's reputation irretrievably.[75] For Addison himself, now sixty, his relatively minor office was a disappointment. After all, for some years, he had held a series of major portfolios, and had wide experience of Cabinet office. He had been an active campaigner for Labour over the past six years, while a man like his friend Wedgwood Benn, whose transition from Liberal to Labour had come as recently as 1927, had gone straight into the Cabinet as Secretary of State for India even though his ministerial experience was negligible. Addison's reaction to his disappointment was a somewhat extreme one. He demanded that the new Prime Minister publish an announcement in the press in the following terms:

At the special request of the Prime Minister, the Rt. Hon. Dr. Addison has consented to fill the post of Under Secretary to the Minister of Agriculture with the title of Deputy Minister, in order that he may participate in promoting the Land Development and Marketing Policy of the Labour Party in the framing of which he has taken an active part.

He went on to write to MacDonald:

In accepting the appointment I have in mind the understanding that you will promote me to the office of Minister on its becoming vacant, as you explained it was likely to be in the near future by the appointment of Noel Buxton [the new minister] to another post. I rely upon your assurance that you would endeavour to afford me the promotion in some other way.

He suggested that Buxton might be moved to some other department. 'It would be unfair to myself to become committed, after my previous experience, to the rank of Under-Secretary for any prolonged period.'[76]

Addison's disappointment, in view of his background of high office and his relative seniority in the party, is understandable. At the same time, in trying to dictate terms (from a weak position) to an incoming Prime Minister, Addison's ambition overreached itself. He was fortunate that MacDonald treated the affair with less than his usual hypersensitivity and proved to be conciliatory. Noel Buxton (who sat for North Norfolk) had been Minister for Agriculture in the 1924 government and had obvious prior claims to the department. As it happened, Addison's role under MacDonald was to give him far more influence upon Cabinet policy in his department than most Under-

Secretaries could reasonably expect. Mrs Addison seems to have been content with the situation. She noted 'marked coldness in some of the denizens' of the Devon village where she lived when they went to morning service at church. 'They appear to think you can't even acknowledge a good morning from your political opponents—ignorant fools!' On the other hand, like her husband, Isobel Addison could be severe towards the political opposition. She refused to congratulate Major S. E. Harvey for retaining Totnes, the constituency in which the Addisons lived, for the Conservatives. 'I felt inclined to say neither on personal or any other grounds could I. He looks an utter nincompoop.'[77]

For all his failure to return immediately to Cabinet office in June 1929, the years since his breach with Lloyd George in 1921 had indeed been ones of fulfilment for Addison. They were years which had witnessed the ruin of the Liberal party as a party of government and the emergence of Labour as the only viable alternative to the Conservatives. As has been noted, the vast majority of the leading Labour recruits from the Liberal ranks in these years, those whom G. T. Garratt termed the 'mugwumps' somewhat misleadingly, men like Morel, Ponsonby, Trevelyan, Norman Angell, were drawn from the opponents of the Lloyd George Coalition in 1918. Usually they had moved left because of their aversion to the foreign and diplomatic policies of the war years and the 'system of Versailles' after 1919. They had moved to Labour after being active in the Union of Democratic Control, which indeed supplied Labour with much of its approach to foreign policy after the armistice. Addison's entry into Labour's ranks was very different. Most of his Liberal colleagues of the days of Coalition—men like Fisher, Shortt, Macnamara, Greenwood, Munro, McCurdy, Kellaway—had gone into political oblivion. Some, like Hilton Young and Sir Edward Grigg, were beginning to carve out new careers in the Conservative party; Grigg had already received the governorship of Kenya under Baldwin. There were only two outstanding survivors from Lloyd George's Liberal entourage from the heady days of 1919, and their experiences had been totally different. Winston Churchill had finally become a Conservative, a move many predicted as early as 1920. He had just concluded five busy but controversial years as Chancellor of the Exchequer under Baldwin; as events turned out, his extreme imperialist views on Indian self-government were about to cast him back into the wilderness again.

The other, who moved in the opposite direction, was Christopher Addison. He joined Labour while remaining faithful to his long cherished convictions on social reform and public control of the economy. He had remained consistent; it was the Liberals and especially Lloyd George, who had betrayed him. And so, after apparently lapsing into hopeless obscurity in 1921 after a colourful five-year period at Munitions, Reconstruction, the Local Government Board, and Health, Addison at the age of sixy launched on a new career as Labour statesman, the colleague of socialists like George Lansbury and Sidney Webb as he had once been of Asquith and Grey. It was a new water-shed in his unusually varied career, It heralded a new phase of Labour activism and of high office, destined to be as creative and controversial—and even longer—than his earlier Liberal incarnation had been.

7

The Second Labour Government

Ramsay MacDonald's second Labour government of 1929-31 is usually considered a disastrous episode in British political and economic history. From the New York stock market crash of October 1929 to the massive run on the pound of July-August 1931 which led to the schism and resignation of a demoralized administration and the formation of the National government, Labour's second period of office was dogged by appalling and uncontrollable economic crises. Unemployment soared from the already severe level of almost two million to nearly four million of the insured population; older industrial working-class communities in Yorkshire, the North-East, Scotland, and South Wales were crucified by a massive social tragedy, the effects of which still reverberate down to the present time.

Yet it is too often forgotten that Labour took office in June 1929 amidst a mood of considerable optimism and public goodwill. After the years of inertia under Baldwin, MacDonald seemed to offer a commanding and inspiring presence at the head of a new progressive administration. Such ministers as Philip Snowden at the Treasury and Arthur Henderson at the Foreign Office, even though suspicious and hostile towards one another, also brought with them authority and experience. The presence in the Cabinet of other able figures—Sidney Webb, Wedgwood Benn, and Lord Parmoor, for example—confirmed that the new government, in which Addison had now taken junior office, was by no means undistinguished. Addison did not have many close acquaintances in the new administration, as he had had in his previous years of office as a Liberal, though he maintained a reasonably warm relationship with MacDonald. From 1930 he was to live near Chequers, when the Addisons moved from Devon to Peterley Farm, near Great Missenden, in Buckinghamshire. With the Foreign Secretary, Henderson, he had had somewhat delicate relations ever since he had opposed Henderson's demand for more executive power as labour adviser for the Ministry of Munitions in the summer of 1916. Philip Snowden, in Mrs Addison's view, was 'very charming' with 'a sweet face'.[1] Unfortunately, he and her husband were locked in conflict on almost every major issue. Addison had no high regard either for several of his other colleagues, such as J. H. Thomas, and the woman Minister of Labour, Margaret Bondfield. He wrote to his wife in July 1929, 'We had an excellent meeting of the whole party this morning and I think it helped and cleared the air a lot—but Margaret B[ondfield] came in for some straight talking and she needed it.' His closest associate in the Cabinet was probably his old Liberal ally, Wedgwood Benn. He did, however, make some good friends in the lesser ranks of the government. Notable among these was the relatively obscure member for Limehouse, Clement Attlee, who succeeded Sir Oswald Mosley as Chancellor of the Duchy of Lancaster in May 1930. Attlee's clipped, precise style of speech somewhat resembled that of Addison himself. They shared a similar quiet sense of humour and also a love of cricket (Addison was an enthusiast for the Radnage cricket team from 1930 until his death). 'Useful and clearheaded' was Addison's early verdict on his colleague.[2] As Labour member for Stepney, Attlee, like Addison, had gained first-hand experience of politics and social conditions in London's East End. In future years Addison's friendship with Attlee was to add a new dimension to his rapidly evolving and lengthy career.

As Parliamentary Secretary to Noel Buxton, Addison soon became unusually active for a junior minister. At first, he had to work out a day-to-day relationship with his Cabinet superior whose post he had coveted. On 24 June he wrote to his wife, 'Buxton is very decent and defers to me a lot.' But two days later he was finding his Minister too meek and acquiescent. 'We were sent across to come to No. 10 this morning because I had screwed up the Dept. to put up a big fight about Forestry. I was vy. sick with Buxton who proceeded with his first sentence to give way and it was only after a big fight that I got anything rescued at all. Our people are vy. sick with him.' This contretemps blew over soon enough, and Buxton and Addison formed an excellent partnership for the next twelve months—largely, it must be said, on the basis that Buxton gave way on practically everything and increasingly let Addison take command of his own department. Agriculture was a vital area of government policy—one in which MacDonald himself was much interested—with the stagnation of

British agriculture in the twenties, the slump in world food prices even in the United States, and the growing arguments over the rival merits of free trade, imperial preference, and protection in assisting the farmer. A vigorous agricultural programme could make a massive improvement in Britain's balance of payments by cutting down on imports. There was also the burning question of the agricultural labourers, amongst whose ranks Labour had recently been recruiting many members in East Anglia and elsewhere. Their votes had helped Labour to capture two Norfolk seats in the 1929 election. Unemployment and low living standards on the land were as grave as in the urban and industrial areas. Thus it was that in the autumn of 1929, shortly after MacDonald's return from a triumphant visit to New York to meet President Herbert Hoover, Addison and Noel Buxton turned their energies to outlining a radical new scheme for agriculture. First, though, there was a reception to mark MacDonald's return from the United States, held by the London Labour party at Friends' House in Euston Road. 'Rather a loud crowd. Humanity is always somewhat queer when you get it en masse,' Mrs Addison ruminated on the event in her diary.[3] Then her husband and Buxton settled down to mastery of the technical complexities of agricultural production and marketing. It generated a profound argument about the future course of agricultural policy which was to have considerable repercussions for the history of the second Labour government.

Labour's return to office was accompanied by a brief revival of trade which lasted for almost six months. During this period, there was an attempt to provide a new initiative in trying to reduce the toll of unemployment; the minister in charge, J. H. Thomas, set about his task with apparent, if misplaced, confidence and formed a co-ordinating committee of permanent secretaries. In the debate on the King's Speech, he claimed that much had been done in a single month—railway managers, business leaders, and civil servants had been interviewed; spacious plans had been drafted. He spoke of building roads, of improvements on the railways, and of public works projects. His activities bore closely on agriculture. In August 1929 he wrote to Noel Buxton enclosing a memorandum which his assistant, George Lansbury, along with Sir Oswald Mosley, had sent him on unemployment. This emphasized that the agricultural industry gave scope for employing more men if it was reorganized. This faith in the capacity of the land to absorb surplus labour and to reverse the drift of population to the cities had been a part of Lloyd George's programme also in 1929. Thomas now asked Buxton to prepare a memorandum on some of the broader aspects relating to agricultural unemployment.[4] This provided a stimulus for Addison and Buxton to get on with the preparations for their marketing and land proposals.

Since the mid-twenties, Addison had been urging the Labour party to place agriculture in the forefront of its policies. With the right kind of organization it could provide new employment and drastically cut the import bill. Once again, his experience of the war socialism between 1914 and 1918 influenced his approach. The post-war 'decontrol' policy for agriculture, with the repeal of the Corn Production Act in 1921, he considered to have been profoundly mistaken; especially calamitous were the ending of guaranteed wheat prices for farmers and of wages boards for agricultural labourers. He was much influenced by the wartime controls when advocating his marketing board schemes in the twenties and thirties. In November 1929 he produced a major memorandum in which he suggested the creation of a Home Produce Marketing Authority. This was considered by a conference on the marketing of agricultural produce on 5 December 1929.[5]

He also produced a memorandum for the Cabinet on 12 December on 'The Marketing of Home Food Produce', which Noel Buxton had circulated.[6] In this, Addison drew the Cabinet's attention to the need for adopting the Marketing Board principle. He emphasized the steady decline of the rural population and the inadequate prices obtained by the grower for his produce. There was an urgent need for a national marketing authority for home produce to improve the handling and marketing of produce, to encourage experimental enterprises, and to draft schemes for commodity marketing organizations. A sum of £100,000, including money now derived from the Empire Marketing Board, should be placed at the disposal of the new authority. He also urged creating a National Agricultural Produce Marketing Council and, in an appendix, advocated an import board for wheat and flour. In circulating this memorandum, Buxton proposed that a committee of ministers be set up, including Addison, so that he could have a proper opportunity to state the case for his ideas. So began a prolonged controversy over import quotas and marketing schemes which was to lock the Treasury and the Ministry of Agriculture in conflict over the next eighteen months.

Addison was extremely active in pressing all aspects of his agricultural schemes. On rural employment, he showed that the Ministry had sanctioned twenty-five schemes of land drainage submitted by fourteen local authorities between July and the end of October 1929; the total cost was approximately £27,000, of which about £16,000 represented a government grant. On these schemes, for which Addison had been pressing, at least five hundred men were to be employed.[7] He also sought to convert the mind of the rural community to his plans for marketing. At the meeting of the Council of Agriculture for England, he stressed that the Empire Marketing Board was highly sympathetic to his Marketing Board ideas. After his speech, a resolution expressing apprehension about the effect on home wheat markets of the existing large supplies of stored wheat was withdrawn.[8] At a meeting of the National Farmers' Union in his Swindon constituency in January 1930 he assured the farmers that the government knew that the import of so-called 'bounty-fed' protected cereals from Germany was unfair to the British producer. The government had directed their representative on the Economic Committee of the League of Nations at Geneva to raise the question. The land drainage policy would be embodied in a bill for early presentation to Parliament, as also would the proposals for the more effective housing of rural workers at rents which they could afford to pay. He appealed to tenant farmers and freeholders to support these reforms, and also to assist in developing plans for the orderly and systematic marketing of British home produce. These plans would yield as good results when applied to wheat, potatoes, and meat as they had in the case of eggs for which procedures had been standardized in the twenties. The government was anxious to lessen the gap in prices between those received by the producer and those paid by the consumer, and to establish a stable financial basis for farming operations over the long term.[9]

Apart from land draining, marketing boards, and rural housing, Addison was also active in working out a policy for land settlement. Here again was a pledge largely ignored by the Lloyd George Coalition in which Addison had served after the war. He prepared a series of memoranda on land settlement in the later months of 1929.[10] For example, in one of them in November he showed the handicaps suffered by the Ministry of Agriculture as a result of its lack of powers to acquire land for smallholdings or allotments. The power which had been conferred on the Minister by the Land Settlement (Facilities) Act

The Second Labour Government 181

of 1919 had been allowed to lapse in 1922. The Minister should now be given powers to acquire land for smallholdings, for farms, and experimental farms, to acquire derelict or neglected land, and to purchase land for reclamation.[11] In December he elaborated these proposals. Facilities should be provided for land settlement in the form of either small-holdings or profit-sharing and co-operative farms. The establishment of farm settlements by the Ministry would result in expanded production of food and a substantial increase in the resident, working population in the countryside.[12]

These useful departmental activities were overshadowed by the economic cataclysm that soon overtook the new Labour administration. In September 1929, MacDonald had written in his diary, 'were it not for industrial condition government looks as if it would live for ever, but the "were" is a big one'. His latter foreboding was to come true and, in the event, to prove critical much earlier than the Prime Minister could have anticipated. After the New York stock market crash at the end of October, the world economy collapsed. Britain's economy subsided with it. By the early months of 1930, the worst trade depression of the century was under way. The now familiar British problem of structural unemployment in the old staple industries such as coal, iron and steel, and shipbuilding, was compounded by the effects of a world crisis. In January 1930, 1,533,000 people were out of work, as against 1,433,000 in January 1929. By June 1931 the total had soared to 2,735,000. The existence of the government, as well as of the economy, was in jeopardy.

Some kind of new initiative by MacDonald and his colleagues was essential. In particular, pressure to protect the home market had built up steadily since the depression first made itself felt. This applied especially to industries where a high level of unemployment arose directly from foreign imports. As early as January 1930, MacDonald had recognized that 'the day is coming when we may have to give up orthodox free trade'. This had major implications for agricultural policy, above all.

New initiatives were needed because Thomas's bravado had come to nothing. Unemployment was becoming more alarming, month by month. Thomas's incompetence led to a profound debate over policy within the Cabinet and to the dramatic resignation of Sir Oswald Mosley from the government in May 1930. Addison and Buxton were amongst those who joined the agricultural and iron and steel industries in pressing for protection of the home market. But their opponents were powerful indeed, since free trade had been one of the foremost tenets of left-wing faith since the days of Cobden and Bright almost a hundred years earlier. Moreover, the Labour government had come to power on a free trade programme and in opposition to the Conservatives' 'safeguarding' policy for industry. A policy of 'safeguarding', so Labour's election manifesto declared in 1929, meant a higher cost of living, sweated wages, and unemployment, misery equally for the consumer and the producer. On the other hand, some Labour ministers were prepared to be convinced that protection could be a partial solution to unemployment; among them was MacDonald himself. Thus, as agriculture was the main industry where the debate over protection and free trade took place, Addison and Buxton became directly involved in a central area of government policy. Indeed, the first big test for MacDonald's government came over agriculture.

Addison, of course, had long felt that agriculture was a key element in the country's economic strategy. In January 1930 he advised MacDonald that it would be diplomatic for the Prime Minister to open the Agricultural Conference and to attend for as long as possible. 'They are exceedingly touchy and any excuse for disparagement would be eagerly seized upon and might have disastrous results.'[13] Hostility to taxes on food lay at the heart of the free trade faith; yet there was no industry where the effects of free trade were now more damaging to those who were engaged in it than in agriculture. Addison himself, as has been shown, was never a doctrinaire on the question of free trade. He knew that cereal growers in particular were hard hit by the importation of corn from abroad. By February 1930 he and Buxton were pressing for the establishment of a marketing board to protect the home wheat crop, coupled with quotas and import boards. Buxton was preparing the draft of an Agricultural Marketing Bill in accordance with a Cabinet decision of January 1930.[14] Mac-Donald, too, was alarmed at the inflow of 'bounty-fed' cereals. If it were allowed to continue, there was likely to be a serious contraction of British agriculture and a disastrous collapse of wheat farming. The departments concerned should consult as to a joint policy, while the Foreign Office should exert influence over foreign competitors, as unfair and illegal competition of this kind could not be tolerated. The Board of Trade should stir itself to defend the British market against this kind of competition, while the Minister of Agriculture and the Board of Agriculture for Scotland should confer and report on the problem.[15]

In February the proposals of the Ministry of Agriculture for the establishment of a marketing board for the home wheat crop, coupled with quotas and import boards, came before the Cabinet. MacDonald circulated a memorandum on 24 February, however, to the effect that he was not wholly convinced that the details of the organization, functions, and finance of these boards had been worked out satisfactorily.[16] Snowden, an arch free trader at the Treasury, resisted them fiercely; Willie Graham, the President of the Board of Trade, backed him up, as did Parmoor, the Lord President, and Arthur Henderson, the Foreign Secretary. Snowden's hostility to marketing boards had already been revealed. As early as December 1929 he had written to Buxton to express his 'grave doubts' about the marketing proposals and stating that he could not at present agree to provide funds for publicity and propaganda on behalf of home produce.[17] He had also opposed the circulation of Addison's paper on agriculture to the Cabinet in December on the grounds, as P. J. Grigg put it, that 'other departments should be consulted, as to the practicability of the scheme before it is circulated'. Grigg, however, later noted in his memoirs that Snowden's increased readiness at this time to 'have recourse to his unrivalled powers of denunciation and invective' somewhat weakened the impact of his arguments in Cabinet.[18]

After lengthy discussions, the Cabinet decided that 'no proposal that involved either crude subsidy or protective tariffs should be considered'. It also decided that a committee consisting of ministers, officials, and various agricultural representatives should be set up to examine agricultural policy in the light of the Ministry's proposals.[19] Addison had suggested the latter expedient in his memorandum of 12 December. In spite of opposition from Snowden and others, MacDonald in fact seemed to favour the line of Addison and Buxton in agricultural matters and wanted to bring about the protection of home cereals quickly. He suggested imposing a registration fee on imperial grain and spending the proceeds to keep the cost of home wheat up to the cost of the productive level.[20] However, the Cabinet continued its opposition and nothing was done.[21]

In March 1930 the Committee on Agricultural Policy reported tepidly and indecisively on co-operative marketing, quotas, and import boards. The Cabinet, however, decided that a Marketing Bill should be drafted as soon as possible. Addison now took the opportunity to press the real need for marketing legislation upon MacDonald. He sent him an encouraging report of a campaign in which he had been involved to steady beef prices and to promote the sale of good quality beef during the early months of 1930. Average weekly sales had risen from 2,750 in December–January to 4,627 for the week ending 22 March 1930. 'The whole campaign has cost less than £1,000 and gives a small glimpse of what a little intelligent direction could do in promoting good marketing.'[22] He added that 'the mood of the industry is thoroughly friendly and more ready to consider and adopt new methods than I think it has been in our time'. The vital need in agriculture was not the ability to produce but rather to market its produce.[23]

In accordance with a Cabinet directive which went contrary to the recommendations of the Committee on Agricultural Policy, the Ministry of Agriculture prepared a draft White Paper for the Prime Minister at the end of April. This advocated a quota, but was later amended by MacDonald who felt that the quota scheme was not sufficiently settled in detail to justify inclusion in the White Paper.[24] An alternative proposal was circulated by Philip Snowden to cut down the amount of arable land available for the production of corn as a way of solving the present difficulties.[25] This precursor of part of the 'Triple A' policies put through by Roosevelt in the United States after 1933 was deplored by Addison. Writing to MacDonald, he urged 'The message of the White Paper should not be one of despair, but one of encouragement and hope and keenness to help. . . . If this composite paper were published, so far as England is concerned, there would certainly be anger and a good deal of derision, and our political credit, so far as agriculture is concerned, would be gone.' He gathered that the import board scheme had been set aside.

> We are all opposed to the lame expedients of subsidies and protection. Apart from the active encouragement of marketing boards, so far as cereals are concerned, the suggested quota has emerged as the only alternative method of help. . . . Nothing, of course, would please everybody, but the suggested method of working would certainly meet the difficulties presented by the Scottish bankers and the Quota proposals would be eagerly welcomed by the farmers.

He knew that the Tories had promised support.

The Second Labour Government 185

Personally I should like to see an active marketing policy with a Board working the Quota for at least a limited period, followed by an active policy to develop smallholdings in suitable districts on much more economical lines than have been adopted before. This should be coupled with the acceptance of the principle of unemployment insurance for labourers.[26]

He strongly rebutted the conclusions of the Treasury and the memorandum of the Chancellor on the wheat quota. It revealed a

misunderstanding both of the nature of the proposal itself and of its implications as well as the reasons for it. . . . He appears to base his preference upon the policy of the late Government. . . . The Labour Party has never accepted the policy of impotence as set out by the late Government. The Chancellor of the Exchequer supposes that the passage of the necessary legislation through Parliament would raise 'formidable' difficulties.

But these difficulties were 'not comparable with those which would arise otherwise'. Addison realized that there was some opposition from the flour importers, but the most grotesque misrepresentation had characterized the way they presented the case in Canada. 'The proposal would probably increase the importance of Canadian hard wheat or flour . . . subsidies and tariffs are ruled out. The import board to which we were committed at the election is apparently in cold storage.' He added that 'it is a political impossibility and a certain precursor to political disaster to present our supporters with a negative when they demand proposals for the assistance and maintenance of the cultivation of land in England'.[27]

Addison's exhortations to the Prime Minister were not made in vain. As David Marquand points out, MacDonald had 'long ago come to the conclusion that agriculture's problems could not be solved without state aid'. An undated note in his papers, apparently written during the summer of 1930, makes it clear that, although he saw practical difficulties in the idea of a quota, he supported the principle that lay behind it.[28] Nevertheless, with Snowden's opposition still unyielding, by the time that Noel Buxton left the Cabinet in June 1930, no decision on the shape of agricultural policy had been taken.

By now, as has been seen, Addison had become a figure of stature in the government through his advocacy of a strong initiative in agricultural policy in an effort to provide a solution to the country's economic difficulties. He worked closely with agricultural specialists such as George Dallas. He presided over agricultural conferences dealing with issues like cottage holdings, allotments, and the control of cultivation.²⁹ One body of much future significance that he chaired was that set up in 1929 to 'consider and report upon the desirability and possibility of establishing one or more National Parks in Great Britain'. Britain was almost alone amongst major countries in having no national parks and in its wanton neglect of the environment, especially areas of outstanding natural beauty. The committee over which Addison presided heard impressive and convincing evidence from conservationist bodies such as the National Trust of the need to preserve the countryside from speculators, jerry-builders, and profit-seeking landowners. The report and recommendations of this committee, when presented to the government in 1931, were a major landmark in the history of environmental planning. Even though its proposal of an annual grant of £100,000 for five years (an amount carefully trimmed down by the Treasury official who served as its secretary) was too modest, it did lay the foundations for the later decision to create a National Parks Commission. Areas of outstanding beauty such as the Lake District, Snowdonia, and the Cairngorms were set aside as National Parks under public protection on the same lines as Yellowstone, Yosemite, and the rest in the United States.³⁰ Addison's committee began a process (still very far from complete in rural areas in 1979) of protecting beautiful countryside from the depredations of private interests and of conserving it for the enjoyment and recreation of ordinary people. In addition to these activities, Addison also served as chairman of the subcommittee of civil research to inquire into the Fishing Industry—Fisheries as well as Agriculture came within the orbit of the Ministry³¹—while, as has been seen, he was active in preparing legislation on land drainage, rural housing, marketing boards, and land utilization in 1929–30.

It came as no surprise, therefore, when, on the resignation of Noel Buxton and his elevation to a peerage, Addison succeeded him as the Minister of Agriculture on 5 June 1930. Like Haldane, he now enjoyed the distinction of having served in the Cabinets of both a Liberal and a Labour prime minister. He had been in effective charge of the Ministry for many months and needed no preparation for his new role; this was probably one of the reasons why the ambitious Addison and Buxton got on so well. Even Snowden, a consistent political opponent, wrote in his memoirs later, 'I was surprised that Dr. Addison and Mr. Buxton had been able to work together even for twelve months. Dr. Addison was an energetic, pugnacious person and

The Second Labour Government 187

not likely to be satisfied with a subordinate ministerial post. Mr. Buxton, on the other hand, had a kind and unassertive nature.'[32] Hugh Dalton, now a junior minister, was one who had 'great confidence' in Addison as the new Minister.[33] There was no major reconstruction of the government at this time, but J. H. Thomas relinquished the post of Lord Privy Seal to move to the Dominions Office, having totally failed to make any impression on the swelling total of unemployed, or even to show any sign of understanding the nature of the problem. Vernon Hartshorn, a Welsh miner, succeeded him as Lord Privy Seal, while Lord Passfield (Sidney Webb in his new incarnation) retained the Colonies. Outside the Cabinet, the vacancy caused by Mosley's resignation as Chancellor of the Duchy of Lancaster was filled by Clement Attlee, whose career and Addison's were soon to be much intertwined.

Addison was now a political figure of importance in a wider sense. The second Labour government was a minority administration dependent on Liberal support. Lloyd George had thus put Labour in power for the second time; he made the best of it by claiming, before Parliament sat, that the electorate had really endorsed the Liberals' programme for public works, and that they would support the government if they carried it out. During the debate on the King's Speech in July 1929 the government had made it clear that they would accept the Liberals' offer of collaboration between the parties on their tactics and programme, though somewhat guardedly. The political prospects for the new government seemed, indeed, reasonably bright in this first phase. The Conservatives had their own interal difficulties. There was discontent within the party over Baldwin's leadership, intensified after the defeat in the 1929 election. Churchill was mounting a vehement protest over the granting of any form of self-government to India. There was also Beaverbrook's crusade for 'empire free trade' as a panacea for economic recovery; there would be freedom of trade between the countries of the empire, with a tariff wall to keep out imports from the rest of the world. This produced a considerable division of opinion within Conservative ranks: it was pointed out that the dominions would be the first to refuse freedom of entry for British manufactures which competed with their own, in 1930 as in 1903. Empire free trade was not a form of protection for which Addison had any sympathy, of course. However, he enjoyed a reasonably warm relationship with Beaverbrook, an old associate of his since December 1916. Beaverbrook warmly endorsed some of Addison's agricultural proposals. He wrote on 6 June 1930, 'May I be allowed to say how pleased I am at your appointment to the Ministry of Agriculture. I feel quite sure the farmers' case will now be presented to the Cabinet.' He appreciated that if the government took up Addison's proposals enthusiastically, 'in all probability my movement will be torpedoed'. For all that, he welcomed the prospect of new legislation to rescue British agriculture 'with all my heart'.[34]

It looked as if the dependence of the Labour government upon the Liberals for support would place it constantly at risk. Several leading right-wing Liberals, including Walter Runciman, Donald Maclean, and Ernest Brown rejected Lloyd George's leadership. But the Liberals needed the alliance even more desperately than did the Labour party; as in the 'Lib–Lab pact' concluded by James Callaghan and David Steel in 1977, it was the weaker partner whose dependence was greatest. Despite all their campaigns and Lloyd George's support from his 'fund', the Liberals had increased their parliamentary representation only from 40 to 59 in the general election. This was immediately reduced to 58 when William Jowitt, member for Preston, promptly joined Labour. The Liberals would have to think long and hard before turning out the government and facing possible extinction at the polls. The range of options was narrowing for the Liberals all the time. In 1930, with mounting depression and unemployment, the economic situation grew more desperate. With repeated attacks from his opponents on his failures to promote economic recovery, MacDonald had to seek the co-operation of other parties in a far more determined fashion than before.

For some time, the Liberals' support of the government had been highly tentative. In January 1930, shortly after the government had come close to defeat over its Coal Mines Bill, Lloyd George announced that his party's continued co-operation with it was dependent on concessions being offered to the Liberals. In particular, the government should agree to some form of electoral reform to give the Liberals parliamentary representation more commensurate with their popular vote. This was a distasteful prospect for MacDonald. Since 1922 he had been bent on the destruction of the Liberals as Labour's main rivals for the leadership of the left. With proportional representation or some other form of electoral reform introduced, the Liberals would be likely to survive as a serious force in British politics for an indefinite period. From late March until late May 1930, the Liberals kept the government in office in the expectation of some concession on electoral reform. Finally, the national executive of the Labour party turned it down. Even so, on 3 June Lloyd George told Hankey that he had decided to accept MacDonald's invitation to co-operate with the government on the condition that he saw Cabinet papers and had access to government officials.[35] He was 'full of tactics', Hankey recorded. This was clearly a far more intimate form of collaboration that was envisaged than had been the case between Liberals and Labour in the 1906–14 period. The Cabinet then endorsed a letter from MacDonald to Lloyd George which invited the latter to confer regularly with a committee of ministers appointed for the purpose, and promising him access to papers and officials. A similar offer was made to Baldwin, who predictably refused. Meetings then followed at regular intervals between representatives of the Labour and Liberal parties even though MacDonald and Lloyd George continued to eye each other with considerable distrust.

It was here that Addison emerged as an important link figure. He had been very hostile to Lloyd George at the start of the 1929 Parliament, especially after the bitterness between them in the recent election. On the election of the Speaker in June 1929, Addison had written to his wife, 'L. G. was received rather badly and offended the House by introducing a party note.' But he had always felt that the reorganization of agriculture required the co-operation of all parties. The Liberals' agricultural programme was not too different from his own, and he publicly welcomed Lloyd George's intervention in the House of Commons on agricultural questions.[36] Lloyd George for his part appealed for the treatment of agriculture on non-party lines. Throughout the period of office of the second Labour government, the co-operation of the Liberals was constantly sought over agricultural policy: it became an important bridge between the two parties. In June 1929, at the very outset of the new government, Buxton had written to Addison, 'We must be careful about committing ourselves beyond administrative actions till we know where the Liberals stand.'[37] Both parties held that a 'radical change of agricultural policy' was urgently necessary. In a memorandum he prepared on 'the common ground between the Liberal and Labour agricultural policies', Addison wrote that both attributed the decline on the land to 'government neglect and to the breakdown of the old landlord–tenant system'.³⁸ The similarities between the two parties' views on agriculture far outweighed the differences. On the other hand, there remained a background of distrust. Like MacDonald, Addison was deeply suspicious of Lloyd George, and with even better reason. Although he wrote on 7 June 1930 that 'a real agreement might emerge' out of the co-operation agreed upon between the two parties, he felt that Lloyd George would require 'careful watching',³⁹ a judgement which was indeed borne out.

In August Lloyd George wrote to MacDonald to complain that he had not been informed, as the Cabinet and the Prime Minister had promised in June, about the government's policy proposals. 'Up to the present I know no more about the government's proposals than any other M.P.' He complained about the inadequate policies adopted by the government with regard to roads, public works, and unemployment. He stated bluntly,

> The clear impression I and my colleagues have formed from such conferences as we have already had is that there is no evidence of that driving energy behind the Government as a whole which is essential in the emergency in which we stand. . . . There is certainly no proposal, especially for helping the agriculturist to meet the exceptional stresses of the present time, to which I and my colleagues are not prepared to give fair consideration. . . . We are prepared and anxious to place at the disposal of the Government both our experience and such expert assistance as we command.⁴⁰

MacDonald responded at once. Addison and other ministers were asked to be present at a meeting which Lloyd George and his Liberal colleagues were invited to attend.⁴¹ This appears to have been the first formal contact which Lloyd George and Addison had had since the schism of 1921. Lloyd George's requests for information about government policy were now handled in a diplomatic fashion. For example, Addison's secretary informed the Minister in late August, 'I handed him [Lloyd George's representative] a considerable number of documents. . . . They gave very considerable information, without including any that would be embarrassing.'⁴²

Perhaps in part because of his old friendship with Addison, more because on agriculture, of all subjects, the Liberals had most in common with Labour, in September Lloyd George emphasized again his willingness to co-operate with Labour. This time he sent a message to Addison through Seebohm Rowntree, the distinguished social reformer. Rowntree was an old Liberal colleague of Addison's, from

The Second Labour Government

the days at Munitions in 1916, one with whom Addison had remained in touch over the years. On 10 September Addison reported to MacDonald that he had had 'what was clearly intended to be a message from Lloyd George to the effect that Lloyd George was anxious to arrive at an understanding with us as to unemployment and the agriculture programme, and if we could agree was prepared to back it, and if need be to secure special procedures for forcing it through Parliament'. Rowntree had cited Lloyd George as believing that 'unless we can do something to save the situation, the whole lot of us, Liberals and Labour alike, will be swept away by a great protectionist wave'.[43] MacDonald must have felt some relief at receiving this message from Addison, as he had also received reports that Lloyd George had been sounding out the Conservatives in August and September about a possible (national) government. Marquand rightly comments, 'MacDonald had no faith in Lloyd George's unemployment policy . . . but on agriculture he probably saw him as a potential ally.'[44] He responded quickly to Addison's message and asked for a meeting with the Liberal leader.

MacDonald's reply shows how important agricultural policy was at this time for the government.

> I really do not think we can do much to build things up, except as regards agriculture, and undoubtedly a very heavy party attack is to be made on us in consequence. Should that attack be successful, the mind of the country is such that we cannot prevent a real national protectionist government being returned for a full period of parltiamentary life; but I think that an agricultural programme might just provide the time necessary to enable the country to do a little more thinking and to come to steadier conclusion.[45]

Marquand's conclusion is that the reply cannot have been altogether welcome to Lloyd George. 'He was being asked to keep an increasingly unpopular Government in office in order to carry through an agricultural programme of distinctly modest dimensions, and had been offered nothing in return.'[46] This is a just verdict, save that it underestimates the novelty of Addison's agricultural programmes. In addition, the fear of a general election led MacDonald and his colleagues once again to offer the Liberals tentative promises on electoral reform, in return for their support in the Commons.

The Liberals, for their part, were still anxious to co-operate with the government on agriculture. In early October, Lloyd George had a private meeting with Addison at the specific request of the Liberal leader. Addison believed that the purpose of it was 'first to put Lloyd George on speaking terms with myself and secondly to have, quite fairly, an informal talk on the agricultural position'. They discussed the land, marketing boards, import boards, and the wheat quota. Lloyd George told Addison of Liberal, or at least his own, views on these and kindred topics.[47] The discussions went well and seem to have done much to heal the nine-year breach between the two men. Lloyd George wrote to MacDonald after the meeting that the talks had put him into a co-operative frame of mind with regard to agricultural policy.

> I and my colleagues would like to pay tribute to the willingness shown by Dr. Addison to put at our disposal the information bearing upon agricultural problems. We have already met him and if the Government feel that there is a broad general basis for discussion we shall be very glad to take up with him a friendly examination of the whole of the agricultural problems at the earliest possible date.[48]

For the historian, there is an irony in comparing the standing of the two men at this time—Lloyd George, once so all-powerful, now the suppliant for a struggling minor party; Addison, apparently once crushed beyond any hope of revival, now a leading minister and calling the tune. But at least Addison played an important role in bringing Lloyd George and MacDonald closer together, and served as an important go-between in the political manœuvres of the autumn and winter of 1930–1. They might yet salvage the tottering Labour government and rekindle the old 'Progressive alliance' of pre-war days.

When he became Minister of Agriculture in June, Addison as has been seen was a figure of some stature in the government. He had been preparing new programmes throughout his tenure as Under-Secretary; by the summer of 1930, these policies were in the forefront of the government's agenda. The implication given by Dr Skidelsky[49] that the Labour party largely took over the Liberal policies on agriculture is not correct; the two policies were quite distinct on marketing, quotas, and other matters. The new agricultural programme drawn up by Addison came up before the Cabinet in June and July. He addressed meetings all over the country to promote it. He said that it fell into three main parts—the Marketing Bill; the provision of large-scale farming and the letting of farms to suitable tenants; and the provision for housing and agricultural research. Britain, he

The Second Labour-Government

declared, offered one of the finest agricultural markets in the world. Within easy reach of that market, there were efficient food-producing districts and yet a large part of that market was being supplied by food products from overseas. There had also been a progressive decline of agriculture since the war, with 100,000 fewer people employed, and 1,100,000 acres of land taken out of cultivation. A massive new effort was needed to reverse these trends. The government now proposed that, in addition to new marketing boards, the Ministry itself, as well as the local authorities, would have powers to acquire land and make it available to suitable cultivators.[50]

The second part of the policy was an emergency measure for helping to redress unemployment by giving acres of land to suitable men who were unemployed. The Ministry should have powers to acquire land with three classes of provision in mind—something larger than allotments for those with the training and aptitude, smaller-scale allotments, and large-scale farming in certain cases. On housing, the government intended to draw up a schedule of insanitary cottages in rural areas. This policy would mean several bills. They would be drafted before the House reassembled in the autumn of 1930 and, subject to the government's remaining in office, would be carried into effect.

One especial area of need was the plight of cereal growers. Mac-Donald had supported Addison's proposals for a wheat quota, and defended them in Cabinet, while proposing no new initiatives to translate this economic heresy into reality. He did, however, ask Clement Attlee to examine the question. Attlee reported that, unless the government set up an import board or established a quota, a serious situation would arise. Addison now pressed hard for import boards, with the object of presenting firm proposals from the British government to the Imperial Conference due to meet in October. In a memorandum on the Marketing Bill prepared on 11 June, he stressed that, with a home import board under the proposed Marketing Bill and an agreed quota for British wheat, it would be possible to give much assistance to the arable wheat farmer. He had heard that both MacDonald and Attlee favoured a guaranteed price for home-grown wheat.' If they decided on a guaranteed minimum price which was above that of the world market it would have to be paid for either by the consumer or by the taxpayer unless corresponding reductions in supplies were made. The only way of effecting these reductions seemed to be the creation of import boards. From a parliamentary point of view, too, there was much to be said for coupling the guaranteed price with the import board scheme.[51] But this was difficult for a traditionally free-trade party to swallow. The Cabinet was faced with a choice between higher unemployment and higher food prices; not surprisingly, it dithered. Addison's efforts met little success at first, and a decision regarding import boards and a wheat quota was adjourned until the Imperial Conference in October. Even Addison himself saw the need, in political terms, for moving cautiously. Labour wanted to avoid the kind of splits that Churchill and Beaverbrook were now generating within the Conservative party.

On 1 August, Snowden, the Chancellor, announced in the Commons that the government would bring in a Marketing Bill. Once the Imperial Conference was over, it would take 'whatever practical steps can be devised to put cereal growing in this country on an economic foundation'.[52] MacDonald now asked Addison to prepare legislation for a Marketing Bill. However, he felt that Addison must discuss with agriculturists, such as Sir Alan Anderson and Christopher Turnor, the methods to be used in bringing pressure to bear on the farmer to modernize British agriculture. MacDonald 'did not at all like your idea that marketing boards should do this'. It was not the business of marketing boards at all.[53]

The government was still no nearer any solution to the basic stagnation of the economy. By the end of August, the Prime Minister's hopes for speeding up the processes of co-operation between the central banks had come to nothing. His concern for a large expansion in public works programmes had been frustrated. To a minority of the Cabinet there was only one solution left. Since it was clear that little more could be done through public works, production within the home market should be encouraged at the expense of imports; in other words some form of modified protection should be introduced. Addison reflected this view when speaking in his constituency at Swindon in late August. He repudiated the 'present fashionable mood to represent ourselves as played out'. With regard to agriculture, he felt that there was positive evidence for the possibility of settling more people on the land. This was perhaps a view that owed much to his lifelong sentimental attachment to rural life, dating from his childhood in Lincolnshire.[54] The free trade system, he felt, was dead or dying. A scheme had now to be devised to give the home grower a

The Second Labour Government

secure livelihood and yet retain the advantage of tax-free imports. There were two ways of realizing this ideal. Either secure markets could be created for home produce, or the same result could be achieved by a board to deal with imported supplies of foodstuffs. He emphasized again his support for a quota system for wheat.[55]

Addison was congratulated by George Lansbury for the stand he took at Swindon. It caused some alarm to Neville Chamberlain and the Conservative Research Department which was now working on a quota scheme and feared that Labour might now seize the imperial initiative. At the forthcoming Imperial Conference, Labour could present itself as the truly imperial party through the new emphasis in its agricultural policy.[56] But, as has been seen, no decision was taken about import boards and quotas until after the Imperial Conference met in October 1930. The free trade section of the Cabinet was uneasy about a quasi-protectionist programme somewhat similar to the McNary–Haugen scheme that was advocated by champions of the Midwestern American farmer in the US Senate. The free traders had already gained one victory on import boards and the wheat quota. Snowden had argued successfully that they implied higher food prices and this would have the same effect as fiscal protection. This was followed by another victory on the whole strategy of the government for overseas trade. There was a wide-spread belief in Labour ranks that if exports could be increased, then unemployment might significantly diminish. In February 1930, eleven countries, including Britain, signed a covenant at Geneva in which they committed themselves not to raise tariffs until April 1931; these proposals, however, had to be ratified by November 1930. At a meeting of the Cabinet in August, most Ministers opposed ratification until the results of the trade negotiations at Geneva had become clearer. However, at a further meeting of the Cabinet on 2 September (with Philip Snowden chairing the discussion as MacDonald had incomprehensibly departed to Lossiemouth) the free traders, headed by Snowden, Graham, Henderson, and Parmoor, dominated the discussion. The Cabinet voted by eight to two (Thomas and Addison) in favour of ratification, a further pledge of support for free trade.[57]

Addison's continuing enthusiasm for import boards, quotas, and similar protectionist experiments, in the course of his speeches throughout the country about the government's agricultural programme, aroused much opposition. He created particular dismay with a bold speech he delivered at Leicester on 13 September. He declared there that 'in my opinion the import board is the only way to deal with the problem of imported wheat. I think we shall have to adopt it for a number of commodities.' This led to a severe reproof from MacDonald who wrote:

> I now see the cause of the trouble. If you look at the *Manchester Guardian* report and read the third sentence, under the heading 'Imported Food' you will see that you have gone further than the Cabinet decision. . . . I am having the greatest difficulty keeping sections together in the hopes that we may get an agreed policy, but when these pronouncements are made of the private opinion of ministers expressed in public in precisely the same way as they are expressed in the Cabinet where they draw out hostile comments, you will see some of your colleagues, instead of being helped to agree are driven away from it; and I am afraid that the result is that to get an agreement now in the Cabinet is much more difficult than it was when the last session ended. Matters were then left in quite a hopeful position and had we now been able to resume these talks exactly where we left off an agreement could have been come to, I think. The feeling that some of our colleagues now have is that they are being rushed; that things have been said in public which indicate that the Government have to all intents and purposes decided its policy and that the agreement which has been come to is in accordance with the opinions which you have expressed. . . . I am afraid as soon as you meet Parliament you will have questions put to you which you will find very difficult to answer on behalf of the Government, and which if answered in accordance with your speeches may well produce a very serious division of opinion amongst us. For the time being you have seriously upset the method of handling which I had adopted and before anything can be done of a practical kind I must now try to restore the position to what it was at the end of July.[58]

So Addison was accused by the Prime Minister of setting back the cause of import boards and the wheat quota, and, more crucial still, of disturbing the precariously balanced factions within the Labour government. There is, however, no evidence that he was any more contrite when rebuked by MacDonald than he had been towards Lloyd George.

Nothing was done until December about Snowden's statement on agricultural policy made in August. This was not surprising as the doctrinaire free trader, Snowden, had always resisted marketing boards. Nor was he enthusiastic about 'too definite a commitment to provide unemployment insurance to agricultural workers'.[59] Indeed Dalton was later to note that Addison was a lonely champion of this policy in 1929–31. But the economy was now deteriorating so fast that urgent action could not be delayed. In December MacDonald

The Second Labour Government

persuaded the Cabinet to set up a committee to work out the government's future policy on agriculture. In March 1931 this committee produced a majority report in favour of a wheat quota. In April MacDonald wrote to Addison asking him to lobby Lloyd George so that the Liberals would support the wheat quota, if the Cabinet decided in its favour.[60] But there was still much resistance in the Cabinet. According to Lord Parmoor, Addison had already been trying 'to force his wheat quota policy on the Cabinet'. The free trader, Parmoor, added that he had received many letters from farmers 'objecting strongly to any form of fiscal policy which might increase the price of cereals since their interest is to buy all cereals cheaply. An imperial quota based on a world price is a very different matter and open to further discussion.'[61]

Parmoor's cautious views seemed to have been shared by most of the Cabinet in April. At two meetings on 15th April, it was decided that no decision should be taken on the wheat quota, but that Addison should work out a satisfactory alternative. Three weeks later, he reported that this was impossible. Thus, after a long battle over many months, deadlock remained. Skidelsky has taken the debatable view that the refusal to give protection to agriculture 'cost the government its last chance of getting the farmers on its side'.[62] However, it was agreed by the Cabinet on 4 June that Addison and William Adamson, the Secretary of State for Scotland, in consultation with the Treasury, should prepare plans for the encouragement and stimulation of the transfer of agricultural effort from the cultivation of cereals to other forms of produce in all cases where it was likely to be profitable.[63] Addison submitted preliminary proposals to give effect to this policy on 30 June. But a policy which proposed to solve the problems of wheat farmers by thinning out their ranks was hardly comparable to Addison's favoured scheme for a wheat quota.

His other agricultural proposals had a better reception. On 24 June 1930 he moved the second reading of a Land Drainage Bill 'to amend and consolidate enactments relating to the drainage of land'. It was a non-party contribution to the subject, as it was based largely on the recommendations of a Royal Commission representing all parties.[64] More innovative was Addison's Land Utilization Bill; this was, according to Snowden, 'the most important measure presented to Parliament up to that time by the Labour Government'.[65] In introducing this Bill on the occasion of its second reading on 13 November

1930 Addison was anxious to rebut charges that the 'Labour Party is so urban that it has no understanding nor pity for the rural population' and was 'very ignorant of agricultural conditions'.[66] His whole career from the mid-twenties was, in part, a crusade to combat this kind of misconception.

The Bill did two things. It empowered the Minister of Agriculture, working through an Agricultural Land Corporation, to buy land for large-scale experimental farms, and for demonstration farms in fruit-growing, dairying, and other branches of production, and also for the purposes of reclamation of land, drainage, and other work, compulsorily if need be, Secondly, it contemplated the development of a vast system of land settlement. It would, for example, give an opportunity to a large number of unemployed persons who had rural aptitudes to be offered a chance on the land. It provided a scheme for their selection and training and for a system of smallholdings for specialized purposes. The Ministry was to be empowered to provide smallholdings and allotments, with financial assistance for equipping them. No financial limit was to be set, but it was estimated that it would cost about £1 million for each thousand holdings.

The Liberals (or that majority of them who followed Lloyd George) supported the Land Utilization Bill. They 'thought nationalisation was the aim and approved the proposals if not the tactics'. Lloyd George was most enthusiastic—it gave him 'real joy', he wrote to Lansbury.[67] On the second reading, the Bill received an appreciative welcome from the Liberal leader. He declared, 'This is a measure after my own heart. . . . So far as I am concerned and my friends also, I will give him [Addison] wholehearted support in any measure he likes to carry through committee.' The Conservatives opposed the Bill and it had a rough passage through the Commons as it did through the Upper House. It was severely criticized by some organs of the press. *The Times*, for example, commented, 'It is only too clear that Dr. Addison's measure cannot be regarded as an attempt to carry out the promise to make farming pay. It leaves existing farmers in their present plight and will make it worse. Its real purpose is to carry out the election pledges of the Government to reduce the number of unemployed.'[68] One historian has wrongly described the passage into law of this Bill in August 1931 as 'an irrelevant epilogue', in which the wrecking amendments of the Lords were fudged by the usual compromise. He has written that the Bill was 'dead before it ever reached the statute book'.[69] But it is quite wrong to refer to the Bill as a failure. It reached the statute book shorn only of what was originally its first clause, relating to the setting-up of a business farming corporation with a working capital of £1 million, to try out improved methods of cultivation. Addison felt that this was 'a social crime' but 'it ought to come about and I am sure it will'. Otherwise the main fabric of his measure survived. It was not unreasonably described by its author as 'the greatest land reform measure for some generations. . . . Its possibilities are immense.'[70]

The Agricultural Marketing Bill, however, was to prove more significant in the long term. It was given its second reading on 9 February 1931 and passed through the Commons on 13 July, despite the opposition of a large section of the National Farmers' Union and even of colleagues at the Ministry of Agriculture. The farmer-author, A. G. Street, was later to praise Addison warmly for fighting on behalf of the Bill despite prophecies that 'it would be a wash-out'. The Milk Marketing Board, set up in the aftermath of Addison's Act, had saved the British dairy industry from 'perdition'.[71] This is undeniable. The production of liquid milk in Wales, for instance, began a process of revival for the dairying industry of the principality, and for this the existence of the Milk Marketing Board was wholly responsible.[72] As Addison had so often emphasized, Britain possessed the finest food market in the world. Some of the chief elements in that, and who were holding their own in the difficult time now faced by the nation's agricultural industry, were those catering for that market either by specialized farming or as small cultivators. The British agriculturist could not possibly meet the requirements of that market until the standardization and marketing of British supplies had been organized to enable the producer, by combination and scientific direction, to obtain a greater share of the product of his own labours.[73]

The Marketing Bill aimed to set up marketing boards to eliminate the middle man who, until that time, had obtained a great percentage of the price paid for agricultural produce by the consumer. To raise the price for the producer and to lower it for the consumer, and thus make agricultural expansion possible, Addison proposed to allow the producers of certain agricultural products—milk, potatoes, cheese, hops, wools, cereals, livestock (and, later, fruit)—regulate the marketing of their own products by boards elected by themselves. These boards would have the power to buy the particular products from the farmer, sell it, and fix its selling-price. All the producers of a given product would be compelled to take part in the scheme, provided that a majority of producers were in favour, but the Minister himself was not to be given the power to establish a board. A high degree of autonomy was thus given to the food producers. The Agricultural Marketing Bill was passed by 190 votes to 128 when it was read a third time in July 1931.[74]

The Bill was remarkable in providing an illustration of that all-party agreement which Addison had sought in promoting agricultural reform. For example, Addison frequently conferred with Liberal members of the Standing Committee on the Bill, and adopted several Liberal suggestions for improving it.[75] The Act survived the crisis of 1931 and was widely operated by the National government thereafter, especially after the principle of protection was conceded. The governing principle of the Marketing Act was a revolutionary one in the history of British agriculture. It provided that a substantial number of farmers might compel their colleagues to market their produce in the manner, place, and quantity to be determined by a control board elected by the industry. Viscount Wolmer, a Tory, later wrote in an article in 1933,

As a political opponent of Dr. Addison, I take my hat off to him for his courage in introducing a measure that was very unpopular in the farming community at that time and which, in other hands, might have been roundly condemned by his own party as an attempt to increase the price of food. It was indeed a remarkable achievement on his part to induce a Socialist government to accept the principle that farmers, under certain safeguards, should be empowered to fix the prices of their produce at figures that gave them a fair return. In doing so, he went a long way towards the much-desired goal of taking agriculture out of party politics. A new chapter in British agriculture had begun.[76]

Walter Elliot, the Minister of Agriculture in the National government after 1931, and a good friend of Addison's since his support for the Ministry of Health in 1919, also paid warm tribute to his predecessor's pioneering work on behalf of marketing schemes and import quotas. Regulation of the home market was accompanied by the Board of Trade quota scheme developed by Elliot in 1933. The Milk Marketing Board of the same year, with similar programmes later for bacon and for eggs, was a direct legacy of Addison's achievement. Nor was endorsement of Addison's experiment in planning absent on the

The Second Labour Government

Labour side. On the contrary, Hugh Dalton and George Dallas were but two influential Labour authors who warmly commended Addison's marketing schemes.[77] The Agriculture Act passed by Tom Williams, the Minister of Agriculture under Attlee in 1947, acknowledged the success and importance of these marketing activities by putting the marketing boards and subsidies for farmers, which had loomed so large during the second world war, into more permanent form. Addison, then Labour's leader in the House of Lords, was delighted to give them public commendation.[78]

But his effective and energetic activity at the Ministry of Agriculture was overshadowed by the worsening economic crisis. The underlying stagnation in trade and unemployment, with the total of unemployed now approaching two and a half million, had continued unabated during the early months of 1931. Despite (or perhaps because of) the rival stimulus proposed by Sir Oswald Mosley's New party and by the Conservatives' pressure for protection and imperial preferences the Labour government seemed quite unable to find any remedy. The crisis suddenly became immensely more serious after the Austrian bank, Kredit Anstalt, collapsed in May; by the beginning of July the German banking system was equally in ruins. It could only be a matter of time before British gold and currency reserves and the value of the pound were also under pressure. By mid-July the flight from the pound was reaching alarming proportions and from 15 to 31 July the Bank of England was losing gold at the rate of £22 millions a day.

At the height of the crisis, the May Committee reported in dire terms—and at first without any Government pronouncement owing to the August bank holiday. The May Committee declared that by the following spring the budget would be in deficit to the total of £120 millions. It recommended the early implementation of cuts in public spending, especially in welfare payments, to the shattering amount of £96 million. The dire sense of drama conveyed in the May Report, and its forecasts of total calamity unless massive economies were introduced within a matter of weeks or even days had a traumatic effect upon the public mind. The Labour government reassembled after the holidays on 8 August to try to stem the tide. Since the government was united at least in rejecting the abandonment of the gold standard or altering the parity of the pound through devaluation, as Keynes had proposed, and with tariffs ruled out, there seemed no alternative but to implement huge cuts and then to seek a loan from bankers abroad, probably in the United States. The outcome has been fully described by Mowat, Bassett, Skidelsky, and Marquand. The Cabinet's Economy Committee came up with a package of £78.5 million, including a cut in unemployment insurance of £43.5 million (instead of the £67 million for which the Treasury had originally called in high panic). These proposals now led to deep divisions within the government. Meanwhile, on 20 August, Neville Chamberlain and Samuel Hoare, on behalf of the Conservatives, told MacDonald that in their view these huge cuts were far from sufficient. Even more critically, the General Council of the TUC told the Cabinet's Economy Committee that the cuts were far too sweeping and quite unacceptable, and that in any event the benefits paid under the unemployment insurance system must be left untouched.

This pressure by its powerful industrial wing tore the Labour movement apart. Arthur Henderson now became the spokesman of those in the Cabinet who fiercely resisted the 10 per cent cut proposed in unemployment benefit. MacDonald and a narrow majority fought in favour of it, to save the pound at its existing parity. Several Cabinet Ministers announced that they would resign if the cuts were accepted by the government. The result was that the government could agree on cuts of £56 million and no more. After hopeless disagreements between Ministers, on the evening of 23 August the Cabinet voted in favour of the cuts by 11 votes to 9. Most of these nine stated that they would now resign. Exhausted and shattered, MacDonald went to Buckingham Palace just after ten o'clock that evening to submit the resignation of the second Labour government to King George V. No one imagined that he would re-emerge the next morning as the head of a 'National' government ranged in opposition to his Labour ex-colleagues.

Christopher Addison was one of those tired, angry, bewildered ministers who took part in these fateful discussions. In a 'very confidential' series of notes on the August Cabinet crisis, apparently written some time in September, he provided a chronological account of the days of 19–24 August. It generally confirms the version accepted by most historians.[79] He emphasized here that 'no general decision was arrived at' by the Cabinet on the Economy Committee's proposals of 19 August. He also noted that MacDonald specifically brought up the suggestion of some kind of inter-party national government on 22 August (a fact not referred to in Marquand's otherwise comprehensive biography), but that the Cabinet was strongly hostile, not least Philip Snowden. Unlike some of his colleagues, Addison's position seems to have been clear and consistent throughout. Much of his career had been devoted to building up the nation's social, health, and educational services; in this there is a clear continuity between Addison the medical practitioner and Addison the politician. This had provided the cause of his violent breach with Lloyd George and resignation from the Coalition government in July 1921. No professional economist himself, Addison felt instinctively that the well-being of the poorest sections of the community was being sacrificed to placate the demands of the bankers for savage cuts in public expenditure; the government was being dictated to by the Tory minority, and by the New York banks. As an alternative policy, Addison even suggested in Cabinet that Britain might leave the gold standard, a heresy which no one else seems to have supported and which Snowden violently denounced.[80]

In the final crisis, therefore, Addison voted consistently against the 10 per cent cuts in unemployment benefit, not because of that instinctive class loyalty to the TUC which motivated Henderson, but because he felt that slashing social spending in this way was profoundly wrong, even immoral. He was one of that dissident minority of nine on 23 August who refused to support the cuts in unemployment benefit. Indeed, as A. J. P. Taylor has pointed out, he was the only middle-class member of the nine.[81] The other eight (Henderson, Clynes, Lansbury, A. V. Alexander, Adamson, Arthur Greenwood, Tom Johnston, and Graham) were all responding to the call of their working-class origins. Addison, in 1931 as in 1921, was simply responding to the call of conscience. His wife in some comparatively rare political entries in her diary, warmly applauded his decision. On 24 August, she noted: 'Daddy telephoned about saying Ramsey was going to form a National Govt. This of course puts the lid on him and for the Party's sake it is the best thing he could do. He and Snowden and Thomas will all presumably be in it so we shall be rid of these old men of the sea.' She noted that E. F. Wise of the ILP promptly rang up to congratulate her husband on his stand. When Addison attended a meeting of the parliamentary Labour party a few days later, his wife's comment was 'they seem to be preparing a pretty socialistic programme and I do hope they will put some real vim into it'.[82] She wrote to *The Times* to denounce MacDonald and Snowden for failing to show any sign of socialism over the past two years.[83]

A bitter atmosphere followed MacDonald's emergence as head of a 'National' government, including Conservatives and Liberals, but only four members of the late Labour Cabinet. Addison was the first ex-Minister to refer publicly to the events that caused the political crisis. In a speech which he made before the Swindon divisional Labour party on 26 August, he described the crisis of the past weeks. 'We were willing to balance the budget; we were all willing to make immense sacrifices; but we refused to believe that the propriety and soundness of this country is dependent upon the depression of the standard of life among working people.' He also declared that 'the break-up of the Labour Government was clearly a definite objective' in the recent crisis. This objective had for the time being been attained but in obtaining it an issue had been raised which led to only one conclusion, namely that the industry and security of the country could not be left to the dictation of the great, private banking corporations. 'The pistol that had been put to our heads was put by the controllers of the money market . . . it was utterly unconstitutional.'[74]

Addison deplored the fall of the Labour government on account of the farmers as well as the unemployed. He felt that the farmers had reasons as solid as anyone for regretting its fall. Many of the Labour government's plans for meeting the economic crises of the agricultural industry had almost matured. Understandings had been reached within the industry which cleared the way for an agricultural policy satisfactory to both farmer and worker. In other important respects the provisions of the Marketing Act were to be immediately used. He had been on the eve of producing a plan for a non-trading, regulatory wheat import board which would approach the wheat quota problem from a new angle. On the import side it contemplated a non-trading flour import board co-ordinated with a Home Flour Marketing Board.[85]

Addison repeatedly urged that the serious plight of farming could only be worsened by the National government.[86] In an outspoken article in *The Clarion* he went on to argue that the crisis had not been solved and could only be met in other ways.[87] In the press and in Parliament in September 1931 he condemned the National government, especially for passing the Gold Standard (Amendment) Bill on 21 September. This took Britain off gold. Never had a new govern-

The Second Labour Government

ment had to make such a conspicuous confession of failure in such a short time. They had been brought into being to maintain the gold standard and yet within a fortnight they had to introduce a bill to destroy the fabric which they were created to build up. While the opposition could not refuse a second reading of this Bill, the House should have some assurance that the government would do something to protect the poorest people against the rise of the cost of living.[88] Addison's advocacy of leaving the gold standard during Cabinet discussions in the last days of the Labour government added to his bitterness at his opponents' deception. Henderson had made a conciliatory speech advising the Labour party not to oppose the Gold Standard (Amendment) Bill. But, as Marquand records, in spite of his advice, 112 Labour members voted against the second reading.[89] Addison (who spoke in the debate) abstained, but he was amongst those who criticized Henderson's over-moderate approach at a meeting of the parliamentary Labour party. The former wrote to Addison in irritated terms though with predictably little effect:

> I note what you say regarding the necessity for my services as leader if there is to be any revival of progress in this country, but I am not yet free from the feeling that when a successor to MacDonald had to be appointed not sufficient consideration was given to the claims upon my time.
>
> Further, if I am to be called upon to make speeches, I must be free to exercise my own judgement as to the nature of the speeches necessary to suit the occasion. . . . May I say that I also felt that whatever your intentions were, when I had stated that we were not to oppose the Bill, the matter might have been left there without running the risk of encouraging, by another speech, a very definite opposition, which was indeed manifest even up to the Second Reading of the Bill . . . the position not only of the country but of the Party is so serious that we really must pull together as much as possible. It is only by the most limited co-operation that we are going to survive these very difficult times.[90]

Addison also attacked the government's Economy Bill in Parliament, especially the fact that the details were not going to be discussed in the House of Commons even though it was going to leave multitudes of the population with much less money to spend at a time when prices were going to rise.[91] Here again, he reflected Labour's bitterness at the formation of the National government: earlier he had strongly supported the expulsion of MacDonald, Snowden, and Thomas, those 'old men of the sea', from the parliamentary Labour party on 28 August.

By the end of September 1931 pressure for a general election to give a 'doctor's mandate' for the government was mounting. Addison was well prepared. He had kept in close touch with his Swindon constituency since his election in 1929. He had contributed a weekly article to the *Swindon Advertiser* on parliamentary notes and sent a monthly news-sheet as to the record to date of the Labour government.[92] His election address declared that the election had been forced unnecessarily upon the country by the so-called National government, even though the sections which comprised it were unable to agree on any sort of policy and represented only the great financial interests and the protectionists. The main issue in the election was whether the country was to be ruled by financiers and consent to all-round reductions in the standard of living, or was the country to rule them and be free to develop its own resources for the benefit of all. Stafford Cripps spoke at one election meeting in his support.[93] Behind the atmosphere of panic in which the election had been called there was, he claimed, an attempt to smash socialism. Addison conducted a vigorous, aggressive campaign in Swindon. He was supported by both Labour and Lloyd George Liberals and was assisted by a squad of canvassers from Oxford University Labour Club.[94] But he was defeated by his old rival, the former Conservative member for Swindon, Sir Reginald Mitchell Banks, by 4,794 votes.[95] Addison did remarkably well in the circumstances, to increase the Labour vote by 1,000, and his share of the poll from 43 per cent to 44.1 per cent. No Liberal stood in 1931, and the flight of 7,000 Liberal voters to the Tories cost him his seat.

Thus, like most of his colleagues, Addison was swept away in the 'doctor's mandate' general election of October 1931. The tally of Labour MPs fell from 280 to 46. His career, for a second time, was apparently over. However, his reputation had been fully sustained at the Ministry of Agriculture. Indeed, the National government, as has been shown, were to make ample use of the marketing and other agricultural measures he inaugurated during his period as Minister of Agriculture and the Liberals, too, endorsed his policies. In October 1931 Lloyd George commented that they 'constituted by far and away the best contribution to the revival of agriculture and rural life which I recall during the whole of my experience'.[96] Beaverbrook, when congratulating Addison on his term of administration, felt that 'if you had had good colleagues, I know you would have been the greatest Minister of Agriculture in history'.[97] Addison had achieved his ambition of removing agricultural questions from the field of party politics. In the event, his capacity for survival was far from exhausted. His career was only beginning a new chapter. Although now in his sixty-third year, his health remained good and his zest for public service undiminished. The years of opposition after 1931 were to give him a new creative role and a new authority. As in 1921, his political odyssey had far from concluded. With further years of ministerial experience behind him, he was admirably placed to help inaugurate a new phase in the British progressive tradition.

8
From Slump to Victory

After the crisis of 1931 the Labour party moved left, and Addison moved left with it. The way in which the second Labour government had been driven from office had a profound impact on party workers throughout the country. Memories of the so-called 'bankers' ramp' of 1931 convinced many people on the left that a Labour or Socialist government would never be given a fair opportunity to carry out its programme so long as the capitalist system remained. The Crown, the Civil Service, the banks, the heads of privately owned industries, were all, it was claimed, determined to ensure that a democratically elected Labour government could never fulfil its mandate and carry out socialist change. In the annual party conferences at Leicester in 1932, Hastings in 1933, and Southport in 1934, motions were carried which denounced the private capitalist system in Marxist terms and committed Labour to sweeping programmes of public ownership of the banks, transport, major industries, and the land. The newly formed Socialist League, founded in 1932, pressed for more extreme policies still. Through spokesmen such as Stafford Cripps, it demanded that the next Labour government pass a programme of emergency powers on attaining office, and institute a kind of temporary dictatorship. Cripps also urged that the Labour party join with the Communists in an anti-fascist 'United Front'. Although these more extreme proposals never became official Labour party policy, their prominence, especially at the Hastings party conference in 1933 showed how profound had been the reaction of Labour activists after the 1931 crisis.

Addison, himself, reflected these changes. He was now in a position of considerable seniority within the party. According to Hugh Dalton, had Addison or any other members of the parliamentary executive (Henderson, Clynes, Graham, Johnston, Dalton, Greenwood, Pethick-Lawrence, Shinwell, and Lees-Smith) been re-elected to Parliament, almost any one of this list would either have been chosen leader in the next Parliament, in preference to Lansbury, or deputy leader in preference to Attlee, particularly as both of these were London MP's and the latter not a member of either the national or late parliamentary executive.[1] Many of the older generation of leaders—Henderson, Lansbury, Clynes, and Graham, for instance—gradually retired from front-line politics, while others, of course, had joined the National government. Addison, however, remained as a senior and authoritative figure in the party's ranks. He was never an adherent of the Socialist League, even though it included such old colleagues as E. F. Wise and Sir Charles Trevelyan. Wise had written to congratulate Addison on his stand in 1931 and Addison did lecture to the League in March 1933. In 1937 he and G. D. H. Cole were to try to resist the expulsion of Socialist League members from the party.[2] But he remained anchored in the centrist mainstream, rather than in leftish backwaters.

Addison's speeches in the period he spent out of Parliament after the 1931 election clearly reflect an increasingly radical tone in Labour thinking. It was an outlook that, as usual, his wife strongly shared. She felt that the very existence of the National government was a triumph for 'dirty work' and 'false tongues'.[3] As Addison himself wrote when preparing notes for a talk to a Labour party week-end conference at Easton Lodge in April 1932, the previous general election had witnessed 'an almost unique opportunity for a combination of forces—propagandist, financial, industrial and pseudo-patriotic—against us'.[4] Fifteen years later, in a debate on the creation of the International Monetary Fund, Addison took the opportunity to reiterate his disgust for the pressures of international finance and of the banks upon the Labour government in 1931.[5]

One result of the concern in Labour ranks with the events of 1931 was the new attention paid to the structure of the party and the workings of Parliament. Addison was a leading figure in the Labour party inquiries which were set up to overhaul the machinery of the party. In April 1932 he was sent a memorandum by his friend, Frank Wise; this reflected the views of the committee of the Independent Labour party, including Fenner Brockway, David Kirkwood, John Paton, and Wise himself. It had been given official approval by the National Administrative Council, the executive body of the ILP. It urged that any future Labour government must be subjected to control by the party rank and file. It should conform to the spirit of standing orders by carrying out decisions of the annual party conference or else gain the approval of the parliamentary Labour party for matters not covered by conference decisions. The consultative committee of the last Labour government was thought to have been entirely ineffective; the gulf between the party workers in the constituencies and the government at Westminster had been a major factor in the schism of 1931.[6] The ILP was now too peripheral a body to carry much weight, and Addison could not do much with this memorandum. But pressure for greater party democracy in Labour's ranks did yield results, notably the reform of the composition of the national executive of the party in 1932.

Addison also attended a meeting of the joint committee of the national and parliamentary party, and of the party national executive, called in April 1932 to consider internal party cohesion. The main discussion concerned a resolution from the parliamentary Labour party which called for an inquiry into the procedure to be followed after any future victorious election, with reference to the choice of a Prime Minister, the membership of a Labour government, and the policy to be outlined in the King's Speech.[7] Here again was another attempt to make Labour's leaders accountable to the rank and file and to curb the excesses of leadership which were thought to have led to the aberrant policies of MacDonald and Snowden.

The most important body created to discuss these and other matters was the Labour party's 'House of Commons group'. This was a powerful team drawn from all sections of the party. It included trade unionists like Charlie Cramp and Arthur Pugh, academics and intellectuals like G. D. H. Cole, Mary Agnes Hamilton, R. H. Tawney, Edward Radice, and Harold Laski, members of parliament like Attlee, Cripps, and Shinwell, and other notable Labour politicians among them J. F. Horrabin and Addison. This produced a 'Labour Programme for Action' in May 1932.[8] This draft became the basis for continuing discussions by the group which went on throughout 1932. In October of that year it was decided that it should meet weekly on Fridays, so the name 'Friday Group' was adopted. This was one of several new bodies created at this time with the object of rethinking Labour policy in fundamental respects; the 'XYZ' body, in which Nicholas Davenport, Dalton, the young Hugh Gaitskell, and Douglas Jay among others tried to direct Labour thinking towards problems of

From Slump to Victory 211

credit and finance, was a similar creation. The Friday Group conducted purely informal discussions on constitutional aspects of Labour party policy on a confidential, non-publishable basis.[9] Various memoranda were produced by its members, Dalton on the reform of parliamentary procedure, Cole on Parliament, Shinwell on the reconstruction of the Cabinet. Addison himself wrote on the procedure of the House of Commons.[10] In this, he laid especial emphasis on the need to give more power to private members of parliament. He frequently took the chair at meetings of the Friday Group, which confirmed his stature and seniority in the party.

Like others in the party, Addison fully shared the general anxiety about the nature of Labour's leadership after MacDonald's recent conduct as Prime Minister. At the annual party conference in 1933, he gave strong support to a motion designed to tie the hands of the leader of any future Labour government. He declared again that special efforts should be made to ensure that no future Labour government should be subjected to dictation by the Treasury as the last one had been.[11] In 1934, he argued that the same financial policy which had destroyed the Labour administration in 1931 was still dictating the programme of the present National government. Even in 1944 he was to refer bitterly to memories of the 'bankers' ramp'.

I, for my part, can never get away from the horrid memories of the years from 1929 to 1935 during which the management of our fate nationally was largely in the control of the central banks. It is essential in future that national control of major matters of financial policy should remain within the government of the country and must not be the business of any semi-independent private corporation.[12]

The conclusion he reached, of course, was the need for the public ownership of the Bank of England.

His criticisms of the National government at this period were unrelenting. He attacked it for its lack of a constructive policy on housing, and took an active part in the Labour party's Housing Committee which proposed the creation of a central housing authority.[13] These were years when the ribbon development of cheap suburban houses for the middle-class owner-occupier extended around most major cities. But, as Addison argued, so far as the reclamation of slum property in deprived parts of inner cities was concerned, Britain was no better off than it had been in 1919. There was cheap money, a supply of raw materials, and labour available—and yet the need for a large number of houses at rents which working people could afford to pay was as urgent as ever. Nor had housing been placed under the direction of any specific authority. He also savaged the government for its failures to reduce significantly the toll of unemployment and for the inadequacies of its 'depressed areas' policy for the older industrial regions. He told the Friday Group, 'I hope we shall never repeat the quackeries of J. H. Thomas.'[14]

On the other hand, it would have been quite unlike Addison to take a wholly partisan view of the nation's social and economic problems. In particular, he was concerned that agriculture should, as far as possible, be removed from partisan contention. While he denounced the National government's policy as the traditional Tory one of 'higher tariffs and lower wages',[15] he found much to applaud in the policies carried out by Walter Elliot at the Ministry of Agriculture after 1932. With Elliot himself (an old Unionist supporter of the Coalition in 1918–22), he enjoyed a good relationship. Elliot, once a doctor like Addison, had gained a reputation as a health reformer when he first became an MP in 1918 and had warmly supported Addison's housing and health reforms in the post-war years.[16] The Marketing Act, initiated by Addison and passed through the Commons by the Labour government in July 1931, was retained. Marketing boards for farm produce were set up extensively by Elliot with powers given to the Board of Trade for fixing quotas for the importation of certain specified products from abroad. The Milk Marketing Board of 1933 was the largest marketing scheme and was generally approved by Addison. On the other hand, when quotas and tariffs failed to give adequate protection or incentive to the farmer, direct subsidies and guaranteed prices were increasingly advocated. The marketing boards were more concerned with profit margins than with efficient distribution of foodstuffs.

Throughout the thirties, Addison remained Labour's chief spokesman on agriculture. At the Labour party conference at Leicester in 1932, he strongly supported a resolution which called for a comprehensive national plan for agriculture. This meant the national ownership and management of land, to secure financial stability and a decent standard of living for the competent producer. The next socialist government should be equipped with powers to deal with the control of food prices, with marketing and supply, and with the protection of the standards of production.[17]

His experience at the Ministry of Agriculture had convinced him that marketing schemes for produce would flourish only if they had the financial backing of the Treasury. At the Labour party conference in 1933, a resolution was carried which endorsed a scheme whereby socialized credit applied to retail prices was to be used to enable the home market to absorb as much as it needed of the home industry's output of consumable goods. Addison warned in this debate, 'as one who has suffered at the hands of the Treasury', that they would be paralysed until they settled basic questions of finance, both for producers and for agricultural labourers. One of his regrets about the débâcle of 1931 was that his proposals for improvements for the standard of living of farm labourers had disappeared. Labour, he declared, was still the only party that had put forward a comprehensive policy for land and for agriculture.[18]

He was a natural choice for the Labour party Policy Committee on Agriculture set up in 1932. He wrote to Jim Middleton, the national party agent in 1932, of the members of this Committee,

> I found them determined upon the development of a definite Socialist policy and eager for it to be prepared and stated in a very practical form so that they could use the present opportunity for conducting propaganda in its support. . . . It is most urgent that in respect of such governing questions as Finance, Banking, Trade and Industrial Development, including land and rural development, that we should satisfy their demand with the least possible delay.[19]

There was a political aspect to all this—Labour's need to win more of the rural vote. The party was still heavily based on the industrial and urban areas of Britain, especially those associated with the old staple industries. Such few seats as Labour had held in East Anglia or rural Wales had been lost in 1931. In the summer of 1933, under Addison's direction, Labour launched a rural campaign in 'one hundred and fifty villages and country towns'.[20] At these, speakers addressed the voters on aspects of Labour's agricultural policy, Addison himself spoke at many of them, with Stafford Cripps as one of his main assistants.[21] He and George Dallas organized a series of week-end schools at Oxford to back up this propaganda drive.[22] Despite a meagre budget, this campaign had some impact. The Agricultural Workers' Union increased in membership by 15,000, partly as a result of its efforts, while constituency Labour parties in rural areas were much strengthened. The campaign was continued in

1934 and 1935. Even so, Labour's foothold in the rural parts of Britain, apart from the special circumstances of a traditional radical vote in parts of Wales and Scotland, remained relatively weak.

In 1933, Gollancz published a volume on *The Problems of a Socialist Government*. Its authors were distinctly on the left of the party, and formed a distinguished group—Attlee, C. P. Trevelyan, Wise, Cripps, Horrabin, and G. D. H. Cole amongst others. Addison wrote on 'Socialist Policy and the Problem of Food Supply'; here he reiterated his previous defence of marketing and quota schemes which were now firmly established policy. Despite this partisan company, however, Addison as has been seen always sought to transcend party politics when agriculture was involved. In his enthusiasm for the Marketing Acts, in particular, he reflected something of the bipartisan zeal for 'planning' and for 'the middle way', current throughout the thirties. The 'Next Five Years' group, associated with Harold Macmillan and others in the middle years of the decade gave a general, if modified, support to policies on marketing and land settlement which Addison had sponsored.[23] His concern to remove agriculture from partisan controversy was well known to the Minister of Agriculture, Walter Elliot, himself a broad-minded and imaginative man as well as an old friend. In October 1933, Elliot appointed a new Reorganization Commission to direct the marketing of eggs and poultry, and asked Addison to become its chairman. After checking with Lansbury that it had Labour's approval, he agreed.[24] *The Times*, for once, welcomed Addison's appointment. It hoped that it marked 'the beginning of a real success in devising a beneficial policy for agriculture, exempt from the cries of "dear food" and immune from the consequences of political change'.[25] These hopes were not to be disappointed. Addison (whose precarious finances no doubt benefited from this appointment) worked hard at his new post. He travelled as far as Northern Ireland to work out a scheme for co-operation between poultry-keepers there and in England and Wales.[26] When he resigned as chairman in October 1934 to stand as Labour candidate in the by-election at Swindon, he wrote to Elliot,

> I should be even more sorry than I am to be obliged to take this step were it not that I and my colleagues have reached agreement upon all the essentials of the scheme and are so well advanced on the detailed consideration of our report that the important interests concerned need not be jeopardised by delay. I feel confident that the results obtained will justify the effort and that the spirit of

From Slump to Victory 215

co-operation shown by all interests will be a valuable example for the future.[27]

Although the highly individualist producers of eggs and poultry rejected a marketing board on the same lines as that set up for milk and for bacon, co-operative methods within this specialized section of agriculture were notably enhanced.

Addison the political activist was never far below the surface despite all this bipartisan work. In particular, he continued to be involved in trying to build up the contacts established in 1930-1 between the Labour party and David Lloyd George. In that period, much of the old intimacy between the two former Liberal colleagues had been restored. Addison's enthusiasm for working with Lloyd George was certainly not shared by his wife. She well remembered the bad old days of 1921, and sensed that Lloyd George was not to be relied upon. 'It would be fatal to work with him . . . a great misfortune he is not to be trusted, because there is no doubt he could lead', she wrote on 11 November 1931 after her husband had had a further meeting with his former chief.[28] In fact, Lloyd George's political strength was very limited after the general election of 1931. He had declared against the National government at that election, but only a family group of three other members, all representing rural Welsh constituencies, followed his lead. Nevertheless, Lloyd George's cross-party prestige in domestic and foreign affairs alike was still very high. It was by no means inconceivable that he might yet again enter the government, perhaps to press home his public works schemes for grappling with unemployment. Addison was one of those anxious to bring the ex premier more directly into mainstream politics by enabling him to work with Labour. Certainly he and Lloyd George were increasingly amicable at this time. This is reflected in the highly complimentary references to Addison contained in Lloyd George's *War Memoirs* which were being written in the early thirties.[29] Addison consulted him at Churt on detailed matters affecting agriculture, as early as March 1932; later in 1937 he was to seek his advice on the desirability of accepting a peerage.[30] In the by-election at Swindon in 1934, Lloyd George declared that if he had a vote in that constituency he would cast it for Addison and urged Liberals to do the same.

This was very far from being the first reconciliation between the two former friends as the press sometimes maintained. Lloyd George was well aware of Addison's enthusiasm for his co-operating with Labour in the thirties. He discussed with Addison an interview he had had with George Lansbury in late 1934 on the prospects of arranging an understanding between the Labour and Liberal parties, 'which would avoid mere cut-throat fights between progressives in all parties at the next election'. He went on:

I made it clear to them that I had no desire to make any terms about office for myself or any of my friends. I was only anxious the next Parliament should be neither reactionary, nor like the Parliament of 1929 purely futile owing to lack of co-operation between those who, in the main, are strong for the same thing—a betterment in the conditions of life for the multitude. I suggested that the test of common action in the constituencies should be the programme for which candidates stand. You and I have the same purpose in mind—the return of a Parliament which will carry through a real progressive policy. . . . I have never put party first, nor have you. I shall do my best between now and the next election to promote the return of men who will help to make the next Parliament one of real and beneficial action. . . . I have been hoping that all persons who wanted things done would come together. . . . But I am afraid the party demon will prove too strong for us. Attlee and Lansbury . . . are genuinely distressed with the present social and economic muddle and they are disgusted with the failure of this Government to grapple with it. . . . Why not act with them to the limit of possible agreement?[31]

On 14 November, a month before receiving this letter, Addison had met Lloyd George at Churt and they had discussed 'the possibility of Lloyd George and Labour coming to a bargain over seats at the next election'. Addison had then arranged Lloyd George's meeting with Lansbury.[32] He also agreed to discuss Lloyd George's letter of 12 December with Attlee and Lansbury.[33] Nothing came of these electoral plans; but in June 1935 Lloyd George again dined with Addison, at the Reform Club. Lloyd George declared here that the leadership of the Labour party was 'about as bad as that of the generals in the war'. Sylvester, Lloyd George's secretary who was present at this lunch meeting, noted that 'Addison demurred'.[34] Addison and Lansbury, however, accepted an invitation to the convention that summer that was to launch Lloyd George's Council of Action for Peace and Reconstruction. But they played no subsequent direct part in Lloyd George's ultimately abortive campaign. Nevertheless, Addison remained sufficiently close to his former leader to be invited to serve as a trustee of the Lloyd George Fund, which indeed he had himself strongly condemned in the twenties. He was apparently willing, but his appointment was vetoed by another trustee, Lord St. David's, on the ground that the fund was solely Liberal in origins whereas Addison was a prominent figure in the Labour party.[35] On balance, Addison's continuing flirtation with Lloyd George was a testimony to the fluid cross-party patterns of the thirties without suggesting any permanent deviation from the Labour party and its main lines of strategy.

Addison's first concern during the years after 1931, of course, was to get back into Parliament. He had now to continue this quest alone. His wife, his loyal, radical supporter for thirty-two years, died on 22 August. Addison continued to live at Peterley Farm in Buckinghamshire, with his eldest son, Christopher, and his wife, Bridget. His daughters, Isobel and Kate, and the younger son, Michael, all got married during the thirties, but the family remained a closely knit one. His bereavement merely launched Addison, for all his sixty-five years, even more determinedly into political activity. He had kept up his contact with his former constituency at Swindon; such leading Labour figures as Lansbury, Henderson, Cripps, Arthur Greenwood, and Ernest Bevin had addressed meetings there on his behalf since 1931. Now he got his chance. In October 1934 a by-election was called at Swindon after the appointment to a judgeship of Sir Reginald Mitchell-Banks, the Tory member whom Addison had defeated in 1929 but who had beaten him in 1931. Addison's pre-election speeches took the usual Labour line of stressing the ineptitude and drift of the National government in the past three years. Like Labour men generally, he placed much emphasis now on foreign affairs. There had been a drift towards war; Britain had failed to exercise her influence with determination in the councils of the League of Nations; the work of the Disarmament Conference had been interrupted by frequent postponements. At home, there was poverty and mass unemployment. His election address called for public controls of the banks and the currency supply, and a policy of planning for industry, together with social themes like abolishing the means test.[36]

It was reported in the press that 'a big rally of Liberals to Dr. Addison's support is anticipated as a result of Lloyd George having given his blessing to the Labour fight against the National Conservative candidate'.[37] The omens nationally were favourable to Labour after big swings at Rotherham, East Fulham, and other recent contests. Even in the election of 1931, after all, Addison had increased

Labour's poll. The Liberal *News Chronicle* considered that Addison's election was 'virtually certain'.[38] His opponent was Wavell Wakefield, a former English rugby captain of much sporting celebrity. One of Labour's campaign songs included the chorus, 'Who'll beat "Rugger" Wakefield?', to be sung to the tune of 'Who killed Cock Robin?' In the event, Addison achieved a swing of over 9 per cent and was returned with a majority of 2,649. Thus Labour gained its eighth seat since the election of 1931 (the others being Wednesbury, Rotherham, Wakefield, North Lambeth, East Fulham, Upton, and North Hammersmith). Attlee wrote in rare delight, 'It will be splendid having you in the House again, what with yours and Strauss and G. L.'s return we shall have a great first day of it.'[39] G. R. Strauss had a few days earlier retained Vauxhall with a handsome majority. After the poll, Addison had lunch with Wakefield, his defeated and much younger Conservative opponent. He gave him, in all amiability, the advice that he should seek a safer seat elsewhere as he had no hope of defeating himself at Swindon.[40]

During his second period as member for Swindon, Addison took a vigorous part in House of Commons debates. He launched a fierce attack on the government's feeble efforts to relieve unemployment by their Depressed Areas Bill. One of the worst things the government had done was to end the excellent organization for allotments which Sir William Waterlow had developed with the assistance of the Ministry of Agriculture and the county councils, by which 60,000 men had been provided with allotments and had been trained at the trivial cost of 7*s.* per head per year.[41] He also pressed for the setting up of a National Investment Board, which Labour now demanded. 'We stand for the safeguarding of the uninformed public against exploitation'.[42]

He was also active in condemning government policy on peace and disarmament. In 1932 he had written an article for the National Press Bureau on 'The Power of Nations to Prevent War'. In this, he had urged positive action from the International Disarmament Conference. Arms provided no security, but the absence of an alternative forced the French, for instance, to cling to them.[43] In March 1935 he and other Labour members attacked the government's arms policy in the light of the new Defence White Paper. This Paper provided for increased armaments, notably the air force, at a time when the Foreign Secretary, Simon, was engaged on a peace mission. This, in

Addison's quasi-pacifist view, was a piece of monumental idiocy.[44] Here and in other respects, Addison fully reflected the anti-war mood of the socialist left at the time. In a further debate on 29 May he urged the government to assume the necessary powers to compel the limiting of profits for industries involved in the rearmament programme. This led to a fierce exchange with Sir Philip Cunliffe-Lister (formerly Lloyd-Graeme, his ministerial colleague of Coalition days in 1920 and now Secretary for Air). He claimed that the government preferred to act by agreement whereas Addison had a 'passion for coercion'.[45]

Addison gave evidence before the Royal Commission set up in 1935 to consider the private manufacture of and trading in arms. He described his experiences at the Ministry of Munitions when reliance on private enterprise methods of manufacture had proved to be a total failure. Efficiency had only been achieved when a state department responsible for the manufacture, assembly, and distribution of all munitions of war, was set up. His evidence before the Royal Commission was regarded as being of considerable value. In the view of A. J. Cummings in the *News Chronicle*, he had presented a devastating case against the manufacture of arms for private profit.[46] His expertise in the general field of munitions production and armaments policy was well known in Labour circles; it was a field in which Labour speakers tended to rely on emotion rather than on factual knowledge. Thus, Addison wrote for the editor of *Labour* in July 1935 an article dealing with the government's control of prices and of costing procedures in the manufacture of armaments. Even though the recommendations of the Royal Commission achieved relatively little, Addison had made his own contribution to the 'merchants of death' controversy, similar to that aroused by the Nye Committee in the United States at about the same time.

Addison seems to have somewhat neglected his Swindon constituency after his return as its member in 1934. In the general election of October 1935, he faced Wavell Wakefield as his opponent once again, despite having tried to warn him off previously. In his election address, Addison repeated his criticisms of the government's objectives and foreign policy. The real reason for the election being called was for the government to receive a mandate for a huge rearmament programme which would screen its failures to deal with unemployment at home. The government's foreign policy had not continued the determinedly peacemaking policy of Arthur Henderson. If it had, there would have been no breakdown of the Disarmament Conference, no desertion of the League of Nations by Japan and Germany, no reversion of Europe to a state of peril and armed confrontation. Addison emphasized Labour's support for the League of Nations—though, apparently, without the arms to make collective security function. Wakefield, by contrast, dwelt on the need to build up the air force, partly on grounds of increased employment. Addison then produced posters which used W. W. W., his opponent's initials—'Wakefield Wants War'. To Wakefield himself, these tactics seemed a great political error.[47] A bigger majority for Addison was predicted by the local Swindon newspaper. In the election, Labour regained some lost ground. It returned 154 MPs compared with only 46 in 1931. But Addison was not amongst them. Very surprisingly, he was defeated by Wavell Wakefield who achieved a swing of 4.6 per cent and a majority of 975 votes.

After the election, the Swindon Labour party held an inquiry into this unexpected defeat. One fact often mentioned was Addison's relative failure to nurse the constituency in the way that Wakefield had done.[48] He had certainly shown signs of over-confidence prior to the poll, and less than his usual thoroughness and obsessive attention to detail. However, the historian may see the fundamental cause of his defeat in the likelihood of a marginal seat like Swindon (and, indeed, East Fulham, which the Conservatives also regained) proving more sympathetic to the government at a general election than in a by-election protest vote. There was great dismay in Labour circles. One defeated candidate called it 'disgraceful' that 'a mere sportsman' should have defeated Addison. Frederick Pethick-Lawrence thought it 'a great loss to the House'. William Jowitt, ex-Liberal and ex-National Labour, felt that the Swindon electors, who had voted for the rugby international, Wakefield, had 'obviously preferred brawn to brains'.[49] This last explanation is unlikely. Swindon was no citadel of rugby football: its main sporting institution was Swindon Town, a soccer team. The election result, however, did not cause universal grief. Neville Chamberlain, the Chancellor of the Exchequer, wrote to his sister, Ida, 'I am thankful that Samuel is out [at Darwen] and I rejoice too that that miserable cur Addison has been defeated.'[50] Addison for his part retained sour memories of Chamberlain's mishandling of labour problems in 1917. It was an ironic twist that, two

From Slump to Victory

years later, Addison was to become the only Labour peer that Neville Chamberlain created.

Addison did not seem to be in the least downcast by his defeat at Swindon, and continued his work on behalf of the Labour party. He now played an important senior role in the planning cadres of the party. His stature was enhanced when his good friend, Clement Attlee, was elected leader of the party on 26 November 1935. Attlee had greatly deplored Addison's defeat in the election. 'We should especially have needed your services in this Parliament. We must hope that some by-election will come along to get you back.'[51] This gave Addison further zest for the fight. In 1937, he made a bid to be elected to the constituency section of the national executive of the Labour party. Although unsuccessful, he polled well, gaining 117,000 votes, only 38,000 less than D. N. Pritt, the lowest polling of the seven elected.[52]

Another sign of Addison's importance lay in his association with the Fabian Society (of which he was a member until his death). More specifically, he was associated with the New Fabian Research Bureau, a broad-based ideas group founded by G. D. H. Cole and others in March 1931 and now including most of Labour's leading intellectuals.[53] Addison was asked whether he would serve as its chairman in succession to Attlee. The secretary, Margaret Cole, wrote that it was 'very important for us to have a chairman who is a keen socialist, in touch with the party and alive to the importance of research'. Her husband, G. D. H. Cole, had strongly urged Addison to continue as chairman in 1935 because it was important to have 'someone of outstanding position in the party in order to give it the requisite status with Transport House'.[54] In fact, Addison was to serve as chairman from 1933 until he became a peer in 1937. Harold Clay and G. D. H. Cole were the vice-chairmen of this intellectually formidable body, with G. R. Mitchison as treasurer and Margaret Cole as secretary. The executive members included such coming men as the young economist, Hugh Gaitskell. Addison happened to preside over a thriving period in the NFRB's fortunes. Its membership increased, according to the NFRB journal, from 400 to 637 in the period 1935–7, while the Bureau's 'Second Five year Plan' was inaugurated at this period.[55] He was elected an honorary member of the Fabian Society in 1939 for his services rendered to the New Fabian Research Bureau.[56] The Fabians also enabled him to extend his contacts with distinguished overseas socialists, for instance with Walter Nash, then the Minister of Finance in the New Zealand Labour government, with whom he was to have a fruitful association years later when at the Dominions Office under Attlee.

Addison also took part in more mundane aspects of Labour activism. As has been seen, he was heavily involved in the party's intensive recruiting and propaganda campaign, especially in rural areas. He continued to crusade for agricultural reform. In 1938, he summarized the agricultural policy being pursued under three headings—that the best productive use be made of the land, that the producer should have an assured price for his produce in the home market and be protected from exploitation so that he could keep his production costs at a stable level, and that every worker on the land should have decent wages and conditions of work. When farming was made prosperous all over Britain after implementing Labour's plan, then unemployment would be directly reduced by the thousands who would be attracted back to the land. A vital object of Labour's programme was to impress upon the whole of the community the close relationship between the interests of the countryside and the town[57]

He was also active as an author in these years. In 1934 he produced two further volumes of important reminiscences, *Four and a Half Years*, published by Hutchinson. They covered somewhat similar ground to *Politics from Within* but had the added value for the historian of being full of verbatim entries from Addison's diary for the years 1914 to 1918. Even the *British Medical Journal*, which felt constrained to make petty criticisms of the layout and illustrations of the books, nevertheless admitted their value as a mine of information for these crucial years in British political history.[58] Addison's published diaries have been a staple for historians of the period ever since. But he was more involved in writing about the present and future than about the past, with agriculture his major priority. He produced two major policy documents, *Labour's Policy for our Countryside*, published by the Labour Publishing Company in 1937, and *A Policy for British Agriculture* in 1939. In the former, he advocated the national ownership of land; fair rents and financial assistance for tenant farmers; guaranteed prices for produce; the control of imperial produce along with marketing boards for home produce; a national minimum wage; improved housing and better water and light supplies for agricultural labourers. It was a neat and comprehensive survey of the range of agricultural proposals that Addison had been pouring forth over the last ten years. *A Policy for British Agriculture* was a substantial, well-documented volume of three hundred pages, published by Gollancz for the Left Book Club early in 1939. It was actually completed during Addison's second honeymoon in the late autumn of 1937. Here he spelt out his views on long-term agricultural policy at length; it may serve as his political testament in his lifelong crusade to secure a new deal for the countryside. As he had done since 1910, he urged that land be nationally owned. But this was only a means to an end. The Labour party should build upon this basis a structure which would lead to the more efficient and productive use of land, which would stem the tide of emigration from rural areas, give security of tenure to farmers, and a happier and more fulfilling life to all who worked in agriculture. He described in much detail the action needed in raising prices for producers, the machinery for land management, the procedure for the public acquisition of land, its mortgaging and development, and the control of imports. An important section of the book was an argument in favour of the more imaginative use of the Marketing Boards set up since 1931, including a much more extensive use of them in the supply and transportation of foodstuffs. The whole work was a plea for reversing the neglect and disuse of the countryside. In passing, Lloyd George's plans in 1930 for settling 100,000 families as smallholders or family farmers on three million acres of land were generally commended. The book ended on a note of unusual passion for Addison; it revealed that deep attachment to his native soil that underlay a somewhat laconic exterior. 'It is our Land. We love it, every one of us. Let us throw down the challenge to adversity.'[59]

The book sold well and was widely reviewed. One London newspaper welcomed it as giving Addison deserved prominence after some years' relative obscurity since 1931[60]—though this would surely weigh little with so modest a public figure. The *Yorkshire Post* heralded it as 'the most elaborate statement of his party's agricultural policy so far made. . . . In his role of critic, Dr. Addison is devastating.'[61] *The Spectator* thought his description of the present state of farming and his analysis of current problems to be 'in the main accurate and fair'. The *Glasgow Herald* struck a more critical note. It thought the book too vague on the details of the guaranteed price system. 'In this respect, Lord Addison's book has the same fault as the Labour party's official farming policy. It seems to avoid the task of making price policy clear and definite.'[62] The *Listener*, however, felt that the work would 'find a place by the side of Thomas Tusser, William Cobbett, Lord Ernle and Sir Daniel Hall', while even the National Farmers' Union, critical of anything that resembled nationalization of the land, wrote amiably on Addison's book.[63] On balance, his book, while inevitably unspectacular and somewhat stilted in presentation, is a major contribution to the literature on British agriculture. It shows how its now septuagenarian author was still very much in the vanguard of reform and improvement. In terms of developments on the land during and after the second world war, it is a work of remarkably prophetic insight. Addison's last major work on practical political issues, it serves as a worthy monument to his enterprise and imagination as a creative public figure.

His private and public lives were both transformed at this time. As has been noted his wife had died in August 1934; since then he had lived with his eldest son, Christopher, and his wife. Then in November 1937 he remarried. His second wife, Dorothy Low, came from a contrasting political background.[64] Her father, Percy, was a Conservative agent for the Spelthorne division of Middlesex. He had also been a cycling enthusiast and president of the National Cyclists Union. She first met Addison soon after his parliamentary defeat in 1931; she was active in journalism, an agent for the press, and she helped arrange for the publication of interviews by Addison in the daily newspapers. Addison's second marriage was to prove quite as happy as the first. His second wife was no less of a loyal support in his still active public career; poised and attractive, she was thoroughly at ease in the political world, while always treasuring their week-ends together in the quiet Buckinghamshire countryside. From the outset, Addison's political career impinged massively on their private lives; as has been seen, he completed the draft of his book on agriculture during his honeymoon and his wife typed it out for him then. He still had many years of active and creative work in political life ahead of him. It is difficult to visualize this elderly man with his slight physique surviving them in such good fettle without the devotion and moral support of his loyal domestic partner.

Politically, the great change in Addion's life came in June 1937 when the new Prime Minister, Neville Chamberlain, his old enemy, had the ironic task of elevating Addison to the peerage as the first

Baron Addison of Stallingborough. He was introduced in the House of Lords on 30 June 1937. He had been very much in two minds about Baldwin's original offer of a peerage and had consulted Lloyd George, among others. Addison wrote to Baldwin 'It tears my heart to be separated from the House of Commons.'[65] In Shoreditch in 1910 he had campaigned for the abolition of the House of Lords; this body had gravely obstructed his work while at the Ministries of Health and Agriculture. But he had since come to acknowledge that the Lords might serve some constructive purpose.[66] Of course, a peerage would assure him an active part in parliamentary life, whereas he was now in his late sixties, without a seat in the Commons, and no immediate likelihood of returning there. His entry into the Upper House was a notable reinforcement for the thin ranks of Labour peers, and he was greeted with much enthusiasm by Lord Strabolgi, formerly J. M. Kenworthy MP and another ex-Liberal.[67] Addison felt at once thoroughly at home in his new surroundings. He began to take a vigorous part in Lords' debates where he soon became an influential spokesman.

His main immediate target was, inevitably, the government's agricultural policy. Things had not gone well, in his view, in recent years, especially since Elliot had been replaced as Minister in 1936 by W. S. Morrison: in January 1939 he was to be followed by the undistinguished Sir Reginald Dorman-Smith, later lost to view as Governor of Burma. Addison forcefully attacked the government's Livestock Industry Bill, its Agriculture and Milk Bills. In 1938 he turned to a much more significant and congenial target, the Prime Minister, his *bête noire*, Neville Chamberlain, for a recent speech about agriculture delivered at Kettering. Addison declared that the government had allowed large tracts of cultivable land to go out of productive use, whereas Britain was fully capable of increasing her food production by £100,000,000 worth a year. The Prime Minister, he declared, had the mind of a city-dweller: this had dictated agricultural policy for half a century and had ruined the countryside.[68] Meanwhile Addison became president of the Milk Publicity Council in July.[69] He was also active in the Labour party Agricultural Subcommittee on Food Policy. By the late 1930s, indeed, thanks in large part to the work of Addison with the assistance of rural socialists such as Sidney Dye in East Anglia, it seemed as if Labour was at last making real headway as the party of the countryside as well as of the industrial regions of Britain. By-elections in 1939 brought an improved Labour poll in North Norfolk and Ripon in England, and the capture of Brecon and Radnor in mid-Wales.

But these years were dominated not by the problems of the farmer and rural labourer, but by the transcendent issues of foreign policy. Throughout the thirties, Addison took a keen interest in foreign affairs. His speeches here tended to be less well briefed than those on domestic issues such as health or agriculture, but he made an informed contribution to debate, nevertheless. He frequently criticized the appeasement of foreign dictators conducted by the National government, though often displaying the ambiguities common to the left in their view of foreign affairs at this time. In 1935 he spoke out forcefully, linking collective security with disarmament as was general in Labour speeches.

> If you want a condemnation of policy, here it is. . . . The situation has come about as the result of the failure of our statement to give effect to the pledges they made at the conclusion of the war. . . . If the Government display the same pusillanimity in the Italian dispute with Abyssinia as they did in the case of Japan and Shanghai we shall be presented with votes for increased armaments.[70]

Britain, he argued, should uphold the League of Nations. If its government had taken a lead at Geneva in organizing an effective system of economic sanctions to control essential supplies, Japan could never have launched her attacks upon China, nor would Mussolini be able to pursue his nationalistic designs in Abyssinia. The government should seize the initiative in working out an international policy for enforcing sanctions which could be operated without involving the world in the risks of war.[71] Once again, no doubt, Addison's memories of the first world war, the policies of blockade and economic warfare conducted then, were foremost in his mind.

At the height of the Italian–Abyssinian crisis in September 1935, Addison went further. He was one of those who took a strong line in demanding collective action through the League against aggression by Mussolini. He applauded the government's apparent resolve, voiced by Hoare, the Foreign Secretary, at Geneva, to enforce collective security through the League and to impose economic sanctions such as an oil embargo upon Italy. But he doubted whether the government had the administrative equipment to enforce the operation of sanctions upon private traders. In fact, the Hoare–Laval pact of 7 December 1935 showed that the government was prepared to sacrifice the independence of Abyssinia in the interests of the appeasement of Italy. Addison strongly backed up Lloyd George in regarding this as a craven surrender to aggression. The Hoare–Laval pact was 'an act of perfidy that makes every Briton ashamed before all the world, especially before the Abyssinians'.[72] Subsequent research has largely borne out his criticisms. It is quite clear that the Cabinet had reached a firm decision, well before Hoare left to meet Laval in Paris, to yield to all of Mussolini's territorial demands. This had always been the view of Vansittart and other leading officials in the Foreign Office who were anxious to detach Mussolini from Hitler. Hoare was offered up as a scapegoat to an enraged public opinion by Baldwin and the Cabinet. Yet in reality he was merely executing agreed government policy decided before Hoare became Foreign Secretary.[73]

Addison moved well to the left in his view of foreign affairs at this time. He even looked indulgently on the idea of a broad anti-government front, a kind of Popular Front on the lines of those existing in France and Spain in 1936, ranging from Lloyd George to the Communists. This concept no doubt appealed to Addison's penchant for coalitions as well. He supported the Popular Front movement in 1936. Three years later, he was associated, along with Tawney, the Webbs, Leonard Woolf, and J. A. Hobson, in pressing the Labour party executive not to expel his old colleague, Sir Stafford Cripps, who was now advocating an anti-fascist Popular Front with the Communists and left-wing Liberals. Addison wrote to the *New Statesman* in March 1939 setting out his views: basically, they were a plea for tolerance rather than an endorsement of Cripps's ideas. 'I, for one, resent the irresponsible putting out of a half-baked programme of a dozen headings which I am perfectly sure would not endure a fortnight in a Cabinet of Liberals and Labour leaders. . . . On the other hand, I cannot imagine a case for expulsion and heresy-hunting in a party that professes to loyalty to freedom of speech and opinion.'[74] But the Labour party's national executive remained unmoved. Cripps was expelled from the party, as were Aneurin Bevan, George Strauss, and Sir Charles Trevelyan. Addison also was active in connection with the Left Book Club, a strong advocate of a Popular Front with the Liberals and others on the left against the fascist threat. He spoke at large meetings at the Albert Hall and Queen's Hall in London in January 1938, rallies organized by the Left Book Club on behalf of a Popular Front, along with Victor Gollancz, Charles Trevelyan, John Strachey, and the secretary of the Communist party, Harry Pollitt.

Most of the Labour party criticized the endorsement of neutrality and of 'non-intervention' in the Spanish civil war that was the policy of the British government and its new Foreign Secretary, Anthony Eden. However, the National Council of Labour endorsed non-intervention. At the Labour party conference in Edinburgh in September 1936, two months after the outbreak of civil war in Spain, Addison spoke out against a resolution moved on behalf of the executive by Arthur Greenwood, his old assistant at the Ministry of Reconstruction. Addison's speech was one of the most important he delivered on foreign affairs. The British Labour party would make a profound mistake if, even by inference, it supported the so-called non-intervention policy which was now being conducted. It was not an alternative, Addison assured the conference, between non-intervention and plunging Europe into war over Spain. 'The alternative was and is for us to demand that the British Government takes a lead at Geneva and in the world by insisting on those conditions of international law and usage which it is pledged to support.' Like Aneurin Bevan and Philip Noel Baker, he did not believe that Britain should remain aloof. Non-intervention was a farce. It had not prevented arms being sent from Britain to Spain to assist the Nationalist rebels under Franco, and from fascist countries, while the legitimate Popular Front government was left unsupported.

We know perfectly well, those of us who have first-hand information from Spain—and I have no doubt that my friends who supported non-intervention have first-hand information—that the supply of aeroplanes and munitions is four or five times more than six weeks ago, and those supplies we know well enough have come from fascist countries. . . . There is a wholesale leakage going on every day to the assistance of the rebels in Spain.[75]

Addison's speech was one of the first demonstrations of the wider international dimension of the war in Spain.

From the autumn of 1936, he was very active in the Spanish Medical Aid Committee of which he was the chairman. Behind this and other pro-Republican committees, according to Hugh Thomas, 'lurked the shadow of the Comintern'. But this is a great exaggeration. The Spanish Medical Aid Committee was largely the creation of the pro-Labour Socialist Medical Association, founded in 1930 by Dr Somerville Hastings, then the Labour MP for Reading. Addison was a prominent figure in the SMA and gave much personal and moral encouragement to its journal, *Medicine Today and Tomorrow*, launched in 1937 to promote the idea of a free national health service. In a speech to a well-attended meeting of the Spanish Medical Aid Committee in November 1936, Addison argued that neutrality should never denote indifference to the sufferings of the victims of war and trying to help them, even if the war should on no account be allowed to spread beyond the confines of Spain.[76] As a medical authority and as a socialist, he was much involved in the subsequent progress of the Spanish Medical Aid movement. Through its help, a British hospital was established at Granen on the Aragon front. In August 1937, he wrote a letter to *The Times* appealing for funds for the British ambulance service which had been on duty in Spain for the past year.[77] On balance, Addison's attitude towards Spain illustrates the complex of views prevalent on the left, compassion, indignation, anti-fascism, together with a profound apprehension of involvement in war.

In the country and in debates in the House of Lords, Addison played a leading part in Labour's attacks on the government's policy of appeasement. One source of information was another critic, Winston Churchill, an old ministerial colleague of first world war days. In 1937 Addison met Wing-Commander Anderson, Churchill's adviser on questions of air defence, who lived near him. He told Anderson that he 'viewed with much anxiety what was coming in the future'. Churchill agreed with Anderson that Addison seemed 'a good ally to have'.[78] Henceforth, Wing-Commander Anderson kept Addison informed of developments at the Air Ministry. In 1938 he gave him notes on the Air Estimates and extracts from the report of the Air Chief Marshal.[79] Anderson, until recently director of Air Training at the Ministry, aptly illustrates that cross-party collaboration in pinpointing the weaknesses of the national defences common in the later thirties. He and Churchill were anxious for Addison to alert Attlee and other Labour colleagues to the defects in the air defences, and Addison did so. With his authority as a former Minister of Munitions, he was asked by the party's Air Subcommittee to prepare a memorandum on the subject. In May 1938 he produced a powerful note on 'The Essentials of Armaments Supply Organization with special reference to the Air Ministry'. The main point here was that the only method of efficiently dealing with the provision of armaments was the creation of a central Ministry of Supply.[80] As it happened, such a Ministry was to be set up in July 1939 under the undistinguished headship of the National Liberal, Leslie Burgin.

On wider issues of policy, Addison criticized the government's approach to the resignation of Anthony Eden as Foreign Secretary in February 1938. This arose nominally over policy towards Italy. Addison felt that the former Foreign Secretary had been singled out for victimization by the appeasers who comprised the majority of the government.

> The Prime Minister has felt himself obliged to open conversations with a foreign power, Italy, in a manner that is against the advice of two colleagues in the Foreign Office who have, in consequence, resigned. Of a more serious character, this happened at a time when the Foreign Secretary was being abused in a singularly hostile way by broadcasts, by agencies of the very power with which it is proposed to negotiate . . . and France is not to be party to these conversations.[81]

Shortly afterwards, at the time of the annexation of Austria by Hitler in March, the *Anschluss*, Addison took the more unusual view that Germany and Austria ought never to have been separated at Versailles.[82]

He took a close interest in Anglo-French relations in 1938–9, the period of Munich, the invasion of Czechoslovakia, and the guarantee to Poland. He did not take part in the debates in the Lords on either the Czech or the Polish crises, though he would surely have agreed with Lloyd George's criticisms of the foolhardy nature of concluding an alliance to defend Poland without first securing the assistance of Soviet Russia in the East. Addison took, in fact, a somewhat ambivalent line at this period, similar to that of Lloyd George. He demanded a firm stand against the totalitarian dictators along with an attempt to redress their legitimate grievances. France, he declared, had tried to use the League of Nations to set up an iron ring to enforce many of the unjust territorial provisions of the Treaty of Versailles.[83] In his outlook, Addison echoed many of the criticisms of his former leader, Lloyd George, in recent books on reparations and the peace treaties. As in 1919, he looked for the revision of the peace treaties to make an accommodation with Germany feasible; like Lloyd George, however, he sought to pursue his concept of appeasement from a policy of armed strength, not of timidity and weakness. It is notable that Addison's name was mentioned as one of several 'leading British public figures' (the others were R. A. Butler, Leslie Burgin, General Ironside, and Lord Chatsfield) to serve as possible go-betweens to establish contact between the British government and Hitler in the summer of 1939.[84] It is truly fortunate for his reputation that there was no Addison mission to Berlin in September 1939 to parallel that of the other ex-Liberal, Walter Runciman, to Prague in September 1938.

As Addison had long predicted, Neville Chamberlain's version of appeasement brought total failure. Hitler invaded Poland, and Britain declared war on 3 September 1939. There followed a tantalizing winter and spring of 'phoney war' in which Lloyd George and others (though not Addison) called for peace overtures to Hitler. Addison's speeches in the Lords concentrated largely on the inadequacies of the Ministry of Supply under Leslie Burgin, a view taken by the Liberal MP, Clement Davies, in powerful speeches in the Commons. Addison had also much to say on the continuing problem of unemployment even after the outbreak of war, and various aspects of agricultural policy. Then in April and May 1940 there came successively the failures to stem the German occupation of Norway, and the invasion of the Low Countries and of France. After a critical vote in the Commons on 8 May, Neville Chamberlain was forced out of the premiership. On 10 May 1940, Churchill was summoned to Buckingham Palace and accepted the King's commission to form a government. His Coalition included a War Cabinet of five, on the same lines as 1916—himself as Prime Minister and Minister of Defence, Chamberlain and Lord Halifax from the Conservatives, Attlee and Arthur Greenwood for the Labour party. Other leading Labour ministers in the government included Ernest Bevin, the Minister of Labour, Herbert Morrison, Minister of Supply and then Home Secretary, A. V. Alexander, at the Admiralty, Hugh Dalton, and later Sir Stafford Cripps. On this basis, it is surprising that Addison, a senior and distinguished Labour spokesman on domestic and foreign matters and an old ally of Churchill who had recently collaborated with him in criticisms of the air defence system, should be left out. At all events, Addison was not offered a position in the government. Perhaps

Churchill thought he was too closely associated with the peacemongering Lloyd George; perhaps he thought Addison was too old. There is no evidence either way. There is no suggestion that Addison, ever modest, was distressed at not receiving office. He continued to live happily with his wife in rural Buckinghamshire, first in a new farm rented on the Chequers' estate, later in a more imposing new house they had built, 'Neighbours', at Radnage a few miles further west beside the Chilterns. He took pleasure in hearing that Lloyd George, who was indeed six years older than himself, had been offered a place in the government, and hoped that Lloyd George would accept. 'You will get rid of the duds who have landed us in this mess.' Addison added that two crucial priorities were the organization of the local defence volunteers which was 'completely chaotic' and the higher administration of the Admiralty, so cruelly exposed in the operations at Narvik in the Norwegian campaign. 'It reminds me of Jellicoe's proceedings and is evidently causing almost mutiny amongst the keen service men.'[85] Unfortunately for his hopes, Lloyd George and Churchill kept a wary distance from one another. It wasn't L. G.'s war. An offer at the end of the year of the embassy in Washington was predictably refused, and he reverted to the gloomy defeatism of an old man.

Addison was now leader of the Labour party in the House of Lords and took, therefore, a prominent part in debates in the Upper House. One of his favourite themes in the early months of the war was the working of the new Ministry of Supply. It showed no sign of having a programme for the effective mobilization of labour, and had failed to work in intimate contact with the unions and with employers' organizations.[86] In fact, even when Herbert Morrison went to the Ministry of Supply in May 1940, the new Ministry failed to function effectively. It was caught in the cross-fire of forces pressing for raw materials and labour, and was a victim of the personal clashes of Beaverbrook and Ernest Bevin, respectively Ministers of Aircraft Production and of Labour. Addison also launched forth frequently in discussions of war policy. After the episode at Dakar, when a British expedition to capture this West African port was beaten off, Addison commented 'We are always coming in after the event. . . . One longs to see some success arising out of Britain getting in first and proportionate drive in our policy.'[87] He warmly acclaimed the Atlantic Charter agreed between Churchill and President Franklin D.

Roosevelt in August 1941. 'However long postponed victory may be it is undoubtedly certain that this great association of nations will provide the beginning of an effective and powerful instrument that will secure peace for the world.'[88] As in 1914–18, Addison was anticipating the need for some post-war organization to promote international security and lasting peace. He was a particularly forceful critic of the fall of Singapore to the Japanese in March 1942, a shattering blow to Churchill, to Britain's imperialist pretensions, and to the general Allied position in the Far East. The defences of Singapore had been inadequate both on land and on sea. 'We have to search in our annals for an event so shocking to the public mind as the loss of Singapore. . . . This was not sudden, but the finale of a two-months series of events during which one event after another betrayed unmistakable evidence of lack of forethought by those on the spot.'[89]

Like many Labour men during the war, Addison was a warm admirer of the Soviet Union at this time. He does not appear to have been unduly stirred either by the Molotov–Ribbentrop pact to carve up Poland in August 1939 or by the Russo–Finnish war the following year. After the German invasion of Russia in June 1941, Addison called, on behalf of the Labour peers, for unstinted help to be given to Britain's new ally. Later, he welcomed the new accord established between the Soviet Union and the English-speaking peoples at the Moscow Conference in 1943.[90] He was a member of the Anglo-Soviet Public Relations Committee, at a time when the official authorities were anxious to depoliticize and defuse public enthusiasm for Russia, and dampen calls for a second front in western Europe. This Committee, although looked on indulgently by the Foreign Office and presided over by the eminent physician, Lord Horder, was none the less a body of distinctly left-wing appearance. Its members included Aneurin Bevan, H. N. Brailsford, Arthur Creech-Jones, Harold Laski, Kingsley Martin, George Strauss, and Leonard Woolf, as well as Addison, a fair panoply of politicians, editors, and intellectuals on the socialist left.[91] Between them, they gave the Russian cause much effective publicity and a chorus of warm support in Labour party circles until disillusion with Russian policy began to set in during 1944.

Addison remained, therefore, an influential politician during the second world war, even though kept out of office by Churchill.

Beaverbrook even called him 'the most expert parliamentarian in the House'. He was to be one of the two peers chosen to take part in the parliamentary delegation to survey the horrors of Buchenwald in April 1945. On his return, Addison delivered some stern judgements on 'the German mind' and the Teutonic delusion of being 'a special and superior race'.[92] He remained on warm terms with Attlee, his close neighbour in Buckinghamshire. In 1941 the two consulted about possible reinforcements for Labour in the Upper House; H. B. Lees-Smith, Jack Lawson, and Tom Williams, the future Minister of Agriculture, were all sounded out about peerages, but none could be persuaded.[93] Addison's main public activity at this time, outside party politics, was his post as chairman of the Buckinghamshire War Agricultural Committee, in which his expert knowledge was invaluable. Labour's election manifesto was to cite the work of these county agricultural committees in increasing efficiency and giving aid to small farmers. Addison himself often referred to them in the Cabinets of 1945–51. Churchill did offer him something more ambitious, the vice-chairmanship of the new Development Commission 'because of the efforts you have been making for some time past to promote accord with regard to future agricultural policy'. The Ministry of Agriculture, Churchill went on, would 'welcome your help and influence in promoting agreement upon future agricultural policy in any way that might be found practicable'. This proposition was attractive to Addison with his long-held view that agricultural development should stand above party considerations. But he felt compelled to decline because of his commitments as Labour's leader in the Lords.[94]

Much of his energy, as in 1916–18, was consumed by pressure for post-war reconstruction. He pressed hard for a coherent planning programme. Better than most, he recalled only too well the fiasco that occurred after 1918 when too many detailed plans for social and economic rehabilitation were delayed or forgotten. He and the Labour party welcomed the appointment of a Ministry of Reconstruction in 1943.[95] Churchill's first thought had been to appoint Beaverbrook; but in the end he chose Lord Woolton, a non-party business man very much on the lines of those who flourished under Lloyd George in 1916–18. Woolton was to chair the Cabinet Committee on Reconstruction which was rapidly to be dominated by Ministers from the Labour party. Addison also took great encouragement from the publication of the Beveridge Report at the end of 1942. This was a natural sequel to his own achievements in the fields of social insurance and public health. It proposed a comprehensive 'cradle to the grave' scheme for the insurance services and the extension of the social services in a wide variety of directions. Addison felt they 'cannot afford not to afford this scheme'[96] and joined those Labour men in both Houses who pressed in vain for Churchill's government to commit itself to implementing it.

Agriculture, as always, remained one of Addison's passions. He wrote a chapter in *A Programme for Agriculture*, published in 1941, with Sir Daniel Hall, A. G. Street, Lord Cranworth, and Sir Ralph Glyn as its other contributors. Addison's chapter was a plea for effective agricultural planning and land use after the war. In the Lords he called for a new agricultural policy, in part to deal with post-war unemployment. He was a vigorous critic of the milk programmes of Woolton, the Minister of Food, who complained of the attacks of 'Addison and his satellites'. He backed up the experiment of the Land Settlement Association in training men to work on smallholdings which he believed would assist in food production and selling.[97] In 1943 he joined with other members of the House of Lords Agricultural Group in issuing a manifesto setting out all-party views on post-war planning for agriculture.[98] In this body he developed an association with Lord Cranborne, the son of his colleague Lord Salisbury, in promoting housing programmes in 1917–18, and this friendship was to be of much political value in the future.

On other issues, too, Addison was endlessly active. In late 1944, he brought up a suggestion from the Liberal peer, Lord Samuel, to his Labour party colleagues that a joint committee be set up in both Houses of Parliament to consider colonial questions. This, Samuel argued, would both stimulate the Colonial Office and generate public interest in colonial issues. Lord Listowel and Lord Ammon were amongst the Labour peers to take part in this Committee and it met at frequent intervals.[99] In its modest way, it helped on public debate on the principles of post-war decolonization.

In 1944 he also took the lead on a very different issue, namely the reform of the House of Lords, a theme dormant since 1911. He sent to the Labour members of the War Cabinet, Attlee, Bevin, Morrison, and Greenwood, a circular letter which referred to inquiries made by himself and Lord Salisbury on the possibility of inter-party agreement on the reform of the composition of the Upper House. Addison himself felt certain that no proposal could be considered that retained the hereditary basis of the Upper House nor one that enlarged its powers of controlling legislation passed by the House of Commons. The suggestion had been made to him that membership of the House should be limited to certain circumscribed groups of peers, together with a limited number of life peers to be appointed as a recognition of their distinguished qualifications in public life.[100] Since the Labour party was not committed to the abolition of the Lords, it had to respond, and inter-party conferences of Labour, Conservative, and Liberal party leaders then took place. It was agreed that there was at least a basis for further discussion.[101] In fact, House of Lords reform was to remain a dormant issue, long after the end of the war. The main significance of this episode is to be seen in more personal terms. It helped cement further the friendly relationship between Addison and the Unionist leader, Lord Cranborne. Also it confirmed Addison's stature as a distinguished figure in the Upper House, one still of ministerial timber. Another ex-Liberal Labour peer, Lord Nathan, had written to him in 1942 that

the standard which you have set is a high standard which is difficult even for yourself to follow. . . . It has had a marked influence and has been reflected not merely in the improved position of the House of Lords in the public estimation, but for our own party in that House, which, I am sure, is more highly esteemed both among our fellow peers and outside than it was only a short time ago. . . . For this, the main credit rests with you.[102]

Partly as a result of this factor, Labour's election manifesto in 1945 was to be silent on the existence of the House of Lords. The Upper House was to play a useful and constructive role in furthering governmental legislation between 1945 and 1951.

In May 1945, Churchill's wartime Coalition wound up, when the Labour ministers resigned on the ending of the war in Europe. In July, a general election was held and to the popular astonishment Churchill was overwhelmingly defeated. Labour returned to power with 393 members and a clear majority for the first time in its history. Clement Attlee now became Prime Minister. As the leader of the Labour peers and a man with an unparalleled record of ministerial experience within his party, Addison was now clearly destined for a key 'elder statesman' role. On 27 July he was confirmed by Attlee as his government's leader in the Lords. Rather surprisingly, he was told

From Slump to Victory 237

by Attlee, when he returned from the Potsdam Conference, that he was also to be Dominions Secretary. This was frequently a portfolio for senior politicians but one of unusual significance for commonwealth and overseas relations in 1945. He also received a viscountcy. So opened the third, and in many ways most satisfying period of Addison's lengthy career as a Cabinet minister, one free from the rancour of 1916–21 and of the external pressures of 1930–1. Addison in Labour's third Cabinet was very far from being merely a survivor from a previous age. Although now seventy-six, he was still physically healthy and intellectually formidable. He was still a substantial and respected figure in left-wing and progressive politics, poised to take his full share of responsibility in government at yet another crucial watershed in his nation's history.

9

Labour's Elder Statesman

Labour's landslide election victory in 1945 in which 393 Labour members were returned, seemed to herald a brave new world of social reform and exciting dynamic reconstruction. And yet Addison, taking office under his fourth Prime Minister at the age of seventy-six, was an elder statesman in a government of elder statesmen. The major figures in the Labour government, Attlee himself, Morrison, Bevin, and Dalton, had all entered politics before the first world war. Other ministers were equally senior. Arthur Greenwood, Lord Privy Seal, had been a civil servant under Addison in 1916–18. Lord Stansgate, as Wedgwood Benn was now known, had been a Liberal back-bencher with Addison, at the time of the Parliament Bill of 1911. With Pethick-Lawrence (74), Chuter Ede (63), George Isaacs (62), and other veterans, it was truly a Cabinet rich in experience. Not until Harold Wilson entered the Cabinet, at the age of thirty-one, was there a youthful face. In this senior and respectable government, Addison was foremost among its voices of experience. When he succeeded Arthur Greenwood as Lord Privy Seal in 1947, it was noted ironically that Greenwood dismissed ostensibly on grounds of age, was, at sixty-eight, ten years younger than his successor.

Amongst the members of the Labour government, Addison was unique both for his length of service as a Cabinet minister, dating from 1916, and for the variety of different portfolios he had held. He could speak with authority on defence, health, housing, agriculture, and many other issues. Sir Harold Wilson, who joined the Cabinet in September 1947 as President of the Board of Trade, later recalled Addison as 'a wise old man' whose interventions in Cabinet and committee discussions commanded great respect. He also noted that Attlee allowed Addison more scope than most other Cabinet members in speaking at length during Cabinet discussions, for instance over agricultural matters, though even he did not receive the unique

Labour's Elder Statesman

latitude that Attlee allowed Ernest Bevin.[1] Alone of the members of the Attlee government, Addison had first-hand experience of that earlier post-war government after 1918, and the difficulties and failures that the Lloyd George Coalition encountered then. He frequently intervened in Cabinet discussions, often with recollections of the government of 1918–22. For instance, he reminded the Minister of Health, Aneurin Bevan, of the technical supply problems that had led to the failure of the post-1918 housing programme and the difficulties of carrying through ambitious plans. The Cabinet also reflected on the circumstances that had led to the passing of the Emergency Powers Act at a time of labour unrest in 1920.[2] It was agreed to renew this act to maintain essential services at times of industrial disputes; Bevin and other union leaders in the Cabinet agreed that such a measure did not amount to strike-breaking. With his wealth of experience of those past events following the previous war, and his close personal relationship to the Prime Minister, it is not surprising that Addison played an important role in this administration, far more so than was realized by the general public. For Attlee his Buckinghamshire neighbour, perhaps, Addison played the kind of role that Granville had done for Gladstone and Lord Crewe for Asquith—a wise, experienced figure without personal ambitions with whom the Prime Minister could commune intimately and on personal terms. For six years, 'Clem' and 'Chris' reflected on the state of the nation over lunch or tea at week-ends at Chequers. As a voice in Cabinet, as a chairman of major committees, as a practical guide on difficult legislative problems, his influence on the third Labour government was considerable. He deserves his meed of credit for the far-ranging social and political achievements of this government between 1945 and 1951.

In one crucial area, indeed, Addison was involved with a government committee that was to be of profound significance for Britain's international defence and energy requirements. Attlee appointed him to the highly secret body deputed to develop Britain's atomic bomb and nuclear energy programme. Despite his avowed hostility to armaments in the inter-war years, Addison had never been a pacifist. Even the awesome horror of the atomic bomb did not lead him to despair; indeed, his experiences in the second world war convinced him of the necessity for Britain to develop her own atomic bomb and nuclear energy programme. In the Lords debate on the King's Speech in August 1945, at the start of the new Parliament, he endorsed Attlee's recent statement about the future use of the bomb. 'It commits the British government to the fullest possible co-operation in seeing, if possible, in the future that the best use of this discovery is made and that in any case we co-operate with other free nations in seeing that it is not turned to destructive ends.'[3] Addison stressed that no apparatus for imposing secrecy of manufacture or testing would safeguard the human race from the peril of the atomic bomb and other nuclear weapons. Therefore, the nation's first effort must be directed to increasing the efficiency of international machinery to secure collaboration in the handling of these destructive weapons, and to removing the causes of world war.[4] He professed his faith in the United Nations Organization, when it came into being after the San Francisco Conference. In particular, its atomic energy commission would apply nuclear power to peaceful industrial uses, while the security council would help build up a fabric which would remove international tension.[5]

In explaining the government's Atomic Energy Bill to the Lords in April 1947, Addison emphasized that Britain was warmly disposed to the UN Atomic Energy Commission which had resulted from the Prime Minister's visit to the United States in November 1945. Attlee had reached agreement there with President Truman and Mackenzie King, the Canadian Prime Minister, for international collaboration in the use of atomic power.[6] At home, the government had already set up an atomic research establishment at Harwell.[7] The government's Bill did not nationalize atomic energy. Rather it gave the Minister of Supply, who was responsible for the conduct of the work at Harwell, the power to control developments in the light of the best advice he could obtain. Addison denied that there was any contradiction between supporting the United Nations as a peaceful agency and at the same time spending time and money on secret deliberations to decide how to improve Britain's own defence arrangements. He spoke with special knowledge on the work of the Ministry of Defence. One aspect of its work was the setting-up of the Defence Research Committee and the Joint War Production Board which would bring the requirements of supplies into the inmost councils of government.[8] As always, the precedent of the Munitions Ministry in 1915–17 was a guide and inspiration.

Addison's usual theme was that open international co-operation

Labour's Elder Statesman

was vital for the future development of nuclear energy, and that secretive national manœuvres should be avoided.[9] But in 1947 he was made by Attlee a member of the highly secret committee known as Gen. 163, which took the momentous decision that Britain should manufacture its own atomic bomb. The other members were Attlee, Morrison, Bevin, Alexander (First Lord of the Admiralty), and John Wilmot (Minister of Supply). The Cabinet seems to have been bypassed by this committee: here was a supreme move away from traditional Cabinet government towards a presidential style of executive decision-making.[10] During the six years of Attlee's government, in fact, atomic energy or the manufacture of nuclear weapons appeared less than ten times on the agenda of the Cabinet. It is evident that Addison himself knew nothing before the meetings of Gen. 163. For instance, a standing committee on atomic energy known as Gen. 75 had been in existence for eighteen months as a forum for discussion and decision-making on atomic energy policy, but this seems to have been unknown to him. The new Gen. 163 was a ministerial committee on atomic energy to 'deal with questions of policy in the field of atomic energy which require the consideration of ministers'. It was composed of all the members of the old Gen. 75, together with Addison and A. V. Alexander. Little is known of the decisions taken, or even the issues discussed by this clandestine body; as Professor Gowing comments, the pattern of decision-making was confused since so many different, overlapping groups were involved. However, at the first meeting of Gen. 163 in January 1947 it was apparently agreed that work on atomic weapons and all aspects of atomic energy should be undertaken. The committee approved the special administrative arrangements drawn up by Lord Portal, formerly at the Ministry of Supply, to develop atomic weapons on a totally secret basis.[11] Although there was much unrest in Labour ranks about Ernest Bevin's foreign policy, especially his antagonism towards the Soviet Union, the atomic bomb was protected by this veil of secrecy from intruding in public debate.

So Lord Addison was a member of the government committee which finally embarked in early 1947 on the manufacture of Britain's own nuclear deterrent, or so-called deterrent. However, in 1949, he welcomed the formation of NATO, designed to create international defence collaboration in the North Atlantic area, as the beginning of a wider and more effective political co-operation, not as the harbinger of any nuclear shield. He played down the fact that NATO had come into existence because of East–West tension, following the invasion of Czechoslovakia by the Red army and the airlift by the West to relieve West Berlin.[12] In March 1950, when speaking in the Lords, Addison now claimed that it was no use pretending that it was possible to devise any effective international control over the manufacture of atomic bombs: the question of testing them was set on one side. By implication, he justified Britain's retention of her own nuclear arsenal. Whether the Labour government's commitment to a British atomic and later hydrogen bomb programme was a betrayal of the party's basic principles or a symbol of a new realism in foreign policy is open to debate. In practical, party terms, Britain's independent nuclear weapons programme was to plague and divide the Labour party years after Addison's death, down to the crisis over the Campaign for Nuclear Disarmament in 1959–61. It is ironic that so humane a man, a distinguished doctor, a dedicated opponent of armaments, the father of a pacifist daughter herself active in CND, should have played a part in the origins of this controversy. Such, however, are the unpalatable choices that constantly face radicals in government.

In addition to this, as has been seen, Addison was in August 1945 appointed Secretary of State for Dominion Affairs, a post which he retained until October 1947. He had not previously in his long career been particularly associated with Commonwealth affairs, apart from being a well-known friend of colonial freedom and of Indian independence. Indeed, Attlee's choice of department for him initially surprised Addison when he received the crucial telephone call from Downing Street in August 1945, just after Attlee's return from the Potsdam Conference. His appointment was no doubt intended to leave him with some free time to lead the House of Lords, as the Dominions Office was traditionally regarded as one of relatively secondary importance. The main problems of the old Empire fell on the desks of the Secretary of State for India and the Colonial Secretary, posts held respectively by Frederick Pethick-Lawrence, and by George Hall and then (from 1946) Arthur Creech-Jones. One advantage of combining the post of Dominions Secretary with that of leadership of the Lords, as Addison's predecessor, Lord Cranborne had done, was that many important debates on Commonwealth affairs were in fact launched in the Upper House. On the other hand, as Sir Harold Wilson later reminded the authors of this book, Attlee gave the Dominions Office a considerably more important status than it had received prior to 1939. This was partly because of his personal commitment to the concept of the Commonwealth, partly because of the undeniable significance of the Commonwealth, new and old, to Britain in defence, economic, and other respects after 1945. To combine such a post with the leadership of the Lords, as Addison had to do, was a formidable undertaking for a man of any age, especially for one of 76.

Certainly, the Dominions presented the new Secretary with complexities enough. At the end of the war in 1945, the British Commonwealth had been freed from enemy occupation, notably in Asia. But it was a formidable task to restore ordered government, to disarm and repatriate enemy troops found within the confines of the Commonwealth, and above all to reach an accommodation with colonial nationalist movements: Britain had a clear obligation to respond to declarations on behalf of colonial independence made at the San Francisco Conference in 1945. Addison frequently declared his faith in the British Commonwealth of Nations as an example of international, multi-racial co-operation. Since we 'were all partners in the war, we must be partners in the peace'.[13] As Dominions Secretary he had an important role to play in this, to act as a link figure with the governments of the British Commonwealth. He claimed that he had 'daily consultation' with such Dominions statesmen as Dr Herbert Evatt, the Australian Minister of External Affairs, with Mackenzie King, the Prime Minister of Canada, and with Peter Fraser, the Prime Minister of New Zealand. The fact that Australia and New Zealand both had Labour governments was a help towards governmental collaboration. Addison described the Commonwealth as 'the strangest and most illogical association that was ever devised'. But for all that, the relationship enabled independent states in many continents to arrive at a common viewpoint.[14]

During his tenure of the Dominions Office, Addison was often directly involved in efforts to promote contact between Dominions leaders. In April 1946 he took part in the Conference of Dominions' Prime Ministers in London. Here major discussions took place on the disposal of strategic bases and on the defence of the Pacific. The discussions were broadened by the attendance of General Smuts, the South African Prime Minister, Mackenzie King from Canada, and a delegation from India.[15] Addison was also a leading participant at another major Commonwealth Conference held at Canberra in August 1947 at the invitation of the Australian government. The purpose here was for Dominions representatives to share their thoughts on a Japanese peace treaty and to amplify previous declarations on the future of Japan. In Cabinet, Addison had fought successfully to ensure that Australia received reparation for damage caused by the Japanese invasion of Papua–New Guinea, comparable with that received by the United States. At a press conference, he struck a bold imperial note. 'We are anxious to safeguard and develop our interests in the Pacific. The representative of the British government in the Far East, Lord Killearn, has set up an organization to develop the welfare and resources of British countries in those areas. . . . We have no intention of jeopardising or surrendering our rights in the Pacific.'[16] It was reported that complete agreement was reached at Canberra and that delegates to the Conference agreed that post-war Japan should be a 'self-supporting unit'.[17] An Australian newspaper complimented Addison on his handling of the Conference on the British side. The information and instructions of the British delegation were 'more precise and detailed than that of any other delegation, except perhaps the Australian'.[18]

In these formal conferences, the Dominions Secretary was largely expounding the brief prepared for the British delegation by the Foreign Office and the Ministry of Defence. However, he also took the opportunity of making a more personal contribution to good relations between the mother country and the Dominions. During his visit to Australia in August 1947, he was anxious to strike themes appropriate to Anglo-Australian co-operation. Friendly conversations were held with the Labour premier, Ben Chifley. He expressed gratification at the efforts being made by the Australian government to expand food supplies to Britain at a time of shortages; Britain would supply sufficient merchant ships to take all the food that Australia could produce. In return, emphasis was laid on Britain's determination to fulfil her responsibilities in Australasia and the Far East as part of a Commonwealth defence and security system in the Pacific.[19]

From Australia, he and his wife went on to New Zealand in September 1947, as the guests of Lord and Lady Freyberg. It was reported that the country greatly impressed him, not least for its efficient and productive system of agriculture.[20] He told the Auckland Labour party that Britain was anxious to import more meat and other foodstuffs from New Zealand; they could be paid for in sterling which was a vital factor for Britain in view of the shortage of dollars after the crisis of currency convertibility.[21] He struck up a good relationship with Peter Fraser, the Labour premier of New Zealand; Addison told Attlee in October 1947 that he found Fraser 'as forthcoming as ever'.[22] Another close friend in New Zealand was the Finance Minister, Walter Nash, whom he had formerly met during his Fabian Research days in the thirties. Writing to Nash in 1948, he stated that 'New Zealand has left on me enduring impressions. . . . I still feel a bit of misgiving that your housing developments are so much in urban areas, for I can see that your country, as well as ours, needs lots more houses in the country for agricultural workers. In this country, anyhow, it is the key to increased production.'[23]

But of all the Commonwealth leaders, Addison established the warmest friendship with Mackenzie King, the Liberal Prime Minister of Canada. At first glance, there might not appear to be a basis for personal rapport between the British Dominions Secretary, with his brisk, no-nonsense directness, and the Canadian premier, a brooding bachelor, an ardent spiritualist, mournfully worshipping the memory of his mother in the sombre rooms of the Laurier house in Ottawa. Lady Addison found King agreeable but sentimental. Nevertheless, the two septuagenarian statesmen soon built up a cordial and close relationship. In the autumn of 1946, Lord and Lady Addison went on a cross-Canada tour at the invitation of Mackenzie King; Addison seized every opportunity to speak out for good Anglo-Canadian relations. He praised Canada's active work in the United Nations and expressed gratitude for exports of Canadian wheat to Britain.[24] Mackenzie King, for his part, was deeply impressed by Addison's energy and sagacity as their correspondence shows. His friendship with Lord and Lady Addison was 'the most joyous of many happy memories'.[25] Indeed, this visit in 1946 was a great success. The British High Commissioner later wrote to Addison, 'We were lost in admiration at the way you stood up to all you had to do, taking everything so cheerfully in your stride. From the official standpoint, I do not think your visit could have been better timed. . . . We have abundant evidence of how pleased the people in the west were to have had the opportunity of seeing and hearing you.'[26]

The friendship between Addison and Mackenzie King lasted until the Canadian's death in 1950. In 1948, for example, Addison wrote to congratulate King for becoming the longest-serving Commonwealth Prime Minister. In his reply Mackenzie King underlined the sympathetic rapport between the two old men.

I felt that we were again having one of those delightful talks where each is conscious of the complete sympathy and understanding of the other—talks which mean so much in one's personal life and which are of such great value in relation to public affairs. I shall never forget how quick you were in June 1946 to perceive a certain historic significance in my having gained, at that time, a certain lead over my predecessors in office in Canada and how you sought, indeed, succeeded, in giving to that record a place in the history of the British Empire and Commonwealth. Of the many other messages received in the last few weeks, none could possibly have meant more to me than your own.[27]

In 1949 there were to be financial difficulties between Britain and Canada over the dollar shortage. But Addison wrote to King that in spite of this, and 'apart from a bit of Treasury sickness . . . there is an abundance of goodwill and affection towards Canada in every quarter here. For example, last week I had to pilot the Canada Bill, involving an amendment to the North America Act through the House, everybody was anxious to do it in all stages straight away, simply because Canada wanted it.' He congratulated Mackenzie King on the great victory achieved by the Liberals in the recent Canadian election. Meanwhile in 1948 he had persuaded the Cabinet to allow BOAC to buy twenty-two 'Canadair' aircraft as part of a 'Fly Commonwealth' policy.[28] In this and other ways, Addison helped sustain the bonds between the mother country and the white, English-speaking dominions.

The Dominions Secretary also enjoyed a good relationship with Field Marshal Smuts, the South African Prime Minister and an old colleague of his from the days at the Ministry of Munitions in 1917. 'We have no better friends in the world than the South Africans,' he told the Lords on 20 February 1946. The friendship of the two veterans helped smooth over some difficult passages in Anglo-South African relations including the transfer of the High Commission territories. Indeed, over one issue, Addison may have taken too lenient a view of South African intentions on racial relations. This was the much contested topic of South African trusteeship over South West Africa, once a German colony. With reluctance, the Cabinet accepted in April–May 1946 Addison's proposal that Britain support Smuts's demand for the union of South West Africa with South

Africa, and the winding-up of the old mandate system. Eventually the issue was to drag on until the UN General Assembly finally ended the mandate in 1966.[29] Even in the late 1970s, the authority of South Africa over 'Namibia', as South West Africa was now called, and the holding of elections there provided a delicate international issue. The later history of Namibia did not confirm Addison's optimistic outlook, any more than that of Rhodesia confirmed his colleagues' hopes for the future of the Central African Federation. On the other hand, it might be stressed that it was only after the Nationalist party under Dr Malan gained power in South Africa in May 1948, with a defeat for Smuts and his mainly English-speaking United party, that the full rigours of apartheid became apparent. In any case, Addison's commitment to racial equality was beyond question.

In July 1947 the Secretary of State for Dominions Affairs was rechristened the Secretary of State for Commonwealth Relations, and his department became the Commonwealth Relations Office. Addison expressed gratification with this change, a logical one in the light of developments since 1945. There had been dramatic transformations during these years. Several countries of the old Empire secured full independence within the Commonwealth, including India, Pakistan, Burma, and Ceylon. They were countries in which the idea of self-government had made substantial progress during the thirties. The independence of India and of Pakistan was foreshadowed by the constitutional changes of the pre-war years, notably the Government of India Act in 1935 which granted responsible government at both the provincial and central levels. On the other hand, it was considerably easier for a Labour government, with its heritage of anti-colonialism, than for a Conservative party headed by the imperialist Churchill, to adjust itself to these changes. Henceforward, India's leaders could assume not only that full self-government was the long-term goal of British policy but that there would be a sympathetic response to the demand for its early attainment.

As a senior minister, Addison had been involved in the movement towards the independence of India. In July 1946, he had been present at a meeting in Attlee's room when members of the Labour party and of the Opposition parties, including Bevin and Morrison, Churchill, Eden, and Samuel heard the statement from the Cabinet mission which had just returned from India.[30] When the Independence of India Act was introduced in the Lords in February 1947, Addison strongly rebutted Conservative attacks. Labour had always believed in self-government for India. More broadly, it had been British policy over the decades to help develop in India a system of public service manned by Indians. Since the Cabinet mission the previous year, there had been a transformation of Indian opinion and a firm realization of the moral commitment of the British government to independence. A free India would be far more likely to be a friendly India as far as Britain was concerned. He told Mackenzie King that Mountbatten had persuaded Gandhi and Jinnah to make a joint appeal to the Hindu and Muslim population to avoid violence.[31]

It fell to Addison, as leader of the Lords, to handle the Independence of India Bill during its passage through the Upper House in July 1947. He largely dismissed fears for religious and other minorities. The best way to safeguard them was to hand over powers of self-government to the country in which they lived. From 1948 India and Pakistan would share with Britain, Canada, Australia, New Zealand, and the Union of South Africa the status of a self-governing member of the Commonwealth. The India Bill was passed by the Lords on 16 July, and opened up a much wider concept of a multi-racial, self-governing Commonwealth based on equality of statehood. On his way to the Canberra Conference in the summer of 1947, Addison had stopped in both India and Pakistan to welcome them into the Commonwealth.[32] On his way home in October, he accepted invitations to visit Delhi and Karachi at the time of independence. He met here respectively the Indian Muslim leader, Mohammed Jinnah, and then, on 18 October 1947, Mahatma Gandhi. They discussed the country's political problems for an hour.[33] Amongst others, Addison met Dr B. C. Roy, Gandhi's personal physician, and a student of his at St. Bartholomew's forty years earlier. As elsewhere, he seems to have left a favourable impression in India. In 1951, Gandhi's successor, Nehru, wrote to him, 'I hope that it might be possible for you to pay us a visit sometime.... You will be surprised to find how many friends and admirers you have in India.'[34]

The work of the Dominions Secretary was varied and wide-ranging. It spanned the globe from the Straits Settlements to Newfoundland. Also, until 1949, it included relations with Eire. He was much involved with the Commonwealth security arrangements notably for North America and the southern Pacific made in the 1946 Defence White Paper.[35] On the economic side, Britain was anxious in the years following the end of the war in 1945 to increase her bulk purchase of Dominions cereals and other foodstuffs from the Commonwealth. With his experience and knowledge of problems of food supply, Addison was an ideal emissary to ensure a steady flow of produce from Commonwealth countries. He also reminded his colleagues of the sacrifices they were making to feed Britain. Australia and New Zealand 'are depriving themselves of butter and meat in order that we may get supplies'.[36] One of his major tasks was to provide reassurance to such knowledgeable critics as Woolton and Cherwell that Britain's bulk food purchase programme was adequate. In 1946 he told the Lords of efforts being made to obtain supplies from South Africa and from Argentina. In 1947 he was telling them of a long-term wheat contract with Canada and that Britain was buying this wheat at 35 cents per bushel cheaper than the world price. In October of the same year, he spoke of an agreement signed by seventeen countries at Geneva, including member states of the British Commonwealth, to secure co-operation over bulk food purchase over a three-year period. He predicted that an increase of exports from Britain to countries with the dollar as a currency would now follow.[37]

It was frequently observed, for example by the influential imperial journal *Round Table*, in September 1946, that Addison's handling of the various ramifications of Commonwealth relations was exceptionally statesmanlike and fair-minded.[38] Undoubtedly his tenure of this post was a further demonstration of his capacity for effective administration of a major government portfolio. But in early October 1947 he moved from the Commonwealth Relations Office to become Lord Privy Seal. Philip Noel Baker succeeded him as Commonwealth Secretary. His published letter told Attlee that he now sought to concentrate on his task as leader of the House of Lords. In fact, his wife recalled this as one rare occasion when he was somewhat irritated by Attlee, who moved him from his post while he was in Australia in the course of his Commonwealth tour following the Canberra Conference.[39] However, any resentment was very temporary, since Addison returned to continue as a staunch supporter of Attlee's leadership and a vigorous defender of him against Herbert Morrison and others who plotted to depose him as premier. Addison's move, in fact, resulted from the internal Cabinet crisis of that autumn, following from the manœuvre partly organized by Cripps, to replace Attlee with Bevin as Prime Minister. The move of Addison from Commonwealth Relations was part of the Prime Minister's strategy in overcoming that crisis. As Lord Privy Seal, Addison continued to fulfil a wide variety of roles, remarkable for a man of seventy-eight. His salary of £5,000 was used to finance his activity as leader of the Lords, and also his work at Commonwealth Relations which he continued to conduct on a voluntary basis in collaboration with Noel Baker as a result of his passion for the work of the old Dominions.

After leaving the Commonwealth Relations Office he gave Mackenzie King other reasons for the move.

> We had agreed to establish a small Economic Policy Committee of senior ministers and I am one of them. As you can imagine, we have had to meet very frequently and the amount of work that is involved is very great. So, although it cut me to the heart to leave the Commonwealth Office, it would have been physically impossible for me to serve on this new, higher committee, with India and Pakistan questions added to the Commonwealth Relations responsibilities, apart from the House of Lords and all the rest of it.

On the other hand, he continued to take a personal interest in Commonwealth matters and to attend ministerial meetings dealing with them. 'I keep in close touch with all that goes on at the Commonwealth Relations Office because we have established a Commonwealth Relations Committee of which I am a member, and, apart from that, as you know in these days of straitened finance, practically all the big issues have come somehow or another into the Commonwealth field.'[40] In January 1949 Patrick Gordon Walker recorded Addison as being present at a meeting of the Commonwealth Affairs Committee of the Cabinet; those present included Attlee, Cripps, Bevin, Philip Noel Baker, Sir Hartley Shawcross, Arthur Creech-Jones, and the Lord Chancellor, Jowitt. Here they discussed the report on a meeting on India between Attlee, Cripps, and Krishna Menon. At this a signed note on the concept of Commonwealth citizenship had been put forward by Krishna Menon, and also a memorandum on the problem of the nature of India's membership of the Commonwealth. Addison also attended a meeting later to discuss India's membership again: here, he 'kept clearly in mind the need to keep India in'.[41] In November 1949 he deputized in superintending the Commonwealth Relations Office for Philip Noel Baker, while the latter was abroad.[42] Then in February 1950 he was present at discussions between Noel Baker and Seretse Khama on the future of Bechuanaland.[43]

One bill in which Addison took a particular interest, even though it was not passed until February 1948 when he was no longer at the Commonwealth Office, was that giving independence to Ceylon. In addition, Ceylon (later Sri Lanka) attained Dominion status within the Commonwealth. Addison spoke in solemn, measured terms on the advance of Ceylon to self-government. 'This is the first occasion in our history upon which a colony, developing this system of self-government of its own accord, has deliberately sought to become a Dominion State in our Commonwealth but we hope and expect that it will not be the last.'[44]

This myriad of Commonwealth issues, then, kept Addison busily occupied long after he formally left the Commonwealth Office. But he had, in addition, a far more fundamental role in the workings of the Cabinet and government. As has been seen, he was in intimate contact with Attlee throughout these six years. By all accounts, Attlee leaned heavily on Addison's experience and judgement, not least in coping with difficult subordinates such as Herbert Morrison, whose intrigues against Attlee's leadership Addison greatly resented. And there was the vital position of leader of the Lords. Here was a potentially crucial post since, at least in theory, the Upper House, with its hereditary base and built-in Tory majority had the power to embarrass the Labour government in 1945 just as effectively as the Upper House had obstructed the Liberals after a similar electoral landslide in 1906. Here, Addison's calming influence and sane judgement were of immense value to the government. The impression he created as leader of the Lords was happily summed up by the *Manchester Guardian* in August 1946. 'He is ruddy, sanguine and imperturbable. Indeed, he is a sedative. When he is on his feet you feel everything is alright with the Planet, Great Britain and the Government.'[45]

However, in dealing with Lords–Commons relations from 1945, Addison faced a task which taxed his diplomatic skill and human understanding to the full. In the face of an overwhelming Conservative majority, he was responsible for the safe passage of a large and far-reaching, even revolutionary legislative programme. Under the Parliament Act of 1911, the Lords retained the right to delay bills that had passed through the Commons (other than money bills as so certified by the Speaker) for two years. This could cause a government real embarrassment, as it had done to some degree the second Labour government of 1929–31; it could lead to the last two years in the life of a Parliament becoming moribund. If there had been difficulty between the two Houses in 1906–10 it could, in theory, be all the more intense now since the political differences between a socialist-dominated House of Commons and a largely Tory Upper House were all the more profound. In fact, by general agreement, Addison handled this difficult task of political management quite superbly, and proved to be one of the most able leaders that the Lords had ever known. He was much aided by the cordial personal relationship that he enjoyed with Lord Salisbury, the leader of the Conservative peers. The two struck up a personal understanding that does much credit to the wisdom of both men: Salisbury himself, twenty-four years the younger, called it a 'father and son' relationship. But Addison's own abilities were remarkable, too. He was now an exceptionally adroit debater, as even the normally hostile *Daily Telegraph* conceded early in 1947. He was able to deal faithfully even with one as expert as Lord Woolton, on the question of food shortages. He operated with an adept blend of firmness and flexibility, while his honesty, urbanity, and good humour averted many difficult passages for the government. He proved much more competent in this respect than his deputy, Jowitt, the Lord Chancellor. The Labour administration of 1945–51 faced an immense, almost shattering array of difficulties, political and economic. Thanks in large measure to Addison's experienced statesmanship, difficulties with the Upper House were not among them, at least until 1948. For the first three years of Labour's period of office, clashes between the two Houses of Parliament were exceptionally rare.

Of course, Addison well appreciated the stern task that he faced when he became leader of the Lords in July 1945. In an article in the journal *Forward*, in July 1946 (that same journal which had caused so many problems for the Ministry of Munitions in the first world war), he wrote of the tasks confronted by the Labour peers during their first year of government. He professed great enthusiasm for the parliamentary management of Herbert Morrison, the Lord President, in handling the House of Commons. But he also envied him and his colleagues their lot as compared with the herculean burden faced by the small band of Labour peers. In the Commons, the Lord President normally had a working majority of nearly two hundred. In the Upper House, the Labour peers were 'but a tiny atoll in the vast ocean of Tory reaction'. They faced the task of putting through the Labour pro-

Labour's Elder Statesman 253

gramme punctually and in good order. The Coal Nationalization Bill, for example, had taken five months to pass through the House of Commons, yet the Labour peers were expected to have it carried in the Lords and safeguarded from mutilation by the beginning of July 1946. Nevertheless, he claimed, cheerfully (and, indeed, accurately) that the Labour peers were well up to schedule with all government legislation. He felt privileged to be the leader of 'as gallant a band of Labour upholders as could be found anywhere'. Up to the summer of 1946 they had not suffered defeat on any of the more important and contentious bills that had been sent up to them by the Lower House. He did not claim all the credit for the Labour peers. In the House of Lords, while they had party loyalties, 'we wear our rue with a difference'. Under the leadership of Lord Cranborne (as Lord Salisbury was known until he succeeded his father in April 1947), the Tory opposition had shown a healthy inclination to sink partisan prejudice, 'and join with us on the government benches in helping the House of Lords to perform its proper function as a second chamber, namely that of revision and acceptable amendment, rather than using it as a Tory engine for the frustration of the Labour government'.[47]

The Labour peers in the Lords worked as an efficient legislative group. They included several other veterans or near-veterans who served as members of the government, including Lords Pethick-Lawrence, Stansgate, Winster, Ammon, Huntingdon, Nathan, and Listowel. There were also some other figures, recently elevated to the peerage, like Lords Hall, Pakenham, and Calverley. They were by no means undistinguished in calibre: Hugh Dalton's earlier observation that only three Labour peers were fit for office (Listowel, Latham, and Winster were those he specified)[48] was shown to be a piece of characteristic exaggeration. The number of Labour peers slowly rose. In 1947, four more were added in the New Year's Honours List and Labour's nominal tally in the Upper House now stood at 46. There was also a distant prospect of another distinguished recruit to the Labour peers. Lord Reith of the BBC was approached by Addison about the prospect of joining the Labour party: Labour ministers generally felt that he should join the party before being offered the government office for which he craved. Addison, however, sent Reith's letter on to Attlee with the comment, 'Can't see any way of making use of his great abilities.'[49] Very seldom were these peers defeated on a vote: only nine times, in fact, in eighteen months, despite the numerical odds stacked against them.[50] It was arranged that there were always about fifteen who attended each debate to monitor the proceedings for their colleagues. One peer in particularly close touch with Addison on these matters was Lord Nathan. He was another Liberal turned Labour (in 1934 in his case) who acted as Addison's deputy. In August 1947 he wrote to his leader (then in Australia),

Since you and I last met a whole heap of things have happened. In the first place I managed to get through the difficult business of the Supplies and Services Bill. . . . After discussing it with Herbert [Morrison] and Frank Pakenham, I have written a letter to Listowel. I selected him rather than George Hall as he after all is the only remaining member of the Cabinet. I hope you will think I have acted wisely.[51]

Throughout, it was Addison who ensured, by authority and by personal example in debate, that the Labour peers acted as an efficient and cohesive unit. He handled them equably but firmly, to ensure that all of them, even the most senior, were prompt in attendance and effective in debate. One ministerial recruit, Lord Pakenham, was somewhat disconcerted, when in full flow in the course of a speech, to have Addison pass him a short note telling him to take his hand out of his pocket. But the affection and respect with which his peers (Pakenham most of all) regarded him made Addison's disciplinary and admonitory role a minor one.

The leader of the Lords had another role, in addition to leading his troops in the heat and battle of parliamentary debate. He was a major figure in the structural working of the central government. In 1945, the wartime system of Cabinet committees was maintained; indeed, Attlee was the first Prime Minister to retain a permanent structure of Cabinet committees in peacetime. Some were chaired by the Prime Minister himself, others by ministers, either the minister principally concerned or else co-ordinating ministers without a department like Morrison, Arthur Greenwood, or Addison. In this respect, quite apart from his close personal relationship to the Prime Minister, Addison played an important part in sustaining the internal coherence of the government. He was also concerned with another innovation devised by Morrison, the 'Future Legislation Committee' designed to ensure that Labour's programme of radical reform was carried out, efficiently and in sequence. Morrison himself felt that 'the Labour

Labour's Elder Statesman

government of 1945–51 organised their legislative programme and parliamentary business more thoroughly than any previous administration'. The members of the Future Legislation Committee were Morrison himself, William Whiteley, the Labour chief whip, and Addison, the leader of the Lords.[52] The main function of this Committee was to work out a precise timetable for each parliamentary session and then present a programme for the approval of the Cabinet. If revisions were needed, the Committee would meet again after the start of a session, and would also consider progress reports. This Future Legislation Committee was vital for the smooth running of the government's ambitious programme. Morrison himself noted that his Committee processed 347 Acts of Parliament, involving 8,640 pages of legislation; a complicated measure like the Transport Nationalization Bill went into no less than twenty-three drafts as a result of the redrafting and reviewing conducted by Morrison, Whiteley, and Addison.[53] Without this committee work of co-ordination and parliamentary management, it is difficult to see how so wide-ranging a legislative programme could have been forced through within the life of a single Parliament. Yet again, Addison was an important figure in the central decision-making and planning cadres of the Attlee administration.

His main task in the Lords, though, consumed most of his time and energies. Labour's manifesto, *Let Us Face the Future* in 1945 had outlined a clear, sweeping programme of public ownership and social reform. The issues were clearly itemized and Labour could claim an unmistakable mandate at the polls to carry this precisely defined legislative programme into immediate effect.

The most controversial legislation introduced by the new government after 1945 concerned the nationalization of basic industries and services. The case for retaining and extending the state controls of wartime was powerful both on grounds of efficiency and of social justice. The general consensus of wartime economic and social ideas, symbolized by the influence of such figures as Keynes and Beveridge, was clearly sympathetic to planning and centralized management. Addison himself well recalled, and often evoked, the ill-starred 'decontrol' policy of 1919–21 which had, he believed, hamstrung efficient governmental planning after the previous war. Even so, to propose so massive a programme of public ownership and control was inevitably controversial and liable to arouse high passion from root-

and-branch defenders of private capitalism. In the Commons, the nationalization programme was passed only as a result of the free use of the guillotine procedure by the government. It was in some measure due to Addison's patience, shrewdness, and diplomatic skill that these measures passed through the Upper House with such ease. Indeed, as Bromhead notes, all the bills which translated into legislative terms the main themes of Labour's 1945 election manifesto were given a second reading without a division.[54]

The three chief bills of the session of 1945–6 were those to nationalize the Bank of England, to establish a public corporation for civil aviation, and to take the coal mines into public ownership. On the Bank of England measure, one Labour peer (Calverley), making his maiden speech, took the opportunity to reflect in bitter terms on the role played by private bankers in Britain and the United States, in dictating terms to the Labour government in 1931.[55] This measure was relatively uncontroversial. On civil aviation, there was more debate. Addison tried in the Lords to dispel the gloomy pronouncements made by Lord Swinton (formerly Lloyd-Greame and Cunliffe-Lister and a ministerial colleague of his in 1920) about a state take-over of the privately owned aviation industry. In fact, as Dominions Secretary, Addison had chaired the Cabinet Committee which drew up the Civil Aviation Bill: he was also to be one of those who drew up the memorandum as a result of which Heathrow Airport was established on the west of London. He was later said to be largely responsible for the success of BOAC. In July 1948, as chairman of the Civil Aviation Committee, he criticized the lack of co-ordination between the Ministers of Supply and of Civil Aviation, and between both and BOAC.[56] Addison in the Lords emphasized the advantages in terms of safety and public confidence of having the air services under the continuous oversight of a responsible central organization rather than being at the mercy of a miscellaneous assortment of private companies. The government's method of approach would also make the co-operation of the Dominions over aviation matters far easier to secure—a factor to which Addison, of course, attached great importance. Addison told Hugh Dalton, with much satisfaction, that the Bill produced 'a terrific hub-bub' in the Lords: 'Swinton and co. gesticulated in incoherent indignation.'[57] Despite this, the Bill passed the Upper House easily enough, while Addison and Swinton remained on excellent terms.

The bill to nationalize the coal mines also did not face too many difficulties. One journalist noted in the *Star*, 'the Tory peers have accepted Labour's challenge with remarkable meekness . . . As a result the Coal Nationalization Bill, with a few agreed changes, has passed to the Statute Book in the form proposed by Mr. Shinwell and his colleagues.'[58] The Transport Bill in 1947, however, proved to be more complicated. Addison had an added burden here as the government spokesman, Lord Inman, fell ill and he had to take over himself the responsibility of handling the Bill somewhat at the last moment. Even so, he briefed himself with his usual efficiency, and cheerfully invited his wife down to the Lords to hear him hold forth. Many of the parts of the Transport Bill had not been discussed in the Commons, owing to the guillotine procedure, and the Lords had, therefore, to devote nine days to the committee stage, with a vast range of amendments. Addison, however, rose to the task with his usual aplomb and good humour. The management of the railways had long been subject to severe criticism: they had been unable to make steady profits, partly owing to the competition of road transport. The growth of the Transport Workers Union and the relative decline of the National Union of Railwaymen reflected this change. It was vital to have an integrated transport service with both the railways and road haulage under public ownership and direction. A policy-making corporation would be established for the railways, on the lines long favoured and advocated by Herbert Morrison, to consider wider aspects of transport integration and planning, free from detailed executive duties.[59] As ever, Addison was ready with historical analogies drawn from his own long experience. He could cite here the amalgamation of the railway companies put through by Sir Eric Geddes for the Lloyd George Coalition in 1921 as a clear precedent for a wider policy of public ownership.

Addison's skill in piloting this difficult measure through the Upper House was widely recognized by ministerial colleagues. Alfred Barnes, the Minister of Transport, wrote to Addison after the Bill had gone through its third reading in the Lords

a personal note . . . to express my admiration of all you have done during these two strenuous months. It became clear before the Bill left the House of Commons that it would be subjected to exceptionally thorough scrutiny in the other place. It was a long, intricate measure. . . . As leader you had to inspire other peers, some of them already hard pressed by departmental responsibilities, with your sense of the importance and urgency of grappling with this tough material. Nor was it merely a question of meeting the opposition critically with counter arguments. Constructive and statesmanlike handling of this important measure was required to an exceptional degree in the Upper House. All this and more have you achieved with wonderful success. The Bill comes back to me in a form which fully justified the hard work done in your house.[60]

The historian who reads these complicated debates on the Transport Bill must conclude that this praise of Addison's skill and management was thoroughly justified. He might conclude, too, that on this occasion, at least, the House of Lords as a revising and amending chamber still proved to have its uses. By contrast with the somewhat Homeric conflict over Transport, the bill to nationalize gas and electricity industries passed with relatively little difficulty in 1948. Here, especially in electricity, the principle of the public corporation was already well established.

The Labour government also had a far-reaching social programme. It sought to create a welfare state, very much on the comprehensive lines laid down by the Beveridge Report during the war. It fell to Addison to pilot the National Insurance Act and the accompanying measure to introduce a National Health Service through the Lords in 1946. His profound knowledge of the health and hospital services proved invaluable on the committee stage. He subsequently received the warm thanks of Aneurin Bevan for his work in securing the passage of these measures.[61] The National Health Service was especially appealing to Addison, with his medical background; it was in many ways the fulfilment of the health reforms that he had initiated at the Ministry of Health in 1919–21. The reorganization of the hospitals proposed by the Dawson Report in 1920 for instance was now implemented, a generation later. Throughout these years, in fact, Addison's lifelong concern with health policies was fully maintained. In October 1948, he was appointed Chairman of the Medical Research Council with which he had been closely connected since its formation. He also resumed contact with another old passion, that of housing. He was amongst a group of ministers who pressed for housing associations and who criticized the cautious approach of the Ministry of Health under Bevan to new programmes. Ironically perhaps, it was Bevan who seemed to be insisting on executive-type, higher-standard housing being set up in development areas, to assist in the recruitment

Labour's Elder Statesman 259

of management for regional industrial policies, and men like Addison who argued that housing ought to be regarded as a basic public service designed for those in greatest economic need. In November 1948 he criticized Bevan's Housing Bill for not giving improvement grants to 'tied' cottages occupied by farm labourers, especially those let under tenancy agreements. It was Addison's view rather than Bevan's that the Cabinet finally adopted.[62]

A different measure which Addison had to carry through the Lords was the Agriculture Act framed by Tom Williams, the Minister, in 1947. Indeed, after the hard fight on the Transport Bill, the Agriculture Bill which was supported on all sides of the House came to him as a tonic and a relaxation.[63] Since the thirties the condition of agriculture and the standard of living of those who worked on the land had begun to improve. Addison was especially gratified that the principles of his Marketing Act of 1931, developed further by Conservative Ministers of Agriculture like Walter Elliot and R. A. Hudson, had become the conventional wisdom. The 1947 Agriculture Act now put into permanent form the marketing boards and subsidies for farmers, which had been developing from the early thirties and had assumed new importance during the war. The 1947 Act provided for an annual review of farm prices each February; as Addison pointed out, it was the essential corollary of the policy of rationing and price controls for the consumer. In 1951, at the end of his life, Addison wrote at the request of Attlee a pamphlet, *How the Labour Party has Saved Agriculture*. This included a warm personal tribute to Tom Williams as Minister and his efforts to assist the farmer and the farm labourer. He took delight in quoting *The Economist*, no left-wing journal, as endorsing Labour's support for agriculture and its revitalization of the countryside.[64] He was able to spell out, from a position of almost incomparable experience, how during his long lifetime the gulf in the quality of life for the town- and the country-dweller had steadily narrowed, and new hope and dignity been brought to those who worked on the land and on whom the nation so depended.

These, then, were busy and fruitful years for Addison. Their achievement, especially in ferrying so much important legislation through the Lords, was warmly commended by Attlee. Writing to Lord Nathan, the Prime Minister wrote in mid-1947, 'You have done a wonderful job in the Lords and we owe you and Christopher a great deal for the way you have managed that difficult other place. . . .'[65]

In addition to this work in the Lords, as has been seen, a wide range of other responsibilities fell to Addison. After resigning as Secretary of State for Commonwealth Relations, he acted as Paymaster General in 1948–9. The purpose of this was to enable him to serve on major Cabinet committees. Norman Brook, the Secretary to the Cabinet, itemized them for him at one point. Other than the Atomic Energy, Future Legislation, and Commonwealth Affairs Committees, Addison also served on the Economic Policy Committee, chaired the Civil Aviation Committee, was Vice-Chairman of the Overseas Reconstruction Committee and sat on the Machinery of Government Committee.[66] Of all the Labour peers, he sat on the largest number of committees, astonishing enough for a man in his late seventies. He once wrote to A. D. Lindsay, the Master of Balliol, that he was 'a member of more than I sometimes think is good for me'.[67] He was to be consulted by Attlee as to whether ministers who acted as government spokesmen in the House of Lords were kept in sufficient touch with discussions of policy in Cabinet Committees.[68] One procedural innovation which he proposed and which was supported by several peers from all parties was that the Upper House should imitate the Lower and have a regular question time at the start of each sitting. Down to 1946 if a peer put down a question to which he wanted an answer without generating a debate on the topic, he had to wait until the end of the sitting. There was much criticism of this in the Lords, both by ministers and by other peers, as it involved much wasting of time.[69] The proposed reform, however, was not to be adopted.

In the summer of 1947, a series of storms struck the previously impregnable Labour government because of the mishandling of two main areas of policy. These were finance, after the disastrous crisis of the convertibility of sterling into dollars, and the nationalization of iron and steel. As has been seen, until then the Lords had presented few obstacles to the government's radical legislative programme. This was partly because the government's own commitment to them, and mandate for them, was beyond question. But the nationalization of iron and steel was highly controversial within the Labour Cabinet itself. There had been reservations felt by Morrison among others about including it on the 1945 party manifesto. Wilmot, the Minister of Supply (later replaced by the vigorous Strauss in 1947), cited doubts felt about steel nationalization in the City. The party had no detailed blueprints for the public ownership of steel and little progress was made in the government's early period towards implementing this part of its programme. Attlee was well aware of the divisions within the Cabinet. He wrote to Nathan in August 1947, 'I have intimations of resignation whichever course we take and frankly I do not like them. . . . We shall get through our present difficulties but only if we stick together.'[70] Here at last was an area of policy where the Lords might indeed prove a real stumbling-block.

The government finally resolved to bring forward the bill to take iron and steel into public ownership in the 1948–9 session of Parliament. It was now believed that the Conservative peers would vote the second reading down in the Lords because it would be then too late for the government to have the bill passed in three consecutive sessions in the Commons before the Parliament of 1945 came to an end some time before the summer of 1950. Therefore the government armed itself in advance by introducing in the 1947–8 session of Parliament a bill to amend the 1911 Parliament Act. This would reduce the delaying power of the House of Lords from two years to one. Attlee wrote in his memoirs, 'It was clear that the Iron and Steel Bill would not get through the House without the use of the Parliament Bill.'[71]

When it fell to Addison to bring the Parliament Bill before the Lords, it was clear that the Conservative peers were determined to resist it fiercely. He emphasized that the government regarded its passage, with or without agreed amendments, as vital to its programme. If the House of Lords rejected the Bill, it would be passed under the Parliament Act of 1911. No attack was intended on the second chamber; it was calculated to minimize social and political conflict. In this instance, however, their lordships refused to accept Addison's pacifying assurances.

The question of the composition of the Lords, as well as of its formal powers in relation to the Commons, now came into discussion. This was a theme that had exercised Addison since his discussions with the Conservative peers in 1944. In Cabinet discussions on the Parliament Bill in October 1947, he had attacked the Bill for being too timid and not abolishing 'the hereditary right to vote' but the majority felt that this would make the Bill too wide-ranging.[72] Early in 1948, inter-party consultations were held with leading Conservative peers to consider the reform of the second chamber. These disclosed 'a great measure of agreement as to what should be recommended in amending the composition of the House whilst retaining its best qualities'.[73]

Even so, Addison wrote to his friend Mackenzie King in April 1948 that 'we are stuck with the failure to get an accommodation on the length of time, as affecting its powers, that the House of Lords should be able to hold up a Bill'. But he remained optimistic.

You will be glad to know, however, that there is complete agreement that the hereditary right to attend and vote shall be completely abolished and there should be a House that represents a fair balance of parties; that it should be constituted by people on grounds of public service or distinction; that it should be possible to create life peers and that the sex disqualification should be removed. In any case, it would mean that something like 600 of the present members of the House would not be qualified and I must say I admire the Conservative Party in agreeing to this.

He recognized that 'there may be a breakdown in the near future on the subject of powers'. But 'even if there is I am not yet prepared to give up hope on an agreed scheme of reformation on the Chamber's composition. As you can well imagine I had a pretty considerable struggle to get my own political friends in the party to agree to these proceedings.'[74] Ever admiring, Mackenzie King replied that he doubted whether 'any living person other than yourself could have brought the movement so far along the way in so short a time as you have been able to do'.[75]

But these proposals, anticipating the Life Peerages measure of 1958, came to nothing. Nor was there agreement on the limitation of the powers of the Lords. To Addison's disappointment, the Lords rejected the second reading of the Parliament Bill by 177 votes to 81 after five days of debate.[76] A conflict between the two Houses of Parliament was inevitable, with a new test of Addison's capacity for conciliation and statesmanship.

The government pressed on, nevertheless, with their bill to nationalize the iron and steel industry. This had produced much difference of opinion within the Cabinet. While Dalton, Bevan, and Cripps were in favour (and eventually won their point), Addison was one of a group who fought against the Bill. They included Jowitt, Greenwood, and Tom Williams, and at first they had the backing of the Prime Minister and Herbert Morrison. Addison frequently took part in the lengthy debates on iron and steel that preoccupied the Cabinet in the spring and summer of 1947. On 24 April he urged that the government would have to show that nationalization would provide an 'effective incentive for the iron and steel companies to

Labour's Elder Statesman

develop their undertakings on enterprising lines'. On 24 July he spoke out against schemes either to acquire the physical assets of the steel industry or to buy up the shares of selected firms: he gained the support here of Morrison. On 7 August he argued that the scheme for public ownership outlined by Wilmot's Cabinet Paper 212 would 'lead to a reduced output of steel which would be disastrous in the present critical economic situation'. After prolonged disagreement, the Cabinet agreed on 14 October not to introduce the Iron and Steel Bill in the 1947–8 session but to make the amendment of the 1911 Parliament Act its main new measure.

Disagreement between ministers on the outlines of an iron and steel nationalization bill continued in 1948. On 2 June Addison took it upon himself to circulate a memorandum on the subject. He pointed out that 'I have no objection as such to large-scale national acquisition where the case is made out. For example, I myself, for many years past, have recommended the national ownership of land.' But he believed that it was much more difficult to make out a convincing case for nationalizing iron and steel, by comparison with coal, electricity, and gas where the reasons for public ownership had been 'abundantly displayed'. He doubted whether the output of steel or the efficiency of the industry would be improved by nationalization. From the political standpoint, the new measure would come into effect, with all its early transitional problems, at the time of the next general election in 1950. Addison's conclusion was that a 'well thought-out bill' should either be left until the beginning of the next Parliament, after the general election, or else that Morrison should resume talks with the heads of the iron and steel industry with the object of producing a moderate bill based on state control rather than ownership. The majority in the Cabinet was now against such an approach, however, and a bill to nationalize the iron and steel industry was introduced in the autumn of 1948, although, as will be seen, it took a much modified form.[77]

It may seem curious that Addison, with his long commitment to state ownership and control, dating from the first world war, should be amongst those who now resisted nationalization of a major industry, especially one where, as Strauss pointed out to the Cabinet, the pre-war record of private management in terms of modernization and efficiency, and also of cartelization and restrictive practices, had been so dismal. However, Addison's enthusiasm for nationalization had largely focused on public services and utilities such as the railways or electricity, or else extractive heavy industry like coal. There was also the special case of land nationalization, though this had now been dropped from Labour's programme. But Addison had never been keen on the public ownership of large sections of manufacturing industry: he was alarmed that the government's Steel Bill in 1948 would take over large firms such as Guest, Keen, and Nettlefolds which were not wholly concerned with iron and steel production. He had always doubted whether a bureaucratic state management would prove any more efficient in manufacturing industry than a modernized private system. His commitment to public ownership, like that of the majority of the Labour Cabinet, was pragmatic and selective, rather than being founded on a doctrinaire view of the essence of socialism: this put him very much at odds with a minister like Aneurin Bevan whose *In Place of Fear* was to regard nationalization and socialism as inseparable, almost identical. Addison would probably have applauded the view expressed a few years later in C. A. R. Crosland's *Future of Socialism* in 1956 that the emergence of a new cadre of autonomous public managers made the debate over the ownership of industries increasingly irrelevant.[78]

Nevertheless, Addison spoke out with much vigour in favour of the nationalizing of iron and steel when he had to bring it before the Lords. There had long been a process of integration within the iron and steel industry. Yet all around the country industrial recovery was being slowed down by the shortage of steel. If steel were to be diverted to internal development, there would have to be some corporate public body to run the industry. Many peers, he noted, accepted the necessity for a large measure of control. But it appeared that the only ones who would not be allowed to exercise it would be the elected representatives of the British people.[79] In fact, the Iron and Steel Bill was far from a revolutionary measure. It took over the shares of major steel companies and set up a consolidating control board. But no radical changes were made in the organizational structure of the industry. It was a form of public ownership that could easily be reversed, and the Conservatives were to denationalize it in 1953. In fact, although the Lords carried amendments to the Bill on almost every point, they gave way when the Commons reversed these decisions of the Upper House.

On one crucial issue, though, the Lords did not give way. This was that the vesting date for the nationalization of iron and steel should be

Labour's Elder Statesman 265

postponed from 1 May 1950 to 1 July 1951—that is, well after the general election which would have to be held in 1950. Addison had declared that the government would not surrender on this vital point. 'We have taken the view and we stand unalterably upon it that we will not accept that this unrepresentative house . . . shall be able to demand a second mandate of the people and shall refuse to give authority to Bills introduced in the fourth session of a Parliament by a Government with a large majority in the representative chamber.'[80] However, the government eventually conceded the point: a new provision was inserted that no member of the Iron and Steel Corporation could be appointed before 1 October 1950.[81] This represented a notable victory for the Tory peers. However by passing the new Parliament Act on 29 November 1949, over the Lords' resistance, the government deprived the Upper House of the effective power of rejecting the Iron and Steel Bill. They could now delay it for only twelve more months. In fact, on 24 November 1949 the Lords gave the Iron and Steel Bill a second reading without a division.[82] Ironically, the Bill then went through without the contentious Parliament Act having to be used at all.

Addison, now eighty, had therefore to handle and defuse a potentially dangerous constitutional crisis. It was in part a tribute to his equable, imperturbable approach that there was not a major conflict. Although they accepted the government's decisions on the Iron and Steel Bill, apart from the vesting date, Lord Salisbury made it clear that the Conservative peers accepted under protest.

I sometimes wonder whether the Labour Party, in spite of all their protestations, really believe in the second chamber at all. That hardly seems credible if they expect this House, with all its talent and experience, to sit long hours over bills with the object of making them more workable, and then, without even facade of serious consideration, reject all the more important amendments that have been made, apparently just because they emanated from the House of Lords.[83]

Meanwhile the Labour government faced crippling and unprecedented economic difficulties. The long years of war had wrought havoc with Britain's overseas trade and led to the sale of many foreign investments. When the war with Japan ended, the American Senate brought the Lend Lease arrangements to an abrupt end late in 1945, and made no alternative provision for British imports. This was a desperate blow for the Attlee government, reminiscent of the isolationism of the United States after 1919. A loan was negotiated with the United States, on severe terms. But with a continuing dollar crisis and a shortage of raw materials slowing down industrial recovery, the economic situation became increasingly grave. At home, there was public resentment at the continuation of food rationing and other forms of 'austerity', rigorously enforced by the puritanical figure of Sir Stafford Cripps who went from the Board of Trade to the Treasury in 1947. Addison had attacked Cripps's clothes rationing scheme in December 1946 as being too restrictive, especially in its reduction of export allocations to the Dominions. On the other hand, he had joined Dalton and Attlee in pressing for the immediate introduction of food rationing on 21 July 1946.[84] The Ministers of Food, first Sir Ben Smith, then John Strachey, became successively popular targets for cheap abuse in the press and on the radio. It was against a background of financial crisis and public discontent that the Labour government had to operate during its later period in office.

Addison often spoke on these complex economic issues in debates in the Lords. Britain had to find a way to pay for her needs. The price of necessary commodities had increased, overseas expenditure remained severe not least because of military commitments in the Middle East and elsewhere, the demands of the rest of the sterling area were heavy ones.[85] He hailed the signing of the European Economic Co-operative convention at Paris on 16 April 1948. The participating countries could now sustain a satisfactory level of economic activity through their own efforts.[86] On the other hand, the introduction of the Marshall Aid scheme showed how dependent western Europe was on American financial and industrial assistance. In discussing these themes, Addison constantly emphasized that the power of the state and centralized planning were beneficent forces in society. In a radio broadcast in June 1948, in reply to one by Lord Salisbury in which he had claimed that Labour sought an all-powerful state with almost divine authority, Addison hailed the government of which he was a member as 'the foremost champion of personal liberty and the most potent enemy of state tyranny'. The power of the state must be harnessed to promote individual choice in a way unattainable if society was to be left to the struggles of competitive private interests. Characteristically, he reflected on his own experiences as a minister after the first world war. He compared the economic indices for three years of largely Conservative government in 1918–21 with those for three years of Labour rule from 1945. He forecast the disastrous results that would accrue, in terms of recession and unemployment, if controls were precipitately abandoned as they had been in Britain after 1918. By contrast with the earlier post-war period, Britain now had full employment, industrial growth, and thriving exports.[87]

By 1949 the economic and financial situation seemed worse still. There appeared to be a permanent shortage of dollars and an acute imbalance of trade. In September, Britain had to devalue the pound by about one-third of its exchange value against the American dollar. Addison spoke on this theme in the Lords. No benefit would result from devaluation unless exports were materially expanded to take advantage of Britain's improved competitive position. There would have to be a concerted policy to hold down wage and price increases so as not to price Britain out of world markets. There should be more determined selling methods for British products. Only in this way could the imports necessary for industrial growth and full employment in Britain be sustained; only thus, too, could government provision be maintained for children, the old, and the sick where Britain was pioneer amongst the nations.[88] This was a difficult theme to handle convincingly, even though in fact British exports did expand materially in the period October 1949 to June 1950, between devaluation and the outbreak of the Korean War. The political atmosphere was tense, too, as the Conservatives sensed that the government was losing control. Even Addison's benign authority in the Lords was at times under challenge. There was a major row when he had to defend the government's record over the 'ground nuts' scheme in East Africa, after the Conservatives had fiercely attacked Labour for waste and inefficiency.[89] The fact remained that £37 millions of public money had been lost on a well-meant, but maladministered scheme of overseas development. With the further scandal of the Gambia eggs scheme, the reputation of the government, especially of the Ministry of Food, continued to fluctuate.

At this critical period, Addison attended several important meetings of ministers to approve the broad package of policy to be put forward by Cripps and Bevin, the Chancellor and Foreign Secretary, at the forthcoming conference in Washington. This was to assist in restoring equilibrium in the sterling/dollar balance of trade and to enable the economy of the sterling area to maintain stability independent of external aid from the United States. The Washington Conference seemed to go well, and the prospects for British external trade now improved. Addison in public and in private remained optimistic, as ever, both about the future of the economy and about the outcome of the forthcoming 1950 general election. He wrote confidently enough to Mackenzie King in late 1949, just after his eightieth birthday:

In this country we are in fact making good progress, solidly, if slowly. . . . As you know we have an election again next year and I am averse to prophesying. . . . I think one of our most considered risks is derived from some of our own friends. Unless they make an unusual lot of bloomers, I see no reason to think that the present Government may not be returned with a majority, although no doubt a substantially smaller one than it has now. That, even if it occurred, would be no loss, as there was a sprinkling of people who got in last time on the wave who are not very helpful and are much inclined, as you know, to run after various stunts. The record of the by-elections, on the whole, has been very remarkable, although it has so happened that in most cases the seats had been previously held by large majorities which nearly always have been very much reduced.

One of the perplexities of this time is that, despite our efforts we are becoming increasingly cluttered up by International Conferences . . . and it rarely happens that our ministers are at home at the same time. . . . On personal matters, I am still going strong . . . on the whole I think we [the House of Lords] set a very good example of co-operation between the two parties without abatement of our political principles. . . . This is, of course, the right job for me, for the time being anyhow.[90]

Somewhat against the advice of Herbert Morrison, Attlee dissolved Parliament and called a general election in February 1950. Mackenzie King wrote encouragingly to Addison that he thought 'Attlee was right in bringing on the campaign at this time rather than waiting till the last moment.' He cited Labour's remarkable record of not losing a single seat in by-elections between 1945 and 1950. 'I am sorry that at your years you have to continue to battle as you have. However, I have long since learned that you were equal to anything.'[91] The eighty-year-old Addison did nothing to disappoint these hopes. He joined in the general election of 1950 with much enthusiasm. At the request of the editor of *The Observer*, he wrote an article 'Then and Now' which appeared in that newspaper on 19 February, concurrently with one by Lord Salisbury.[92] In this, Addison rebutted the standard Tory charge that freedom was in danger under socialism. He pointed to the complete disappearance of the unemployment of the thirties, to the expansion of the formerly 'depressed' older industrial regions, to the

Labour's Elder Statesman 269

establishment of the health service and other components of the welfare state, and to the reorganization of British industry. He also carried out several engagements during the campaign, speaking at High Wycombe, and on behalf of Attlee at West Walthamstow, Lady Pakenham at Oxford, and Ian Mikardo at Reading. There was also a triumphant reception at Swindon, his old constituency.[93] It was an extraordinary performance for a man of his advanced years, not exactly Gladstone at Midlothian but impressive enough.

Labour was again returned to power at the general election, but with a majority reduced from over one hundred and fifty to only six. Lady Addison spent much time packing and then unpacking their family belongings. While Labour's industrial and urban strongholds remained loyal and polled very heavily, middle-class voters in the suburbs swung right, while the redistribution of seats also told against Labour. Addison, for all his years, was reappointed Lord Privy Seal and leader of the Lords. The *Sunday Times* applauded the move. 'He is shrewd and alert and his three careers have taught him much about human nature and political tactics. A very useful man to a government with a small majority which depends in the last resort on the floating vote.'[94]

The early months of the new government were not fraught with as many external difficulties as had been feared. While there were several tense votes in the Commons which threatened the government's survival, the economy appeared to boom and exports to increase. Even coal was at times exported once again from Welsh and other ports. Addison continued to preside urbanely at this time over a hostile Upper House. In one notable debate on 17 May, he took the occasion again to uphold the power of the state as a liberating, enlightened force. In the case of the rationing of scarce commodities, while the government might be restricting the liberty of one, wealthier individual, they might be safeguarding that of another. He was congratulated on this speech by the miners' peer, Jack Lawson, who felt that he had admirably described 'the sweeping social changes due to industry . . . and with amazing discrimination in view of the fact that your life has not been spent in industry'.[95] Labour meanwhile took heart from two by-elections in highly marginal seats, West Dumbartonshire in April, and Brighouse and Spenborough in May. Both these seats were retained on immensely high polls of over 85 per cent, despite the fact that in both only small swings were required for the Conservatives to retain the seat. In working-class areas, Labour morale was still surprisingly high

Then came the Korean War, which brought another desperate passage for the government. This led to renewed economic and political difficulties for the Attlee administration. Addison was, of course, present at Cabinet discussions over the Korean War and approved of the decision to send a United Nations force in to repel aggression from North Korea. He believed that the invasion of South Korea was 'a great and violent wrong' and Britain should therefore supply military support for the United Nations forces. But as the war continued Addison became more and more alarmed at the implications, especially the possibility of Chinese mass involvement as General MacArthur pushed up towards the Yalu river on the borders of China. Britain, Addison wrote to Richard Stokes, was 'on a very dangerous and slippery slope and the U.S.A. are doing their best to push us down it further every day. If they had been prepared to listen to our advice and not to be stampeded by MacArthur, we should not be in this mess now.'[96] Britain's involvement in the Korean War brought economic problems which were to plague the Labour government for the rest of its period of office. There was immensely higher governmental expenditure, and a sharp rise of prices of food and other raw materials. In addition, the government had embarked upon a hitherto unprecedented level of rearmament as a result of entry into the war. Many members of the government, including Addison, felt deeply unhappy at this policy. Attlee's government now moved towards a major internal crisis. It was not assisted when Bevin gave up the Foreign Office owing to ill health in March 1951, and was succeeded by Herbert Morrison. This resulted in Addison's moving to become Lord President of the Council on 11 March.

A difficult period now ensued for the government in which domestic and external issues impinged upon each other. There was ministerial controversy over charges upon welfare at home, especially the financing of the National Health Service, and over the cost of defence and rearmament. In April (while Attlee was absent in hospital and the Cabinet was temporarily under the less adroit leadership of Morrison), Aneurin Bevan and Harold Wilson, the Minister of Labour and President of the Board of Trade respectively, resigned from the Cabinet, and were joined by John Freeman, junior minister at Supply. Addison agreed with Bevan's concern for infringements of

Labour's Elder Statesman 271

the principle of a free health service for which he himself had fought for half a century, but implored him, nevertheless, not to take this extreme step. 'After all, the proposed charges for prescriptions involved the same principles and to resign over charges for false teeth and spectacles (involving identical principles) would seem small and altogether out of proportion. . . . Remember, please, your great powers and possibly great future.'[97] But Addison had served on the Cabinet Committee appointed in 1950 to keep the administration of the Health Service 'under constant review' and to propose economies.[98] Naturally Bevan resented interference by colleagues of this kind, and he stuck to his resignation.

In October 1951, Attlee again dissolved Parliament and called another general election. The timing of it caused some consternation: it may have been influenced by George VI's visit to Africa. With hindsight, it looks as though an election in mid-1952 might have been more fortunate for Labour. In 1976–9 it was to be seen that a government could perfectly well continue with a very small majority or none at all, given adroit parliamentary management. But in truth government and party in 1951 were exhausted. Ministers, some of whom, like Attlee and Morrison, had been in office almost continuously for eleven momentous years in peace and in war, were worn out. The rearmament programme had put the economy under great strain. From the summer of 1951 onwards the over-all balance of payments deficit was worsened by other countries in the sterling area, who ran deficits on their trade. In the event, Labour was very narrowly defeated. Despite gaining fourteen million votes, a record total which showed that grass-roots party workers were still in good heart and loyal to their leaders, the Labour party fell from power. The Conservatives under Churchill scraped home with a majority of only fifteen.

Addison took little part in the general election of October 1951. He had undergone a minor operation at the end of 1950 and required increased nursing attention from his devoted wife. In 1951 his health deteriorated and his appearances in the Lords diminished in number. His last substantial speech was made on the Forestry Bill on 4 April, a sprightly enough affair. That summer, an operation, supposedly to remove a gall bladder, revealed a malignant growth in the pancreas. Addison, with his medical expertise on the ailments of the pancreas, probably knew the sad news before it was broken to him by the surgeon, Sir James Paterson Ross of St. Bartholomew's. Addison reacted to the prospect of his impending death with all his accustomed courage and calmness. Methodically, he made arrangements with leading doctors about having a successor appointed to the Medical Research Council. He also decided with Attlee that Jowitt (who was less popular in the Lords) would succeed him as leader of the Labour peers, pending his replacement by Lord Alexander. There was a final lunch at 10 Downing Street with the Attlees, on the day the election results were known. As they dined, Lady Addison heard the belongings of the new Prime Minister, Sir Winston Churchill, being brought in below them. The Addisons and the Attlees must have known that they were meeting for the last time. There was just time for a friendly note of congratulation to Addison's old associate, Churchill, and for some correspondence about the old man's eligibility for a ministerial pension.[99] Addison now returned home to Radnage to await the end, to bear the intense pain of encroaching cancer, and to be comforted and nursed by his endlessly courageous wife. On 11 December 1951, after a brief final illness, Addison died in the presence of his wife. There was a funeral service at the Norman church of St. Mary's at Radnage, near the home at 'Neighbours' on 14 December. At the graveside, the words of Mr Valiant for Truth from *Pilgrim's Progress* were read out. 'As he went down deeper, he said, "Grave, where is thy victory?" So he passed over, and all the trumpets sounded for him on the other side.' The grave at Radnage is simple, dignified, and unpretentious.

A memorial service was held in Westminster Abbey, on the instructions of Attlee, on 30 January 1952. Tributes were paid in the Lords that day by Salisbury, Jowitt, Samuel, Pethick-Lawrence, Stansgate, and other peers in a genuine outpouring of grief at the passing of so deeply respected and universally beloved a leader. Lady Addison received a torrent of several hundred letters of condolence and tribute to her late husband. Among them were letters from such varied figures as Sir Winston Churchill, Herbert Morrison, Field Marshal Montgomery, Lords Beaverbrook and Vansittart, John Strachey, and Krishna Menon, as well as personal reminiscences from many humbler folk of acts of personal kindness by Addison that they recalled and treasured. Perhaps three of these letters may be briefly cited. Hugh Dalton, an old Cabinet colleague, wrote that 'No one I ever knew grew old more youthfully.' Lord Pakenham, a Labour colleague in the Lords, spoke with deep emotion of Addison's 'greatness of

Labour's Elder Statesman 273

soul'. On their personal relationship, he added simply, 'I owe everything to him.' Lord Swinton, a colleague in the days of the 1918–22 Coalition, a political opponent in the Lords since 1945, quoted a conversation between the young Lewis Douglas and the veteran Georges Clemenceau in the later 1920s. Clemenceau was recorded as having said that only two things mattered in politics—'to love and to be loved, and to be intellectually honest'. As Swinton himself noted, 'Christopher was both.'[100]

It had fallen to Addison to guide the House of Lords through one of the most difficult and potentially dangerous periods in its long history. For the first time, the Upper House, with its built-in Conservative majority, was confronted with an equally large Labour majority in the Commons. Had Labour been led by a man less shrewd and far-sighted than Addison, there might have been endless conflicts involving the very fabric of the constitution. As Lord Salisbury observed, in the debate called in tribute to Addison's memory on 30 January 1952,

> he showed throughout that difficult period a humanity, a sagacity and a moderation which not only made the system workable in these new, untried circumstances, but also won him the warm and enduring affection even of those who were politically most bitterly opposed to him. . . . He was a convinced constitutionalist. He believed in the maintenance of the authority of Parliament over the Government of the country, equally that the state should be the servant not the master of the people.[101]

Addison himself would have presumably not cavilled at these judgements from a political opponent on his over-all public outlook.

The conduct of the Lords during the period 1945–51 has often been warmly commended. It has been seen as showing assiduity and adaptability in new circumstances; it obliged the government to explain, and sometimes to amend its decisions, without coercing it.[102] This happy outcome owed much to the character of Addison's leadership of it. Lord Nathan, his colleague and deputy leader, wrote to him in 1950,

> As a member of the same Government, let me say with what admiration I have regarded your leadership both in opposition and especially during these past difficult years when so many complex questions have arisen and so much profoundly controversial legislation has had to be carried through a hostile house where we were numerically so insignificant a minority. That so much

has been achieved and with so much absence of friction is in great measure due to you personally—the friendly feeling in all quarters of the House, and the loyal devotion of your own small group, that you have earned for yourself the pride all of every party feel in you as leader of the House; the wisdom with which you have dealt with men and matters.[103]

Every Conservative peer of any significance echoed these words.

There is much evidence that for Addison his leadership of the House of Lords provided a most enjoyable and rewarding finale to his political career, an Indian summer of rare serenity. He liked the informal atmosphere of the Lords. He told the Oxford Labour Club in 1949 that it was marked by 'a complete absence of snobbery. . . . I have spoken at hundreds of Labour meetings and I have found more snobbery at many of them than in the House of Lords. There we are supposed to be equal. . . . There is no distinction of class or type and Labour peers who have come new to the place have been received with the same openness and friendliness as anyone else.'[104] On the other hand, he always stressed the undemocratic nature of a hereditary assembly. His period as leader, however, was not only agreeable but exceptionally fruitful. While he always found his wife and home at Radnage a calm refuge, especially at week-ends when he could once again enjoy the sights and smells of the countryside, his ultimate pleasure came from public activity and in piloting through so many of those major social and political reforms for which is adult life had been a joyous crusade. He found time to battle with the Treasury on behalf of pensions for former Indian civil servants.[105] This most unassuming of men received a bounty of honours in this later period, an honorary degree from Cambridge in 1949, one from Oxford in 1950, and perhaps most pleasing of all, one in 1948 from the University of Sheffield where he had begun his medical career and had become Professor of Anatomy back in 1897. He had also become a Knight of the Garter in 1946, the first member of the Labour party to be so honoured.

Twenty-five years after Addison's death, there were still important links with his eventful life. His eldest son, Christopher, who had succeeded him as second Viscount, died in 1976. He was succeeded by Michael, the younger son; as it happened, he took the Conservative whip in the Lords, as his brother had done. The younger daughter, Isobel, lived near Great Missenden, and the dowager Lady Addison, still mentally very sharp for all her eighty-odd years, in High

Wycombe, close to that much loved Buckinghamshire countryside. There was a final act of commemoration in July 1978 when, after some years of application to the church authorities, a memorial window was placed by Lady Addison in the north chancel of the old Norman church of St. Mary's at Radnage, close to the grave. Its symbols included an anchor, a wheat-sheaf, and a serpent, the last two representing Agriculture and Health, two of Addison's major portfolios. It was designed, appropriately, by Joseph Nuttgens, a veteran socialist craftsman from the C. R. Ashbee school at Chipping Campden. It was right that a memorial of this kind should allude to a life spent in public service. It commemorated in dignified fashion a senior and respected leader of a great reforming administration between 1945 and 1951. It indicated the way, not least in his last six years, Addison brought to fulfilment wide-ranging programmes to promote social welfare, economic innovation, and a transformation of Britain's imperial role. The memorial window testified to changes that span the course of British history, as did Addison's own career, from the government of Asquith to that of Attlee.

Conclusion

'... Idealist turned politician, Liberal turned Labour, middling minister turned elder statesman, he epitomises a whole phase of British politics....'[1] The *Sunday Times*'s characterization of his career in 1950 is an apt description of Addison's exceptionally long and varied life. His brilliant medical career before 1910 led him to a concern for social and environmental deprivation. During the years before 1914 he had come to symbolize the New Liberalism with its emphasis on social welfare and reforming policies. One newspaper commented: 'His opportunity came with the introduction of the Insurance Act and in a very short time he knew more about it than did Lloyd George.'[2] Collective action on behalf of social and humanitarian ends appealed to Addison both as a medical doctor and as a 'true radical'. As a result, he was much involved in the application of the New Liberalism both to warfare and to welfare during the first world war. He was the natural choice of Lloyd George to spearhead his crucially important reconstruction policies throughout the latter part of 1917 and 1918 and to plan for post-war social reform. At the Ministry of Health in 1919–21 he promoted a new surge of welfare policy. After the break with Lloyd George in July 1921 he was a notable recruit to the Labour party, seeing it as the only agency capable of carrying out that social reform programme emasculated by the 'anti-waste' campaign and the Geddes 'axe'. He later became an important figure in the development of Labour policies on agriculture, especially over marketing, and also in debates on foreign policy during the thirties. He served as elder statesman under Attlee with his main task that of leading the House of Lords. His career in politics was as long as that of Lloyd George and almost as eventful. But, unlike the latter, it suffered no period of 'long twilight' and was actively creative to the end.

In many ways Addison shows the continuity of the progressive tradition in politics. His enthusiasm for the New Liberalism of the years before 1914 was reinforced by the collectivism of the first world war. He sustained this attitude during the years of post-war government and thus was a natural recruit for Labour after 1922. Although he was a collectivist rather than what some contemporaries termed a 'real' socialist, the progressive tradition is seen in his lifelong commitment to social welfare, to land development, to reform of the Lords, to Irish home rule, to colonial self-government, and to a pacific (though not pacifist) foreign policy. Sometimes he was thought to have had something of a blind spot over women's equality; for example, he challenged the bill introduced by the Labour party to enable women to hold any civil or judicial office. In fact he was to become more enlightened here, too. He supported the bill to give votes to women over twenty-one in 1920.[3] He retained much of the old Liberal heritage after 1923 and moved smoothly towards becoming a democratic socialist. In his late seventies and early eighties he was expounding in the Cabinet, to younger socialists like Bevan and Wilson, progressive principles first imbibed during the years of Campbell-Bannerman and Asquith. He retained his enthusiasm for radical reform down to the end, at a time when more theoretical exponents of pre-1914 progressivism, such as the Hammonds and Gilbert Murray, were lapsing into disillusioned and even racist conservatism.[4]

On the other hand, Addison as a progressive, took an unusual route towards joining Labour. Most of the middle-class Liberal recruits to Labour moved left in reaction against the first world war and the Lloyd George Coalition, as did, for example, Ponsonby, Trevelyan, Morel, and many in the UDC. Addison moved left rather because he embraced the first world war and saw the value of the collectivism it entailed. The experience of the Lloyd George Coalition strengthened rather than weakened his progressivism. This is illustrated admirably in his books *Practical Socialism* and *The Betrayal of the Slums*. Thus, he was the one leading Coalition Liberal who joined those anti-Lloyd George Liberals in the Labour party after 1923, completely at home with MacDonald, the late Coalition's most passionate adversary.

Addison was also a vigorous and generally successful minister; as Lloyd George recognized 'he was a good organiser and a man of tireless energy'.[5] He had his limitations. At first, he was widely recognized as a somewhat pedestrian speaker, as the *Leeds Mercury*, for example, noted in 1915. On the other hand, it added that his speeches had the merit of 'absolute clearness and plainness of language'.[6] At times, he was prickly as his correspondence and the reminiscences of contemporaries show. Lady Beveridge (herself a difficult person), for example, noted in her diary her opinion of Addison when he was Parliamentary Secretary at the Ministry of Munitions. She did not get on well with him. He was, she thought, 'overwhelmed with the importance of the job . . . and was *de haut en bas* to anyone in my humble way of work . . . On one occasion I dropped a fatal brick by inviting him to have a cup of tea with me. He gave me an outraged and prolonged glare and hurried back to the shelter of his enormous room.'[7] He was, however, to become much more mellow after 1945; in the House of Lords he inspired universal affection. He has been criticized, probably rightly, for his undue optimism as a minister, as over housing, for example, in 1919.[8] At the Ministry of Munitions his record was rather mixed; although very successful on the actual manufacturing and costing side of the Ministry, he himself said of his two years in charge of labour questions that they 'seem like a nightmare looking back on them'.[9] However, his years at the Ministries of Reconstruction and Health opened up new vistas of social reform; he has been unfairly criticized, for example by Bentley Gilbert and Paul Barton Johnson, for his handling of these departments. Indeed, the housing programme was a radical new departure in subsidized welfare in that the government, for the first time, recognized housing as a national responsibility and a vital component of public welfare policies. Addison's critics have laid inadequate stress on the obstructive policies pursued by the Treasury. The 'dear money' policy adopted from April 1920 with its high interest rates was in total conflict with an expansionist housing programme by the local authorities, and Addison's reputation suffered unfairly as a result.

He was also a very innovative minister at the Ministry of Agriculture. The marketing policy which he inaugurated in 1930–1 was to be used by successive Ministers of Agriculture, who built upon the foundations which he had laid. Although he had, before 1918, supported the policy of free trade, he had never been dogmatic about it. His agricultural schemes put forward in the 1930s illustrate the move away from the old Liberal policy of unrestricted imports to the support of a diluted form of protectionism. He was said by contemporaries to have educated his party in agricultural matters so that it became the party of the countryside as well as of the industrial regions. Labour became the more representative of the nation as a whole.

At the Dominions Office after 1945 he was to be a great asset to Attlee's government. He promoted cordial relations between the Dominions and the mother country, because of his ability to establish rapport with Commonwealth Prime Ministers and heads of state, and to win over people in the Dominions by his benign manner. However, his major duty in the 1945 Labour government was to lead the House of Lords. This was an onerous task during this period as, for the first time ever, the House of Lords, with its large Conservative majority, was faced with an equally large Labour majority in the other place. In addition, most of the measures proposed in the Lower House during this period were anathema to the House of Lords. However, Addison, with his long ministerial experience to draw upon, avoided the clashes which could so easily have occurred. In addition to proving himself a most accomplished debater, he showed, in the words of the Conservative leader, Lord Salisbury, 'a humanity, a sagacity and a moderation' which not only made the system workable in these new untried circumstances but also won him the warm, enduring affection, even of those who were publicly most bitterly opposed to him.[10] As Earl Jowitt remarked, 'he was successful in the art of leadership because he never practiced it.'[11] Thus he was a consistent and idealistic radical but a radical who could use power. He could blend idealism with pragmatism.

Finally, Addison played an unusually important part in the evolution of British party politics. He was at the centre of the key crises of 1916, 1918, 1931, and 1945. In particular he was a decisive figure in the career of Lloyd George. He became very close to the latter from the controversial passing of the Insurance Act in 1911 onwards. Lloyd George consulted Addison frequently on a wide variety of subjects and they became good friends. As Addison had remarked in 1914 'we encourage each other to dream dreams but we base them on existing realities'.[12] He describes vividly, both in *Four and a Half Years* and in *Politics from Within*, the important role he played in ensuring that Lloyd George became Prime Minister in December 1916 and he was rightly regarded by the Coalition Liberal party as their most systematic electioneer. He became a key radical figure in Lloyd George's government down to the end of 1920, holding the offices of Munitions, Reconstruction, the Local Government Board, and Health and Housing. His departure from office in July 1921 was a dramatic symbol of the Government's failure to sustain its social programme and build a 'land fit for heroes'. It contributed to the ultimate decline of the Coalition. Although he was the only major Lloyd George Liberal to move to the left, the rift with Lloyd George was later healed: throughout the 1930s the two were in frequent contact over such matters as agriculture and the Popular Front. The high regard which they had formerly entertained for one another was largely re-established and remained constant down to Lloyd George's death in 1945.

Addison was also a key figure in Labour party politics. Indeed, it had been regarded as a *coup* to get him to join the party in the first place by such Labour leaders as Henderson and MacDonald. In the crisis of August 1931 he was the only middle-class member of the government who opposed the cuts in unemployment benefit and he played an important role in the decision to expel MacDonald from the Labour party. He was to take an active part in injecting new enthusiasm and raising morale in the Labour party in the disillusionment of the years following 1931. His activities ranged from the Fabian Research Bureau to the Left Book Club. Thus it was natural that, after entering the House of Lords, he should become leader of the Labour peers and ultimately leader of the House of Lords in 1945.

In the third Labour government of 1945, Addison was a figure of much greater prominence than has often been realized. He was very close to Attlee, who made him a key link figure in Cabinet committees and in determining the Commonwealth, defence, and domestic programmes of the government. Addison's leadership of the House of Lords between 1945 and 1951 was even more crucial. These were indeed years of fulfilment for him. He had always been attracted to the supra-party approach to politics. This was illustrated by his support for the Coalition in 1916, his enthusiasm for fusion in 1920, his work on behalf of agricultural marketing boards, and also his cross-party friendships with political opponents like the Unionists, Edward Carson and Walter Elliot, and the anti-Coalitionist Liberals, Herbert Samuel and Wedgwood Benn. This outlook also brought him close to that enthusiastic Coalitionist, Winston Churchill, with whom his friendship extended over forty years. Although a vigorous partisan

Conclusion

when he chose, Addison felt that progressive objectives were more important than party ties. It was in the Upper House between 1945 and 1951 that this outlook found its ultimate fulfilment.

Addison is, indeed, an unjustly neglected figure. He was a major pioneer of the welfare state, of agricultural reform, and the new British Commonwealth. He inspired the trust and admiration of leading figures of his day, Lloyd George and Churchill, MacDonald and Attlee, Bevan and Harold Wilson. Overseas he enjoyed the personal esteem of Commonwealth leaders such as Mackenzie King, Fraser, Smuts, and Nehru. To the end of his life he was a constructive and imaginative political figure. Although he never held the most important offices of state, he played a notable role in making Britain a welfare democracy with a more responsible attitude towards the outside world. To men like Addison may be accorded some of the credit for Britain's surviving its troubles of the twentieth century with its democratic institutions and social cohesion intact. A future generation was to build on foundations laid in no small part by this unassuming doctor-statesman, to help create a more humane and compassionate society.

Notes

FOOTNOTES TO CHAPTER I—PAGES 1-14

[1] Addison, *Politics from Within* (London, 1924), Vol. I, p. 46.
[2] Papers lent by third Viscount Addison; material in Addison Papers (Bodleian Library, Oxford), box 136.
[3] *Parl. Deb.*, 5th ser., Vol. CXXVIII, pp. 1007 ff. (4 August 1943).
[4] R. J. Minney, *Viscount Addison: Leader of the Lords* (London, 1958), p. 104.
[5] *Curriculum Vitae* (Addison Papers, box 136); letter by Sir Ernest Finch, 1958 (press cutting in possession of the Dowager, Lady Addison).
[6] *Journal of Anatomy and Physiology* (1899), Vol. 33, and ibid. (1900), Vol. 34. The Hunterian lectures were published in the *Lancet*, 16 March 1901.
[7] Printed lecture in Addison Papers, box 85.
[8] Tom Driberg, *Ruling Passions* (London, 1977), p. 212.
[9] *Lancet*, 16 October 1937.
[10] See Mrs Addison's diaries, 1901-10 (in the possession of Mrs Isobel Cheshire); also *Swindon Evening Advertiser*, 6 October 1925.
[11] Addison Papers, box 103.
[12] *Reynolds Newspaper*, 24 November 1910.
[13] Addison to the electors of Hoxton, 14 January 1910.
[14] *Looking Glass*, 24 June 1911.
[15] Minney, op. cit., p. 121.
[16] Stephen Koss, *Nonconformity in Modern British Politics* (London, 1976), p. 110.
[17] *Parl. Deb.*, 5th ser., Vol. XIV, p. 434 (24 February 1910).
[18] Henry Pelling, *Social Geography of British Elections* (London, 1967), p. 48; *Shoreditch Observer*, 19 March 1910; Addison, *Four and a Half Years*, Vol. I (London, 1934), p. 125.
[19] Letter on behalf of Addison from Ramsay MacDonald, 22 April 1910 (Addison Papers, box 80).
[20] *Westminster Gazette*, 29 November 1910.
[21] Paul Thompson, *Socialists, Liberals and Labour* (London, 1967), pp. 166-89; Lloyd George to his wife, ? December 1910, printed in Kenneth O. Morgan (ed.), *Lloyd George: Family Letters, 1885-1936* (Oxford and Cardiff, 1973), p. 154.
[22] See Bentley Gilbert, *The Evolution of National Insurance in Great Britain* (London, 1966) pp. 354 ff. for the definitive account.
[23] Kenneth O. Morgan, *The Age of Lloyd George* (London, new edition, 1978), p. 45.
[24] *Punch*, 17 May 1911.
[25] *Parl. Deb.*, 5th ser., Vol. XXVI, pp. 357-68 (24 May 1911).
[26] *Politics from Within*, Vol. I, p. 20.
[27] *Morning Post*, 19 May 1911; Smith Whitaker to Addison, 16 May 1911 (Addison Papers, box 60); Gilbert, op. cit., p. 363.

[28] *Parl. Deb.*, 5th ser., Vol. XXIX, pp. 250–60 (1 August 1911); *Birmingham Post*, 2 August 1911, for the reaction to Addison's speech.
[29] *Parl. Deb.*, 5th ser., Vol. XXI, pp. 442–8 (2 August 1911).
[30] Ibid., pp. 94–6 (31 July 1911).
[31] *Politics from Within*, Vol. I, p. 21.
[32] *Medical Press and Circular*, 1 January 1919; *British Medical Journal*, 24 February 1934.
[33] Addison, *Four and a Half Years* (London, 1934), Vol. I, p. 26.
[34] C. Addison, 'The Controversy over the Medical Benefit under the National Insurance Act', *Contemporary Review* (October 1912); Gilbert, op. cit., p. 382. Addison is not mentioned in John Grigg, *The People's Champion* (London, 1978), which covers Lloyd George's career from 1902 to 1911 comprehensively in other respects.
[35] Addison Papers, box 60; Paul Vaughan, *Doctors, Commons: a Short History of the B.M.A.* (London, 1959), pp. 200–3.
[36] *Nottingham Daily Express*, 17 August 1911.
[37] *Politics from Within*, Vol. I, pp. 21–2.
[38] Op. cit., p. 407.
[39] Addison to Lloyd George, 20, 29 May 1912; Lloyd George to Addison, 21 May 1912 (Addison Papers, box 32).
[40] *Parl. Papers*, 1912–13, Vol. LXXVIII, 679 (Cd. 6305).
[41] *The Times*, 17 August 1912.
[42] *Politics from Within*, Vol. I, p. 24.
[43] Addison Papers, box 80; *Westminster Gazette*, 12 December 1912.
[44] *Politics from Within*, Vol. I, p.24; *Lancet*, 28 December 1912.
[45] Gilbert, op. cit., p. 413.
[46] *The Medical World*, 30 July 1914.
[47] *Parl. Deb.*, 5th ser., Vol. LVI, pp. 3375 ff. (31 July 1913); Cox to Addison, 24 July 1913 (Addison Papers, box 3).
[48] *The Hospital*, 3 January 1914; Addison Papers, box 77 (for a list of those attending); *Morning Post*, 7 February 1914.
[49] Lloyd George to Addison, 18 April 1912 (Addison Papers, box 85). Lloyd George wrote here, 'Drown your sorrow in service. I have tried to do so.'
[50] *Four and a Half Years*, Vol. I, p. 22.
[51] *Interim Report*, Parl. Papers, 1912–13, Vol. XLVIII, 1 (Cd. 6164).
[52] *Parl. Deb.*, 5th ser., Vol. XL, pp. 2197 ff. (11 July 1912); Addison to Lloyd George, 29 May 1912 (Addison Papers, box 3); memorandum by Addison on 'The Possibility and Expediency of beginning to administer hospital benefits on 15 July 1912' (ibid.).
[53] *Final Report*, Parl. Papers, 1912–13, Vol. XLVIII, 29 (Cd. 6641, 6654).
[54] See A. Landsborough Thompson, *Half a Century of Medical Research: Origins and Policy of the Medical Research Council* (HMSO, 1977), pp. 22 ff.
[55] Addison Papers, box 3.
[56] Addison to Moulton, 13 November 1913; Masterman to Moulton, 15 December 1913 (ibid., box 60).
[57] *Four and a Half Years*, Vol. I, p. 46 (19 November 1914).
[58] *Parl. Deb.*, 5th ser., Vol. XXV, pp. 738 ff.
[59] *Time and Tide*, 8 April 1921.
[60] Mrs Addison's diary, 2 March 1911.
[61] Correspondence between Addison and Mrs Ward, November–December 1913 (Addison Papers, box 80).
[62] Ibid., box 8.
[63] *Four and a Half Years*, Vol. I, pp. 124–5.

[64] Mrs Addison's diary, 19 March 1914; Addison to his wife, 26 May 1915 (Addison Papers, box 111).
[65] *Politics from Within*, Vol. I, p. 35.
[66] Addison Papers, box 80.
[67] *Four and a Half Years*, Vol. I, p. 26 (14 July 1914).
[68] Ibid., pp. 14 ff.
[69] Ibid., p. 37.
[70] Addison Papers, box 76.
[71] *Four and a Half Years*, Vol. I, p. 25; *Western Mail*, 24 April 1914.
[72] Cf. Marvin Swartz, *The Union of Democratic Control in British Politics during the First World War* (Oxford, 1971), p. 6, n. 12.
[73] *Four and a Half Years*, Vol. I, p. 32.
[74] Cameron Hazlehurst, *Politicians at War, July 1914 to May 1915* (London, 1971), p. 46, n. 2.
[75] *Four and a Half Years*, Vol. I, p. 32.
[76] Mrs Addison's diary, 4 August 1914.
[77] *Four and a Half Years*, Vol. I, p. 42 (28 October 1914).
[78] Ibid., p. 74 (3 May 1915) —'I wish he were a better fighter.'
[79] Ibid., pp. 59, 61.
[80] Ibid., p. 55 (19 January 1915).
[81] W. A. S. Hewins, *Apologia of an Imperialist*, Vol. II (London, 1929), pp. 153, 156.
[82] *Four and a Half Years*, Vol. I, p. 74 (30 April 1915).
[83] Addison to his wife, 26 May 1915 (Addison Papers, box 111); Lloyd George, *War Memoirs* (London, 1938 edn.), Vol. I, p. 151.
[84] *Four and a Half Years*, Vol. I, pp. 81–2 (21 May 1915).
[85] Addison to his wife, 26, 28 May 1915 (Addison Papers, box 111).

FOOTNOTES TO CHAPTER II

[1] *Four and a Half Years*, Vol. I, p. 86 (30 May 1915).
[2] Addison to his wife, 28 May 1915 (Addison Papers, box 111); R. J. Q. Adams, *Arms and the Wizard* (London, 1978), p. 47.
[3] *Politics from Within*, Vol. I, pp. 133 ff.
[4] *Four and a Half Years*, Vol. I, p. 91 (13 June 1915).
[5] See PRO, MUN 5/362/1121/2 and MUN 5/142/1121/22.
[6] *Four and a Half Years*, Vol. I, pp. 98, 103–4; Addison to Lloyd George, 18 June 1915 (Addison Papers, box 15).
[7] *Politics from Within*, Vol. I, pp. 97 ff.
[8] Ibid., p. 75; Addison to his wife, 28 May 1915 (Addison Papers, box 111).
[9] *Politics from Within*, Vol. I, p. 174.
[10] C. J. Wrigley, *David Lloyd George and the British Labour Movement* (Hassocks, 1976), p. 137.
[11] Addison Papers, box 2.
[12] Addison to Lloyd George, 15 September 1915 (Addison Papers, box 58).
[13] Adams, op. cit., p. 104.
[14] J. Hinton, *The First Shop Stewards' Movement* (London, 1973), pp. 103 ff.
[15] *Four and a Half Years*, Vol. I, pp. 142–3 (26, 27 October 1915).
[16] Quoted in José Harris, *William Beveridge: a Biography* (Oxford, 1977), p. 220.
[17] *Parl. Deb.*, 5th ser., Vol. LXXVI, pp. 2073 ff. (15 December 1915).
[18] Hinton, op. cit., p. 136.

[19] Hinton, op. cit. This view is effectively demolished in Iain McLean, 'The Ministry of Munitions, the Clyde Workers Committee and the Suppression of "Forward" ', *Scottish Journal of Labour History*, 7 (1973).
[20] Addison to Lloyd George, 6 March 1916 (Addison Papers, box 58); memorandum in Addison Papers, box 59.
[21] *Four and a Half Years*, Vol. I, p. 186.
[22] Ibid., pp. 184–5 (27, 31 March 1916).
[23] McLean, op. cit., pp. 16 ff.
[24] *Parl. Deb.*, 5th ser., Vol. LXXXI, pp. 464–6 (28 March 1916).
[25] Ibid., pp. 999–1002 (30 March 1916).
[26] Hinton, op. cit., p. 160 n.
[27] *Four and a Half Years*, Vol. I, p. 189; L. Macassey to Addison, 4 June 1916 (Addison Papers, box 56).
[28] *The Times*, 22 December 1916.
[29] *Four and a Half Years*, Vol. I, p. 238 (5 August 1916).
[30] Addison to Wedgwood Benn, 6 October 1916 (Addison Papers, box 94).
[31] *Four and a Half Years*, Vol. I, pp. 257–7 (13 October 1916).
[32] Ibid., p. 263.
[33] Ibid., p. 263; *Politics from Within*, Vol. I, p. 212.
[34] *Four and a Half Years*, Vol. I, p. 126.
[35] Ibid., p. 131 (26 September 1915).
[36] Ibid., p. 250; Addison to Morley Fletcher, 9 November 1916 (Addison Papers, box 2); Asa Briggs, *Seebohm Rowntree* (London, 1961), pp. 117 ff.
[37] *Parl. Deb.*, 5th ser., Vol. LXXXIII, pp. 1555 ff. (5 July 1916).
[38] *Four and a Half Years*, Vol. I, p. 165.
[39] Ibid., p. 127 (19 September 1915).
[40] Ibid., p. 158 (4 January 1916).
[41] Ibid., pp. 189–90 (7 April 1916).
[42] Ibid., p. 195 (17 April 1916).
[43] Ibid., pp. 202–3 (8 May 1916).
[44] Ibid., p. 155.
[45] Ibid., p. 204 (8 May 1916).
[46] David Davies to Addison, n.d.; Addison to Davies, 23 May 1916 (Addison Papers, box 4).
[47] Addison to his wife, 2 August 1916 (ibid., box 111).
[48] Ibid.; *Four and a Half Years*, Vol. I, p. 239 (5 August 1916).
[49] Ibid., pp. 215–16 (29 May 1916); *Politics from Within*, Vol. I, p. 260.
[50] *Four and a Half Years*, Vol. I, p. 225.
[51] Ibid., p. 84 (27 May 1915).
[52] Ibid., p. 243 (19 September 1916).
[53] Addison to Wedgwood Benn, 6 October 1916 (Addison Papers, box 94).
[54] A. J. P. Taylor, *Politics in the First World War* (London, 1959), p. 84.
[55] *Four and a Half Years*, Vol. I, p. 269.
[56] Lord Hankey, *The Supreme Command*, Vol. II (London, 1961), p. 557.
[57] *Four and a Half Years*, Vol. I, p. 269.
[58] Ibid.
[59] Ibid., p. 274.
[60] Ibid.
[61] Ibid., pp. 272–3.
[62] Ibid., p. 273.
[63] Ibid., pp. 276–7.
[64] Addison to Lloyd George, 8 December 1916 (Addison Papers, box 8).

[65] *Four and a Half Years*, Vol. I, p. 284.
[66] S. D. Waley, *Edwin Montagu* (Bombay, 1964), p. 114.
[67] *Four and a Half Years*, Vol. I, p. 283.
[68] Taylor, op. cit., p. 85.
[69] *Leeds Mercury*, 16 December 1915.
[70] *Reynolds Newspaper*, 19 December 1915.
[71] Michael Bentley, *The Liberal Mind, 1914–1929* (Cambridge, 1976).
[72] *Politics from Within*, Vol. I, p. 46.
[73] *Lloyd George: Rise and Fall* (Cambridge, 1961), p. 26.

FOOTNOTES TO CHAPTER III

[1] *Four and a Half Years*, Vol. I, p. 201 (1 May 1916).
[2] Ibid., p. 282 (12 December 1916).
[3] *Politics from Within*, Vol. II, pp. 9–11.
[4] Haig to Addison, 1 May 1917 (Addison Papers, box 4).
[5] *Four and a Half Years*, Vol. II, p. 377 (9 May 1917); *Politics from Within*, Vol. II, pp. 33, 39.
[6] *Four and a Half Years*, Vol. II, p. 359 (23 April 1917).
[7] *Politics from Within*, Vol. II, p. 113.
[8] Ibid., p. 118; Addison to Neville Chamberlain, 2 February 1917 (Addison Papers, box 25).
[9] *Four and a Half Years*, Vol. II, p. 343 (14 March 1917); Lord Rhondda to Addison, 29 March 1917 (Addison Papers, box 66).
[10] *Four and a Half Years*, Vol. II, p. 368.
[11] *Politics from Within*, Vol. II, pp. 139–40; J. Hinton, *The First Shop Stewards' Movement* (London, 1973), p. 197 ff.
[12] War Cabinet minutes, 16 May 1917 (PRO, CAB 23/2).
[13] *Evening Standard*, 16 May 1917; *Justice*, 17 May 1917; *Daily News*, 18 May 1917.
[14] *Four and a Half Years*, Vol. II, p. 383.
[15] Addison to Lloyd George, 21 May 1917 (House of Lords, Lloyd George Papers, F/1/3/20).
[16] Bridgeman, Political Diary, February 1918, p. 269.
[17] *Four and a Half Years*, Vol. II, p. 382.
[18] Note of 23 May 1917 in Addison Papers, box 70.
[19] Note in Addison Papers, box 98.
[20] *Four and a Half Years*, Vol. II, p. 386.
[21] Addison to W. Edwards, 16 May 1917 (Addison Papers, box 54).
[22] *Four and a Half Years*, Vol. II, p. 396.
[23] C. J. Wrigley, *David Lloyd George and the British Labour Movement* (Hassocks, 1976), p. 203.
[24] Addison to Churchill, 26 April 1918 (Addison Papers, box 47).
[25] *Four and a Half Years*, Vol. II, p. 415.
[26] Addison to Lloyd George, cited in Martin Gilbert, *Winston S. Churchill*, Vol. III (London, 1971), p. 24.
[27] *Four and a Half Years*, Vol. II, p. 395.
[28] Bentley Gilbert, *British Social Policy, 1914–1939* (London, 1970), p. 24; *Manchester Guardian*, 16 May 1917; *Morning Post*, 21 May 1917.
[29] *Four and a Half Years*, Vol. II, p. 392 (31 May 1917).
[30] Ibid., p. 399 (8 June 1917).
[31] Ibid., p. 404 (3 July 1917).

[32] Ibid., p. 416 (18 July 1917); Gilbert, op. cit., p. 32.
[33] Addison to Lloyd George, 3 March 1920 (Lloyd George Papers, F/1/6/4).
[34] Bentley Gilbert, op. cit., p. 72.
[35] Paul Barton Johnson, *Land Fit for Heroes* (Chicago, 1968), p. 72.
[36] *The Times*, 18 July 1917.
[37] A. J. P. Taylor, *Politics in the First World War*, p. 84.
[38] Johnson, op. cit., p. 71.
[39] M. Gilbert, *Churchill* (Companion Volume, 1917–22), Vol. I, pp.189–90.
[40] Rowntree to Addison, 14 January 1917 (Addison Papers, box 21), though cf. A. Briggs, *Social Thought and Social Action: A Study of the Work of Seebohm Rowntree* (London, 1961), p. 141.
[41] Sir J. Wornvald to Addison, 8 May 1928 (Addison Papers, box 67).
[42] *Sunday Times*, 3 June 1917.
[43] *Four and a Half Years*, Vol. II, p. 423.
[44] B. Gilbert, op. cit., p. 9; *Four and a Half Years*, Vol. II, p. 414.
[45] Ibid.
[46] Ibid., p. 357 (13 April 1917); War Cabinet minutes, 7, 19 June 1917 (CAB 23/3).
[47] *Four and a Half Years*, Vol. II, p. 424.
[48] War Cabinet Minutes, 9 October 1917 (CAB 23/4).
[49] *Four and a Half Years*, Vol. II, pp. 424 –35.
[50] *Liverpool Daily Post*, 26 January 1918; *Local Government Journal*, 18 May 1918.
[51] Cabinet memorandum, 10 February 1918, GT 3643 (CAB 24/42).
[52] *Four and a Half Years*, Vol. II, p. 470 (15 January 1918).
[53] Ibid., p. 556 (23 July 1918).
[54] Ibid., p. 560.
[55] *New Statesman*, 31 March 1918.
[56] Lord Beaverbrook, *Men and Power, 1917–1918* (London, 1956), p. 49; *Four and a Half Years*, Vol. II, p. 248 (11 September 1917).
[57] *Housing in England and Wales* P. P. 1918, XXVI, 437; memorandum on housing by Addison (Addison Papers, box 72).
[58] Rowntree to Addison, 25 September 1917, quoted in Briggs, op. cit., p. 140.
[59] Addison to Hayes Fisher, 13 February 1918 (Addison Papers, box 72).
[60] *Four and a Half Years*, Vol. II, p. 494.
[61] Cabinet Paper, 11 March 1918, GT 3877 (CAB 24/46); Cabinet memorandum, 1 August 1918, GT 5282 (CAB 24/59).
[62] HAC, 2 August 1918 (CAB 26/1).
[63] *Politics from Within*, Vol. II, p. 221.
[64] *Four and a Half Years*, Vol. I, p. 278.
[65] Ibid., Vol. II, p. 317 (16 January 1917); Addison to Lloyd George, 2 April 1917 (Lloyd George Papers, F/1/3/11).
[66] *Four and a Half Years*, Vol. II, pp. 358, 370.
[67] *Politics from Within*, Vol. II, p. 223; note on 'The Ministry of Health and Poor Law Reform', 15 July 1918, GT 5111 (CAB 24/58).
[68] *Four and a Half Years*, Vol. II, p. 494 (21 March 1918).
[69] Ibid., p. 498.
[70] Ibid., p. 515 (24 April 1918).
[71] Ibid., p. 535 (3 June 1918).
[72] Addison to Lloyd George, 5 June 1918 (Addison Papers, box 35); *Politics from Within*, Vol. II, p. 228.
[73] HAC minutes, 9 July 1918 (CAB 26/1).
[74] Memorandum on 'Demobilization and Employment', 19 October 1918, GT 6047 (CAB 24/67).

Notes to Pages 79–94   289

[75] *Four and a Half Years*, Vol. II, pp. 570 ff.
[76] Ibid., p. 590.
[77] Ibid., pp. 577 ff.; memorandum by Minister of Reconstruction, 30 October 1918, GT 6148 (CAB 24/68).
[78] *Four and a Half Years*, Vol. II, pp. 584 –5.
[79] *Parl. Deb.*, 5th ser., Vol. CX, p. 2338 ff. (7 November 1918).
[80] *Four and a Half Years*, Vol. II, p. 588.
[81] Below, p. 117.
[82] Johnson, op. cit., chaps. 17 and 18.
[83] Bridgeman, Political Diary, February 1918, p. 275.
[84] P. Abrams, 'The Failure of Social Reform, 1918–20', *Past and Present*, 24 (April 1963), 43 ff.; H. Eckstein, *The English Health Service* (Cambridge, Mass., 1959), p. 85.
[85] *Politics from Within*, Vol. II, pp. 257–9.
[86] Ibid.
[87] *Four and a Half Years*, Vol. II, pp. 603–4.
[88] Ibid.
[89] Ibid., pp. 479–80 (29 January 1918).
[90] Addison Papers, box 94.
[91] Bridgeman, Political Diary, February 1918, p. 275.
[92] *Four and a Half Years*, Vol. II, pp. 458–9 (28 December 1917).
[93] Ibid., p. 528 (16 May 1918).
[94] Ibid., p. 487 (28 January 1918).
[95] Memorandum of 13 December 1917 (Addison Papers, box 8).
[96] *Four and a Half Years*, Vol. II, p. 486 (19 February 1918).
[97] Ibid., p. 523 (9 May 1918).
[98] Ibid., p. 528 (17 May 1918).
[99] Ibid., p. 553 (23 July 1918).
[100] Ibid., p. 563 ff.; Addison to his wife, 22 August 1918 (Addison Papers, box 111).
[101] Guest to Addison, 17 August 1918 (ibid., box 72); *Four and a Half Years*, Vol. II, p. 565 (22 August 1918).
[102] Ibid., pp. 588–9.
[103] *The Times*, 29 November 1918.
[104] *Four and a Half Years*, Vol. II, p. 599 (6 January 1919).
[105] *Daily Chronicle*, 3 December 1918.
[106] *Daily Express*, 30 December 1918.
[107] *Four and a Half Years*, Vol. II, p. 603 (3 January 1919).
[108] Waldorf Astor to J. L. Garvin, 10 January 1919 (University of Texas, Garvin Papers).
[109] *Four and a Half Years*, Vol. II, p. 602 (6 January 1919).

FOOTNOTES TO CHAPTER IV

[1] *Parl. Deb.*, (House of Lords), 5th ser., Vol. CLIII, p. 317 (17 December 1947).
[2] *Politics from Within*, Vol. II, p. 15; *Four and a Half Years*, Vol. I, p. 201.
[3] Cabinet Minutes, 3 March 1919 (CAB 23/9).
[4] Note by Mrs Addison, July 1919 (Addison Papers, box 111).
[5] Addison to Auckland Geddes, 5 November 1919 (ibid., box 47).
[6] Addison to Lloyd George, 25 November 1918 (House of Lords Record Office, J. C. C. Davidson Papers).
[7] Beatrice Webb to Thomas Jones, 16 March 1919, cited in K. Middlemas (ed.), *Thomas Jones: Whitehall Diary*, Vol. I, (Oxford, 1969), p. 106.

[8] *Report of Machinery of Government Committee, Parl. Papers*, 1918, Vol. XII, 1 (Cmd. 9230).
[9] J. T. Davies to Addison, 24 February 1919 (Addison Papers, box 9); Cabinet meetings in CAB 23/9.
[10] *The Times*, 4 February 1919.
[11] *Parl. Deb.*, 5th ser., Vol. XII, p. 1828 ff.; Sir Arthur MacNalty, 'Medicine and the Public Health', *The Lancet*, 3 July 1948.
[12] Memorandum on the Provisions of the Bill as to the work of the Medical Research Committee, *Parl. Papers*, 1919, Vol. XXIX, 651 (Cmd. 69); cf. *The Lancet*, 31 May 1919 for the Medical Services Bill.
[13] *South Wales Daily News*, 21 March 1919.
[14] For example, Thomas Jones Papers (National Library of Wales), II, Vol. 3, nos. 71, 78, and Addison to Sir Herbert Lewis, 5 January 1920 (ibid.). For Sir Percy Watkin's work at the Welsh Board of Health, see his reminiscences, *A Welshman Remembers* (Cardiff, 1944).
[15] Bentley Gilbert, *British Social Policy*, p. 132; Addison to Lloyd George, 26 June 1919 (Addison Papers, box 43).
[16] Cf. War Cabinet Minutes, 12 March 1918, WC 364 (CAB 23/5).
[17] *Report of Committee, Parl. Papers*, 1918, Vol. VII, 493 (Cd. 9197).
[18] *Four and a Half Years*, Vol. II, p. 597.
[19] Addison memorandum to Lloyd George, 8 July 1919 (Addison Papers, box 13).
[20] Lloyd George to Addison, 15 January 1919 (ibid., box 8).
[21] Addison to Lloyd George, 21 January 1919 (ibid.).
[22] Cabinet Minutes, 22 January 1919. WC 518 (CAB 23/9).
[23] *The Times*, 5 February 1919; *The Surveyor*, 7 February 1919.
[24] LGB Circular 12 of 6 February 1919 (CAB 24/5).
[25] *The Times*, 8 February 1919.
[26] *Parl. Deb.*, 5th ser., Vol. CXII, pp. 705-8 (17 February 1919).
[27] *Western Daily Mercury*, 8 February 1919.
[28] GT 235 (CAB 24/5).
[29] Cabinet Minutes, 3 and 4 March 1919 (CAB 23/9).
[30] *Parl. Deb.*, 5th ser., Vol. CXIII, pp. 1925 ff. (18 March 1919).
[31] *New Statesman*, 5 April 1919; Gilbert, *British Social Policy*, pp. 143-4.
[32] *Parl. Deb.*, 5th ser., Vol. CXIV, pp. 1713-40 (7 April 1919).
[33] *Yorkshire Post*, 22 March 1919.
[34] *The Nation*, 12 April 1919.
[35] Memorandum on nationalization of the mines (Addison Papers, box 8).
[36] Beatrice Webb to Thomas Jones, 16 March 1919, Violet Markham to Thomas Jones, 18 March 1919, *Whitehall Diary*, Vol. I, pp. 106-7.
[37] Addison to Bonar Law, 27 August 1919 (J. C. C. Davidson Papers).
[38] Addison to Lloyd George, 4 June 1919 (Lloyd George Papers, F/1/5/13).
[39] *Parl. Deb.*, 5th ser., Vol. CXVII, pp. 659-77 (30 June 1919).
[40] For example, memorandum on financial situation by C. Addison, 28 August 1919 (Addison Papers, box 4).
[41] Lloyd George to Addison, 20 August 1919 (ibid., box 25).
[42] Addison to Lloyd George, 15 September 1919 (ibid., box 25); cf. *The Lancet*, 3 July 1948.
[43] Memorandum on the Four Consultative Councils for England and Wales (Addison Papers, box 12): these councils covered respectively medical and allied services, national health insurance, local health administration, and general health questions. Cf. *Interim Report of Consultative Council on the future provision of medical and allied services, Parl. Papers*, 1920, Vol. XVII, 1001 (Cmd. 693), and *Report of the Consultative Council*

on *Local Health Administration*, *Parl. Papers*, 1921, Vol. XIII, 227 (Cmd. 1113); *Parl. Deb.*, 5th ser., Vol. CXXVI, pp. 1219–24 (9 March 1920).

[44] 'National Health Insurance', 5 December 1919 (CAB 24/94); meeting of Health Insurance Committee, 17 December 1919 (CAB 21/181); Addison to Lloyd George, 22 December 1919 (Lloyd George Papers, F/1/5/37).

[45] Memorandum by Addison on Doctors' Remuneration, 15 January 1920 (Addison Papers, box 38); minutes of conference of the Health Insurance Committee, 9 January 1920 (CAB 21/181).

[46] *The Times*, 19 November 1919, 9 January 1920.

[47] Cabinet Minutes, 14 August 1919 (CAB 23/11); Gilbert, op. cit., p. 60.

[48] José Harris, *William Beveridge: a Biography*, p. 257.

[49] *The Times*, 17 June 1919.

[50] Addison to Bonar Law, 13 June 1919 (Addison Papers, box 53); *Newcastle Journal*, 9 May 1919.

[51] *The Times*, 26 June 1919.

[52] Ibid., 29 July 1919.

[53] *Parl. Deb.*, 5th ser., Vol. CXIX, p. 1668; *Housing*, No. 1 (19 July 1919).

[54] GT 8402, 23 October 1919 (CAB 24/90).

[55] CP 3, 27 October 1919 (CAB 24/92).

[56] *The Times*, 16 October 1919.

[57] CP 107, 11 November 1919 (CAB 24/93); GT 8272 and 8354 (16 October 1919).

[58] Cabinet Minutes, 7, 13, 20 November 1919 (CAB 23/18).

[59] Memorandum by Minister of Health, 15 August 1919 and 27 October 1919 (CAB 24/92).

[60] *Parl. Deb.*, 5th ser., Vol. CXXI, p. 1295 (21 November 1919).

[61] Memorandum by Addison to Cabinet Finance Committee, 28 January 1920 (CAB 27/72).

[62] *The Nation*, 20 December 1919.

[63] *Parl. Deb.*, 5th ser., Vol. CXXII, pp. 953 ff. (8 December 1919); M. Bowley, *Housing and the State* (London, 1945), p. 23.

[64] Waldorf Astor to Auckland Geddes, 10 December 1919 (Addison Papers, box 11); A. C. Pigou, *Aspects of British Economic History, 1918 –1925* (London, 1947) p. 91.

[65] *The Times*, 13 December 1919; Addison to Samuel, 24 December 1919 (House of Lords Record Office, Viscount Samuel Papers, A/155 (V)/26).

[66] Addison to Austen Chamberlain, 29 January 1920 (Addison Papers, box 11); Susan Howson, 'The Origins of Dear Money, 1919–20', *Economic History Review*, XXVII, No. 1 (1974), especially pp. 100–1.

[67] Addison's memorandum to the Cabinet on Housing Bonds, 28 January 1920 (Addison Papers, box 11).

[68] Addison to Lloyd George, 23 January 1920 (ibid., box 33).

[69] H. Aldridge to Addison, 18 November 1919 (ibid., box 7).

[70] Margaret Cole, *The Life of G. D. H. Cole* (London, 1971), pp. 102–3; *Parl. Deb.*, 5th ser., Vol. CXXV, pp. 34–7 (10 February 1920).

[71] *The Nation*, 14 February 1920.

[72] *Parl. Deb.*, 5th ser., Vol. CXXV, pp. 845–56 (17 February 1920).

[73] *Glasgow Herald*, 4 February 1920.

[74] Cabinet Minutes, 14 November 1919 (CAB 23/18).

[75] *Second Annual Report of the Ministry of Health, 1920–1*, *Parl. Papers*, 1921, Vol. XIII (Cmd. 1446), p. 57.

[76] Addison to Bonar Law, 14 July 1919 (Bonar Law Papers, 97/5/18).

[77] Memorandum on the nationalization of the mines, August 1919 (Addison Papers, box 8); Cabinet Minutes, 7 August 1919 (CAB 23/15).

[78] Addison to Lloyd George, 6, 4 January 1919 (Addison Papers, box 47, 25).
[79] For example, War Cabinet Minutes 599 (CAB 23/11), quoted in John Silverlight, *The Victors' Dilemma* (London, 1970), p. 265.
[80] Sir Henry Wilson's diary, 25 July 1919, quoted by Martin Gilbert, *Churchill: Companion Volumes, 1917–22*, Vol. 2, p. 992; CAB 23/11.
[81] H. A. L. Fisher's diary, 29 December 1920 (Bodleian, Fisher Papers).
[82] Ibid., 6 January 1920.
[83] *The Times*, 29 July 1919.
[84] Addison to Lloyd George, 31 July 1919 (Lloyd George Papers, F/1/5/20).
[85] Fisher diary, 23 September 1919.
[86] Addison to Lloyd George, 3 March 1920 (Lloyd George Papers, F/1/6/4).
[87] Draft speech by Addison, ? 1920 (Addison Papers, box 7).
[88] Fisher diary, 4 February 1920.
[89] Addison to Lloyd George, 3 March 1920, loc. cit.
[90] *The Times*, 17, 19 March 1920; *Manchester Guardian*, 17, 19 March 1920.

FOOTNOTES TO CHAPTER V

[1] *The Times*, 8 May 1920.
[2] Addison to Lloyd George, 13 May 1920 (Lloyd George Papers, F/1/6/8).
[3] Secretary of the Horncastle division Central Liberal Association to Addison, 7 January 1919 (Addison Papers, box 94).
[4] Fisher diary, 31 December 1920.
[5] Edwin Montagu to Lloyd George, 8 September 1919 (Trinity College Library, Cambridge, Montagu Papers AS IV-3 /706).
[6] Cf. D. G. Boyce, *Englishmen and Irish Troubles, 1918–1922* (London, 1972), pp. 131–2.
[7] Fisher diary, 25 July 1920.
[8] Davidson to Lord Stamfordham, 23 December 1919 (Davidson Papers).
[9] Hartington to Lord Robert Cecil, n. d. 1920 (British Library, Cecil Papers, Add. MSS 51, 163, f. 43).
[10] A. C. Pigou, *Aspects of British Economic History, 1918–1925* (London, 1947), pp. 92–3.
[11] *Parl. Deb.*, 5th ser., Vol. CXXVIII, p. 2256 (6 May 1920); *The Economist*, 8 May 1920.
[12] Housing and Rents Policy, 1920 (PRO, HLG 48/13); Addison to H. A. L. Fisher, 12 April 1920.
[13] *The Nation*, 8 May 1920.
[14] *Parl. Deb.*, 5th ser., Vol. CXXIX, pp. 2223 ff. (4 June 1920).
[15] *The Times*, 20 April 1920.
[16] Mond to Addison, 7 June 1920 (Addison Papers, box 7).
[17] Addison to Ernest Moir, 17 May 1920 (ibid.).
[18] *Parl. Deb.*, 5th ser., Vol. CXXXI, pp. 2660 ff. (15 July 1920); Report of the Proceedings and Memoranda of the Cabinet Committee on Housing, 1920 (CAB 27/89).
[19] Chamberlain to Addison, 4 November 1920 (Lloyd George Papers, F/1/6/14); Montague Norman to Addison, 2 May 1921 (Addison Papers, box 4).
[20] Addison to Chamberlain, 25 October 1920 (ibid., box 53).
[21] Cf. Bentley Gilbert, *British Social Policy*, p. 151.
[22] Cabinet Minutes, 14 November 1919 (CAB 23/18); *The Nation*, 14 February 1920.
[23] *Sunday Times*, 17 October 1920.

Notes to Pages 125–135   293

[24] *The Times*, 27 October 1920.
[25] Ibid., 4 November 1920.
[26] Conference of Ministers, 25 January 1921 (CAB 23/35); Addison's memorandum (CU-47) to the Committee on Unemployment, 21 October 1920, and minutes of Cabinet Committee on Unemployment, 5 November 1920 (CAB 27/114).
[27] Memorandum by Addison (Addison Papers, box 39).
[28] Comment by 'Cincinnatus', *New Statesman*, 8 November 1919.
[29] *The Nation*, 20 October 1920.
[30] *Daily Mail*, 22 November 1920; *The Times*, 14 December 1920.
[31] M. Cowling, *The Impact of Labour* (Cambridge, 1971), p. 115.
[32] *Newcastle Chronicle*, 15 December 1920.
[33] *The Times*, 16 December 1920.
[34] *North Eastern Daily Gazette*, 16 December 1920.
[35] *Weekly Dispatch*, 16 January 1921; *Report of the Departmental Committee on the High Cost of Building Working Class Dwellings*, Parl. Papers, 1921, Vol. XIII, 919 (Cmd. 1447).
[36] *The Nation*, 8 January 1921; *Daily Telegraph*, 5 January 1921.
[37] Minutes of Finance Committee, 29 November 1920 (CAB 27/71).
[38] Ibid., 7 December 1920, 30 January, and 17 February 1921 (ibid.).
[39] *Daily Chronicle*, 16 December 1920.
[40] *Yorkshire Post*, 17 December 1920.
[41] Addison to Chamberlain, 3 March 1921, Chamberlain to Addison, 9 March 1921 (Addison Papers, box 4).
[42] Morant to the Treasury, 15 January 1920 (ibid., box 33); lecture by Sir Arthur Newsholme, *The Lancet*, 20 June 1925.
[43] *Parl. Deb.*, 5th ser., Vol. CXXXI, pp. 2650–63 (15 July 1920).
[44] Addison to Chamberlain, 25 October 1920 (Addison Papers, box 53).
[45] Addison to Chamberlain, 23 February 1921 (ibid., box 4).
[46] *Interim report of Consultative Council on Medical and Allied Services*, Parl. Papers, 1920, Vol. XVII, 1001 (Cmd. 693); cf. D. Stark Murray, *Why a National Health Service?* (London, 1971), chap. 1.
[47] *Weekly Dispatch*, 13 February 1921.
[48] Derby to Bonar Law, 18 December 1920 (Bonar Law Papers, 99/8/14).
[49] Curzon to Hardinge, 12 January 1921, cited in Alan J. Sharp, 'The Foreign Office in Eclipse', *History* (June 1976), p. 204, n. 47; *Dundee Advertising*, 24 March 1921.
[50] S. W. Roskill, *Hankey, Man of Secrets*, Vol. II (London, 1971), p. 216.
[51] Lloyd George to Addison, 31 March 1921 (Lloyd George Papers, F/1/6/20).
[52] Ibid.
[53] Addison to his wife, 17 March 1921 (Addison Papers, box 135).
[54] Addison to Lloyd George, 31 March 1921 (Lloyd George Papers, F/1/6/20).
[55] Addison to his wife, 5 April 1921 (Addison Papers, box 135).
[56] *The Times*, 4 April 1921.
[57] *Daily Telegraph*, 9 April 1921.
[58] *Medical Press*, 1 January 1919, 20 July 1921; *The Hospital*, 8 April 1921; *The Medical Officer*, 9 April 1921.
[59] *British Medical Journal*, 9 April 1921.
[60] Ibid., 5 June 1948 (quoting Newman in 1921).
[61] Addison diary fragment, 6 April 1921 (Addison Papers, box 135).
[62] Talbot to Addison, 7 April 1921 (ibid.).
[63] Addison diary fragment, 6 April 1921 (ibid.).
[64] Addison to Lloyd George, 22 June 1921 (ibid.).
[65] Memorandum by Addison, 13 April 1921 (CAB 24/122).

[66] Addison to his wife, 2 June 1921 (Addison Papers, box 135).
[67] Addison to his wife, 5 April 1921 (ibid.).
[68] Addison to Lloyd George, 5 April 1921 (ibid., box 8).
[69] Addison diary fragment, 6 April 1921 (ibid., box 135).
[70] Ibid.
[71] Addison to Hodges, 8 April 1921 (Thomas Jones Papers, C/6/23).
[72] Addison to his wife, 14 April 1921 (Addison Papers, box 135).
[73] *The Times*, 16 December 1920.
[74] *New Statesman*, 4 June 1921.
[75] Addison diary fragment, 16 April 1921 (ibid.).
[76] Ibid., 11 April 1921.
[77] Ibid., 1 July 1921.
[78] *Thomas Jones: Whitehall Diary*, Vol. I, p. 152.
[79] Bonar Law to Thomas Jones, 4 May 1921 (Thomas Jones Papers, A/6/6).
[80] *Morning Post*, 7 April 1921.
[81] *The Times*, 2 April 1921.
[82] Addison to his wife, 15 June 1921 (Addison Papers, box 135).
[83] Ibid., 14 April 1921.
[84] *Daily News*, 16 June 1921.
[85] Chamberlain to Addison, 15 June 1921 (Addison Papers, box 135).
[86] Addison to Chamberlain, 16 June 1921 (ibid.).
[87] Chamberlain to Lloyd George, 10, 13 June 1921; Lloyd George to Chamberlain, 9 June 1921 (Lloyd George Papers, F/7/4/48, F/7/4/6).
[88] Lloyd George to McCurdy, 14 June 1921 (ibid., F/34/4/12).
[89] Addison to Lloyd George, 17 June 1921 (Addison Papers, box 135).
[90] Addison to Chamberlain, 16 June 1921 (ibid.).
[91] Addison diary fragment (ibid.).
[92] Addison to Lloyd George, 22 June 1921 (ibid.).
[93] Ibid.
[94] Addison to his wife, 23 June 1921 (ibid.).
[95] Lord Beaverbrook, *The Decline and Fall of Lloyd George* (London, 1963), pp. 61 ff.
[96] A. J. P. Taylor (ed.), *Lloyd George: a Diary by Frances Stevenson* (London, 1971), p. 223 (20 June 1921).
[97] McCurdy to Lloyd George, 17, 20 June 1921 (Lloyd George Papers, F/34/4/12, 13).
[98] Beaverbrook, op. cit., p. 71.
[99] *Parl. Deb.*, 5th ser., Vol. CXLIII, pp. 1593 ff. (23 June 1921).
[100] Addison diary fragment, 23 June 1921 (Addison Papers, box 135).
[101] *Lloyd George: a Diary*, p. 224 (24 June 1921).
[102] Beaverbrook, op. cit., p. 78.
[103] Addison diary fragment (Addison Papers, box 135).
[104] Ibid.
[105] Memorandum by the Minister of Health on the Reduction of Public Expenditure (CP 3067), 22 June 1921 (CAB 24/125).
[106] Addison diary fragment, 1 July 1921.
[107] Ibid.
[108] Minutes of meeting of Finance Committee, 30 June 1921 (CAB 27/71).
[109] Memorandum submitted to Conference of Ministers (CAB 23/39).
[110] Addison to his wife, 6 July 1921 (Addison Papers, box 135).
[111] Addison to his wife, 7 July 1921 (ibid.).
[112] Addison diary fragment, July 1921 (ibid.).
[113] Conclusions of Conference of Ministers, 13 July 1921 (CAB 23/39).

Notes to Pages 144–156   295

[114] Addison to his wife, 12 July 1921 (Addison Papers, box 135).
[115] Addison to Lloyd George, 14 July 1921 (Lloyd George Papers, F/1/6/30).
[116] Lloyd George to Addison, 14 July 1921 (Addison Papers, box 135).
[117] Addison to his wife, 14 July 1921 (ibid.).
[118] *The Nation*, 30 July 1921; *New Statesman*, 16 July 1921.
[119] *Parl. Deb.*, 5th ser., Vol. CXLIV, pp. 1488 ff. (14 July 1921).
[120] *The Nation*, 30 July 1921.
[121] P. Abrams, 'The Failure of Social Reform, 1918–20', *Past and Present*, 24 (April 1963).
[122] Earl Winterton, *Orders of the Day* (London, 1953), p. 92.
[123] H. R. Aldridge, *The National Housing Manual: a guide to National Housing Policy and Administration* (London, 1923).
[124] Gilbert, *British Social Policy*, p. 144.
[125] P. R. Wilding, 'Government and Housing: a study in the Development of Social Policy, 1906–1939' (University of Manchester Ph. D. thesis, 1970).
[126] Cf. Mary Stocks, *Ernest Simon of Manchester* (Manchester, 1964), pp. 63–4; W. G. V. Balchin (ed.), *Swansea and its Region* (Swansea, 1971), p. 188.
[127] MacDonald diary, 19 December 1929, cited in D. Marquand, *Ramsay MacDonald* (London, 1977), p. 527.
[128] J. Barnes and K. Middlemas, *Baldwin* (London, 1969), p. 518.

FOOTNOTES TO CHAPTER VI

[1] *Glasgow Herald*, 15 July 1921.
[2] *Daily News*, 10 October 1921.
[3] *Westminster Gazette*, 11 October 1921.
[4] Wedgwood Benn diary, 8 March 1922 (House of Lords Record Office, Stansgate Papers, ST/66).
[5] *Manchester Guardian*, 19 July 1921.
[6] 'How we are Governed', *Nineteenth Century* (March 1922).
[7] Published by Herbert Jenkins, London, 1922; cf. Slum Clearance: Allocation of Grant Policy, 1920–2 (Ministry of Housing Papers, HLG 48/697).
[8] *Parl. Deb.*, 5th ser., Vol. CXLIV, pp. 2497–512 (21 July 1921) and Vol. CXLVII, pp. 285–99 (20 October 1921).
[9] *Spectator*, 29 October 1921.
[10] *Parl. Deb.*, 5th ser., Vol. CL, pp. 704–10 (13 February 1922).
[11] Ibid., Vol. CLI, pp. 128–35 (27 February 1922).
[12] Ibid., Vol. CLIII, pp. 815–22 (27 April 1922).
[13] Ibid., Vol. CLVI, pp. 887–901 (10 July 1922).
[14] File on 1922 election (Addison Papers, box 82).
[15] *Hackney and Kingsland Gazette*, 19 June 1922.
[16] Addison's message to the Shoreditch electors, 28 July 1922 (Addison Papers, box 82).
[17] Childs to Addison, 4 September 1922 (ibid.).
[18] Election manifesto, 1922 (ibid.).
[19] *Hackney and Kingsland Gazette*, 17 November 1922.
[20] For example, *Manchester Guardian*, 19 July 1921.
[21] Addison to Bonar Law, ? December 1922 (Addison Papers, box 95).
[22] Addison to W. Isaac, 11 December 1922, Isaac to Addison, 18 December 1922 (Addison Papers, box 82).

[23] Addison to Henderson, 13 November 1922 (ibid.); *Liverpool Daily Courier*, 22 November 1923. There is an inadequate account of Addison's motives in joining Labour in Catherine Ann Cline, *Recruits to Labour* (Syracuse, New York, 1963), pp. 38–9.
[24] MacDonald to Addison, 24 November 1923 (Addison Papers, box 82).
[25] *New Leader*, 30 November 1923.
[26] Addison to Henderson, 19 November 1923 (Addison Papers, box 82); material in Addison Papers, boxes 81–2.
[27] Ibid., box 82.
[28] Pethick-Lawrence to Addison, 13 December 1923 (ibid.).
[29] MacDonald to Addison, 14 December 1923 (ibid.).
[30] Addison to MacDonald, 19 December 1923 (ibid.).
[31] *The Times*, 20 October 1924.
[32] Swindon divisional Labour party to Addison, 4 September 1924 (Addison Papers, box 82).
[33] National Labour party agent to Addison, 21 July 1924 (ibid.).
[34] *The Times*, 28 October 1924.
[35] John Wheatley to Addison, 24 January 1924 (Addison Papers, box 95).
[36] *The Times*, 28 October 1924.
[37] Ibid., 31 October 1924.
[38] Hammersmith South Labour agent to Addison, 9 November 1924 (Addison Papers, box 82).
[39] Addison to Wedgwood Benn, 14 November 1924 (Stansgate Papers, ST/80/1-3).
[40] Secretary of the ILP to Addison, 2 December 1924 (Addison Papers, box 82).
[41] *Western Morning News*, 13 October 1924.
[42] *Daily Record* and *Daily Mail*, 15 October 1924.
[43] *Western Morning News*, 16 October 1924.
[44] Carson to Addison, 30 January 1922 (Addison Papers, box 95).
[45] *Western Gazette*, 19 December 1924.
[46] Ibid.
[47] *Daily Mail*, 7 November 1924.
[48] *Spectator*, 10 January 1925.
[49] *Nottingham Guardian*, 7 November 1924.
[50] *New Leader*, 24 December 1926.
[51] *The Nation and its Food* was reprinted in Percy Redfern (ed.), *Self and Society: Twelve Essays* (London, 1930).
[52] C. Addison, *A Programme for Agriculture* (with a foreword by R. S. Hudson, London, 1941).
[53] See 'Wanted – a Labour Agricultural Policy' by 'S. L. B.', *New Statesman*, 3 May 1919; R. I. McKibbin, *The Evolution of the Labour Party, 1910–1924* (Oxford, 1975), pp. 150–6.
[54] *East Dorset Herald*, 6 August 1925.
[55] Hicks to Addison, 10 December 1923 (Addison Papers, box 82).
[56] Addison to Hicks, 12 December 1923 (ibid.).
[57] *The Times*, 17 October 1924.
[58] For example, E. Forber to Addison, 19 November, 17 February 1927 (Addison Papers, box 84).
[59] National Labour party agent to Addison, 29 May 1925 (ibid., box 82).
[60] *Tiverton Gazette and East Devon Herald*, 29 September 1925.
[61] MacDonald to Addison, 1 June 1926, Henderson to Addison, 21 June 1926 (Addison Papers, box 82); *The Times*, 5, 6 October 1925.
[62] *Annual report* of the Labour party conference, 1926.

[63] *The Times*, 18 April 1927.
[64] Barnes to Addison, 3 January 1928.
[65] G. T. Garratt, *The Mugwumps and the Labour Party* (London, 1932), pp. 45 ff.
[66] F. W. S. Craig, *British General Election Manifestos, 1918–1966* (Chichester, 1970), pp. 57–8; C. R. Attlee, *The Labour Party in Perspective* (London, 1937), p. 52.
[67] National Labour party agent to Mrs Addison, 20 March 1925 (Addison Papers, box 82).
[68] *Swindon Evening Advertiser*, 6 October 1925.
[69] Lord Wakefield of Kendal to the authors, 20 January 1978.
[70] National Labour party agent to Addison, 28 September 1925 (Addison Papers, box 81).
[71] Ibid., 11 August 1925.
[72] File on 1929 general election (Addison Papers, ibid.).
[73] *Swindon Evening Advertiser*, 25 May 1929; *Daily Herald*, 28 May 1929.
[74] Middlemas and Barnes, op. cit., p. 518.
[75] *The Times*, 12 June 1929.
[76] Addison to MacDonald, 9 June 1929 (PRO, MacDonald Papers, 5/40).
[77] Mrs Addison's diary, 2 June 1929.

FOOTNOTES TO CHAPTER VII

[1] Mrs Addison's diary, 7 November 1929.
[2] Addison to his wife, 16 July 1929 (Addison Papers, box 111); Addison to MacDonald, 7 June 1920 (MacDonald Papers, 2/10).
[3] Addison to his wife, 24, 26 June 1929 (Addison Papers, box 111); Mrs Addison's diary, 8 November 1929.
[4] Thomas to Buxton, 6 August 1929 (Addison Papers, box 17).
[5] Addison Papers, box 19.
[6] Memorandum in MacDonald Papers, 1/244.
[7] *The Times*, 31 October 1929.
[8] Ibid., 1 November 1929.
[9] Ibid., 8 January 1930.
[10] Memoranda in Addison Papers, boxes 6 and 16.
[11] Memorandum on the acquisition of land (ibid., box 6).
[12] Memorandum on land settlement (18 December 1929).
[13] Addison to MacDonald, 16 January 1930 (MacDonald Papers, 2/10).
[14] Ibid., 1/244.
[15] Note by MacDonald, 11 February 1930 (Addison Papers, box 5).
[16] Note in MacDonald Papers, 1/244.
[17] Snowden to Buxton, 29 December 1929 (ibid.).
[18] P. J. Grigg to H. G. Vincent, 16 December 1929 (ibid.); cf. P. J. Grigg, *Prejudice and Judgement* (London, 1948), p. 226.
[19] CAB 14/30.
[20] Memorandum by MacDonald, 24 February 1930 (MacDonald Papers, 1/244).
[21] Cabinet Minutes, 25 March 1930 (CAB 23/63).
[22] Addison to MacDonald, 8 April 1930 (MacDonald Papers, 2/10).
[23] Addison to MacDonald, 17 April 1930 (ibid.).
[24] Noel Buxton to Addison, 24 April 1930 (Addison Papers, box 5).
[25] Addison Papers, box 35.

[26] Addison to MacDonald, 30 April (ibid., box 5).
[27] Memorandum by Addison on the Wheat Quota, 5 May 1930 (ibid., box 35).
[28] Marquand, *Ramsay MacDonald*, p. 560.
[29] Addison Papers, box 6.
[30] *The Times*, 20 October 1929; Hugh Dalton, *Practical Socialism for Britain* (London, 1935), pp. 284 ff.; *Report of the National Parks Committee*, Parl. *Papers*, 1931, Vol. XVI, 1 (Cmd. 3851).
[31] Ibid., 19 December 1951: obituary note by H. Griffin.
[32] Viscount Snowden, *An Autobiography*, Vol. II (London, 1934), p. 882.
[33] Hugh Dalton, *Memoirs, Vol. I, 1887–1931* (London, 1953), p. 258.
[34] Beaverbrook to Addison, 6 June 1930.
[35] *Thomas Jones: Whitehall Diary*, Vol. II, p. 262 (3 June 1930).
[36] *The Times*, 13 May 1930.
[37] Buxton to Addison, 21 June 1929 (Addison Papers, box 19).
[38] Memorandum, ibid., box 17.
[39] Addison to MacDonald, 7 June 1930 (MacDonald Papers, 2/10).
[40] Lloyd George to MacDonald, 22 August 1930 (Addison Papers, box 19).
[41] MacDonald's secretary to Addison, 23 August 1930 (ibid.).
[42] Addison's secretary to Addison, 28 August 1930 (ibid.).
[43] Addison to MacDonald, 10 September 1930 (MacDonald Papers, 2/10).
[44] Marquand, op. cit., p. 565.
[45] MacDonald to Lloyd George, 12 September 1930 (MacDonald Papers, 5/174).
[46] Marquand, op. cit., p. 565.
[47] Addison to MacDonald, 2 October 1930 (Addison Papers, box 19).
[48] Lloyd George to MacDonald, 23 October 1930 (ibid., box 17).
[49] R. Skidelsky, *Politicians and the Slump* (London, 1968), p. 256.
[50] *The Times*, 2 August 1930.
[51] Memorandum by Addison, 11 June 1930 (Addison Papers, box 17).
[52] *Parl. Deb.*, 5th ser., Vol. CCXLII, pp. 890 ff.
[53] MacDonald to Addison, 7 August 1930 (MacDonald Papers, 2/10).
[54] Cf. centenary speech at Hogsthorpe Methodist church, 12 July 1945 (Addison Papers, box 86).
[55] *News of the World*, 24 August 1930.
[56] Lansbury to Addison, 25 August 1930 (Addison Papers, box 110); Neville Chamberlain MSS, University of Birmingham, NC/1/742, 21 September 1930 (we are indebted to Mr Andy Cooper for this reference).
[57] Cabinet Minutes, 2 September 1930 (CAB 23/64).
[58] *Daily Herald*, 15 September 1930; MacDonald to Addison, 25 September 1930 (Addison Papers, box 1).
[59] P. J. Grigg appends a letter to MacDonald, 30 November 1929 (MacDonald Papers, 30/69).
[60] MacDonald to Addison, 14 April 1931 (MacDonald Papers, 2/10).
[61] Lord Parmoor to MacDonald, 13 April 1931 (ibid.).
[62] Skidelsky, op. cit., p. 262.
[63] Memorandum by the Secretary of State for Scotland (Adamson) on Agricultural Policy (Addison Papers, box 17).
[64] *Parl. Deb.*, 5th ser., Vol. CCCXLII, pp. 67–71 (28 July 1930).
[65] Snowden, op. cit., p. 882.
[66] *The Spectator*, 9 August 1930; *Parl. Deb.*, 5th ser., Vol. CCXLIV, pp. 1891 ff. (13 November 1930).
[67] Lloyd George to Lansbury (Lloyd George Papers, G/11/4/2).
[68] *The Times*, 9 December 1930.

Notes to Pages 199–210

[69] Skidelsky, op. cit., pp. 257 ff.
[70] Memorandum by Addison (Addison Papers, box 5).
[71] A. G. Street to Addison, 2 November 1949 (ibid., box 119).
[72] Brinley Thomas (ed.), *The Welsh Economy* (Cardiff, 1962), p. 82. The number of milk producers in Wales rose from 10,510 in 1934 to 20,223 in 1939.
[73] Memorandum on the Marketing Bill (Addison Papers, box 5).
[74] *Parl. Deb.*, 5th ser., Vol. CCLVI, pp. 186–90 (13 July 1931).
[75] *The Times*, 5 March 1931.
[76] Viscount Wolmer, 'The Agricultural Marketing Act', *National Review*, March 1933.
[77] Hugh Dalton, *Practical Socialism for Britain*, p. 159; G. Dallas, *What Labour has done for Agriculture* (Labour party, 1934).
[78] *Parl. Deb.*, House of Lords, Vol. CL, pp. 600–1 (14 July 1947).
[79] Addison Papers, box 5.
[80] Dalton, op. cit., p. 298.
[81] A. J. P. Taylor, *English History, 1914 –1945* (Oxford, 1965), p. 297.
[82] Mrs Addison's diary, 24, 28 August 1931.
[83] Letter in *The Times*, 9 September 1931.
[84] Ibid., 27 August 1931.
[85] Typed minute by the Secretary of the Ministry of Agriculture and Fisheries, 15 August 1931 (Addison Papers, box 5); note by Addison (ibid.).
[86] *Daily Herald*, 31 August 1931.
[87] *Clarion*, September 1931.
[88] *Parl. Deb.*, 5th ser., Vol. CCLVI, pp. 1345–50 (21 September 1931).
[89] Marquand, op. cit., p. 660.
[90] Henderson to Addison, 23 September 1931 (Addison Papers, box 94).
[91] *Parl. Deb.*, 5th ser., Vol. CCLVI, pp. 1494–8 (25 September 1931).
[92] Addison to secretary of the Swindon Labour party, 22 August 1929; Addison to the Swindon Labour party, 5 December 1921 (Addison Papers, box 110).
[93] *Swindon Evening Advertiser*, 15 October 1931.
[94] Ibid., 22, 24 October 1931.
[95] Ibid., 28 October 1931. The result was Banks (Conservative) 22,756, Addison (Labour) 17,962.
[96] *Daily Herald*, 24 October 1931.
[97] Beaverbrook to Addison, 1 September 1931 (Addison Papers, box 117).

FOOTNOTES TO CHAPTER VIII

[1] Hugh Dalton, *Memoirs*, Vol. I, *Call Back Yesterday*, pp. 297–8.
[2] Mrs Addison's diary, 24 August 1931; Addison and Cole, round robin letter to the national executive of the Labour Party, 31 May 1937 (Nuffield College, G. D. H. Cole Papers, box 5, B3/5/E).
[3] Mrs Addison's diary, 28 September, 27 October 1931.
[4] Notes for the 'House of Commons Committee' week-end conference at Easton Lodge on 16–17 April 1932 (Cole Papers, box 5, B3/5/E).
[5] *Parl. Deb.*, House of Lords, 5th ser., Vol. CXXXIX, pp. 747–53 (19 February 1946).
[6] E. F. Wise to Addison, 5 April 1932 (Addison Papers, box 129).
[7] Addison Papers, ibid.
[8] Addison Papers, box 130.

[9] Cole Papers, box 5, B3/5/E.
[10] Ibid.; Addison Papers, box 130.
[11] *The Times*, 4 October 1933.
[12] *Parl. Deb.*, House of Lords, 5th ser., Vol. CXXXI, pp. 834–8 (23 May 1944).
[13] Minutes of meeting of Labour party Housing Committee, 2 November 1933 (Addison Papers, box 130).
[14] *The Times*, 2 April 1934; Cole Papers, box 5, B3/5/E.
[15] *The Times*, 18 January 1933.
[16] Elliot to Addison, 15 October 1931 (Addison Papers, box 95). For Elliot, see Colin Coote, *A Companion of Honour* (London, 1965).
[17] *Annual Report of the Labour Party Conference*, 1932, speech by Addison, 6 October.
[18] Ibid., 1933.
[19] Addison to Middleton, 16 February 1932 (Addison Papers, box 125).
[20] *Daily Herald*, 23 June 1933.
[21] Addison to Cripps, 23 June 1933 (Addison Papers, box 130).
[22] Ibid., box 130.
[23] See Arthur Marwick, 'Middle Opinion in the Thirties', *English Historical Review*, LXXIX (April 1964); *The Next Five Years* (London, 1935), pp. 160–77.
[24] Elliot to Addison, 29 September 1933, Addison to Elliot, 30 September 1933 (Addison Papers, box 6); *Yorkshire Post*, 11 October 1933.
[25] *The Times*, 10 October 1933.
[26] Addison Papers, box 6.
[27] Addison to Elliot, 10 October 1934 (Addison Papers, box 89).
[28] Mrs Addison's diary, 11 November 1931.
[29] David Lloyd George, *War Memoirs*, Vol. I (1938 edition), p. 151.
[30] A. J. Sylvester to Addison, 22 March 1932 (Addison Papers, box 95); Lloyd George to Addison, 13 May 1937 (ibid., box 100).
[31] For example, *The Times*, 24 October 1934; Lloyd George to Addison, 12 December 1934 (Addison Papers, box 113).
[32] *Lloyd George: a Diary by Frances Stevenson*, p. 290.
[33] Addison to Lloyd George, 13 December 1934 (Addison Papers, box 113).
[34] Colin Cross (ed.), A. J. Sylvester, *Life with Lloyd George* (London, 1975), p. 124.
[35] Frank Owen, *Tempestuous Journey* (London, 1954), p. 691.
[36] Addison Papers, box 81.
[37] *The Times*, 8 October 1931.
[38] *News Chronicle*, 19 October 1934.
[39] Attlee to Addison, 26 October 1934 (Addison Papers, box 94).
[40] Letter from Lord Wakefield of Kendal to the authors, 30 January 1978.
[41] *Parl. Deb.*, 5th ser., Vol. CCXCV, pp. 2030–5 (7 December 1934).
[42] Ibid., Vol. CCXCIX, pp. 1807–13 (26 March 1935).
[43] Addison Papers, box 115.
[44] *Parl. Deb.*, 5th ser., Vol. CCXCVIII, pp. 2243–5 (7 March 1935).
[45] Robert Paul Shay, *British Rearmament in the Thirties: Politics and Profits* (Princeton, New Jersey, 1977), pp. 106–7.
[46] *News Chronicle*, 20 June 1935; *The Times*, 20 June 1935.
[47] Letter to the authors, 30 January 1978.
[48] Addison Papers, box 82.
[49] H. H. Mills to Addison, 16 November 1935; F. Pethick-Lawrence to Addison, 17 November 1935; W. A. Jowitt to Addison, 16 November 1935 (ibid., box 94).
[50] Neville Chamberlain to Ida Chamberlain, 17 November 1935 (Birmingham University Library—Neville Chamberlain Papers, NC/18/1/939). We are grateful to Dr R. A. C. Parker for this reference.

[51] Attlee to Addison, 18 November 1935 (Addison Papers, box 94).
[52] *Annual Conference Report of the Labour Party*, 1937.
[53] Ben Pimlott, *Labour and the Left in the 1930s* (Cambridge, 1977), p. 36.
[54] Margaret Cole to Addison, 4 June 1933, G. D. H. Cole to Addison, 11 March 1935 (Addison Papers, box 95).
[55] *Quarterly Journal of the New Fabian Research Bureau*, 10 (June 1936), 11 (Autumn 1936) and 14 (Summer 1937); Margaret Cole, *The Life of G. D. H. Cole*, p. 194.
[56] General Secretary of the Fabian Society to Addison, 22 June 1939 (Addison Papers, box 117).
[57] *The Times*, 7 July 1938.
[58] *British Medical Journal*, 24 February 1934.
[59] *A Policy for British Agriculture* (London, 1939), p. 284.
[60] *Westminster Gazette*, 28 January 1939.
[61] *Yorkshire Post*, 6 February 1939.
[62] *Spectator*, 10 February 1939; *Glasgow Herald*, 16 January 1939.
[63] National Farmers' Union *Newssheet*, 23 January 1939.
[64] Interview with Lady Addison, 13 July 1978.
[66] Addison Papers, box 135.
[67] Strabolgi to Addison, 11 May 1937 (ibid., box 100).
[68] *Parl. Deb.*, House of Lords, 5th ser., Vol. CX, pp. 767–72 (12 July 1938).
[69] *The Times*, 27 July 1938.
[70] *Parl. Deb.*, 5th ser., Vol. CCCII, pp. 427–34 (22 May 1935).
[71] Ibid.
[72] *Evening Advertiser*, n. d. (Addison Papers, box 83).
[73] J. A. Cross, *Sir Samuel Hoare* (London, 1977), pp. 225 ff.
[74] *New Statesman*, 25 March 1939.
[75] *Annual Report of the Labour Party Conference*, 1936.
[76] *News Chronicle*, 30 November 1936; Hugh Thomas, *The Spanish Civil War* (London, 1961 edition), p. 305; D. Stark Murray, *Why a National Health Service? The Part Played by the Socialist Medical Association* (London, 1971); letter from Addison in *Medicine Today and Tomorrow*, October 1937.
[77] *The Times*, 31 August 1937.
[78] Cf. 'The Muddle at the Air Ministry', *News Chronicle*, 30 October 1936; Martin Gilbert, *Winston S. Churchill*, Vol. V (London, 1976), p. 874.
[79] Wing-Commander J. Anderson to Addison, 8 March 1938 (Addison Papers, box 6).
[80] Notes for Labour party Air Subcommittee, No. 5, May 1938 (ibid., box 83).
[81] *Parl. Deb.*, House of Lords, 5th ser., Vol. CVII, pp. 886–93 (24 February 1938).
[82] *Skegness News*, 23 March 1938.
[83] *Parl. Deb.*, House of Lords, 5th ser., Vol. CVII, pp. 931–4 (23 March 1939).
[84] Martin Gilbert and Richard Gott, *The Appeasers* (London, 1963), p. 212.
[85] Addison to Lloyd George, 19 June 1940 (Lloyd George Papers, G/1/4/13).
[86] *Parl. Deb.*, House of Lords, 5th ser., Vol. CXIV, pp. 1169–78 (27 September 1939).
[87] Ibid., Vol. CXX, pp. 12–15 (9 September 1941).
[88] Ibid., Vol. CXXI, pp. 379–84 (8 January 1942).
[89] Ibid., Vol. CXXII, pp. 429–35 (25 March 1942).
[90] Ibid., Vol. CXXIX, p. 693 (11 November 1943).
[91] Paul Addison, *The Road to 1945* (London, 1975), p. 138.
[92] Beaverbrook to Addison, 29 January 1943 (Addison Papers, box 119); *The Times*, 20, 23 April, 2 May 1945.
[93] Addison to Attlee, 25 September 1941 (ibid., box 136).

[94] Churchill to Addison, 3 October 1941, Addison to Churchill, 2 October 1941 (ibid.).
[95] *Parl. Deb.*, House of Lords, 5th ser., Vol. CXXX, p. 162 (8 December 1943).
[96] Ibid., Vol. CXXVI, pp. 307–15 (25 February 1943).
[97] Ibid., Vol. CXXXI, pp. 494–9 (25 April 1944); Woolton Diaries, 3 June 1942, 27 July 1943 (Bodleian Library).
[98] *The Times*, 26 February 1943.
[99] Addison to Samuel, 31 October 1944 (Samuel Papers, A/121/77, 100).
[100] Circular letter to Attlee *et al.*, 22 June 1944 (Addison Papers, box 18).
[101] Document C: House of Lords Reform. Party Leaders' Conference (ibid.).
[102] Nathan to Addison, 2 July 1942 (ibid., box 136).

FOOTNOTES TO CHAPTER IX

[1] Interview with Sir Harold Wilson, 15 December 1978.
[2] Cabinet Minutes, 20 November 1945 (CAB 128/2); ibid., 28 March 1946 (CAB 128/5).
[3] *Parl. Deb.*, House of Lords, 5th ser., Vol. CXXXVII, p. 76 (16 August 1945).
[4] Ibid., pp. 310 –16 (16 October 1945).
[5] Ibid., Vol. CXXXVIII, pp. 40–4 (27 November 1945).
[6] Ibid., Vol. CXLVII, pp. 284–9 (30 April 1947).
[7] Ibid., Vol. CXLIII, pp. 569–72 (23 October 1946).
[8] Ibid., pp. 327–38 (16 October 1946).
[9] *The Times*, 1 May 1947.
[10] M. Gowing, *Independence and Deterrence: Britain and Atomic Energy, 1945–52*, Vol. I, (London, 1974), pp. 19 ff.
[11] Ibid., p. 23.
[12] *Parl. Deb.*, House of Lords, 5th ser., Vol. CLXII, pp. 803–5 (18 May 1949).
[13] *The Times*, 19 October 1945; *Parl. Deb.*, House of Lords, 5th ser., Vol. CXXXVII, pp. 523–8 (25 October 1945).
[14] Ibid., p. 523.
[15] *Evening Standard*, 23 April 1946.
[16] *The Times*, 13, 26 August 1947.
[17] Ibid., 27 August 1947.
[18] *Sunday Morning Herald*, 28 August 1947.
[19] *The Times*, 26 August 1947; *Northern Daily Leader*, 25 August 1947.
[20] *Rotura Morning Post*, 3 October 1947.
[21] Account in Addison Papers, box 102.
[22] Addison to Attlee, 15 October 1947 (University College, Oxford, Attlee Papers, box 4).
[23] Addison to Walter Nash, 19 January 1948 (Addison Papers, box 137).
[24] *Montreal Star*, 24 September 1946; interview with Lady Addison, 13 December 1978.
[25] Mackenzie King to Addison, 31 December 1946 (Addison Papers, box 102).
[26] High Commissioner of UK in Canada to Addison, 31 October 1946 (ibid.).
[27] Mackenzie King to Addison, 2 May 1948 (ibid., box 119).
[28] Addison to Mackenzie King, 30 November 1948 (ibid., box 137); memorandum on 'Civil Aircraft Programme', 9 July 1948, CP (48), 179 (CAB 129/28).
[29] Correspondence with Sir E. Baring on High Commission territories, 1946 (DO 35/1172/Y. 706/12); Cabinet Minutes, 24 April, 13 May 1946 (CAB 128/5); also see William Roger Louis, *Imperialism at Bay* (Oxford, 1977), pp. 17–18, 507–8, 564 –5.

[30] Note on conference (Samuel Papers, A/155 (xii)/26).
[31] *Parl. Deb.*, House of Lords, 5th ser., Vol. CLXV, pp. 1062–7 (28 February 1947); Mackenzie King to Addison, 31 April 1947 (Addison Papers, box 102).
[32] Ibid., Vol. CL, pp. 846–50 (16 July 1947); *The Times*, 14, 19 August 1947.
[33] Addison to Attlee, 15 October 1947); (Addison Papers, box 4); *Karachi Daily*, 20 October 1947.
[34] Nehru to Addison, 13 May 1951 (Addison Papers, box 137).
[35] Minutes of meetings of Addison and Attlee on the constitution of Newfoundland, 1946 (PRO, DO35/1344/N.402/39); *Parl. Deb.*, House of Lords, 5th ser., Vol. CXLIII, pp. 337–8 (16 October 1946). For a general survey of the work of the Dominions (later Commonwealth) Secretary, see J. Garner, *The Commonwealth Office, 1925–1968* (London, 1979).
[36] Cabinet Minutes, 24 April 1946 (CAB 128/5); Addison's memorandum on 'Clothes Rationing', 13 December 1946 (CAB 129/15).
[37] *Parl. Deb.*, House of Lords, 5th ser., Vol. CXLI, pp. 679–83 (30 May 1946); ibid., Vol. CXLV, pp. 94–103 (22 January 1947); ibid., Vol. CLII, pp. 358–65 (30 October 1947).
[38] *Round Table*, Vols. XXXVI–XXXVII (September 1946).
[39] Interview with Lady Addison, 13 July 1978; *The Times*, 8 October 1947.
[40] Addison to Mackenzie King, 9 April 1948 (Addison Papers, box 137).
[41] P. Gordon Walker, *The Cabinet* (London, 1970), pp. 135–7.
[42] P. Noel Baker to Addison, 8 November 1949 (Addison Papers, box 119).
[43] *The Times*, 17 February 1950.
[44] *Parl. Deb.*, House of Lords, 5th ser., Vol. CLIII, pp. 1203–7 (4 December 1947).
[45] *Manchester Guardian*, 31 August 1946.
[46] *Daily Telegraph*, 23 January 1947; *Parl. Deb.*, House of Lords, 5th ser., Vol. CXXXIX, pp. 768–78 (20 February 1946).
[47] 'It's Hard Work for the Labour Peers', *Forward*, 27 July 1946.
[48] Dalton Diary, 25 April 1945 (London School of Economics, Dalton Papers, 32).
[49] Reith to Addison, 1 January 1946 (Attlee Papers, box 7); Charles Stuart (ed.), *The Reith Diaries* (London, 1975), pp. 354–6.
[50] *News Review*, 16 January 1947.
[51] Nathan to Addison, 14 August 1947 (Addison Papers, box 18).
[52] B. Donoghue and G. W. Jones, *Herbert Morrison: Portrait of a Politician* (London, 1973), pp. 356–7; F. Williams, *A Prime Minister Remembers* (London, 1961), p. 81.
[53] Herbert Morrison, *Government and Parliament* (Oxford, 1954), pp. 238–42; cf. memorandum by Addison on 1948–9 parliamentary session, CP (48), 68 (CAB 129/25).
[54] P. A. Bromhead, *The House of Lords and Contemporary Politics* (London, 1958), p. 157.
[55] *Parl. Deb.*, 5th ser., Vol. CXXXVIII, pp. 1001 ff. (Calverley was formerly George Muff, MP).
[56] Cabinet Minutes, 10 January, 18 March 1946 (CAB 128/5); H. Hartley to Lady Addison, 16 December 1951 (Bodleian, MS Eng. Let. d. 332, f. 192); Addison's remarks on civil aviation appear in Cabinet Minutes, 15 July 1948 (CAB 128/13).
[57] *Parl. Deb.*, 5th ser., Vol. CXXXVII, pp. 680–6 (6 November 1945); Dalton Diaries, 1 November 1945 (Dalton Papers, 33).
[58] *The Star*, 15 July 1946.
[59] *Parl. Deb.*, House of Lords, 5th ser., Vol. CXLVII, pp. 1045–56 (21 May 1947) and ibid., Vol. CXLVIII, pp. 287–90 (9 June 1947).
[60] Barnes to Addison, 15 July 1947 (Addison Papers, box 135).
[61] Bevan to Addison, 6 November 1946 (ibid., box 136).

[62] Memorandum on 'The Housing Bill', 23 November 1948, CP (48), 279 (CAB 129/31); Cabinet Minutes, 25 November 1948 (CAB 128/13).
[63] *Parl. Deb.*, House of Lords, 5th ser., Vol. CXLIX, pp. 163–9 (24 June 1947).
[64] *How the Labour Party has saved Agriculture* (Labour party Publications, 1951), p. 7.
[65] Nathan to Addison, 19 August 1947 (Addison Papers, box 18).
[66] Brook to Addison, 28 October 1947 (ibid.).
[67] Addison to Lindsay, 14 April 1947 (ibid.).
[68] Memorandum from Sir Norman Brook to Attlee, 10 October 1947 (ibid.).
[69] Note in Addison Papers, box 135.
[70] Interview with Sir Harold Wilson, 15 December 1978; Nathan to Addison, 19 August 1947 (ibid., box 18).
[71] C. R. Attlee, *As it Happened* (London, 1954), p. 167.
[72] Cabinet Minutes, 30 October 1947 (CAB 128/10).
[73] *The Listener*, 17 June 1948; party political broadcast by Lord Addison.
[74] Addison to Mackenzie King, 9 April 1948 (Addison Papers, box 137).
[75] Mackenzie King to Addison, 2 May 1948 (ibid.).
[76] *Parl. Deb.*, House of Lords, 5th ser., Vol. CLVI, pp. 589–98 (9 June 1948).
[77] For Addison's part in the Cabinet debate on iron and steel nationalization, see Cabinet Minutes, 24 April 1947 (CAB 128/9), and 31 July and 7 August 1947 (CAB 128/10); also Addison's memorandum on 'Iron and Steel Bill', 2 June 1948, CP (48), 139 (CAB 129/27); cf. Dalton Diaries, 28 April, 8 August 1947 (Dalton Papers, 35). For an effective exposition of the arguments in favour of iron and steel nationalization, see G. R. Strauss's memorandum of June 1948, CP (48), 145 (CAB 129/27).
[78] C. A. R. Crosland, *The Future of Socialism* (London, 1956), esp. Part One.
[79] *Parl. Deb.*, House of Lords, 5th ser., Vol. CLXII, pp. 1134–43 (25 May 1949).
[80] Ibid., Vol. CLXIII, p. 566 (29 June 1949).
[81] Ibid., Vol. CLXV, pp. 958–9 (24 November 1949).
[82] Ibid.
[83] Ibid., Vol. CLXIV, p. 626 (28 July 1949).
[84] Memorandum on 'Clothes Rationing', 13 December 1946 (CAB 129/15); Dalton Diaries, 1 August 1946 (Dalton Papers, 34). Cripps was briefly Minister for Economic Affairs, September–November 1947.
[85] Parl. Deb., House of Lords, 5th ser., Vol. CLIV, pp. 88–97 (24 February 1948).
[86] Ibid., Vol. CLVII, pp. 381–9 (6 July 1948).
[87] *The Listener*, 17 June 1948.
[88] *Parl. Deb.*, House of Lords, 5th ser., Vol. CLXIV, pp. 709–19 (27 September 1949).
[89] Ibid., Vol. CLXV, pp. 1602–14 (14 December 1949).
[90] Ibid., Vol. CLXIV, pp. 709–19 (27 September 1949); Addison to Mackenzie King, 30 November 1949 (Addison Papers, box 137).
[91] Mackenzie King to Addison, 3 February 1950 (ibid., box 119).
[92] D. Astor to Addison, 1 February 1950 (Addison Papers, box 101); *The Observer*, loc. cit.
[93] Divisional Labour parties of High Wycombe, West Walthamstow, Oxford City, and Reading to Addison, 12 February, 31 January, 27 January, and 27 January 1950 (Addison Papers, box 101); W. Dixon to Lady Addison, 19 December 1951 (Bodleian, MSS Eng. Lett. d. 333, f. 158).
[94] *Sunday Times*, 5 March 1950.
[95] Lawson to Addison, 18 May 1950 (Addison Papers, box 135).
[96] *Parl. Deb.*, House of Lords, 5th ser., Vol. CLXVIII, pp. 887–94 (27 July 1950); Addison to Stokes, 7 May 1951 (Addison Papers, box 137).

[97] Addison to Bevan, March 1951, quoted in Michael Foot, *Aneurin Bevan*, Vol. II (London, 1973), p.325.
[98] Hugh Dalton, *Memoirs*, Vol. III, *High Tide and After* (London, 1962), p. 365.
[99] Addison to Churchill, November 1951 (Addison Papers, box 137); interview with Lady Addison, 13 December 1978.
[100] Bodleian, MSS Eng. Lett. d. 332, f. 115 and d. 333, ff. 78, 159.
[101] *Parl. Deb.*, House of Lords, 5th ser., Vol. CLXXIV, pp. 949–51 (30 January 1952).
[102] Bromhead, op. cit., p. 176.
[103] Nathan to Addison, 6 January 1950 (Addison Papers, box 119).
[104] *The Times*, 5 November 1949.
[105] Lord Clydesmuir to Lady Addison, 13 December 1951 (Bodleian, d. 332).

FOOTNOTES TO CONCLUSION

[1] The Sunday Times, 5 March 1950.
[2] *Sunday Herald*, 8 August 1915.
[3] See pages 25–6, above; also *Review of Reviews*, May 1919. For the disillusion of many progressive intellectuals in their old age, see Peter Clarke, *Liberals and Social Democrats* (Cambridge, 1978), especially the Epilogue.
[4] *The Times*, 28 February 1920.
[5] *Daily Chronicle*, 2 November 1915.
[6] *Leeds Mercury*, 16 December 1915.
[7] Quoted in José Harris, *William Beveridge: a Biography*, p. 228.
[8] Paul Barton Johnson, *Land Fit for Heroes*, pp. 435 ff.
[9] *Politics from Within*, Vol. I, p. 176.
[10] *Parl. Deb.*, House of Lords, 5th ser., Vol. CLXXIV, p. 950 (30 January 1952).
[11] Ibid., pp. 952–3.
[12] *Four and a Half Years*, Vol. I, p. 22.

Bibliography

A. Manuscript Collections

B. Official Papers

C. Newspapers, Periodicals, and Reports

D. Addison's Publications

E. Other Printed Primary Sources

F. Biographies and Memoirs

G. Other Published Works

H. Articles in Learned Journals

I. Unpublished Theses

A. Manuscript Collections

1. Public Records

CAB 23	(Cabinet Minutes, 1916–21, 1929–31).
CAB 24	(Cabinet Papers).
CAB 26	(Cabinet Home Affairs Committee).
CAB 27	(Cabinet Committees).
CAB 128	(Cabinet Minutes, 1945–8).
CAB 129	(Cabinet Papers, 1945–8).
DO 35	(Dominions Office Papers).
HLG 48	(Ministry of Health and Housing Papers).
MUN 5	(Ministry of Munitions Papers).

Bibliography

2. Private Papers

Addison MSS (in private hands, courtesy of Lord Addison and Mrs Cheshire).
Addison Papers (Bodleian Library). This is a large, miscellaneous collection of 137 boxes, poorly catalogued. In addition to much private correspondence, MSS of books and diaries and press cuttings, there are large quantities of official papers and memoranda relating to Addison's period as a Cabinet Minister, 1916–21, 1930 –1, and 1945–51. There are also some letters of condolence, 1951, in Bodleian, Eng. Lett. d. 332–3.
Attlee Papers (University College Library, Oxford).
Beveridge Papers (Collection on Munitions: London School of Economics Library).
Bridgeman Papers (Courtesy of Lord Bridgeman).
Neville Chamberlain Papers (University of Birmingham Library).
Cole Papers (Nuffield College Library, Oxford).
Dalton Papers (LSE Library).
Davidson Papers (House of Lords Record Office).
Fisher Papers (Bodleian Library).
Garvin Papers (University of Texas, by courtesy of Professor John Stubbs).
Lloyd George of Dwyfor Papers (House of Lords Record Office).
Thomas Jones Papers (National Library of Wales: Courtesy of Mr Tristan Jones).
Bonar Law Papers (House of Lords Record Office).
Sir Herbert Lewis Papers (National Library of Wales).
Ramsay MacDonald Papers (Public Record Office).
Montagu Papers (Trinity College Library, Cambridge).
Samuel Papers (House of Lords Record Office).
Stansgate Papers (House of Lords Record Office).
Viscount Wakefield of Kendal (personal recollections).
Woolton Papers (Bodleian Library).

B. Official Papers

Interim Report of the Departmental Committee on Tuberculosis (Cd. 6164) *P.P.* (1912–13), XLVIII, 1.
Final Report of the Departmental Committee on Tuberculosis (Cd. 6641) *P.P.* (1912–13), XLVIII, 29 anrid *Appendices* (Cd. 6654) *P.P.* (1912–13), XLVIII, 47.
Report of Sir William Plender to the Chancellor of the Exchequer on the result of his investigation into existing conditions in respect of medical attendance and remuneration in certain towns (Cd. 6305), *P.P.* (1912–13), LXXVIII, 679.
Index to the Health Provisions of the Insurance Act (Cd. 6468), *P.P.* (1912–13), LXXVIII, 899.

Report of the Committee appointed to consider questions of building construction in connection with the provision of working-class dwellings (Cd. 9191), *P.P.* (1918), VII, 319.
Interim Report of the Health of Munition Workers Committee on Industrial Efficiency and Fatigue (Cd. 8511), *P.P.* (1917–18, XVI, 1019.
Final Report (Cd. 9065), *P.P.* (1918), XII, 195.
Report of the Committee on the Building Industry after the war (Cd. 9197), *P.P.* (1918), VII, 493.
Report of the Chief Medical Officer of Health 1917–18 (Cd. 9169), *P.P.* (1918), XI, 301.
Report of the Machinery of Government Committee (Cmd. 9230), *P.P.* (1918), XII, 1.
Memorandum of the Ministry of Reconstruction on the Ministry of Health Bill 1918 (Cd. 9211), *P.P.* (1918), XX, 863, *and Memorandum* (in continuation) (C 45), *P.P.* 1919, XXXIX, 647.
Memorandum of the Advisory Panel on Housing in England and Wales (Cd. 9087), *P.P.* (1918), XXVI, 437.
Interim Report of the Treasury Committee on Housing Finance (Cmd. 444), *P.P.* (1919), XXII, 1179.
Regulations for the training of health visitors (Cmd. 354), *P.P.* (1919), XXXIX, 159.
Memorandum on the provisions of the Ministry of Health Bill as to the work of the Medical Research Committee (Cmd. 69), *P.P.* (1919), XXXIX, 651.
An outline of the practice of preventive medicine. A memorandum by Sir George Newman, Chief Medical Officer of Health (Cmd. 363), *P.P.* (1919), XXXIX, 677.
First Report of the Ministry of Health 1919–20: Part I, Public Health, Local Administration, Local Taxation, and Valuation (Cmd. 923), *P.P.* (1920), XVII, 49. *Part II, Housing and Town Planning* (Cmd. 917), *P.P.* (1920), XVII, 227. *Part III, Administration of the Poor Law, Unemployed Workman's Act, and the Old Age Pensions Act* (Cmd. 932), *P.P.* (1920), XVII, 283. *Part IV, National Health Insurance Administration 1917–20 and Welsh Board of Health* (Cmd. 913), *P.P.* (1920), XVII, 447.
Annual Report of the Chief Medical Officer 1919–20 (Cmd. 978), *P.P.* (1920), XVII, 573; *1920–1* (Cmd. 1397), *P.P.* (1921), XII, 889.
Interim Report of the Consultative Council on the future provision of medical and allied services (Cmd. 693), *P.P.* (1920), XVII, 1001.
Second Annual Report of the Ministry of Health (Cmd. 1446), *P.P.* (1921), XIII, 1.
Report of the Consultative Council on Local Health Administration (Cmd. 1113) *P.P.* 1921, xiii, 227.
Report of the Departmental Committee on the high cost of Building Working Class Dwellings (Cmd. 1447), *P.P.* (1921), XIII, 919.
Third Annual Report of the Ministry of Health (Cmd. 1713), *P.P.* (1922), VIII, 1.
Report of the National Parks Committee (Cmd. 3851), *P.P.* (1931), XVI, 1.

Statement of Policy on Constitutional Reform in Ceylon 1945–6 (Cmd. 6690), P.P. (1945–6), XIX, 47.

C. Newspapers, Periodicals, and Reports

1. Newspapers

Birmingham Daily Mail
Birmingham Post
Daily Chronicle
Daily Express
Daily Herald
Daily Mail
Daily News
Daily Telegraph
Glasgow Herald
Hackney and Kingsland Gazette
Justice
Manchester Guardian
Morning Post
News of the World
North Eastern Daily Gazette
North Wiltshire Herald
Reynolds Newspaper
The Scotsman
Shoreditch Observer
South Wales Daily News
The Standard
The Star
Sunday Pictorial
Sunday Times
Swindon Evening Advertizer
The Times
Weekly Despatch
Western Mail
Westminster Gazette
Yorkshire Post

2. Periodicals

British Medical Journal
Clarion
Economist
The Hospital

Housing
Lancet
Liberal Magazine
Listener
Lloyd George Liberal Magazine
Local Government Journal
Medical Officer
Medical Press and Circular
Nation
National Review
New Leader
New Statesman
Outlook
Punch
Quarterly Journal of the New Fabian Research Bureau
Review of Reviews
Round Table
Spectator
The Surveyor

3. Reports

Hansard, Parliamentary Debates, 5th Series.
Labour Party Annual Conference *Reports*, 1924–36.
London County Council, *Reports* of the Housing of the Working Classes Committee, 191–22.

D. Addison's Publications

1. Books

With the Abyssinians in Somaliland, by Major J. Willes Jennings and C. Addison (Hodder and Stoughton, London, 1905).
The Law and Practice of Housing, by Sir Kingsley Wood with a preface by Lord Addison (Hodder and Stoughton, London, 1921).
The Betrayal of the Slums (Herbert Jenkins, London, 1922).
Politics from Within, vols. I and II, 1911–18 (Herbert Jenkins, London, 1924).
Practical Socialism, 2 vols. (Labour Publishing Co., London, 1926).
Four and a Half Years, vols. I and II, 1914–19 (Hutchinson, London, 1934).
Labour's Policy for our Countryside (Labour Publishing Co., 1937).
A Policy for British Agriculture (Gollancz, London, 1939).

Bibliography

2. Pamphlets

The Health of the People and how it may be Improved (London, 1914).
'The Boy in Industry' (with a foreword by C. Addison) (Ministry of Munitions, 1917).
British Workshops and the War: Speech delivered in the House of Commons on the work of the Ministry of Munitions, 28 June 1917 (T. Fisher Unwin Ltd., London, 1917).
Why Food is Dear (Labour party Publications, 1925).
Religion and Politics (The Social Service Lecture, 1931, Epworth Press, London).
How the Labour Party has saved Agriculture (Labour party Publications, 1951).

3. Articles

'Education in regard to the feeding and care of infants', *The Child*, December 1910.
'The Controversy over Medical Benefit under the National Insurance Act', *Contemporary Review*, October 1912.
'The Future of the Panel Practitioner: His Aims and Ideals', *Medical World*, 30 July 1914.
'The Budget and the Worker', *London Liberal*, No. 2, August 1914.
'Healthy Houses Make a Happy People', *The Future* (September 1919).
'Economising on Human Life: the trying cost of a great reform' (n. d.).
'The Part of the State in the Prevention of Disease': the Cavendish Lecture delivered on 17 June 1921 and reprinted.
'How We Are Governed', *Nineteenth Century* (March 1922).
'The Nation and its Food' (1929): reprinted in *Self and Society, Second Twelve Essays*, ed. Percy Redfern (Ernest Benn, London, 1930).
'Agriculture and the Future. The Beginning of Great Developments', *Forward*, 15 August 1931.
'The Power of Nations to Prevent Wars', The General Press Agency, 24 February 1932.
Chapter on 'Socialist Policy and the Problem of Food Supply' in *The Problems of a Socialist Government* (Gollancz, London, 1933).
'Fundamentals in Marketing Schemes', *Farmer and Stockbreeder*, January 1933.
'A Great Opportunity', *The Labour Candidate*, May 1933.
'The Cost of Beef Subsidy Failure', *New Statesman*, 1 August 1936.
Chapter in *A Programme for Agriculture* (Michael Joseph, London, 1941).
'It's Hard Work for the Labour Peers', *Forward*, 27 July 1946.
'Party Political Broadcast by Viscount Addison', *The Listener*, 17 June 1948.
'Then and Now', *The Observer*, 19 February 1950.

E. Other Printed Primary Sources

Bunbury, Sir H. (ed.), *Lloyd George's Ambulance Wagon* (Methuen, London, 1957).
Cole, Margaret (ed.), *Beatrice Webb's Diaries, 1912–1929* (Longmans, London, 1952).
—— *Beatrice Webb's Diaries, 1929–1932* (Longmans, London, 1956).
Cross, Colin (ed.), *A. J. Sylvester, Life with Lloyd George* (Macmillan, London, 1975).
Dalton, Hugh, *Memories: Call Back Yesterday, 1887–1931* (Muller, London, 1953).
—— *Memories: High Tide and After, 1945–1960* (Muller, London, 1962).
Gilbert, Martin (ed.), *Churchill*, Companion Volumes, vol. III; 2 vols. (Heinemann, London, 1972); Vol. IV, 3 vols. (1977).
Mansergh, Nicholas, *Documents and Speeches on British Commonwealth Affairs, 1931–1952* (Oxford University Press, 1953).
Middlemas, Keith (ed.), *Thomas Jones: Whitehall Diary*, vols. I and III (Oxford University Press, London, 1969).
Morgan, Kenneth O. (ed.), *Lloyd George: Family Letters, 1885–1936* (Oxford University Press, 1973).
Stuart, Charles (ed.), *The Reith Diaries* (Collins, London, 1975).
Taylor, A. J. P. (ed.), *Lloyd George, A Diary by Frances Stevenson* (Hutchinson, London, 1971).
Wilson, Trevor (ed.), *Political Diaries of C. P. Scott* (Collins, London, 1970).

F. Biographies and Memoirs

Attlee, C. R., *As it Happened* (Windmill Press, London, 1954).
Briggs, Asa, *Social Thought and Social Action: A Study of the Work of Seebohm Rowntree* (Longmans, London, 1961).
Cole, Margaret, *The Life of G. D. H. Cole* (Macmillan, London, 1971).
Coote, Colin, *A Companion of Honour* (Collins, London, 1965).
Cross, J. A., *Sir Samuel Hoare* (Cape, London, 1977).
Donoghue, B. and Jones, G. W., *Herbert Morrison: Portrait of a Politician* (Weidenfeld and Nicolson, London, 1973).
Foot, Michael, *Aneurin Bevan*, vol. II, 1945–60 (Davis Poynter, London, 1973).
Gilbert, Martin, *Winston S. Churchill*, vols. III, IV, and V (Heinemann, London, 1971, 1975, 1976).
Harris, José, *William Beveridge: A Biography* (Oxford, 1977).
Hewins, W. A. S., *The Apologia of an Imperialist*, 2 vols. (Constable, London, 1929).
Kirkwood, David, *My Life of Revolt* (Harrap, London, 1935).

Bibliography

Koss, Stephen, *Fleet Street Radical* (Archon Books, Connecticut, 1973).
Lloyd George, David, *War Memoirs* (Odhams, new edition, London, 1938).
Marquand, David, *Ramsay MacDonald* (Cape, London, 1977).
Middlemas, K. and Barnes J., *Baldwin* (Weidenfeld and Nicolson, London, 1969).
Minney, R. J., *Viscount Addison: Leader of the Lords* (Odhams, London, 1958).
Owen, Frank, *Tempestuous Journey* (Hutchinson, London, 1954).
Pakenham, Lord, *Born to Believe* (Cape, London, 1953).
Roskill, S. W., *Hankey: Man of Secrets*, vols. I and II (Collins, London, 1970).
Rowland, Peter, *Lloyd George* (Barrie and Jenkins, London, 1976).
Shock, M., *Dictionary of National Biography, 1951-60*, under 'Addison'.
Taylor, A. J. P., *Lloyd George: Rise and Fall* (Cambridge University Press, 1961).
—— *Beaverbrook* (Hamish Hamilton, London, 1972).
Thomas, Hugh, *John Strachey* (Eyre Methuen, London, 1973).
Snowden, Viscount, *An Autobiography*, 2 vols. (Ivor Nicholson and Watson, London, 1934).
Waley, S. D., *Edwin Montagu* (Asia Publishing House, Bombay, 1964).
Williams, Francis, *A Prime Minister Remembers* (Heinemann, London, 1961).
Winterton, Earl, *Orders of the Day* (Cassell, London, 1953).

G. Other Published Works

Adams, R. J. Q., *Arms and the Wizard* (Cassell, London, 1978).
Addison, Paul, *The Road to 1945* (Cape, London, 1975).
Aldred, G. A., *Socialism and Parliament* (The Bakunin Press, Glasgow, 1923).
Aldridge, H. R., *The National Housing Manual* (National Housing and Town Planning Council, 1923).
Astor, W. and Murray, K. A. H., *The Planning of Agriculture* (Oxford University Press, 1933).
Attlee, C. R., *The Will and the Way to Socialism* (Eyre Methuen, London, 1935).
—— *The Labour Party in Perspective* (Gollancz, London, 1937).
—— *The Labour Party in Perspective and Twelve Years Later* (Gollancz, London, 1949).
Barker, M., *Gladstone and Radicalism* (Harvester Press, Hassocks, 1975).
Bassett, R., *Nineteen thirty-one: Political Crisis* (Macmillan, London, 1958).
Bateson, F. W., *Towards a Socialist Agriculture* (Gollancz, London, 1946).
Beaverbrook, Lord, *Politicians and the War 1914-16* (Collins, new ed., London, 1960.)
—— *Men and Power, 1917-18* (Hutchinson, London, 1956)
—— *The Decline and Fall of Lloyd George* (Collins, London, 1963).
Bentley, Michael, *The Liberal Mind, 1914-1929* (Cambridge University Press, 1976).

Blundell, F. N., *A New Policy for Agriculture* (Phillip Allan, London, 1931).
Bowley, Marian, *Housing and the State 1919–1944* (Allen and Unwin, London, 1945).
Boyce, D. G., *Englishmen and Irish Troubles, 1918–22* (Cape, London, 1972).
Bromhead, P. A., *The House of Lords and Contemporary Politics* (Routledge and Kegan Paul, London, 1958).
Bruce, Maurice, *The Coming of the Welfare State* (Batsford, London, 1966).
Churchill, Winston S., *The World Crisis 1914–18* (Butterworth, London, 1927).
Clarke, P. F., *Lancashire and the New Liberalism* (Cambridge University Press, 1971).
Cline, Catherine Ann, *Recruits to Labour: The British Labour Party 1914–1931* (Syracuse University Press, Syracuse, New York, 1963).
Cowling, Maurice, *The Impact of Labour, 1920–1924* (Cambridge University Press, 1971).
Currie, G. W., *The Growth of Socialist Opinion in Britain* (Nishet and Co., London, 1922).
Dewar, G. A. B., *The Great Munitions Feat, 1914–1918* (Constable, London, 1921).
Emy, H. V., *Liberals, Radicals and Social Politics* (Cambridge University Press, 1972).
Ford, P. & G., *A Breviate of Parliamentary Papers, 1900–1916* (Blackwell, Oxford, 1957).
Freeden, Michael, *The New Liberalism* (Clarendon Press, Oxford, 1978).
Garner, J., *The Commonwealth Office, 1925–1968* (Heinemann, London, 1979).
Garratt, G. T., *The Farmer and the Labour Party* (Labour party Publications, 1927).
—— *The Mugwumps and the Labour Party* (Woolf, London, 1932).
Garrod, H. W., *Worms and Epitaphs* (Clarendon Press, Oxford, 1920).
Gilbert, Bentley, *The Evolution of National Insurance in Great Britain* (Michael Joseph, London, 1966).
—— *British Social Policy 1914–1939* (Batsford, London, 1970).
Gilbert, Martin and Gott, Richard, *The Appeasers* (Weidenfeld and Nicolson, London, 1963).
Gordon-Walker, Patrick, *The Cabinet* (Cape, London, 1970).
Gowing, Margaret, *Independence and Deterrence; Britain and Atomic Energy, 1945–52*, vol. I (Macmillan, London, 1974).
Gupta, Partha Sarathi, *Imperialism and the British Labour Movement* (Macmillan, London, 1975).
Hall, D. A., *Reconstruction and the Land* (Macmillan, London, 1941).
Harris, Richard W., *National Health Insurance 1911–1946* (Allen and Unwin, London, 1946).
Hazlehurst, C., *Politicians at War, July 1914 to May 1915* (Cape, London, 1971).
Hewart, G., *The Lloyd George Government: What it has done and why it is still needed* (1920).

Bibliography 315

Hinton, J., *The First Shop Stewards' Movement* (Allen and Unwin, London, 1973).
Johnson, Paul Barton, *Land Fit for Heroes* (University of Chicago Press, 1968).
Koss, Stephen, *Nonconformity in Modern British Politics* (Batsford, London, 1976).
Landsborough Thompson, A., *Half a Century of Medical Research: Origins and Policy of the Medical Research Council*. (HMSO 1977).
Lloyd, T. O., *Empire to Welfare State: English History 1906–1967* (Oxford University Press, 1970).
Louis, William Roger, *Imperialism at Bay* (Clarendon Press, Oxford, 1978).
Lyman, R. W., *The First Labour Government* (Chapman and Hall, London, 1957).
Mansergh, Nicholas, *A Survey of British Commonwealth Affairs 1939–52* (Frank Cass, London, 1958).
McKibbin, R. I., *The Evolution of the Labour Party 1910 –24* (Oxford University Press, 1975).
Morgan, Kenneth O., *The Age of Lloyd George* (Allen and Unwin, London, new edn., 1978).
Morris, A. J., *Radicalism against War, 1906–1914* (Longmans, London, 1973).
Mowat, C. L., *Britain Between the Wars 1918–1940* (Methuen, London, 1955).
Murray, D. Stark, *Why a National Health Service?* (Pemberton Books, London, 1971).
Mustoe, M. E., *The Agricultural Marketing Acts and Schemes* (London Estates Gazette, Ltd., 1935).
Naylor, John F., *Labour's International Policy* (Weidenfeld and Nicolson, London, 1969).
Newman, G. H., *Health and Social Evolution* (Allen and Unwin, London, 1931).
—— *The Building of the Nation's Health* (Macmillan, London, 1939).
Newsholme, Arthur, *The Ministry of Health* (Putnam, London, 1926).
—— *The Last Thirty Years in Public Health* (Allen and Unwin, London, 1936).
Pelling, Henry, *Social Geography of British Elections 1885–1910* (Macmillan, London, 1968).
Pigou, A. C., *Aspects of British Economic History 1918–1925* (Macmillan, London, 1947).
Pimlott, Ben, *Labour and the Left in the 1930's* (Cambridge University Press, 1977).
'Politicus', *Party Not Faction* (1920).
Richardson, Harry W. and Aldcroft, Derek H., *Building in the British Economy between the Wars* (Allen and Unwin, London, 1968).
Shay, Robert Paul, *British Rearmament in the Thirties: Politics and Profits* (Princeton University Press, Princeton, New Jersey, 1977).
Silverlight, John, *The Victor's Dilemma* (Barrie and Jenkins, London, 1970).

Skidelsky, Robert, *Politicians and the Slump: The Labour Government 1929–31* (Macmillan, London, 1967).
Swartz, Marvin, *The Union of Democratic Control in British Politics during the First World War* (Clarendon Press, Oxford, 1971).
Taylor, A. J. P., *Politics in the First World War* (Oxford University Press, 1959).
—— *English History 1914–1945* (Oxford University Press, 1965).
Thompson, Paul, *Socialists, Liberals and Labour* (Routledge and Kegan Paul, London, 1967).
Vaughan, Paul, *Doctors Commons: A Short History of the British Medical Association* (Heinemann, London, 1959).
Webb, Sidney and Beatrice, *English Poor Law History, part II: The Last Hundred Years*, vol. 2 (Longmans Green, London, 1929).
Wilson, Trevor, *The Downfall of the Liberal Party, 1914–1935* (Collins, London, 1966).
Worsfold, W. B., *The War and Social Reform* (Murray, London, 1919).
Wrigley, C. J. *David Lloyd George and the British Labour Movement* (Harvester Press/Barnes and Noble, Hassocks, 1976).

H. Articles in Learned Journals

P. Abrams, 'The Failure of Social Reform, 1918–20', *Past and Present*, No. 24 (April 1963).
Roger Davidson, 'Wartime Labour Policy 1914–16', *Scottish Journal of Labour History*, 8 (June 1974).
Bentley B. Gilbert, 'David Lloyd George: the Reform of British Landholding and the Budget of 1914', *Historical Journal*, 21, 1 (March 1978).
W. Golant, 'The Emergence of C. R. Attlee as Leader of the Parliamentary Labour Party in 1935', *Historical Journal*, XIII, 2 (1970).
J. Hinton, 'The Suppression of *Forward*', *Scottish Journal of Labour History*, 7 (1973).
Susan Howson, 'The Origins of Dear Money 1919–20', *Economic History Review*, XXVII, No. 1 (February 1974).
Iain McLean, 'The Ministry of Munitions, the Clyde Workers Committee and the suppression of "Forward": an alternative view', *Scottish Journal of Labour History*, 6 (December 1972).
Arthur Marwick, 'Middle Opinion in the Thirties', *English Historical Review*, LXXIX (April 1964).
Kenneth O. Morgan, 'Lloyd George's Premiership: a Study in "Prime Ministerial Government"', *Historical Journal*, XIII, 1 (1970).
Alan J. Sharp, 'The Foreign Office in Eclipse, 1919–22', *History*, 61 (1976).
J. A. Turner, 'The Formation of Lloyd George's "Garden Suburb": "Fabian-Like Milnerite Penetration"?', *Historical Journal*, XX, 1 (1977).

J. M. Winter, 'The Impact of the First World War on Civilian Health in Britain', *Economic History Review*, XXX, No.3 (August 1977).

I. Unpublished Theses

G. M. Bayliss, 'The Outsider: Aspects of the Political Career of Alfred Mond, First Lord Melchett' (University of Wales Ph.D., 1969).

Roger Eatwell, 'The Labour Party and the Popular Front Movement in Britain in the 1930s' (Oxford University D.Phil., 1975).

John Turner, 'Lloyd George's Private Secretariat, 1917–18' (Oxford University D.Phil., 1976).

Paul R. Wilding, 'Government and Housing; A Study in the Development of Social Policy 1906–1939' (University of Manchester Ph.D., 1970).

Index

Aberavon, 160
Abyssinia, 226–7
Adams, W.G.S., 60
Adamson, William, 197, 203
Addison, Dr Christopher,
    Career: early life, 1–2; medical career, 2–4; marriage, 5–6; enters politics, 4–7; elected to Parliament, 7–10; and National Insurance Bill, 10–22; personal relationship with Lloyd George, 22–3, 28, 34, 147–8, 189, 190, 215–17; serves on Tuberculosis Commission, 23–4; and Medical Research Council, 24–5, 258; and women's rights, 25–6, 277; and labour unrest, 26, 114, 135–6, 167–8; and Ireland, 27, 115, 121, 135; and land question, 27–8; at Education department, 29–31; and outbreak of 1914 war, 29–30; at Ministry of Munitions, 32–47; and wartime labour troubles, 38–45, 62–7; and conscription crisis, 48–50; and Lloyd George becoming premier, 50–8; as Minister of Munitions, 59–70, 278; as Minister of Reconstruction, 70–82; and wartime politics, 82–6; in 'coupon' election, 87–8; role in post-war politics, 90–3; at Local Government Board, 93–6; and housing policy, 96–102, 106–13, 121–9, 211–12, 258–9; work as Minister of Health, 102–5, 129–31, 276; on foreign affairs, 114–15, 121, 128–9, 226–31; and 'fusion', 115–20; attacked by 'anti-waste' movement, 131–2, 136; leaves Ministry of Health, 132–4; break with Lloyd George Coalition, 137–48; a critic of the Coalition government, 149–53; defeated in 1922 election, 154–5; joins the Labour Party, 156–60; financial difficulties, 158–9; in 1924 election, 161–2; and Labour's agricultural policy, 165–6, 168–71; elected for Swindon, 171–2; enters second Labour government, 173–5; at Ministry of Agriculture, 177–86; friendship with Attlee, 177, 239; negotiations with Lloyd George, 187–92, 215–17; policy as Minister of Agriculture, 192–201, 278; and 1931 crisis, 202–7; defeated in 1931 election, 206; role in opposition in the thirties, 208–15; in 'Friday group', 210–11; and arms trade, 219; re-elected for Swindon, 218; defeated at Swindon, 219–20; and New Fabian Research Bureau, 221–2; second marriage, 224; enters House of Lords, 224–5; and Spanish Civil War, 228–9; role during second world war, 232–6; enters Attlee government, 237; role in Attlee government, 238–9, 251, 254, 255; and the atomic bomb, 239–42; work at Dominions Office, 242–50, 279; friendship with Mackenzie King, 245–6; and Indian independence, 247–8; leadership of the House of Lords, 251–4, 265–7, 273–4; and

nationalization, 255–8; and the 1947 Agriculture Act, 259; and iron and steel bill, 259–64; in 1950 election, 268–9; and Korean War, 270; and fall of Attlee government, 271; death of, 271–3, 275; wider significance of, 276–81.
Writings:
Four and a Half Years, 16, 222, 279
Politics from Within, 18, 46, 163–4, 279
The Betrayal of the Slums, 150–1, 277
Practical Socialism, 33, 165, 277
Why Food is Dear, 165–6
The Nation and its Food, 165–7, 170
An Exposure of the Government's Trade Union Bill, 167–8
Labour's Policy for the Countryside, 222
A Policy for British Agriculture, 223–4
A Programme for Agriculture, 235
How the Labour Party has saved Agriculture, 259
Addison, Christopher (son), 5, 93, 274
Addison, Dorothy, Dowager Lady (second wife), 224, 232, 245, 249, 271, 272, 274–5
Addison, Isobel (first wife), 5–6, 27, 32, 51, 78, 92–3, 143, 157, 160, 174, 189, 203–4, 209, 215
Addison, Isobel (daughter), 5, 217, 242, 274
Addison, Michael (son), 5, 217, 274
Addison, Paul (son), 22
Addison, Robert (elder brother), 1
Agadir, 29
Agriculture, 1, 165–71, 173, 177–86, 189–201, 204, 206–7, 212–15, 222–6, 234, 235, 259, 278, 279
Air Policy, 67, 220, 229–30, 246, *See also* Civil Aviation
Aitken, Max. *See* Beaverbrook
Aldridge, H. R., 145
Alexander, A. V., 203, 231, 241, 272
Amalgamated Society of Engineers. *See* Engineers

Ammon, Lord, 235, 253
Amritsar, 115
Anderson, Sir Alan, 194
Anderson, Sir John, 18, 94, 102
Anderson, Wing-Commander, 229
Anglo-Soviet Committee, 233
Anti-Dumping Bill, 119
Anti-waste, 113, 122, 137, 138, 146, 276
Armaments, 218–19, 242
Asquith, Herbert H., 25, 33, 48–55, 70, 83–5, 88, 112, 117, 120, 145, 175, 239, 275, 277
Asquith, Margot, 1–2, 57
Astor, Waldorf, 22–4, 55, 59, 60, 83, 88, 109
Atomic Bomb, 239–42
Attlee, Clement R., 1, 171, 177, 193, 201, 209, 210, 216, 221, 229, 231, 235–42, 245, 249–51, 259–62, 268–72, 275, 280, 281
Australia, 243, 244
Austria, 201, 230

Baldwin, Stanley, 91, 158, 167, 174, 176, 187, 189, 225
Balfour, Arthur J., 25, 121
Barnes, Alfred, 170, 257–8
Barnes, George, 114, 117
Beaverbrook, Lord, 53, 57, 73, 139–41, 147, 187–8, 206, 232, 234, 272
Belgium, 30
Benn, Ernest, 71
Benn, W. Wedgwood, 9, 29, 44, 53, 119, 150, 162, 173, 176, 238, 253, 272, 280
Bevan, Aneurin, 146, 227, 228, 233, 239, 258–9, 264, 270, 271, 277, 281
Beveridge, Lady, 278
Beveridge, Sir William, 33, 39, 105, 255
Bevin, Ernest, 217, 231, 232, 235, 238, 239, 241, 249, 250, 267, 270
Birchenough, Sir Henry, 71
Birkenhead, Earl of, 139, 143, 154
Black, Sir Frederick, 33
'Black Friday', 136
Bondfield, Margaret, 177
Booth, George M., 33
Bradbury, Sir John, 18
Brailsford, H. N., 233
Bridgeman, W. C., 64, 81, 83
British Medical Association, 11–14, 16–21, 105

Index

British Medical Journal, 16, 133, 222
Brockway, Fenner, 162–3, 209
Brown, Ernest, 188
Brownlie, J., 43, 65
Buchenwald, 4, 234
Buckinghamshire, 5, 93, 177, 217, 224, 234, 275
Budgets, of 1909, 7; of 1914, 27, 28; of 1915, 31
Building Trades, 106–8, 123, 152
Bull, Sir William, 162
Burgin, Leslie, 230, 231
Burmah, 247
Burns, John, 30
Butler, R. A., 231
Buxton, Noel, 166, 173, 177–9, 181–3, 185–7, 189

Calverley, Lord, 253, 256
Campbell, J. R., 161
Campbell, The Revd R. J., 6
Campbell-Bannerman, Sir Henry, 6, 277
Canada, 245–6, 248
Canberra Conference, 244, 248
Cardiff, 29
Carmichael, Sir James, 71, 97
Carr, A. Comyns, 8
Carson, Sir Edward, 27, 53, 55, 137, 141, 163–4, 280
Cave, George, 55, 78
Ceylon, 251
Chamberlain, Austen, 15, 91, 100, 109, 110, 113, 124, 125, 128–30, 132, 135, 137–9, 142, 144, 154
Chamberlain, Neville, 63, 64, 88, 146, 195, 202, 220, 221, 224, 231
Charing Cross Hospital, 3, 4
Chatsfield, Lord, 231
Cherwell, Lord, 249
Chifley, Ben, 244
Childs, R., 154, 159
Churchill, Winston, 7, 9, 26, 31, 66–7, 69–70, 84, 85, 90–1, 114, 116, 139, 143, 147, 153, 157, 174, 187, 229–31, 234, 236, 247, 271, 272
Civil Aviation Bill, 256
Clay, H., 221
Clemenceau, Georges, 273
Clyde, 38–43

Clynes, J. R., 203, 209, 210
Coal Industry, 91–2, 102, 113–14, 135–6, 167, 188, 253, 257, 264
Coalition, of 1915, 31–2; of 1916, 55–7; of 1918, 85–7, 116–19, 145, 147, 149, 154, 239
Coalition Liberals, 85–6, 118–20, 147, 148, 157, 275
Cole, G. D. H., 209–11, 221
Cole, Margaret, 221
Conscription, 48–50
Conservative Party, 156, 187, 195
Cox, Alfred, 21
Cramp, Charles T., 210
Cranborne. *See* Salisbury, 5th Marquess of
Creech-Jones, Arthur, 233, 242, 250
Crewe, Lord, 52, 239
Cripps, Sir Stafford, 208, 210, 213, 214, 227, 231, 247, 249, 250
Crosland, C. A. R., 264
Cummings, A. J., 219
Cunliffe, Lord, 113
Cunliffe-Lister. *See* Swinton
Curzon, Lord, 61, 115, 121, 131
Czechoslovakia, 230

Daily Mail, 127, 164
Daily News, 48, 50, 64, 138, 150
Dallas, George, 170, 185, 201
Dalton, Hugh, 187, 196, 201, 208, 210, 211, 231, 238, 253, 256, 272
Davenport, Nicholas, 210
Davidson, J. C. C., 122
Davies, Clement, 231
Davies, David, 19, 50, 51, 59, 60
Davies, Joseph, 60
Davies, Sir J. T., 34, 54
Dawson, Bertrand, 86, 130–1, 134, 258
Defence of the Realm Bill, 47
Demobilization, 72, 97
Derby, Lord, 131
Derby scheme, 48, 49
Devaluation, 267
Dilution, 37–8, 41–3, 65, 66, 111, 124, 125, 168
Dominions Office, 242–4, 247, 279
Dorman-Smith, Sir Reginald, 225
Driberg, Tom, 4
Duckham, Sir Arthur, 114
Dye, Sidney, 225
Dyer, General, 115

322 Index

Ede, J. Chuter, 238
Eden, Anthony, 228, 230, 247
Edge, William, 120
Education, 29–31, 52, 149, 150, 152–3
Egypt, 115, 121, 150
Elibank, Master of, 12, 29
Elliot, Walter, 200, 212, 259, 280
Engineers, 38, 40–5, 62–7
Ernle. *See* Prothero
Evatt, Dr H. V., 243
Evening Standard, 138

Fairfield Yard, 39
Faringdon, Lord, 171
Finance Committee, 108, 129, 141–4
Fisher, Hayes, 73–4, 76–8, 80, 93, 96
Fisher, Herbert A. L., 55–7, 78, 86, 90, 114–18, 121, 122, 123, 128, 131, 136, 152–3, 174
Fisher, Sir John, 31
Fisher, Victor, 83
Foreign Affairs Group, 29–30
Foreign Policy, 29–30, 114–15, 121, 150, 161, 217, 219–20, 226–31
Forward, 40, 41, 252
France, 30, 230, 231
Francis, F., 10
Franz Ferdinand, 29
Fraser, Peter, 243, 245, 281
Free Trade, 118–19, 158, 194
Freeman, John, 271
Freyberg, General, 244
Friendly Societies, 11, 13, 14, 16–17, 78
Friday Group, 210–11
Fusion, 115–20, 147
Future Legislation Committee, 254–5

Gairloch proposals, 149, 151
Gaitskell, Hugh, 210, 221
Gallacher, William, 38–40, 42, 43
Gandhi, Mahatma, 3, 248
Garden Suburb, 59–60
Gardiner, A. G., 48, 90
Geddes, Sir Auckland, 4, 61, 90, 93, 98, 109, 115
Geddes, Sir Eric, 131, 146, 257
Geddes Axe, 91, 146, 152–3, 276
General Elections, of January 1910, 7–8; of December 1910, 9–10; of 1918, 87–8; of 1922, 154–5; of 1923, 159–60; of 1924, 161–3; of 1929, 171–2; of 1931, 206; of 1935, 219–20; of 1945, 236; of 1950, 268, 269; of 1951, 271
General Strike, 167
George V, 16, 54, 55, 122, 202
Germany, 87, 230, 231
Girouard, Sir Percy, 34
Gladstone, Viscount, 157
Glasgow, 40, 91, 151
Glyn, Sir R., 235
Glyn-Jones, Sir W. S., 83, 132
Gold Standard, 113, 203–5
Gollancz, Victor, 228
Graham, William, 183, 195, 203, 208, 209
Greece, 115
Greenwood, Arthur, 71, 203, 209, 217, 231, 235, 238, 254, 262
Greenwood, Sir Hamar, 121, 157, 174
Grey, Sir Edward, 29, 30, 175
Griffith, Sir Ellis, 49
Grigg, Sir Edward, 157, 174
Grigg, P. J., 183
Guest, Freddie, 49, 83–6, 131, 157
Guild Socialism, 110–11

Haig, Field-Marshal Earl, 61, 84, 85
Haldane, Lord, 31, 70, 94, 186
Halifax, Lord, 231
Hall, D., 235
Hall, George, 242, 253, 254
Hamilton, Mary Agnes, 210
Hammersmith, South, 161
Hankey, Lord, 53, 132, 142, 189
Harcourt, Lewis, 25, 54
Hardie, Keir, 12
Hargreaves, L., 45, 62
Hartington, Lord, 122
Hartshorn, Vernon, 135, 187
Harvey, Major S.E., 174
Hastings, Dr Somerville, 229
Hay, Hon. Claude, 7, 8
Health, 4, 6, 46, 69, 75, 82, 95, 103–5, 129–31, 151, 155
Health, Ministry of, 35, 75–8, 80, 88, 93–5, 102–3, 126, 131, 132, 144, 147, 276
Henderson, Arthur, 26, 36, 37, 55, 57, 64, 157, 158, 168, 169, 176, 183, 195, 202, 203, 205, 208, 209, 217, 280
Heseltine, Michael, 94

Index

Hewart, Sir Gordon, 117, 120
Hicks, George, 168
Hitler, Adolf, 227, 230, 231
Hoare, Sir Samuel, 202, 227
Hobhouse, L. T., 6
Hobson, J. A., 6, 166, 174, 227
Hodge, John, 55, 64
Hodges, Frank, 136
Home Affairs Committee, 74, 78, 134
Horder, Lord, 233
Horncastle, 120
Horne, Sir Robert, 91, 105, 128, 131, 135, 142, 143, 154
Horrabin, J. F., 210
Housing, 73–5, 81, 82, 96–102, 106–13, 121–9, 141–5, 149–53, 168, 172, 211–12, 239, 258–9, 278
Housing and Town Planning Bill, 100–1
Housing Bonds, 108, 110, 123
Hudson, R. A., 259
Huntingdon, Lord, 253

Illingworth, Alfred, 132, 141
Imperial Mineral Resources Bureau, 61, 62
Independent Labour Party, 162, 163, 209–10
India, 115, 173, 187, 243, 247–8
Industrial Assurance Companies, 12, 76, 78
Inman, Lord, 257
Insurance. *See.* National Health Insurance
Ireland, 25, 26, 51–2, 84, 115, 121, 135, 248
Iron and Steel nationalization, 260–5
Ironside, General, 231
Isaacs, George, 238

Japan, 147, 220, 233, 244, 265
Jay, Douglas, 210
Jinnah, Mohammed Ali, 248
Jobson, G. H., 154, 159
Johnston, Tom, 164, 203, 208
Jones, Thomas, 11, 60, 96, 137
Jowitt, Lord, 188, 220, 250, 252, 262, 272, 279
Joynson-Hicks, Sir William, 136

Kellaway, F. G., 50, 54, 61, 64, 117, 120, 136, 174

Kemp, Sir George, 25
Kerr, Philip, 60
Keynes, John Maynard, 109, 201, 255
Khama, Seretse, 251
King, W. L. Mackenzie, 240, 243, 245–6, 248, 250, 262, 268, 281
Kirkwood, David, 39–41, 164, 209
Kitchener, Field-Marshal Earl, 31, 52
Korean War, 267, 270

Labour, 25–6, 36–45, 62–6, 135–6, 157, 167–8. *See also* Trade Unions
Labour Party, 12, 26, 55, 88, 116, 117, 154, 158, 160, 168–72, 189, 202–6, 208–13, 216–18, 228–9, 234–6, 255, 277, 280
Land question, 27–8, 169–70, 180, 223
Land Utilisation Bill, 197–9
Lansbury, George, 12, 172, 175, 178, 195, 203, 209, 216, 217
Laski, Harold, 210, 233
Law, A. Bonar, 25, 31, 53–7, 80, 85, 91, 102, 131, 132, 137, 156–8, 163
Lawson, J. J., 234, 269
Layton, Walter, 33, 34
Leamington Spa, 120
Lee of Fareham, Lord, 131
Lees-Smith, H. B., 208, 234
Left Book Club, 227–8
Leicester, 160, 196, 208
Lever, Sir Hardman, 35
Lewis, Sir Herbert, 96
Liberal Party, 7, 47–50, 54, 56, 57, 82–5, 116–18, 120–1, 156, 158, 167, 188–92. *See also* Coalition Liberals
Liberalism, 4, 6, 57, 83, 162, 276–7
Lincolnshire, 1, 12, 27, 159, 165, 194
Lindsay, A. D., 260
Listowel, Lord, 235, 253, 254
Llewellyn-Smith, Sir Hubert, 34, 39, 114
Lloyd George, David, compared with Addison, 2; and People's Budget, 7–8; and National Insurance Bill, 10–19, 21–2; personal relationship with Addison, 22–3, 28, 34, 147–8, 189–90, 215–17; and 1914 budget, 27, 28; and outbreak of first world war, 30–2; as Minister of Munitions, 32–4, 36–8, 40–2, 45–7; and conscription crisis, 48–

50; becomes Prime Minister, 50–7, 59, 163; and the Garden Suburb, 59–60; and wartime labour unrest, 64, 65; makes Addison Minister of Reconstruction, 66–8, 70; and Ministry of Health, 76–8, 80; and wartime politics, 82–6; in 'coupon' election, 87–8; as post-war premier, 89–92, 96, 102; and housing policy, 98, 109–11, 125, 141–4; and post-war labour troubles, 114, 135–6; and foreign policy, 115, 121; and 'fusion', 115–20; and Ireland, 52, 121; and dismissal of Addison from Ministry of Health, 131–4; and Addison's departure from the Coalition government, 136–44, 147–8, 151, 203; and the fall of his government, 153–5; attacked by Addison, 155, 159, 168, 169, 172, 175; negotiations with second Labour government, 188–92, 198; praises Addison, 206, 215, 217, 277; with Addison in the thirties, 215–17; praised by Addison, 223, 232; on appeasement, 227, 230, 231; in second world war, 232; general relationship with Addison, 276, 277, 279–8; also mentioned, 25, 174

Lloyd George Fund, 216–17
Lloyd George Liberal Magazine, 131
Local Government Board, 23, 55, 73–7, 88, 90, 93, 98
London, 4, 6, 7, 10, 28, 30, 87, 149, 256
Long, Walter, 77
Lords, House of, 2, 7–9, 20, 26, 127, 201, 225, 229, 234, 235, 236, 240, 249, 251–9, 261–5, 273–4, 278, 279
Low, Percy, 224

MacArthur, General Douglas, 271
Macassey, Lynden, 41, 42
McCurdy, Charles A., 138, 140, 174
MacDonald, James Ramsay, 9, 26, 42, 62, 119, 157, 158, 160, 161, 169, 172–4, 176–9, 188–97, 202–5, 211, 277, 280
McKenna, Reginald, 49, 54
Maclean, Donald, 188
Maclean, John, 40

MacNalty, Sir Arthur, 95
Macnamara, Thomas J., 107, 117, 120, 125, 126, 128, 131, 143, 174
McNary-Haugen Scheme, 195
Macphail, Dr A., 5
Malan, Dr D., 247
Manchester Guardian, 150, 196, 251
Marketing Boards, 170, 179–83, 192–7, 199–201, 212–13, 223, 259
Markham, Violet, 102
Martin, Kingsley, 233
Masterman, C. F. G., 1, 13, 28
Maurice Debate, 84, 85
May Committee, 201
Medical Officer, 133
Medical Research Council, 24–5, 95–6, 130, 258
Medical World, 21
Menon, Krishna, 272
Middleton, Jim, 213
Mikardo, Ian, 269
Milner, Alfred, Lord, 55, 60, 67, 75, 83, 114
Mitchell Banks, Sir R., 171, 172, 206, 217
Mitchison, G. R., 221
Mond, Sir Alfred, 49, 56, 107, 118, 142–4, 146, 152, 157, 160
Money, Sir L. Chiozza, 6
Montagu, Edwin, 28, 44, 52, 56, 61, 90, 114, 115, 118, 121, 147, 153
Montgomery, Field Marshal, 272
Morant, Sir Robert, 18, 28, 77, 94
Morel, E. D., 157, 174, 277
Morley, John, 30
Morrison, Herbert, 231, 232, 235, 238, 241, 247, 249, 251, 252, 254, 255, 257, 260, 262, 263, 269–72
Morrison, W. S., 225
Mosley, Lt.-Col. E. H., 172
Mosley, Sir Oswald, 177, 178, 181, 201
Moulton, Lord, 24
Mountbatten, Earl, 248
Muir, James, 42–3
Muir, Ramsey, 160
Muir, Ramsay, 160
Munitions, Ministry of, 23, 32–47, 59–70, 117, 158, 168, 240
Munitions of War Act, 36, 38, 42, 56, 63, 64, 66
Munro, Ronald, 117, 121, 131, 174
Mussolini, Benito, 226, 227

Index

Nash, Walter, 22, 245
Nathan, Lord, 236, 253, 254, 259, 261, 273–4
Nation, The, 100, 101, 144, 145
National Health Insurance, 10–23, 29, 57, 60, 79, 105–6, 258, 279
National Health Service, 131, 258, 270–1
National Labour Advisory Committee, 36–7, 63
National Parks, 186
Nationalization, 114, 167, 171–2, 198, 224, 253, 256–8, 260–5
New Fabian Research Bureau, 221, 245
New Leader, 158, 165
New Liberalism. *See* Liberalism
New Statesman, 73, 100, 136, 144, 227
New Zealand, 222, 243–5, 249
Newman, Sir George, 28, 46, 75, 94, 133, 134
Newsholme, Sir Arthur, 23, 129
Noel-Baker, P., 228, 249, 250
Norman, Sir Montague, 124
North Atlantic Treaty Organization, 241, 242
Northcliffe, Lord, 122
Nurses, 105
Nuttgens, J., 275

Observer, 59, 268
Owen, Dr David, 1

Paisley, 112, 120
Pakenham, Lady, 269
Pakenham, Lord, 253, 254, 272–3
Pakistan, 247
Paris Peace Conference, 98, 99, 114, 115
Parliament Act, of 1911, 16, 238, 251, 261; of 1949, 261, 262, 265
Parmoor, Lord, 176, 183, 195, 197
Paterson-Ross, Sir James, 271
Paton, John, 209
Pethick-Lawrence, 160, 208, 220, 242, 253, 272
Phillips, L., 71
Plender, Sir William, 19
Pollitt, Harry, 228
Ponsonby, Arthur, 29, 157, 174, 277
Poor Law, 9, 77, 78, 81, 103, 130, 132
Popular Front, 227–8
Price, E. G., 155, 157
Pringle, W. M. R., 42

Prothero, G. W., 55, 169
Pritt, D. N., 221
Pugh, Arthur, 210

Quota schemes, 178–80, 183–5, 192, 195–7, 212

Radice, E. A., 210
Radnage, 177, 232, 272, 275
Reconstruction, Ministry of, 68, 70–82, 91, 150
Redmond, John, 52
Reid, W. M., 162
Reith, Sir John, 253
Representation of the People Bill, 82
Rhondda, Lady, 25, 94
Rhondda, Lord, 35, 55, 73
Roberts, G. H., 114
Robertson, General Sir William, 53, 84, 85
Robinson, Sir Arthur, 102
Robinson, Sir Thomas, 132
Roosevelt, Franklin D., 184, 232–3
Rothermere, Lord, 122
Roumania, 53
Rowntree, Seebohm, 46, 69, 73, 190–1
Roy, B. C., 3, 248
Runciman, Walter, 36, 49, 188, 231
Russia, 62, 91, 92, 103, 114–15, 161, 233

St. Bartholomew's Hospital, 2
St. David's, Lord, 217
Salisbury, 4th Marquess of, 70, 74, 96, 97, 127, 235
Salisbury, 5th Marquess of, 235, 236, 242, 252, 253, 265, 266, 272, 273
Salter, Sir Arthur, 11, 18
Samuel, Lord, 109, 249, 272, 280
Sankey Commission, 91, 102, 114
Schuster, Sir Claude, 11, 18
Scott-Robertson, Sir George, 30
Selborne, Lord, 70, 127
Shackleton, David, 64
Shawcross, Sir Hartley, 250
Sheffield, 2, 3, 44–5, 62, 274
Shinwell, Emanuel, 208, 210, 211, 257
Shoreditch, 1, 7–10, 87, 154–5, 159, 225
Shortt, Edward, 118, 121, 131, 141, 174
Simon, Sir John, 49, 54, 164
Singapore, 233
Sinn Fein, 84, 115, 121, 147
Smillie, Robert, 164

326 Index

Smith, Sir Ben, 266
Smuts, Field Marshal, 79, 181, 243
Snowden, Philip, 12, 172, 176, 177, 195, 203, 205
Socialist League, 208, 209
Socialist Medical Association, 131, 229
South Africa, 246–7, 249
South-West Africa, 246–7
Spanish Civil War, 227–9
Spanish Medical Aid Association, 228–9
Spectator, 164
Spen Valley, 116, 117
Stamfordham, Lord, 122
Stanley, Sir Albert, 55
Stansgate. See Benn, Wedgwood
Stevenson, Frances, 139, 141
Stokes, Richard, 270
Strabolgi, Lord, 225
Strachey, John, 228, 266, 272
Strauss, G. R., 218, 227, 233, 260, 263
Street, A. G., 199, 235
Suffragettes, 25–6
Sutherland, Sir William, 49, 65, 131
Swansea, 146, 160
Swindon, 161, 171–2, 180, 194, 195, 204, 206, 217–18, 269
Swinton, Earl of, 219, 256, 273
Sylvester, A. J., 216

Talbot, Lord Edmund, 55, 134
Tariffs, 9, 136, 158, 183, 195, 201
Tawney, R. H., 161, 210
Thomas, Albert, 35
Thomas, D. A., See Rhondda, Lord
Thomas, J. H., 55, 177, 178, 181, 195, 203, 205, 212
Thompson, F. C., 117
Thring, Sir A., 71
Thurtle, Ernest, 155
Times, The, 19, 54, 68, 87, 133, 137, 161, 162, 169, 173, 198, 204, 229
Trade Card scheme, 45, 62, 63, 66
Trade unions, 36–45, 62–6, 110, 111, 113, 124–6, 167–8, 202, 203, 239. See also Labour
Treasury agreement, 36
Trevelyan, Sir Charles P., 30, 157, 174, 209, 227, 228, 277
Truman, Harry S., 240
Tuberculosis Commission, 23–4
Turkey, 115, 121, 153

Turnor, Christopher, 194

Ulster, 25, 27, 51
Unemployment insurance, 79, 105, 196
Unionist Party, 49, 51–4, 85, 86, 118, 138, 153–4. See also Conservative Party
United Nations, 240, 270
United States of America, 35, 68, 184, 195, 240, 256, 265–7, 270

Vansittart, Lord, 272
Versailles, Treaty of, 92, 230

Wakefield, Sir Wavell, 218–20
Wales, 19, 24, 29, 96
Walters, Tudor, 74, 106, 109, 126
Ward, Dudley, 120
Ward, Mrs Humphrey, 26
Waterlow, Sir W., 218
Watkins, Percy, 11, 96
Webb, Beatrice, 94, 102, 227
Webb, Sidney, 175, 176, 227
Wheatley, John, 161
Whitaker, Smith, 12, 13, 17
Whiteley, William 255
Whitley Councils, 70–2, 88, 91
Wilkinson, Ellen, 172
Williams, Tom, 201, 234, 259, 262
Wilmot, John, 241, 260, 263
Wilson, Sir Harold, 238, 271, 277, 281
Wilson, Field Marshal Sir Henry, 85
Wilson, Leslie, 140
Wilson, Woodrow, 59
Winster, Lord, 253
Winterton, Lord, 145
Wise, E. F., 166, 170, 203, 209
Wolmer, Viscount, 200
Women, 25–6, 33, 37, 39, 277
Wood, Sir Kingsley, 12, 94
Woolf, Leonard, 227, 233
World War, First, 30, 48, 51–3, 59, 86, 88, 165, 170; Second, 231–6
Wormold, Sir John, 71
Worthington-Evans, Laming, 64, 86, 91, 143

XYZ Group, 210–11

Young, Sir Hilton, 157, 174

Zinoviev letter, 161, 162

OXFORD POLYTECHNIC LIBRARY